P9-CQH-511

The Professor of Secrets

The Professor of Secrets

Mystery, Medicine, and Alchemy in Renaissance Italy

WILLIAM EAMON

NATIONAL GEOGRAPHIC
WASHINGTON, D.C.

para Elbita con amor,
y para Miguelito con esperanza

Published by the National Geographic Society
1145 17th Street N.W., Washington, D.C. 20036

ISBN: 978-1-4262-0650-4

Library of Congress cataloging-in-publication information available upon request.

The National Geographic Society is one of the world's largest nonprofit scientific and educational organizations. Founded in 1888 to "increase and diffuse geographic knowledge," the Society works to inspire people to care about the planet. It reaches more than 325 million people worldwide each month through its official journal, *National Geographic,* and other magazines; National Geographic Channel; television documentaries; music; radio; films; books; DVDs; maps; exhibitions; school publishing programs; interactive media; and merchandise. National Geographic has funded more than 9,000 scientific research, conservation and exploration projects and supports an education program combating geographic illiteracy.

For more information, please call 1-800-NGS LINE (647-5463) or write to the following address:

National Geographic Society
1145 17th Street N.W.
Washington, D.C. 20036-4688 U.S.A.

Visit us online at www.nationalgeographic.com

For information about special discounts for bulk purchases, please contact
National Geographic Books Special Sales: ngspecsales@ngs.org

For rights or permissions inquiries, please contact National Geographic Books
Subsidiary Rights: ngbookrights@ngs.org

Interior design: Cameron Zotter

Printed in the United States of America

10/WCPF-CML/1

CONTENTS

prologue

EXPERIENCE AND MEMORY

Bolognese doctor Leonardo Fioravanti paced his cell, outraged by the indignity he'd suffered. And who wouldn't be? Ever since he arrived in Milan in the early 1570s, the city's physicians had been plotting against him. But this time they'd gone too far, sending officers of the Provveditori alla Sanità, or Public Health Board, to arrest him and throw him in prison on the dubious charge of "not medicating in the canonical way."

Fioravanti was no common barber-surgeon. Nor was he one of those wandering charlatans who would suddenly show up in the town square, hawk a few nostrums, then just as quickly disappear. He was a physician, holding degrees from Italy's preeminent medical school, the University of Bologna. Yet he'd languished in jail for eight days now without anyone's heeding his protestations of innocence.

Unable to contain his anger any longer, Fioravanti asked the prison guard for pen and paper. He then drafted a letter to Milan's public health minister, taking care to address him in the proper—that is to say obsequious—manner. He introduced himself as "Leonardo Fioravanti of Bologna, Doctor of Arts and Medicine, and Knight." He wrote his protest in a measured tone, but didn't hold back, demanding to be allowed to "medicate freely as a legitimate doctor." Then he sealed the letter, dated it 22 April 1573, and paid the jailhouse guard to entrust it to a messenger, who would carry it to the Sanità office at the ducal palace in the Piazza del Duomo.

The next day, Niccolo Boldoni plucked Fioravanti's letter from the pile of documents on his desk. As Milan's protophysician *(protofisico),* or public health minister, Boldoni oversaw every aspect of the city's medical profession. His duties entailed a seemingly endless grind of routine bureaucratic tasks: examining barber-surgeons and midwives, collecting fees, imposing fines, inspecting pharmacies, ruling on petitions and appeals.

On the face of it, there was nothing unusual about the letter Boldoni was about to open: He would have read plenty of complaints from disgruntled healers. After breaking the wax seal that fastened the edges of the letter and opening it, however, Boldoni must have immediately recognized that the appeal before him was like no other.

A vile plot was afoot, the angry supplicant protested. The town physicians were behind it. They had accused him of poisoning his patients, yet the real reason for his incarceration was "pure and simple envy":

> Seeing that I've cured and saved so many sick people in this and many other cities of Italy with such beautiful and excellent remedies unknown to any of them, and seeing that my fame continues to grow because of it, the physicians don't want me, a foreigner settled in Milan, to demonstrate the virtue that God, nature, and long experience have taught me.

To prove the worth of his doctrine, which he called the "New Way of Healing," Fioravanti issued a challenge: "Let there be consigned to me alone twenty or twenty-five sick people with diverse ailments and an equal number with similar infirmities to all the physicians of Milan. If I don't cure my patients quicker and better than they do theirs, I'm willing to be banished forever from this city." The results, he predicted, would demonstrate once and for all that "true medicine is proved only by experience."

We can only imagine what Boldoni made of this preposterous challenge. Did the town physicians accept Fioravanti's dare? It seems unlikely, but the historical record is mute. In any event, the court set him free.

LEONARDO THE MIRACULOUS

This was hardly the first time that Leonardo Fioravanti had run afoul of the medical establishment. By 1573 his defiance of conventional medical doctrine was legendary. He had journeyed to Milan from Venice, where the College of Physicians had accused him of fraud and endangering the people's health with his unorthodox treatments. Before that, Fioravanti had been chased out of Rome by a "cabal" of physicians. Yet when he visited Sicily in 1548, his miraculous cures earned him accolades as a "new Asclepius." And while serving as a military surgeon in the Spanish navy during the war against the Turkish corsairs in Africa, Fioravanti became famous for his novel treatment of gunshot wounds. Only a few years after the Milan affair, he would travel to Spain and to the court of King Philip II, where the people would proclaim Leonardo Fioravanti a saint, a prophet, and a necromancer.

Contemporaries lavished similar paeans on his healing prowess. A Venetian poet called him "an angel of paradise, sent by God to earth for the health and preservation of human life" after Fioravanti cured him "with miraculous success" of a brutal gunshot wound to the head. Abrasive and contentious, Fioravanti made enemies wherever he went; his battles with the medical establishment made him a virtual symbol of the Renaissance charlatan—a reputation that would shadow him long past death.

To some, Leonardo Fioravanti was a ridiculous and dangerous quack; to others, he was a veritable savior. Unlike the commonplace charlatans of the day, Fioravanti didn't mount a portable scaffold and pitch his remedies to a crowd in a piazza. Yet he was a prolific author who marketed his cures with equal parts originality and theatricality. In the books he wrote for middlebrow readers, he launched a new kind of medical advertising that would survive for centuries, even as his cures faded from memory. Fioravanti was an ordinary surgeon who catapulted himself from obscurity to become one of the most famous healers of the Renaissance. The scourge of the regular doctors, he lashed out against their "abuses" and accused them of having extinguished the light of "true medicine." In so doing, he became one of history's first medical celebrities. In the minds of his readers he was "Fioravanti of the miracles," and through the miraculous medium of print he gained a devoted following.

Yet Fioravanti's successes did not stem purely from clever advertising. For better or for worse, his style of medicine pointed the way to modern practices. Although premodern medicine offered few effective cures for most maladies, Fioravanti insisted on attacking every illness head-on, using robust drugs that he promised would drive out the sickness and return the body to "pristine" health. Diseases to him were not benign humoral imbalances, as they were to the run-of-the-mill doctors of the day, but rather alien forces that invaded the body and had to be violently beaten back. His martial therapeutics prefigured a confident age of "magic bullets" that would promise instant panaceas. At the same time, it heralded the emergence of medical messiahs who prey upon helpless patients desperate to be healed.

A PASSION FOR SECRETS

Fioravanti was also a zealous Renaissance experimenter—not the kind we normally associate with the great scientific revolution that ushered in modern science, but rather one who practiced a more typically Renaissance style of experimenting: avid, daring, devouring—and utterly random. Throughout his life, he wrote, he had followed in the footsteps of the "masters of experience," whom he identified as the original school of doctors who practiced in ancient times. Among *contemporary* masters of experience he named naturalists such as Vincenzo Cantone of Siena, who "has walked the world and ploughed many seas in order to discover diverse secrets of nature," and many others whose names have been eclipsed by the standard heroes of Renaissance science.

Without such vibrant figures, however, our picture of the scientific and medical world of the 16th century is incomplete. In many ways, they typify the most novel aspect of Renaissance science: For a growing number of men and women interested in natural philosophy (as the study of nature was called at the time), trueness to nature was measured not by the yardstick of ancient authority but by direct experience. For them, the secrets of nature had to be discovered by experiment—a vague concept that often meant little more than trying out a procedure that had never been attempted before.

The practitioners of this chemistry-kit approach to science were known to contemporaries as "professors of secrets." The sobriquet had been bestowed on them by Dominican friar Tommaso Garzoni, whose 1585 book, *The Universal Plaza of All the World's Professions*, identified the pursuit of the secrets of nature as one of the "professions" or preoccupations of the day. In his encyclopedic tome, Garzoni depicted society as a teeming piazza filled with an infinite variety of occupations and professions, each one unique. Somewhere in that buzzing swarm Fra Tommaso located the "professors of secrets," creating an indelible portrait of them as a community of hypercharged experimenters who burned with such passion for secrets that "they desire them more than any of life's daily necessities."

Three decades before Garzoni wrote *The Universal Plaza*, the very first professor of secrets—the model for them all—was portrayed in one of Renaissance Italy's most popular scientific books, *The Secrets of Alessio Piemontese*. The book's author identified himself as a nobleman from the Piedmont region of Italy who had spent a lifetime traveling from place to place collecting hundreds of secrets and experiments, some drawn from books and others obtained simply by drawing out people. Alessio had gathered them "not just from very learned men and noblemen, but also from poor women, artisans, peasants, and all sorts of people." His secrets included remedies unknown to doctors, exotic perfumes, and alchemical formulas tried out by Alessio himself. Like other collectors, he'd always carefully guarded his discoveries lest they be "profaned by the common people."

One day Alessio was approached by a surgeon who had gotten wind of his cache of rare secrets. He begged Alessio to divulge one that would enable him to cure an artisan he was treating; tormented by a bladder stone, the poor man was near death. Alessio demurred, apprehensive that the surgeon would claim sole credit for the cure. The surgeon, for his part, refused Alessio's offer to treat the man gratis, fearing that it would ruin his reputation if word got out that he had consulted another healer.

The artisan paid the ultimate price for their reciprocal vanity, eventually succumbing to his painful ailment. Racked with remorse over his role in the affair, Alessio gave away his wealth and retired, monklike, to a secluded villa. There he renounced his adherence to secrecy—and vowed to publish his secrets for the benefit of the world.

Garzoni creates the impression that professors of secrets like Alessio Piemontese roved all over early modern Italy, members of a Europe-wide network of experimenters who made up an underworld of 16th-century science. Only their obscurity has made it difficult for historians to reconstruct that community.

Among these "masters of experience," Leonardo Fioravanti stands out because he reveals so much about himself, making him pivotal to the history of early modern science. A prolific author, he published books that were reprinted and translated into several languages well into the 18th century. In fact, almost all that we know of the man comes from his own writings. Although the archives provide a check to his exuberant and often embellished recollections, they provide only scant glimpses of his wanderings. Fioravanti worked hard to dictate how posterity would define him, taking pains to disclose neither fault nor flaw. Theatrical, larger-than-life, barely believable episodes are offset by exasperating silences. He was a master at shaping and remaking his image.

REBUILDING A LOST WORLD

A friend of mine, the Italian historian Andrea Carlino, once remarked that Fioravanti was a *trucco*—a trick. With him, Andrea said, what you think you see is never quite what really is: Just when you think you've uncovered the truth, the trickster changes the rules of the game. In reading Fioravanti's autobiographical fragments, I often found myself frowning in disbelief at how brazenly he would exaggerate, hide, or make the same facts serve different ends as the occasion suited him. The more I thought about how to make sense of Fioravanti's life, the more Andrea's advice came back to me. What kind of trick might *I* use, I wondered, to uncover the sleight of hand behind his contradictory and sometimes dubious self-representations? How might I trick Leonardo Fioravanti into confessing the truth about himself?

I decided to play his game: I would probe his memory through his books and try to make it tell a story, just as he had manipulated the facts in creating his own persona. Some of the details can be teased out of his medical autobiography, *The Treasury of Human Life,* which he published in 1570. Further details can be gleaned from recollections contained in his other seven books on medicine and natural philosophy, including his last, *Della fisica (Of Physic),* which he completed in Naples after returning from Spain in 1577. A dark, brooding, pessimistic work, it barely conceals the fact that something had gone terribly wrong.

Archival documents and the testimony of contemporaries can augment our knowledge, but Fioravanti himself was the principal witness to his life—a fact that renders a conventional biography almost hopeless. An obsessive autobiographer, he continually colored the events of his past to build an image of himself among his admiring public. At best, we are left with an incomplete and selective record of his memory. Although I rely on Fioravanti's memory and use it as a guide, I do not accept it at face value. Instead, I have strived to craft it into a more multilayered story than the one-dimensional, biased version we encounter in his writings.

Precisely because so little is known about marginal figures such as Fioravanti, the effort of reconstructing his memory can bring all of us closer to a world that has otherwise been lost. Because he is the principal source of information about himself and the members of his cultural circles, his recollection of events is precious to us. If we cannot accept his memory at face value, our reconstruction of his life can serve as a window into the remarkable world of late Renaissance Italy.

1

MIA DOLCE PATRIA

"My sweet homeland" was how Leonardo Fioravanti remembered his birthplace, Bologna. When viewed from the historical perspective, however, it's difficult to imagine a more unlikely depiction either of the city or of Italy as a whole during the late Renaissance. Like other cities dotting the long peninsula, 16th-century Bologna exhibited both the glories that had epitomized the High Renaissance and the detritus of decades of social conflict and political turmoil.

"*La misera Italia*" (unhappy Italy) was the description more commonly used by Fioravanti's contemporaries. Indeed, an entire literature was devoted to Italy's woes in the late Renaissance. The lament can be traced all the way back to the 13th-century poet Dante, who exclaimed, "Ah, servile Italy, hostel of grief, ship without pilot in great tempest, no mistress of provinces, but brothel!" The brooding over Italy's condition crescendoed in the 16th century, as writers and poets competed with one another to mourn the country's current chaos while exalting her past glory. Machiavelli considered Italy to be a beaten, stripped, and plundered captive, reduced to a state of misery from which only a strong leader could free her. "So now, left lifeless, Italy is waiting to see who can be the one to heal her wounds," he wrote in *The Prince,* "and cleanse those sores which have now been festering so long."

What had happened to "poor Italy" to warrant these gloomy depictions of a land where, everyone agreed, civilization had once flourished as nowhere else? How had the age that produced Leonardo da Vinci turned into the age of Leonardo Fioravanti?

In many ways, historian Guido Ruggiero has pointed out, the Renaissance has always been little more than "a fantasy, a dream." Intellectuals and writers of the 14th century imagined that they were giving birth anew to the grandeur of ancient civilization and, as Florentine novelist Boccaccio wrote, "breaking through and tearing away the brambles and bushes with which, by the negligence of men, the road was covered." Boccaccio described Dante as the poet who "opened the way for the return of the Muses, who had been banished from Italy." The notion of reviving an age of glory was born in the period we call the Renaissance.

If the Italian Renaissance was a dream, the late Renaissance in Italy was a nightmare. As a checkerboard of independent principalities, Italy was tantalizing territory for the powerful, centralized monarchies newly arrived on the Continental scene. The French monarchy, which had consolidated its domestic power following the Hundred Years' War, and the Catholic monarchs of Spain—Ferdinand of Aragon and Isabella of Castile, who in 1492 had completed the *reconquista* of the Spanish peninsula by taking the last Muslim stronghold, Granada—regarded Italy as a region of vast wealth and strategic importance. For both France and Spain, the prospect of expansion into the Italian peninsula held a powerful appeal.

Whenever they faced a crisis, all too often the Italian city-states called upon some foreign ally to tip the balance of power in their favor. In 1494, the Duke of Milan, Ludovico Sforza, "Il Moro," invited the King of France to invade Naples in order to punish his old enemy, Ferrante II, the Aragonese king of Naples. French King Charles VIII, who had just come of age, wanted to do something bold, and Il Moro gave him his chance. Pressing an ancient claim to the Kingdom of Naples, Charles gathered an army of 25,000 men and invaded the peninsula. Unexpectedly, city after city capitulated to him, and within a few short months Charles marched into Naples, having conquered virtually all of Italy.

The French invasion heralded a period of foreign involvement in Italian affairs that would last for more than 60 years. Machiavelli found the situation so desperate that he exhorted some "new prince"—a thinly veiled reference to Lorenzo de' Medici of Florence—to step forth and "liberate Italy from the barbarians." What happened instead was a succession of foreign incursions, culminating in the humiliating Sack of Rome in 1527—a fitting measure of Italy's impotence. Even if it was only a dream, to many of Leonardo Fioravanti's contemporaries the age of Italy's glory seemed far in the past.

BOLOGNA ASCENDANT

Bologna's early history, like that of its fellow Italian city-states, was rent with violence and political discord. Founded as a self-governing commune in 1123, when privileged townspeople seized power from their overlord, the Holy Roman Emperor, the city's governing body was initially aristocratic *(signorile).* In 1278, the city again became part of the Papal States; for the next two centuries, it passed back and forth from papal rule to aristocratic rule to republican regimes as "the people" *(popolo)* and the nobility *(nobiltà)* vied for power. This to-and-fro of political conflict manifested itself in Bologna's urban architecture, as the armed castles of the feudal countryside were brought into the city. Soaring fortresses belonging to noble families popped up all over town. At one time, 145 towers—rising as high as 97 meters (318 feet), in the case of the Asinelli tower—dominated the cityscape, standing like sentinels primed for the next outbreak of hostilities.

The political turmoil of the 14th century demonstrated that the survival of the city depended on the concentration of power in a single leader. Pressured from within by political conflict and from without by the prospect of a papal takeover, Bologna finally succumbed to signorial government. In 1446, Sante Bentivoglio became prince of Bologna in everything but name. He ruled until his death in 1463, thus securing the hold of the Bentivoglio family on Bolognese politics.

Under the benevolent despotism of the Bentivoglio family, which governed the city until 1506, Renaissance Bologna experienced a golden age during the 15th century. As a modern historian remarks, however, the Bentivoglios "were not among the more resplendent

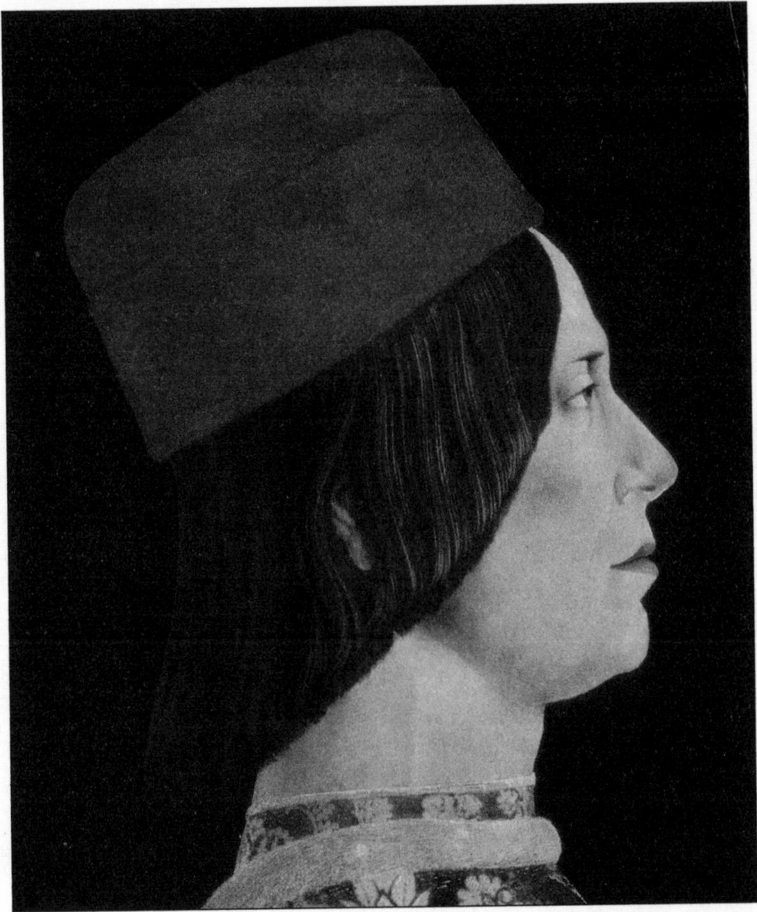

Though Renaissance condottiere Giovanni Bentivoglio had been out of power for more than a decade by the time Leonardo Fioravanti was born, the memory of his benevolent despotism was still alive in Bologna.

of the princely dynasties" of Italy. They did not establish a princely court and, like the Medici in Florence, did not hold formal office. Yet they were generous patrons of the arts: Under Giovanni II Bentivoglio, who ruled the city for nearly half a century, Bologna underwent an urban makeover. It was said of Giovanni that "he received a clay and rough-wooden Bologna [and] returned it as brick and polished marble."

During Giovanni's rule, the University of Bologna rose to world prominence. Enrolling 1,000 to 2,000 students, plus hundreds of foreign scholars and their servants, the university furnished the city a steady source of income—and global renown. Bologna emerged as a university town, its major economic activity the housing and provisioning of students.

The university's influence was everywhere apparent. Doctors in sumptuous purple robes figured in all civic ceremonies, and every candidate for a degree was conducted in state to the cathedral, there to expound his thesis and (if all went well) to receive the insignia of the doctorate. The city accommodated the university even in its architecture: Bologna's famous porticoes, which overhang its sidewalks and give the town its distinctive modern-day charm, originated as shelters from the harsh climate for students forced out-of-doors from their cramped lodgings.

During the lifetime of Leonardo Fioravanti, the political situation in Bologna—indeed, in all of Italy—was nothing short of depressing. The papacy, intent on bringing the Papal States, hitherto ruled nominally by the pope, under the direct rule of Rome, took advantage of this weakness. Within days of becoming pope in 1506, Julius II informed Bologna of his intentions. Giovanni resisted, whereupon Julius placed the city under interdict, preventing any of its citizens from participating in the sacraments. But with the people tired of arming themselves at their own expense, Giovanni enjoyed scant support. The churches closed. The clergy began to depart. A gloom settled over the city.

Finally, on All Souls' Day, Giovanni, accompanied by his sons and grandsons, rode out of Bologna. Eleven days later Julius II personally took control of the city, ending its long and prosperous period of independence.

After the French invasion of 1494, hostilities dragged on almost continuously in Italy for another 65 years. The warfare was made more horrifying by the introduction of some innovations known collectively as the "military revolution." The major technological and strategic changes of the time included the eclipse of cavalry by infantry, improvements in fortification design, an increased reliance on battlefield firepower, a dramatic increase in the size of armies, and new tactics that took advantage of artillery. The destructiveness of the prolonged Italian wars inspired awe in all who witnessed it. Gravediggers reported burying 16,500 bodies after the battle at Marignano in 1515, when French forces under the command of King François I defeated an army of Swiss mercenaries commanded by the Sforza Duke of Milan. At Ravenna in 1512, more than 13,000 Spanish and French troops were slain. The Italian wars ended in 1559 with the Peace of Cateau-Cambrésis, which confirmed Spain's dominance in Italy through its control of Milan and Naples, as well as its alliance with the papacy. The accord left the Republic of Venice as the sole independent entity on the Italian peninsula.

"A MOST PRESUMPTUOUS POX"

Along with the horror of war came famine and disease—including ailments previously unknown. The most frightening of them was syphilis, probably introduced to Spain from the New World by sailors on Columbus's return voyage. Spanish soldiers carried the sickness to Naples, where troops in Charles VIII's army got infected and took the illness back to France. For this reason it gained the name *mal Francese*, or French pox, from the erroneous belief that the Italians had contracted the disease from the French army. The French, meanwhile, believing they had caught it from the Italians, dubbed it the Neapolitan disease.

Whatever name it went by, the pox ravaged its victims, leaving them hideously scarred—and ostracized from society because of the moral opprobrium the disease carried. Although the modern strain of syphilis is relatively mild (and treatable), during the Renaissance it was a deadly scourge. No disease was more contagious, reckoned the Dutch humanist Erasmus, more terrible for its victims, nor more difficult to cure. "It's a most presumptuous pox," exclaims a character in one of his *Colloquies*. "In a showdown, it wouldn't yield to leprosy, elephantiasis, ringworm, gout, or sycosis."

Epidemic typhus was another newcomer to Renaissance Europe. It first appeared in Spain and Italy in the 1490s. Another, more widespread outbreak occurred in 1527–1528, with cases reported from Naples to Milan. A disease of famine and filth, typhus was constantly on the march, accompanying armies on every campaign. The population of Europe had been preconditioned for the malady by unremitting warfare, bad weather, and crop failures, all of which diminished food supplies and weakened immune systems.

In his colorful history of typhus, *Rats, Lice, and History,* Hans Zinsser—the bacteriologist who isolated the germ that causes the illness and developed the first antityphus vaccine—wrote that when typhus broke out in Europe, "the disease was scattered far and wide among the wretched populations under conditions—ideal for typhus—of famine, abject poverty, homeless wandering, and constant warfare." Such was the state of affairs in early 16th-century Italy, a land of grief and despair so deep that a Venetian poet could lament, "War, plague, famine, and these times . . . have made a whore out of all Italy." It must have seemed as if the Four Horsemen of the Apocalypse—War, Pestilence, Famine, and Death—had galloped through Italy, sweeping up victims in their wake.

In January 1514, almost exactly three years before Leonardo Fioravanti's birth date, a deformed infant was born near Bologna. Unlike the many semifantastic "monsters" previously reported to have been born in Ravenna, Florence, and other cities (and taken as portents of dire things to come), this child was a real human being. She was the daughter of a man named Domenico Malatendi, who raised vegetables outside the city. According to chroniclers who described the birth, the child had two faces, two mouths, three eyes, and no nose. On the top of her head was an excrescence described as resembling "a red cockscomb" or "an open vulva." The child was baptized in the cathedral of San Pietro on January 9 and christened Maria. Four days later she was dead.

Little Maria's life, though brief, caused a long-lasting stir. According to contemporaries, the Bolognese astrologers interpreted the infant as "a sign of great pestilence and war." A Roman observer, having seen a printed illustration of the child, interpreted Maria's body as a symbol of "calamity-stricken Italy, now so prostrated and lying with open vulva that many outsiders, whom we have seen before us, have come to luxuriate and run wild." Similar expressions of alarm came from Venice and Florence.

Maria Malatendi became part of Bolognese folklore. Surely the young Fioravanti must have heard these stories, making it reasonable to conclude that Maria's deformed body held special significance for him. The "corruption" of the human body—the cause of its sickness and deformity—would become a symbol not only of Italy's decline, but also of the wretched state of contemporary medicine.

In response, Leonardo Fioravanti would dedicate his life to finding a way back to an age of pristine glory—an age when false theories had not yet despoiled the pure and primitive medicine of olden days. He would revive it, improve it, and anoint it "the new way of healing."

2

THE EMPIRE OF DISEASE

Toward the end of his life, Leonardo Fioravanti recorded that he had spent the past 40 years roaming the world in search of the *Magna Medicina,* or Great Medicine. He documented that long search copiously, if not always factually, in his many books and letters, yet the texts reveal frequent evasions. He led his readers exactly where he wanted them to go and no further. He was a professor of secrets in more ways than one.

As substantiated by his baptismal record, Leonardo Fioravanti was born in Bologna on May 10, 1517. The document also records the names of his parents, Gabriele and Margarita Fioravanti. It was, and still is, a common family name in the Emilia-Romagna region and in Bologna, its capital.

As if purposely erasing the early years of his life, Leonardo reveals little about his boyhood. The only event he recorded from those times was Bologna's violent typhoid epidemic of 1527–28, which swept the city when he was a boy of 10.

Diseases framed the recollection of Fioravanti's life. In that respect, Leonardo was hardly unique. Early modern people marked life's stages not only by rituals of passage—baptisms, marriages, initiations, and funerals—but also by the wars, famines, natural disasters, and diseases that they suffered through and survived.

The physician Girolamo Cardano recorded in his autobiography every illness he contracted during the course of his long life, from a bout with the plague when he was two months old to recurrent attacks of gout in middle age. Few were as assiduous in marking their bodily ailments as Cardano, a hypochondriac who, by his own admission, "considered that pleasure consisted in relief following severe pain." Yet the scrupulousness with which Cardano tallied every sickness reveals less a driving need to understand disease (or to exert some measure of psychological control over it) than complete resignation to its capricious nature.

To the people of the time, disease was arbitrary, inescapable, and ubiquitous. Epidemics struck unexpectedly, killing without mercy, while chronic illnesses lingered and debilitated their victims, exhausting them to the point that they willingly gave up the ghost. Whereas infectious diseases took a heavy toll in health and life, more constant and oppressive were everyday, nonlethal ailments such as skin rashes, ulcers, sores, and pain suffered through trauma.

Medical self-help manuals from the era shed light on these common maladies. Popular writer Girolamo Ruscelli's 1567 book, *Secreti nuovi (New Secrets),* contains about a thousand treatments for illnesses ranging from mange to memory lapse. About 20 percent target skin diseases such as rash and ringworm. Eye ailments and diseases of the teeth and gums were also common, as were intestinal worms, wounds, fractures, and bites. The typical indignities suffered by 16th-century Italians were the chronic pains of life that annoyed and distressed but rarely killed.

Contrary to Leonardo Fioravanti's opinion, doctors were only partly to blame for the high incidence of disease in early modern Italy. Far more culpable were the deplorable living conditions of the day. Lacking adequate housing, food, and drink, the great majority of people lived barely above subsistence level. Famine, poor diet, and chronic malnutrition debilitated rural and urban populations alike. Personal and communal hygiene were deplorable, especially in the cities, where sewage was dumped in the streets and human and animal waste polluted water supplies. Early modern cities bred a vigorous microcosm of microbes that preyed upon the population. giving rise to a wide variety of diseases that people simply lived with, because they had to.

A HOUSEHOLD *PESTE*

Everyday ailments were so common that they often failed to leave an imprint on people's memories. Mostly they remembered epidemics. Bubonic plague, still the century's most feared infection, had not diminished in its fury in the century and a half since its most violent outbreak during the Black Death of 1347–48. Yet many other epidemic diseases struck with nearly equal violence—so many that contemporaries referred to them all, simply, as *peste*.

"Plague" hardly conveys the range of afflictions that word embraced. *Peste* referred not only to bubonic plague but also to influenza, typhus, meningitis, smallpox, and a host of other contagious diseases. Neither do the names people used to distinguish one form of *peste* from another—*pestilenzia, morìa, mal de zucho,* for example—help us much in identifying early epidemics in modern medical terms. Often epidemics coexisted with other infectious and chronic illnesses, making identification extremely difficult. During the epidemic of 1528 that raged in the Po Valley in central Italy, contemporaries reported four different *peste* occurring simultaneously. On the basis of such accounts, rarely is it possible to determine with any degree of precision which diseases early modern people actually experienced.

Even if we could, that alone would not explain the burden people felt. The experience of disease is conditioned by social and cultural factors, as well as by biological ones. The understandings we construct of our illnesses are as important to our experience of them as the pathological agents responsible for them. Leprosy—believed to be a divine punishment for moral depravity—stigmatized its victims, rendering them objects of fear and revulsion. The leper was the archetypal outcast, condemned as "dead to the world" and separated from the rest of society. Leprosariums, refuges for the despised, were ubiquitous in Renaissance Europe.

Even in strictly biological terms, the experience of disease during the Renaissance was often radically different from ours today. In general, diseases that are new to a population strike with greater force than do more familiar illnesses. With time, populations build up natural immunities against recurrent outbreaks of epidemics, while microbes, continually evolving, adapt new strategies enabling them to live upon their hosts without killing them off. Thus syphilis and typhus, both new diseases in early modern Europe, were much more virulent and more widespread when they first appeared than they would later become.

People lived in mortal fear of epidemics. The letters of the Florentine gentlewoman Alessandra Strozzi to her sons, written from 1447 to 1470, a period of recurrent plague epidemics, reveal the panic that gripped people when word reached them that the dreaded disease had arrived. "Now it's in two houses close to here and it's leaving few survivors," she wrote to her son Filippo in November 1465. "So it is beginning, and it is winter. God help us." Reflecting on the death of a relative during the plague of 1458, Strozzi wrote, "There's nothing you can do to prevent it and we all seem to go that way." The suddenness of the man's death baffled her: "Although he'd been feeling ill for some days, he wasn't in a bad way and he was always going out and didn't seem really sick."

Death overshadowed life, and death's mystery made its presence ominous and menacing.

Virtually everyone agreed on the underlying cause of the plague: sin. No one in the 16th century would have doubted that epidemics, like all natural disasters, were sent by an angry God as punishments for humanity's wrongdoing. In the view of Venetian physician Prospero Borgaruccio, plague was "God's great scourge against us sinners."

Few questioned the justice of this harsh judgment. Certainly not Leonardo Fioravanti, who, writing in the 1560s, gave this explanation of the plague:

> The principal and most powerful cause of the plague is put in motion by the Divine Goodness. For it cannot be denied that our Holy God, the creator of all things, is the first cause *(motore)* of all creation, as the sacred and divine histories have testified. . . . Infinite times He has sent plague to the world to punish those people who rebelled and strayed from Him. And yet when we see such frightful diseases as the plague,

> which strike such terror in the world, we can say in truth that it is God's work and not a natural thing. Such infirmities never come except when it pleases his Divine Majesty, who sends it to punish us for the enormous sins that we continually commit against his divine goodness.

Medicine coexisted with this grim theological understanding of disease. Even popes hired physicians—lots of them. Scipione Mercurio, who had a foot in both camps as a physician and a friar, insisted that religion and medicine must go together, "For God has ordained that health is recovered through medicine." To ask for a cure without medicine would be like asking for a miracle—which would, in effect, be to tempt God.

THE QUEST FOR A CAUSE

If the physicians accepted the underlying supernatural origin of epidemics, they were less certain about the secondary, natural causes of disease. Most agreed with the ancient Greek physician Galen's theory that plagues resulted from some sort of corruption of the air. Borgaruccio took the fact that plague strikes everyone at the same time as proof that it is caused by foul air, for what else does everyone do in common but breathe the air? Once inhaled, he continued, these *miasmas* proceed "in some occult way" to "follow our humors, and above all the innate humidity of the heart, by which putrefaction afterwards proceeds an attack of fever, as I say, most pernicious and dreadful."

Some physicians assigned great weight to astrological factors, which they believed unleashed the foul airs that gave rise to epidemics. Conjunctions of the planets Mars and Saturn were thought to be particularly dangerous. Others insisted that astrological events were merely portents of coming plague, not causes in and of themselves. Physicians also noticed a connection between famine and epidemics, although they were unsure whether famine caused plague or, by weakening the constitution, merely made people more susceptible to it.

The one principle that virtually all authorities agreed upon was that pestilence could be transmitted by personal contact with infected persons or their goods. The Renaissance theory of contagion continues an ancient theme, the belief that disease was brought from the outside by travelers and vagabonds. From there it was but a short step, psychologically speaking, to placing the blame for disease on marginal elements within: beggars, prostitutes, the poor, and Europe's traditional scapegoats, Jews. Such "lower" groups in the population were regarded as particularly vulnerable to the disease because they attracted contagion and vice.

The horrifying symptoms of the plague reinforced the view of the sickness as bodily corruption. In bubonic plague *(Yersinia pestis)*, a rodent disease, fleas typically carry the pathogen from infected rats to humans. Once a person is afflicted, the microbe quickly replicates at the site of the flea bite, causing the area to blacken and produce a swelling in the lymph node nearest the bite. These swellings, or buboes—the characteristic sign that gives the plague the name "bubonic"—gradually grow larger, often reaching the size of an egg or an apple, and are intensely painful. Patients develop high fevers and become alternately listless and frantic. Their eyelids turn blue and their faces become leaden. Then, when the buboes suppurate, they ooze a pus that emits a horrible stench. In up to 90 percent of cases, delirium sets in and the victim lapses into a coma and dies. No wonder that the remedies physicians prescribed against the plague included purgations to drive out bodily corruptions.

Erroneous or not, Renaissance etiologies (explanations of the cause of diseases) dictated urban communities' responses to epidemics. Gioseffo Daciano, the city physician of Udine, wrote, "The first thing that must be done is to immediately have recourse to heartfelt prayers, votive offerings, and fasts to the Lord God our most merciful Redeemer, that he might rectify and return the corrupted air to its purity and natural temperament according to the seasons of the year." Odiferous wood and perfumes should be burned throughout the city to purify the air. During the plague of 1556, Daciano recalled, the health board placed stringent controls on the sale of fresh fruits, meat, and other perishable items. Butchers' and fishmongers' shops were closed; the marketplace was strictly regulated.

Fearing that clothing might be infected, the health board even banned the sale of textiles and leather goods.

This theory of contagion also ushered in regulations that the sick were to be quarantined. City dwellers hated and feared these rules almost as much as the plague itself. Daciano's description of the measures taken in Udine in 1556 mirrors those taken in other cities:

> It was provided, under pain of hanging, that no one should walk around the city, nor engage with infected persons. A public proclamation was issued, that anyone who became ill had to immediately notify the officials, under threat of the aforesaid penalty. Two inspectors *(visitatori)* for each neighborhood visited the houses in their jurisdiction at sunset and reported their findings to the Health Office.... Each day the police took away those who had been denounced as infirm and delivered them to the health officer.... No body was buried until it had first been examined by the inspector. If it was not infected, with written permission the priest could bury it in the church with solemn ceremonies. But if they had died of the peste, the corpse handlers *(beccamorti)* alone buried them.
>
> Those who had relations with infected persons were sequestered in their house for at least two days. The houses that had dead or infected persons were closed for forty days. ... Each day the sick and the dead were brought to the *lazzaretto* of the infected, where their bodily and spiritual needs were provided for. Those who remained at home and were healthy were removed to another *lazzaretto,* and those who were healthy but suspected of having the disease were washed with vinegar and rosewater and had their clothing changed. They were all well purged according to what was determined to be the preservative against the disease, and the families (without their infected things) were separated from one another. The property that was of little value or suspected of being infected was immediately burned by the health officers. But the things that were valuable, provided that they were

not infected, were with great diligence, care, and art faithfully cleaned and purged.

SOMETHING WICKED THIS WAY COMES

In Bologna, reports of the epidemic Fioravanti remembered were first heard from Rome. The Modena notary Tommasino Lancelotti ominously summarized firsthand reports of conditions in the summer of 1527 as the epidemic rapidly moved north: "all the houses abandoned, deserted, full of infected people and dead animals; one cannot celebrate Mass or go to the shops for fear of catching the sickness and dying, because there are no physicians, medicines, or bandages; great and deadly famine, things unheard of since the world began."

The epidemic swept through northern Italy with unusual ferocity. One frightened contemporary reported that 20,000 had died in Bologna—a figure probably inflated by panic, considering that the city's population was only 60,000 at the time. Others reported a figure around 12,000, the same number said to have been killed in Mantua. The disease lingered in northern Italy throughout the summer and fall and continued into the following year, felling hundreds of thousands of victims.

What caused the epidemic of 1527–28? Although diagnosis of historical diseases is speculative at best, contemporary accounts of the epidemic appear to be more consistent with typhus than with plague, even though plague was probably present in some areas as well. (Diseases are notoriously opportunistic that way: When one parasite infects a population and breaks down its resistance, others take advantage of the host's weakened state.) The physician Girolamo Fracastoro's detailed description of the 1527 epidemic reads almost like a textbook account of typhus: fever and fatigue followed by general prostration and delirium in the first few days, then the body erupting in a general rash resembling fleabites or, in some cases, spots about the size of lentils—the classic symptom that gave the disease its 16th-century Italian name, *mal di petecchie* (spotted sickness). Niccolò Massa, another physician, gave a similar account, noting that "the spots appeared throughout the entire body."

Only the timing of the 1527 epidemic appears to contraindicate typhus. Spread by human body lice, typhus normally occurs during the late winter and early spring, when bundling up with clothing encourages the growth of lice. The 1527 epidemic broke out in the late spring and continued through the summer. However, 1527 was an unusually cold and wet year. The layers of heavy, moist clothing that people wore under such conditions would have provided a perfect environment for the growth of body lice. Crops failed due to the severe weather, resulting in extreme famine, which further weakened the population and made it more susceptible to the infection.

Nor was this the end of Bologna's suffering. That same spring the mercenaries who made up Holy Roman Emperor Charles V's army were billeted in the city and its environs on their road to Rome, where they would pillage the city—the infamous Sack of Rome. Unpaid and undisciplined, they lived on plunder and extortion. While Bologna was saved Rome's fate, thanks to a substantial bounty paid out of the city's treasury, the mercenary troops were impossible to control. One witness reported that 34,000 German and Spanish troops entered Bolognese territory in March and "commenced to steal chickens and other animals great and small, to smash houses and jewelry cases, to rob and kill in the countryside, shaming the women, burning the farmhouses, and killing and wounding the country folk."

How did Fioravanti, as a boy of ten at the time, remember this devastation? Surprisingly, he reveals tantalizingly little about that *annus horribilis*. To him it must have seemed as if the Huns had descended on poor Bologna. Loutish, drunken men who spoke a coarse language with harsh, guttural sounds, the imperial German soldiers behaved like barbarians. They commandeered people's homes and looted their food. Adding to Bologna's misery, the cold, damp weather chilled to the bone. For two years a terrible famine had raged. The price of bread, when it could be bought at all, was so high that people starved. Making matters even worse, the city authorities taxed the foodstuff—a levy the people called the "death penny."

So derelict had the city become that it took on an otherworldly aspect. People walked around gaunt and hollow-eyed, resembling ghosts more than humans. Some died in the streets, then rotted there for days before the overwhelmed authorities got around to collecting the bodies.

A BOY'S MEMORY OF MAYHEM

Although the epidemic killed thousands, it was not the disease's mortality that Leonardo remembered about the scourge. Rather, he recalled the strict measures taken against it by the health authorities. Much of the dread generated by epidemics was caused by the rigid restrictions on daily life, the threats and bullying of officials charged with enforcing them, and the abuses that inevitably resulted. The merchant Romolo Amaseo, writing from Bologna in September 1527, reported that the proclamations against the pestilence were "*grandissima*—very extreme" and that most of the citizens had tried to flee, "if they were not already dead or gravely ill."

Not surprisingly, people resented the restrictions. Even as a child, Leonardo would have looked on, terrified, as the health police rapped on people's doors and demanded entry, burned their belongings in gigantic bonfires, and marched the infected off to the *lazzaretto.* Such images must have been seared into his memory. Writing about the event 43 years later, he still could not contain his anger, and he aimed it directly at the medical establishment. During the Bologna epidemic, he reported, the epidemic caused much more damage in the city than in the country, despite the presence of physicians and a medical college in town. For "cities are much more apt to receive corruptions than the countryside, which is more open." Hence the country air is uncontaminated by the "corruption of the natural heat" that infects city air and causes the pestilence.

More important, the villages did not suffer the strict regimentation imposed by the health board. "In the villages there was less fear than in the cities," Fioravanti recalled, "where strict rules and regulations were put into effect, like shutting people up in their houses, burning their belongings, and sending them to the pest houses, things that would terrify the ghosts of hell to say nothing of Christian men and women." Indeed, only after the authorities had lifted the restrictions on people's lives did the plague abate:

> The remedy they found for relieving the pestilence was this: they ended all those restrictions and let people live in their own way. They ordered the physicians to visit the people in their houses and the pharmacists to give them medicines. After this decree went out, the epidemic didn't have as much force, and all of a sudden a great gladness grew in the hearts of the people and thus the plague was completely eradicated.

The end of the plague generated popular images just as profound and moving. In the early modern period, the experience of surviving an epidemic took on deep religious significance. Why was *I* spared, people asked, when so many others were felled? To such questions there could be no certain answers, only the profound gratitude that gives rise to fervent religious devotion. Faced with threats to their collective well-being, townspeople wanted to know who would help them and what they should do in return. Similar queries had been asked thousands of times before, and they are still being asked today. To the people of Bologna in 1528, the answer was the Madonna del Soccorso.

Like many objects of local devotion, the veneration of the Madonna del Soccorso began with the discovery of a buried image of the Virgin. The statue had been disinterred in 1517 by two workers digging near an old gate in the city wall. The men cleaned the battered image and placed it in a shrine, hoping that it would attract devotees and alms, as other shrines had. A confraternity of followers was organized but, to the lay brothers' disappointment, the image failed to demonstrate any miraculous power.

During the pestilence of 1527, the lay brothers intensified their religious services. For many long weeks they prostrated themselves with tears and prayers before the little image, begging her to placate God's anger so that he might lift the plague from the city. They removed the image from its shrine and began carrying it in procession through the neighborhood, singing devotions and pleading with God to remove the sickness.

To the wonderment of everyone, the plague soon subsided. It seemed like a great miracle, and the humble image came to be called the Madonna del Soccorso (Madonna of Succor). To this day, each year on the second Sunday after Easter, the image is solemnly conveyed across the city to the shrine of San Rocco, the patron saint of those who suffer from plague.

Images of the plague, the suffering, the processions, and the lifting of the sickness remained fixed in Leonardo's memory. Did the confraternity's prayers end the epidemic? Or was the procession God's way of telling the people that the doctors' strict regimens were contrary to nature? Leonardo offered no opinion. But of this he was certain: "If what was done at the end had been done in the beginning, the mortality would not have been as great as it was. So you can see how great is the power of joy, that it prevented the pestilence from killing any more people there. This was the remedy they found in Bologna." It is our first indication of his lifelong conviction that "natural ways" of healing were superior to the physicians' strict regimens.

The empire of disease that gripped Bologna in the early 16th century profoundly shaped Leonardo's view of medicine. Even as a child, he saw clearly that piety, suffering, and healing were inextricably linked. Piety teaches that death is natural, yet the physician's duty is to ease suffering, and for that, all the learning in the world could not help. Later in life, he would look back on his time in Bologna, the celebrated capital of Italian medical learning, and reflect that he had discovered true medicine not in books but by way of experience. The physician who possesses only academic knowledge, he would later write, "might be able to talk about medicine but would never be able to actually heal, because there's a big difference between medicating with words and medicating with deeds."

Fioravanti's disillusionment with academic medicine would persuade him that only by leaving Bologna and venturing out into the world—only by searching for cures that he expected to learn from the people themselves—would he find his way to true healing.

3
MEDICAL BOLOGNA

Leonardo Fioravanti grew up in the shadow of Italy's oldest university and most famous medical college. Long celebrated as a law school, the Bologna *studium,* or university, emerged in the 13th century as a prominent center of medical learning, liberal arts, and philosophy. With an enrollment of more than 1,500 students it had the largest faculty and student body of any Italian university. In addition to being a world-famous institution of learning, the University of Bologna was its host city's chief economic asset, so its professors enjoyed lives of privilege.

The extensive perquisites and generous economic benefits conferred upon academics drew eminent scholars to Bologna. The great Florentine teacher Taddeo Alderotti, who taught there from 1260 to 1295, trained an entire generation of distinguished Bologna masters. One of Taddeo's pupils, Mondino de' Liuzzi, pioneered the use of human dissection as a part of medical education. Although autopsies had been performed for some time, as early as 1316 medical students at Bologna would have been able to observe human dissection in a classroom. Surgery—a craft traditionally learned by apprenticeship—also became part of the medical curriculum at Bologna.

In Fioravanti's day, the university's medical school was regarded as Europe's premier center of medical learning, and a model for other European universities. Its faculty boasted such luminaries as the naturalist Luca Ghini, who took his pupils on field trips in the surrounding hills to learn about medicinal plants. Others went on to greater heights: Matteo Corti, after a distinguished career as professor of theoretical medicine, became a personal physician to Pope Clement VII.

The medical curriculum taught at Bologna, and all other European medical schools, was based upon an extensive body of Latin medical literature of Greek and Arabic origin. It included treatises attributed to the ancient Greek physician Hippocrates, whom everyone regarded as the founder of medicine, as well as works by the Hellenistic physician Galen. Added to these were a number books by Arabic writers, notably the 11th-century Persian physician Avicenna (Ibn Sina), whose encyclopedic work, *Canon of Medicine,* occupied a central place in the traditional medical curriculum. Essentially a compendium of Greco-Arabic medicine, the *Canon* was the learned physician's bible, giving chapter and verse for every disease and bodily part, from head to toe.

By Fioravanti's time, however, Avicenna's reputation had noticeably declined. Skepticism about the value of his doctrine had been expressed as early as the 13th century, when the Montpellier professor Arnald of Villanova attacked the "infatuation" with the Arab master as misguided and dangerous. Yet the criticisms launched by humanists in the late 15th and 16th centuries were far broader in scope. The goal of the humanist movement, which had originated in Italy in the 14th century, was to "go back to the sources" *(ad fontes)* of classical culture. The program strove to imitate, however imperfectly, the thought and literary style of Greco-Roman antiquity. As a necessary corollary, the "corrupting" influence of the Arabs had to be expunged. Relentless attacks by Renaissance moderns against Avicenna's "tyranny" over the schools resulted in a body of learning that, ironically, was not modern at all; it was tied to classical Greek and Roman medicine even more closely than the medieval curriculum had been.

DUKES OF DISPUTATION

The classroom experience of a Renaissance medical student was vastly different from that of a modern one. Rather than acquiring a foundation in basic sciences such as biology, chemistry, anatomy, and physiology, the Renaissance medical student studied the works of the ancient authorities and learned to dispute controversial questions that stemmed from their writings. Experts in the art of disputation, the professors were expected to demonstrate the subtleties of argumentation in the classroom.

Besides being an important teaching method, disputation was a favorite form of academic entertainment: Outperforming other masters in disputations was a way of attracting students. The celebrated Bologna professor Dino del Garbo once loudly debated a fine point of Galenic theory with another professor in the street. Students were expected to learn these disputations and be able to imitate them. As historian Roger French notes, the aim of medical education was "to make the ancients so clearly understood [that] it was as if they were in the same room, speaking."

The kinds of questions that students and masters argued about tell us a lot about Renaissance medical education. Certain avenues of inquiry—for example, "Can disease be hereditary?"—resemble important modern medical problems, although in the Renaissance such issues were never resolved on experimental grounds, but purely by argumentation. Other questions were purely theoretical. "Can a physician cure a disease that he does not understand?" asked one professor. "Can a mortal sickness be cured?" demanded another, nonsensically. Other questions were specific to Galen's medical doctrine, such as: "Should vomiting be provoked on two successive days?" Even on matters that were purely empirical or descriptive, such as physiology and anatomy, the professors prized intellectually coherent accounts of bodily processes above anatomical descriptions of human anatomy.

Renaissance medical learning was thus highly theoretical. It was, as historian Nancy Siraisi writes, "a rigorous mental discipline requiring of its devotees a high degree of skill in handling abstract concepts and theoretical systems; simultaneously, it was a fairly simple technology or craft." Academic medicine's main selling point was that it explained the *causes* of things. Practice without theory, the learned physicians insisted, was poor medicine, and knowledge of theory made the physicians stand out from the herd of uneducated practitioners swarming the piazzas and plying their trade in pharmacies and barbershops.

Early modern Bologna was filled with dozens of doctors. As you walked the streets, they were easily recognized by the billowing sleeves of the gowns they were privileged to wear. University-educated and able to command high fees, the physicians were experts on diseases affecting the inner body. Using a number of diagnostic tools, such as reading the pulse and analyzing urine, they could supposedly "see into" the body and determine the underlying causes of infirmities by their outward signs.

BLOOD AND BILE

The theoretical foundation of the physician's art was the ancient doctrine of the four humors, which enabled doctors to understand the all-important origins of sickness and propose a cure. Health and illness were primarily matters of balance and imbalance of the bodily fluids, or humors, which determined a person's complexion. The four bodily humors—blood, yellow bile, phlegm, and black bile—were all naturally present in the body, but during specific seasons they appeared to flow out and unleash illness. For example, winter colds were ascribed to phlegm, while summer dysentery appeared as an overabundant flowing of bile.

Correspondingly, treatment consisted of prescribing a diet and routine of life, or regimen, aimed at maintaining or restoring the natural humoral balance. This was done by regulating the so-called non-naturals—that is, by tailoring a patient's diet, exercise, and environmental conditions to achieve the optimum complexion and restore the humors to their proper equilibrium. Thus if a patient suffered from the disease called catarrh, which is characterized by a surfeit of phlegm—a cold and moist humor—he should be treated with hot and dry remedies, such as hyssop, cumin, licorice, or syrup of ginger. (Other ways to regulate the humors included bloodletting and prescribing hot or cold foods.) The therapy was designed primarily to maintain health; physicians were well aware of their limited power to change the course of an illness.

Strolling along the streets of Renaissance Bologna, you would see the shops of various medical practitioners, each marked by the signboard they were allowed to display. The barber-surgeons' shops were decorated with placards depicting an arm with the sharp-pointed surgical instrument known as a lancet, which symbolized the medical task they were most frequently called upon to perform: bleeding.

In theory, barber-surgeons intervened only under a physician's order, as part of a prescribed cure. In reality, matters were quite different. Seasonal bloodlettings were commonly self-prescribed as part of everyday health management. In addition to performing phlebotomies, barber-surgeons were authorized to set broken bones, treat wounds, and medicate abscesses and skin diseases. They were, in other words, authorized to treat the outer body. (The physiological domain of physicians, by contrast, was the body beneath the skin.) Because their cures were more accessible and less expensive than those of physicians, surgeons routinely treated a much broader range of illnesses than they were officially empowered to.

Farther down the street, you might encounter a sign with three crosses; this signified a midwife's establishment. Beyond assisting at childbirth and delivering virtually all of Bologna's newborns, midwives treated a wide variety of female complaints. The treatment of women's disorders was by no means the exclusive domain of midwives, but men tended to cede women's reproductive health to women on grounds of modesty. Until the 17th century, when male physicians began to take over many of the tasks traditionally assigned to midwives, the feminine body was generally regarded as secretive and the preserve of female practitioners. Midwives were also charged with washing and dressing the dead in preparation for burial. Theirs were the hands, along with those of the barbers, that touched the body, whether alive or dead, whether dirty or covered with sores.

Pharmacies were easily recognized by the distinctive multicolored signs displayed above their doors. A 1568 list of shops included the signs of the Moon, the Cedar, the Doctor, the Swordsman, St. George, the Star, the Angel, and the patron saints of the plague, Sts. Cosmas and Damian. In the early 16th century, apothecaries controlled the quality and pricing of their products through their guild, which also included practitioners of such lower-ranking trades as grocers, candlemakers, brewers, and paint sellers. However, around the middle of the century, the city's health board, the Protomedicato, began to take control of licensing apothecaries and inspecting their shops.

In addition to its settled practitioners, medical Bologna included a host of itinerant healers who came into the city periodically or seasonally to ply their trades. The *norcini,* who specialized in lithotomy (surgery to remove bladder stones) and the cure of hernias, were highly skilled surgeons who were natives of the area of Norcia, a village near Perugia in southern Umbria. Why did hernia specialists hail from Norcia? Historians point to the region's widespread pig farming; castrating pigs to be fattened for market was carried out by specialists who wandered from town to town. This plausible link underscores the empirical, folk origins of many early modern surgical practices. Others specialized in treating cataracts, setting bones, pulling teeth, and treating venereal diseases. Because their skills were so specialized, these healers had to travel from one town to the next to enlarge their clientele. Charlatans and other remedy peddlers also drifted from city to city; in Bologna, their portable stages heightened the hustle and bustle of daily life in the city's piazzas and marketplaces.

A CURIOUS OMISSION

Among the many silences surrounding Fioravanti, perhaps none is more perplexing than the one that veils the first 30 years of his life. In his *Treasury of Human Life,* he begins his autobiography in 1548—when, at the age of 30, Fioravanti "went out into the world" to seek experience. Yet those first three decades were formative, for he does not burst onto the scene in 1548 as an innocent abroad, but as a surgeon and empirical healer whose views of academic medicine had already begun to acquire their jaundiced shape. Reconstructing those years will require inventiveness—and a willingness to hazard some reasonable guesses.

Did Leonardo attend medical school? For once, the local archive is helpful. We know that he did not graduate from the university during those early years because his name does not appear in the *Liber Secretum*, the "Secret Book" that recorded the names of the university's graduates. However, that does not preclude his having taken classes there. Later on, Fioravanti would claim that he had been *"adottorato"* (literally, "made a doctor") three times before returning to Bologna to receive his medical degree, but this claim must have referred to licenses to practice surgery that local authorities granted him. An archival record from Rome documents two such licenses, one in Naples and another in Rome. The third was probably a permit to practice as an "empiric"—a derogatory term for healers lacking university credentials—in Bologna or Palermo. Otherwise, nothing is known of his formal medical education.

Yet Fioravanti was unusually literate for a surgeon. By 1548 he was familiar enough with the herbal of the ancient Greek botanist Dioscorides, first published in Italian four years earlier, to use the herbalist's treatment for quartan fever. He knew some Latin but, by his own admission, was not fluent in the language. Clearly Fioravanti possessed a smattering of medical learning, but he was in no way wedded to academic tradition. If he did go to medical school, in all probability he was a dropout.

And if that was the case, Fioravanti was scarcely atypical. Many students in this era attended a university for a few years, then dropped out or moved on to another school. Bologna's graduation fees were relatively high compared with other universities—a disparity that doubtless fostered the peripatetic character of its student body. Scholars might come to Bologna for its teaching, but they would often transfer elsewhere to complete their degrees. Polish astronomer Nicolaus Copernicus, for example, attended the University of Bologna from 1497 to 1500 before transferring to Ferrara to graduate. Others dropped out altogether, thwarted by the sterility—or, being poorly prepared, the difficulty—of academic medicine.

Milanese physician Francesco Pardo was one who left Bologna as jaded as Fioravanti: In a 1566 letter to Leonardo he declared, "everything I studied at Bologna was nothing but smoke compared to your doctrine." That Leonardo shared Francesco's sentiments about academic medicine would soon become apparent.

4

LEONARDO AND THE ANATOMISTS

Fioravanti was 23 years old in the winter of 1540 when Flemish anatomist Andreas Vesalius arrived in Bologna to perform a series of anatomical demonstrations. Although Vesalius was only 26 at the time and had yet to publish his pioneering work, *On the Fabric of the Human Body,* he was already famous for his dissections. As the professor of anatomy at the University of Padua medical school, Vesalius insisted on dissecting cadavers himself rather than following the customary practice—that is, having a barber-surgeon do the cutting while the professor read the lecture describing the parts of the body.

Vesalius's skill as a dissector was legendary, so the Bologna medical students eagerly awaited his appearance. Whether a medical student or not, Leonardo would certainly have been aware of the demonstration, for it was the most talked-about event that Carnival season. That's because dissections had gradually been opened to the public—provided each spectator paid an entry fee. By the 16th century, the public anatomy lesson had become one of the most anticipated theatrical events on the Carnival program. To some extent, practical concerns dictated that public anatomies (as dissections were known) would be staged during Carnival: Because Carnival took place in early winter, cadavers would be less prone to decay. But the theatrical element was equally important, for Carnival season guaranteed a large crowd at any spectacle.

To heighten the drama, university officials brought together two individuals whose contrasting outlooks, temperaments, and philosophies would make a clash inevitable. The anatomy course at Bologna that term was being taught by Matteo Corti, a distinguished professor of theoretical medicine. Thirty years older than Vesalius, Corti had come to Bologna from Padua in 1538, drawn by an annual salary of 1,200 ducats. Ambitious and vain, he was, like Vesalius, on his way to the top. In 1541 Corti accepted an invitation to become the personal physician of Cosimo de' Medici, the Grand Duke of Tuscany; he then served as a professor of medicine at Pisa before moving on to Rome to become personal physician to the pope.

One of the humanist "moderns" who insisted on returning to the unadulterated original texts of the ancients, Corti made his name as a critic of Avicenna and a staunch defender of Galen. "I certainly don't see what use it would be for you to read the Arabic authors," he admonished his students. "There's nothing in them that isn't explained more clearly by Hippocrates and Galen." The confrontation between the well-established Galenist Corti and the brash young anatomist Vesalius was a clash of the old versus the new.

Among those taking Corti's anatomy course that term was an assiduous German medical student, Baldasar Heseler. Heseler took copious classroom notes, recording every detail of Corti's lectures—and sprinkling his notes with private jabs at the professor. "See how anxious he is to criticize and boast in unimportant and paltry things, always seeking vainglory," Heseler wrote at one point. Impatient with the lectures, Heseler and his fellow students grew anxious to see the things hidden beneath the skin with their own eyes. When the beadle interrupted Corti's fifth lecture to announce that the anatomy subject was finally ready, Heseler reports, "we proceeded to the demonstration in great disorder, as the mad Italians do."

BODY OF EVIDENCE

Corti's lectures took place in the Church of San Salvatore. Each morning and afternoon, the professor declaimed on a particular organ or system and explicated passages of Galen's text. Afterward, the students walked the hundred or so yards to the Church of San Francesco, where Vesalius's anatomy demonstrations were held. The atmosphere within must have been as lively as the scene represented on the title page of Vesalius's famous treatise (see page 44). More than 200 spectators crowded into the candlelit room. Along with the students, a throng of townspeople, who had paid 20 soldi apiece to witness the demonstration, jostled for places on the four tiers of benches that encircled the makeshift dissection table. Infected with the spirit of Carnival, the spectators chattered among themselves, made obscene jokes, and groped at the organs displayed on the anatomical bench. On several occasions during the demonstration, Vesalius had to plead with the crowd to quiet down so that he could proceed with his work.

The three cadavers prepared for the dissections were, as required by law, the bodies of hanged criminals. The first anatomical subject had been hanged on the morning of Corti's third lecture, according to Heseler. "He was a very strong, muscular and fat man, about thirty-four years of age." The following day Heseler looked on as some brothers from the confraternity of Santa Maria della Morte—a company of pious laymen whose religious duties included consoling condemned criminals before they were executed—cut the man's body down from the gallows and carried it to the hospital "in stately procession." We do not know the nature of the man's crime, but in all likelihood it was murder or theft—the two offenses most commonly punished by execution. University statutes governing the subjects for human dissection mandated that he would also have been a foreigner (to avoid bringing shame upon any family from the city). Later, after the anatomy was completed, the brethren of Santa Maria della Morte would collect the parts of his body and prepare them for a proper burial in a Christian cemetery.

Twenty-six demonstrations took place over the course of 14 days, both morning and evening. Old versus new, Galenist against empirical anatomist, Corti and Vesalius clashed again and again, the professor insisting that Galen was infallible and the anatomist urging students to rely on the evidence of their senses. The most dramatic

This 1543 frontispiece depicts Vesalius (center) doing a public dissection in a crowded anatomy theater. The barber-surgeons who formerly performed dissections have been banished to the floor, where they quarrel over who will sharpen Vesalius's razors.

moment came during the hotly debated discussion of venesection, or phlebotomy: Where is the proper place to draw blood—near the infection or on the opposite side? Vesalius had staked out his opinion in a *Letter on Venesection* published in Latin the year before.

In his lecture, Corti refuted Vesalius's theory and vigorously defended Galen against the young anatomist. At the demonstration following the lecture, Vesalius led his older colleague to one of the opened cadavers and pointed to evidence that he claimed proved his theory: "Here Galen is wrong," the Fleming declared, thumping the cadaver's chest, "because he didn't know the true position of the vein. Plainly he errs in this and in many other places, as is evident from these bodies." In the disputation that ensued, Corti stood calmly as Vesalius, gesticulating wildly with bloody hands, protested that he preferred to believe in the visible as opposed to the imaginary.

"HOW CAN WE BELIEVE IN THINGS THAT ARE OCCULT?"

Present or not at this particular demonstration, Fioravanti viewed human dissection differently from any medical student in the room. Later on he made those views known, and they can be summarized in a single word: disgust. To Fioravanti, human dissection was a practice both "pitiless and cruel" *(impia e crudele),* an undertaking that resembled the butcher's art more than the art of medicine, "since both do the same thing, namely skinning, dismembering, cutting up, and taking a body apart into many pieces."

Not only that, Fioravanti argued, but opening up the body and displaying its parts could never substantiate the claims that physicians assert when they talk about things beneath the skin and therefore invisible to the eye, such as choleric humors or vital spirits. "When I saw an anatomy done," he later wrote, "I never saw phlegm, choler, melancholy, or vital spirits, or any of those other fabulous things that the physicians dream up. I saw the tongue, lungs, heart, liver, spleen, ventricle, diaphragm, bowels, kidneys, bladder, nerves, veins, tendons, flesh, skin and bones, but I never saw those imaginary things. How can we believe in things that are occult, things we can't see or touch?"

The only thing the anatomy lesson proved, in Fioravanti's opinion, was that doctors teach and write about things that don't exist.

Fioravanti's extreme views contrasted sharply with those of the academic medical community. During his day, the "anatomical renaissance" being ushered in by Vesalius and others was elevating anatomy to a lofty status within medical faculties. Vesalius held a professorial chair at Padua and later went on to become the Holy Roman Emperor's personal physician. By the 1570s, thanks largely to student demand, every medical school in Italy was teaching anatomy according to methods he had advanced.

The confrontation between Vesalius and Corti, both vain and cocksure men, would have epitomized to Leonardo the futility of learned medicine. That neither man would budge from his version of the truth—one through the open book, the other through the opened body—persuaded Fioravanti that academic medicine was nothing more than a fantasy. Physicians "continually dispute and read about these fabulous things, and none of them has ever been able to show how a specific part of the interior works with all its particularity," he protested. "They just grope around and with their thoughts and chimeras go about imagining them in their minds."

To Fioravanti, the problem with academic medicine was that it consisted of too much theory and too many books—too much argument and too little evidence. It lacked any foundation in experience and served only to keep the physicians on top. "See how the physicians have usurped medicine, taking measures that deprived everyone else who had not graduated with a degree from taking their office: what a malicious thing!" Medicine was God's gift to all, he maintained. Anyone who had the skills to practice the art should be allowed to do so.

Worse, according to Fioravanti, anatomy is "contrary to the order of nature," for nature wants to unite the parts, not tear them asunder. The surgeon's role is not to cut up the body, but to "help nature" to heal the body. That anatomy is an offense against nature, Fioravanti argued, can be plainly seen by observing animals:

> We see that dogs never bother the bodies of dead dogs, nor do wolves, foxes, cats, or any kind bird in the world. This is because nature doesn't permit it. We, on the other hand, use the excuse to perform such cruelty, for which we are well punished and castigated, such that the majority of those who do such cruelties as anatomy die a violent death and almost in despair, as we see over and over again. So I would advise everyone not to ever meddle in this matter of anatomy and to not take apart human bodies, which God our lord made, because in doing so one sins against the law of nature and offends one's own kind.

Many of Fioravanti's contemporaries shared his repugnance at the notion of opening cadavers for public inspection. As historian Andrea Carlino has suggested, the 16th-century opposition to dissection was not religious but anthropological: "The difficulty resided . . . in the contact with the dead and with blood *(contrectare)* and in the desecration of the corporeal structure." To Fioravanti, the anatomist was not much different from a butcher—with the latter enjoying a slight moral edge by performing an art vital to human sustenance.

Thus we might conjecture the reasons why Leonardo left the university and, presumably, apprenticed himself to a surgeon or empiric. His severe judgment of human dissection—a moral (and perhaps religious) reaction that welled up from deep within—typified his reaction to academic medicine in general: Fioravanti was repelled not only by anatomy but by what to him was a sterile and bankrupt academic tradition.

By entering the underworld of medicine, Leonardo Fioravanti chose a different path. He would become the scourge of the doctors and the defender of the empirics.

5

THE EDUCATION OF A SURGEON

Leonardo's recollection of his Bologna years is not terribly helpful for reconstructing his early medical training. All he reveals about his professional life during that period is that he began studying medicine at age 16 and had been practicing since he was 22. We know that he wasn't a physician while he resided in Bologna because he didn't graduate from the medical college and wasn't entered on the rolls of the city's physicians. But that would not have prevented him from being a *medico,* or doctor. Like a host of other practitioners, he might have worked as an empiric, or unlettered healer. Empirics plied their trade, sometimes licensed and sometimes not, in every city of Renaissance Italy, selling patent medicines, or "secrets," vaunted to cure various ailments. As we know from contemporary observers such as Boccaccio, the ranks of such healers swelled in the decades following the Black Death, attracted by a growing demand for medical services amid a severe shortage of physicians. Drifting from town to town, empirics often escaped the notice of the authorities.

Or, as seems more likely, Fioravanti might have apprenticed himself to a barber-surgeon. His substantial knowledge of surgery suggests that he received some early instruction in the art before he left Bologna to seek his fortune. Whatever his training, Fioravanti's jaundiced view of the medical establishment was clearly shaped by his exposure to Bologna's medical oligarchy. In 1517, the year of his birth, the city had placed all medical practitioners under the control of a newly formed public health board called the Assumpti contra empyricos, or Protomedicato, which comprised the dean of the medical college and two professors chosen by lot. In addition to licensing healers, the three *protomedici* were charged with compiling the city's *Antidotaria*, or pharmacopeia—the list of medicinal compounds approved for sale in pharmacies. The protomedici were likewise obligated to visit apothecary shops to verify their drugs were being made according to specifications. They inspected pharmaceuticals at the customs office, set the prices pharmacists charged for drugs, and licensed street vendors wishing to sell medical secrets.

Thus an academic oligarchy controlled virtually every aspect of Bologna's medical practice, from licensing empirics to pricing drugs. If in other cities medical power was not as overtly connected with the academic establishment, the control of medical practice was no less oligarchic. Empirics, surgeons, and apothecaries had little choice but to accept their inferior status vis-à-vis physicians. As Neapolitan barber-surgeon Cintio d'Amato wrote in his treatise on barbering, "in those matters which the learned physician with judgment proposes, the diligent barber with his hands carries out." The authorities repeatedly enforced the regulations that separated the therapeutic domain of the physician from that of the surgeon.

This division of labor in Renaissance medicine was also governed by Galen's theory, which divided therapy into diet, pharmacy, and surgery, all arranged in a hierarchy reflecting their degrees of universality and effectiveness. Whereas drugs and surgery were deemed to have local applications, diet was a treatment directed at the entire body. The ancient Greek meaning of diet was much broader than ours: It embraced not only what we eat and drink but what Venetian physician Giovanni della Croce dubbed "the mode and regimen of life" in general, including exercise, rest, excretion, bathing, and sexual activity. The cornerstone of Renaissance therapeutics, diet was the exclusive domain of the physician; though he did not execute tasks pertaining to drug therapy and surgery, he decided when they should be applied.

The ranking of therapeutic tasks reflected a crucial distinction between diseases of the inner and outer body. This physiological

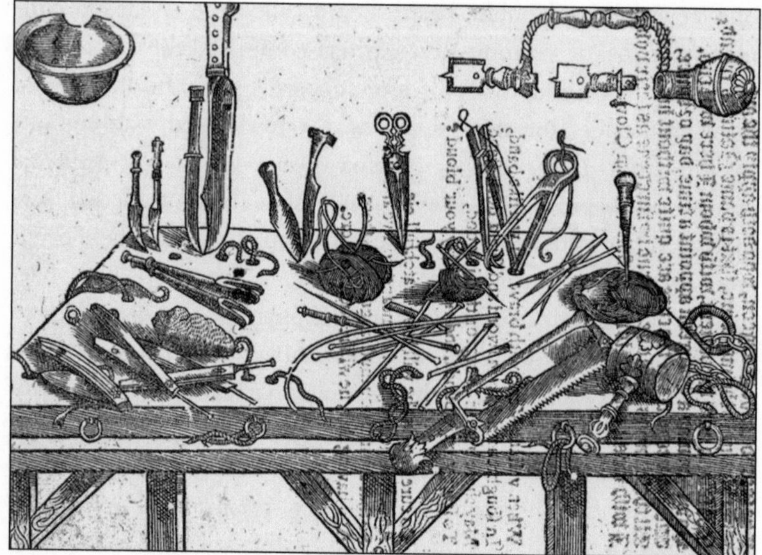

An operating table (with tie rings and ropes to fasten a patient's limbs) holds a variety of instruments used by the Renaissance barber-surgeon: scissors for cutting hair; needles and thread for sutures; dismembering cutters; and, on the upper right, a trepan for boring through the skull.

separation in turn determined the division between the physician's remedies and those of the surgeon. Only the physician could treat the body internally—for example, by prescribing drugs to be taken *per boca,* by mouth. The rule was repeatedly enforced, not only in decrees issued by health boards and colleges of physicians but also in the licenses granted to empirics, surgeons, midwives, and charlatans.

CLEANSING THE BODY

The craft of surgery differed from the science of medicine in another important respect: Most surgeons had no formal academic training. Although surgery was taught in some universities, one didn't need to earn a university degree to practice the art. In the Renaissance, surgeons usually learned their craft via apprenticeship to a practitioner. The mode of training and the degree of literacy that differentiated physicians from surgeons opened a wide gap between the two functions: Whereas physicians were trained in intellectual disciplines and treated diseases with their minds, surgeons plied a craft and treated illnesses with their hands.

Like other crafts, barber-surgeons were organized into a guild, or company, that defined the practitioner's duties and set standards for training. The statutes of the barber-surgeons' guild stated that "a barber's practice does not merely imply shaving, washing, and cutting hair, but also pulling teeth and drawing blood from men in whatever way and from any body part, as well as applying leeches." Tommaso Garzoni, in his encyclopedic book on the professions, *Piazza universale di tutte le professioni del mondo (The Universal Plaza of All the World's Professions),* defined the barber's trade as pertaining to the "cleansing" of the body, adding that "barbers are also useful for drawing blood from the sick and for applying leeches, medicating wounds, applying bandages, pulling decaying teeth and such things, so that their craft . . . is subordinated to the science of medicine."

As an apprentice barber-surgeon, Leonardo would have learned the trade from a master barber, as required by the barber-surgeons' guild. His master, who would have maintained his practice in one of those shops marked by a signboard with an arm and lancet, would have displayed a professional demeanor that served as an example to his apprentice. According to Roman barber-surgeon Pietro Paolo Magni, author of the professional manual *Discorsi sopra il modo di sanguinare (Discourses on the Method of Bloodletting),* the barber must be "clean, gracious, modest, and properly dressed; ugly gestures and dirty words are foreign to him; he must not tell lies about people or be overly curious or gossipy in his establishment, but must be discreet and circumspect in all things." So as not to offend customers, the barber should also be sober and avoid strong perfumes and odors.

First, Leonardo would have learned the tools of the trade. He knew them well and describes them one by one in a chapter on the barber's art in *The Mirror of Universal Science:* a basin, two razors, a lancet, a *gamaut* (or bistoury—a small, narrow surgical knife used for opening abscesses), a forceps for extracting teeth, hair clips, a comb, two aprons, a scalding burner and some coals, some lye, and a water bag with a spout for rinsing the face. Like the art itself, the tools of the trade were both hygienic and surgical; in the barber-surgeon's establishment, no distinction was made between the two functions. What Garzoni described as the "cleansing of the body" entailed more than shaving and cutting hair. It also involved extracting rotten teeth, expelling corrupt matter from the body through bloodletting, and treating rashes and skin lesions. All were considered to fall within the realm of hygiene.

Then the apprentice would have learned surgical techniques. Each master barber followed a particular method developed in the region where he trained. Magni noted, for example, at least four regional techniques for drawing blood: Roman, Neapolitan, Sicilian, and Calabrese. In *Prattica nuova che al diligente barbiero s'appartiene (Barber's New Practice),* Cintio d'Amato, a barber-surgeon from Naples, warned that a certain lancet used by Spanish barbers could be quite dangerous. Much safer, he counseled, was the *zingardola,* the lancet used in d'Amato's hometown, which had been invented around 1590 by Neapolitan barber Maestro Salvatore di Rosa. Whatever bloodletting school the apprentice learned, the art required keen dexterity; the barber had to open veins and lance fistulas without cutting into arteries or damaging nerves. It was no art for the timid.

Menial as their professional status may have been, barber-surgeons were the people's first line of defense against illness. Bloodletting—the barber's principal surgical task—was the remedy of choice in popular culture, because it was thought that periodic bleeding cleansed the body and helped to maintain health. Bloodletting was normally accomplished by venesection, though in some circumstances leeches were also applied. The medical principle behind this ancient therapeutic practice was the idea that bloodletting drained corrupted matter from the body. Because the blood was capable of transporting the humors, bloodletting was also considered an efficient means of eliminating superfluous humors that endangered health.

Phlebotomy was a sophisticated procedure that required considerable knowledge of superficial anatomy and an understanding of the appropriate veins to incise for various complaints. Thus, as we learn from Magni's *Discorsi,* a certain vein in the forehead should be incised to treat madness or delirium *(pazzia o delirio),* while drawing blood from the vein under the tongue was useful in treating angina *(squirentia).* Certain procedures, such as drawing blood from the basilica vein in the arm, could be used as preventive therapies "as many are wont to do in the springtime, in order to be purged." Some veins are exceedingly difficult to locate, Magni advised. Only a few barbers were able to draw blood successfully from the vein on the outer part of the foot, for example—a procedure recommended for sciatica and kidney ailments.

Bloodletting was one of several means by which barber-surgeons drew internal fluids to the outside of the body. They also used sweat baths to cause profuse sweating, vesicants to blister the skin and draw pus, cautery to dissolve humors, cupping glasses to bring them to the skin's surface, and scarification to purge them. All of these techniques were based on the principle of attracting impurities within to the body's surface in order to eliminate them, thus cleansing the body of pollution. Besides drawing fluids out of the body, barber-surgeons were charged with stopping the flow of blood when the body was wounded and with closing up its surface.

MEDICINE ON THE MARGINS

Barber-surgeons thus operated at the periphery of both the medical hierarchy and the human body. Prohibited from prescribing drugs to be taken internally, they plied their trade at the body's surface, healing wounds, setting broken bones, shaving beards and cutting hair, and administering plasters, ointments, and balsams to treat skin eruptions, rashes, and ringworm. The barber-surgeon's craft brought him in daily contact with bodily effluents, giving his task of cleansing the body both a medical and a social significance: He was charged with ordering the physical body and bringing it within the boundaries of social convention. Bloodletting, shaving the beard, cutting the hair and trimming fingernails were all functions of *politezza*—politeness, or cleansing the body in order to make it socially acceptable. As Fioravanti put it, "The art of the barber is very necessary for polite society." Without the barber, he wrote in *The Mirror of Universal Science*, "men would live in filth."

During the period of Leonardo's youth and apprenticeship, however, the system that had once regulated the barber-surgeon's realm was breaking down. Far-reaching changes were taking place in the relationship between physicians and barber-surgeons. Surgery—traditionally considered a craft associated with the barber and hence fulfilling a principally hygienic function—was increasingly being defined as a medical task, which would place it under the purview of the Protomedicato. In Bologna the separation of the surgeon from the barber was not completed until the 18th century, when surgeons were accorded full physician status, but the encroachment of physicians on the traditional territory of the barber-surgeon had already begun during Fioravanti's lifetime. In the course of the 16th century, the Protomedicato, through a series of decrees, gradually assumed control over the licensing of surgeons—and, as a result, came into frequent conflict with the company of barber-surgeons. Eventually surgery would become a university subject, while the barber's craft would remain a trade.

The shift in surgery's status made a profound impression on Fioravanti, shaping not only his view of the medical establishment but his own medical ideas. What did he make of this sea change? He traced it all the way back to ancient times, when certain doctors had invented medical theory and had assumed the mantle of "rational physicians" to distinguish themselves from the empirics. They "usurped" medicine and made laws blocking empirics from practicing medicine using the old, time-tested ways. Sects arose, and soon the physicians were quarreling among themselves about whose theory was the best. Eventually, theory took over and the methods of the "first physicians"—those who had learned their art organically, by imitating the animals—were forgotten. As a consequence of these changes, Leonardo believed, "the sciences of medicine and surgery have never been as confused as they are today."

Fioravanti found the usurpation of medicine by the rational physicians to be a great moral wrong—one that had caused medicine

Holding a lancet between his teeth, a barber-surgeon prepares a woman for a bloodletting. The ancient practice was believed to draw corrupt matter from the body. At right, a physician indicates the proper vein to cut.

to "go straight to the bordello." His reform of medicine aimed to reverse that wrong and return to the methods of the "first physicians." To do that, he would extend the therapeutic-hygienic principles of barber-surgery to all of medicine. In the years of his journeys after leaving Bologna, he began to regard all diseases as the product of pollution and disorder, and would project the hygienic theory of the barber-surgeon onto all forms of sickness. In the medical system that he cobbled together from his experiences as a barber-surgeon and his interactions with ordinary people, he made purgation paramount. He placed great significance in blood and its healing power, calling it "the juice of life." Fioravanti even invented a way of distilling blood to make a "quintessence" that, he claimed, harbored miraculous healing powers.

Throughout his life, Fioravanti remained deeply respectful of the surgeon's craft, resenting its subordination to medicine. Even after earning his medical degree, he proudly displayed the title of "Surgeon" on his books. He contrasted the surgeon's empirical shrewdness with the physician's ineffectual theoretical knowledge. Surgery, born of the vicissitudes of war and the chance accidents of everyday life, required skill, good judgment, and courage. Medicine, by contrast, had become so bogged down in dogmatic disputes that its original foundation in experience had been lost. Medicine and surgery had the same intent, insisted Fioravanti, lamenting the division of the arts into separate spheres with these words:

> It was done because the physicians, who were revered then, didn't want to dirty their hands by touching sores. Just to keep their hands from smelling bad they separated themselves off from the most important part of medicine, which is surgery. Of course, they reserved for themselves the authority to give permission to use surgery, but they didn't want to concede to the surgeon the right to practice internal medicine.

Like the outrage of the dispossessed, Fioravanti's antipathy toward physicians was a bitter gall that he tasted every day. The fanaticism with which he championed empiricism over theory was born of his resentment of the physicians' political power. And the cornerstone of that power, Leonardo believed, was the subordination of practice to theory. The priestly aura surrounding the physicians, who alone graduated in the Bologna Cathedral, fueled his indignation. Defending "true medicine" against the "false physicians" became the crusade that would animate his pursuit of a new way of healing.

6

THE ROAD OF EXPERIENCE

> Many years have passed since I left my sweet home, Bologna, solely with the intention of traveling around the world in order to gain knowledge of natural philosophy, so that I might be able to practice medicine and surgery better than I could in those days when I began my work. And thus I have traveled to various and diverse provinces, always practicing the art wherever I found myself. I never ceased studying but always went looking for precious experiments, whether from learned physicians or simple empirics, yea from all kinds of people, whether peasants, shepherds, soldiers, clerics, old women, and people of all different qualities.

So begins Leonardo's autobiography, a buoyant and self-congratulatory record of his pilgrimage from obscure barber-surgeon to celebrity healer. He was 30 years old, and the wider world beckoned.

The 19th-century Bolognese chronicler Salvatore Muzzi, looking back on the year 1548, wrote, "If ever there was a year in which things in Bologna passed so quietly and normally that there is nothing to say about it, it was this one." But for Leonardo Fioravanti it was a momentous year, the beginning of his apprenticeship as a natural philosopher. Years later he would recall that only when he "went out into the world," leaving books and lectures behind, did his eyes begin to be opened to the truth. He was following the example of the ancient philosopher Apollonius of Tyana, who traveled to many distant parts of the world to learn the secrets of nature. To those who wished to be called philosophers, he offered this advice:

> [Y]ou must go walking the world and live among all sorts of people and understand their nature and the medicines they use. Once you've done that, you have to discover the great variety of things in nature, the diversity of people in the world, and their many different medicines. And when you've seen all these things, only then will you have acquired the name of philosopher.

Leonardo dated his departure from Bologna as October 1548. He remembered the month because it coincided with the arrival in Genoa of Prince Philip of Spain, who was making his first grand tour of the empire that he would inherit from his father, the Holy Roman Emperor Charles V. Hoping to catch a glimpse of the young prince, Leonardo set off for Genoa, where he would stay "for a few days" before embarking for Sicily.

By what means he journeyed to Genoa we don't know. Most likely by foot; that was the customary means of travel in the 16th century—unless you could afford a horse. Traveling by coach or litter was reserved for the very rich. When he refers to his travels, Fioravanti almost always uses the verbs *camminare* or *andare camminando*—literally, "to walk" or "to go walking" (though the verbs can also mean "to take a journey"). Even when he traveled by horseback, as Leonardo did between Palermo and Messina when he lived in Sicily, the trip was arduous; he often slept on stable straw and "ate with the chickens."

Fioravanti may have preferred traveling by foot because it kept him closer to nature. He reports that he "walked the world and ploughed the seas" in search of nature's secrets. And so we should imagine him, walking the world, walking from Bologna to Genoa, later from Naples to Rome and from Rome to Pesaro, walking from city to city and from inland city to port, where he could catch a ship to travel by sea.

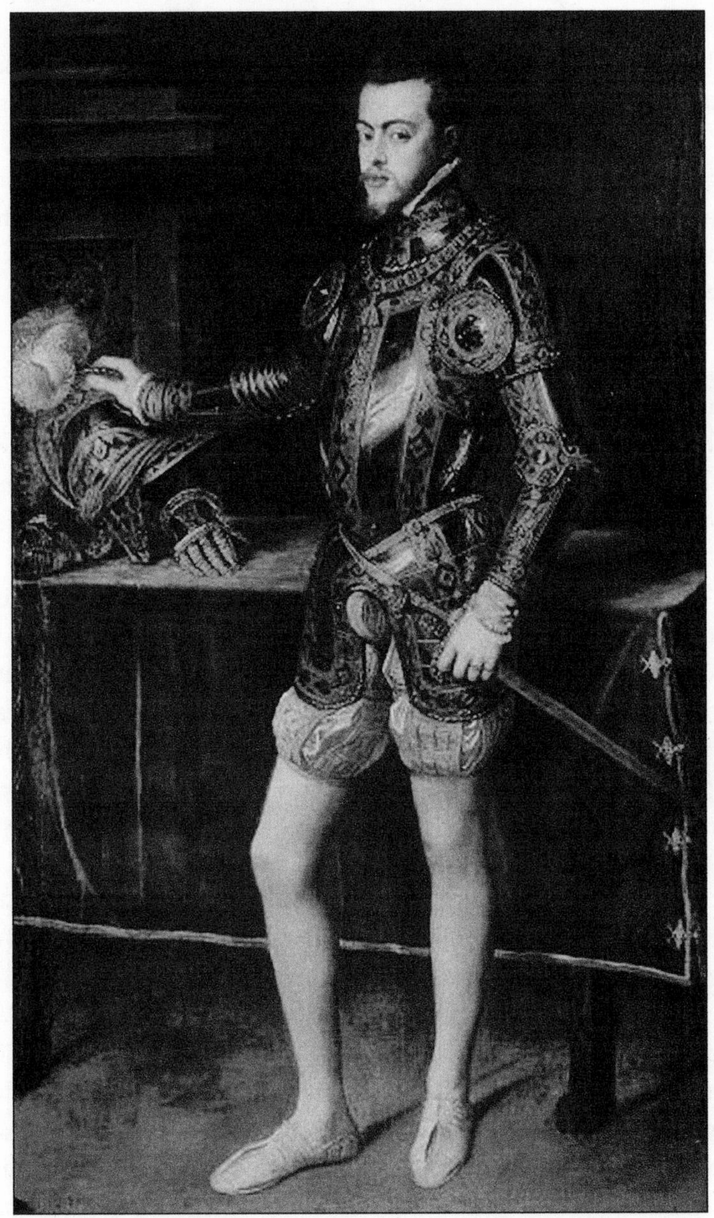

Titian painted this portrait of Prince Philip in 1550, two years after Fioravanti saw the prince in Genoa. The suit of armor symbolically proclaims the prince as the model of chivalry and the defender of the faith.

A PRINCELY SPECTACLE

Thus in late October, toward the end of a bitterly cold autumn, Leonardo made what was, evidently, his first trip away from his birthplace. The approximately 150-mile journey overland would have taken him about ten days. He would have started out before daybreak so that he could travel a familiar way in the dark. Reaching Genoa after this exhausting journey, he stayed "for several days" *(alquanti giorni)* awaiting Prince Philip's arrival.

A huge crowd turned out to greet the prince when his fleet sailed into the harbor. He was accompanied by dozens of Spanish noblemen, and by captains and princes great and small from all over Italy. The Doge of Venice was there to greet him, as were the dukes of Mantova and Ferrara, the prince of Salerno, and Captain Giordano Orsini of Rome. The playing of pipes and the firing of arquebuses filled spectators' ears.

A marble stairway had been constructed to conduct the entourage from the harbor across a bridge built atop two barges and decorated with tapestries and carpets, and thence into the city. As the trim, handsome young prince descended from the bridge, he was an impressive sight. He was dressed in a black velvet tunic of the Spanish style, a white satin jacket with a collar trimmed in braided gold, white stockings and laced buskins, and a black velvet cap with a white feather.

As the retinue entered the city, it arrived at a great triumphal arch constructed for the occasion. Contemporaries described the arch as taking up the entire street. Its four gilded columns formed a large gate. At the arch's pedestal, two wind machines in the form of zephyrs blew flowers on the people who walked through it. A dedication to Philip was inscribed on the frieze. Above one end were the figures of Jupiter and Apollo, with the prince on horseback between them. Below the arch, one side depicted palm trees and nymphs, while the other was decorated with images of green laurels—signs of the prince's triumphs and virtues. On both sides of the arch were representations of the peoples whom Philip's father, Charles V, had conquered: Germans, Turks, even Indians of the New World. The emperor himself was also portrayed, seated on an imperial throne at the door of a great temple. At each piazza along the prince's route to the cathedral stood other triumphal arches, smaller but every bit as ingeniously designed.

Leonardo, an anonymous face in the crowd, stood mesmerized as the young prince stepped down from the archway and walked through the streets to greet his future subjects. For a provincial barber-surgeon from Bologna, it must have been a marvelous sight to behold. Did Leonardo catch the prince's gaze? It would have been a heady experience to look upon the face of the man in whose hands lay the future of Catholic Europe.

Philip stayed on in Genoa for two leisurely weeks as a guest of Prince Andrea Doria at his palace outside the city. The prince's party finally departed on December 8 to continue its grand tour, which proceeded through the Holy Roman Empire for seven more leisurely months.

Fioravanti, too, was in no hurry. As he boarded the first ship bound for Sicily, he had no way of knowing that the two men's paths would not cross again for another 28 years.

7

THE CARNIVAL DOCTOR

Fioravanti's choice of Sicily as the first destination of his long pilgrimage was probably related to that remote island's rich tradition of empirical healers. His glowing portrait of Akron of Agrigento, the founder of the ancient empiricist medical sect, suggests as much. Reflecting on medicine's "good old days," Leonardo wrote:

> Even though in those days there weren't any rational physicians around, that doesn't mean that there weren't any remedies or that doctors didn't use them. For we read that Akron of Agrigento and his disciples knew things only by experience and didn't have any kind of theory. And it's a good thing for all of us who came after who have studied and searched for experiences to accompany method and science, because in following that way, medicine is a glorious thing.

Akron, a physician of the fifth century B.C.E., was reputed to have been a pupil of the Sicilian philosopher Empedocles, who asserted that experience alone should be our guide in the inquiries we make about nature. The empiricists who followed Akron maintained that what is invisible is unknowable; therefore, only the senses could be trusted. Because it is impossible to know the causes of disease, which are hidden, the physician must rely solely on what he observes at the moment, his senses finely tuned to the patient's individual symptoms. Sagacity, not philosophical learning, is the physician's best ally.

Was Leonardo hoping to encounter some new Akron in the hills of Sicily, someone who could teach him the old ways of healing? The scenario perfectly fits his reconstruction of the origins of medicine. He denied that medicine was invented by the ancient Greek god Asclepius. Such foolishness conflicted with the biblical account of creation, which told how God infused plants with their medicinal virtues and gave the animals instinctive knowledge of them:

> Nature gave the animals the gift of knowing, without aid or counsel from anyone, how to cure their infirmities. . . . The dog, when it feels sick, goes into the forest and finds a certain herb, which it recognizes by instinct, and eats it, and that herb immediately makes it vomit and evacuate from behind; and it is cured at once. The ox, horse, and mule, when they are aggravated by some infirmity, bite the end of their tongue until blood flows out, and are healed. When hens get sick they take out a certain membrane under the tongue, and the blood flows from it, and immediately they are healed. Many other animals do similar things to cure various illnesses.

Thus the animals, without ever having studied medicine, know instinctively, as a "gift of nature," that they can cure their illnesses by purging and bleeding. "When men observed these things they realized that evacuation and bloodletting were very useful."

Fioravanti waxed nostalgic when he reflected on those olden days. Back then, he imagined, medicine was perfect and people maintained their health by natural means. "I believe that this was the time when mankind was happiest on this earth," he mused, "because people lived closer to nature and did not suffer as much from the illnesses they had, nor did they have so many diseases as we have today." Only long afterward did the Greeks finally codify the empirical "rules of life" they had discovered in those days and put them into writing. Hippocrates wrote his *Aphorisms,* Galen made commentaries on them, and so on. Soon schools and sects arose, and the disputes among them blurred the empirical foundations of the healing art. Medicine became a science; theory took over from experience. Yet despite being continually persecuted by the physicians, the heroic empirics endured, and "they will endure for eternity." So went the story of the discovery of medicine according to Leonardo Fioravanti.

It made sense to him, therefore, that Sicily, an island far removed from the centers of Italian culture, yet in antiquity the part of Italy closest to Greek influences, was the birthplace of medical empiricism. In Magna Graecia—the ancient colonial cites and settlements of Greece in southern Italy—the mythical Akron gathered his "throng of experimenters" and sent them out into the world to teach the "doctrine of experience." Fioravanti believed that Sicily might still harbor the heirs of those original empirics. Old men, shepherds, herb women, surgeons, and craftsmen bent over their workbenches: They were the ones who, uncorrupted by school learning, were closest to nature. Lacking a university or medical school, Sicily could be idealized as a place where pure medicine flourished.

OUT OF THE SHADOWS

Travel by sea was safer now that peace had at last returned to Italy. The year before he left Bologna, Charles V's nemesis—François I, the warrior-king of France—had died; a month earlier, Henry VIII of England passed on. With the deaths of these great antagonists, international tensions eased considerably. The previous year, 1546, saw the death of Martin Luther, whose radical religious reform split Europe into two warring ideological camps. That same year marked the passing of Admiral Khair al-Din ("Barbarossa" to the Europeans), the Ottoman corsair and scourge of the Mediterranean. An entire epoch of European history had therefore just come to a close. Sicily and the Kingdom of Naples were safely in the hands of the Spanish. Although pirates still menaced the Mediterranean coasts, Leonardo risked a week's voyage to the unfamiliar and "most fertile kingdom of Sicily." For the first time in his life, he experienced being a foreigner in a strange land.

Landing in Palermo, Sicily's main port and the residence of the Spanish viceroys, Fioravanti posed as a tourist. "I stayed for many days to my great pleasure and solace, without anyone discovering that I was a medical man or a Bolognese." He used his anonymity to his advantage, listening, observing, waiting for the right moment to reveal himself. A few months after his arrival, Carnival took place. It was a time to be seriously playful and gaily disrespectful. People came out into the streets and piazzas in outrageous costumes to play at turning the world upside down. Common people dressed as officials, nobles as peasants, men as women, prostitutes as men. Everywhere misrule ruled.

Stepping out of the shadows, Leonardo impersonated a *medico,* or healer. He wasn't a real doctor, of course; he was merely donning a mask, as one does during Carnival, and playing a part. When some local doctors mistook him for a learned Bologna physician, however, and sought his help in a particularly puzzling case, Fioravanti seized his chance:

> When word got out that I was a doctor from Bologna, people surmised that I must have been a man of great knowledge with expert cures, although in fact I was only thirty years old at the time and still didn't know any more about medicine than any ordinary doctor. I still hadn't acquired the gift of truth, as I did much later. Nevertheless, I went along and let them believe that I was an expert Bologna physician. As it happened, in a little while two of the town's physicians, Master Pietro Paro and a Spanish doctor called Maesta, came to me concerning a certain patient they were treating, a Spanish gentleman called Alessandro Sampier di Rosa. The gentleman had a bad case of quartan fever and the doctors asked me whether I, being a foreigner, might have a secret to cure him. If so, they assured me, I'd be well paid for my efforts.

Armed with a few books and his rough-and-ready theory of disease, Fioravanti agreed to try. Although he had no idea how to proceed, he recalled that botanist Pietro Mattioli and others had recommended vomiting for such cases, especially with "Precipitato" *(il precipitato* is mercuric oxide). Taking advantage of the Carnival spirit in the air, he put on the airs of a Bologna professor and made up a little speech. He described the event in comic fashion, inviting the reader to believe that his preposterous harangue fooled the doctors. The speech went like this:

> Most excellent doctors, there can be no doubt whatsoever that this infirmity is no other than double quartan fever. The cause? Good doctors, like lovesickness and the French Pox, it is caused by melancholy humors. The cure? Now, the ancients say that the cure is exceedingly difficult, while the poets, in their fables, have depicted the cure as standing somewhere between a physician and an apothecary, cocking a snook at both of them—inferring by this that it fears neither the doctor's science nor the apothecary's medicine. Be that as it may, my good sirs, if it pleases you, it would seem to me that we ought to give him one remedy or the other, this one or that, but not both, nor neither. What else can we do? Because by evacuating the melancholy the fever will be quickly cured.

The physicians, "much pleased" with Leonardo's oration, agreed to follow his recommendation by attacking the insolent "melancholy humor" head-on: They would purge it with a powerful emetic. The following morning, unsure what would happen, they gave the patient a syrup of ten grains of Precipitato in half an ounce of rose water. To their amazement, the man immediately "vomited up copious amounts of choler and phlegm." The treatment brought some relief, so the doctors agreed to give him another dose. Six days later, following another bout of vomiting, "he was completely cured."

CARNIVAL CATHARSIS

As Leonardo's name spread around the city, people began to seek out his counsel. What followed was a remarkable series of dramatic cures, or perceived cures, highlighted by extreme purging, vomiting, sweating, and faith healing.

In reinventing himself, Fioravanti drew on a long tradition of Carnival characters—a rich vein of popular lore and spectacle that Bolognese ballad singer and pamphleteer Giulio Cesare Croce would later mine to hilarious comic effect. Croce's pamphlets are populated with outrageous caricatures of fawning courtesans, swooning lovers, foolish simpletons, conniving lawyers, lusty prostitutes, and grandiloquent academics. In one of his booklets, *The Marvelous Secrets of Medicine,* a pompous physician named Doctor Braggart touts his "marvelous" prescriptions. Composed more to be recited or sung than read, the verses are almost impossible to translate. Here, for example, is one of Croce's recipes for a medicine to cure syphilis:

Take the foolishness of a buffoon,
add to it a concubine's charms
and three drams of a fatty's blubber;
anoint with a cudgel,
throw in a hen's song,
and smear it on his cock.
If this doesn't do the trick
pickle it in brine for a year and one month:
that'll cure him of the French Pox.

The macaronic language of Croce's pamphlets—pure Carnival—mimicked the comic speech of the *ciarlatani,* an Italian word whose English equivalent, "charlatans," does not remotely capture the meaning of the original. The Italian *ciarlatano* comes from *ciarlare,* meaning "to chatter"—a reference to the itinerant actors who sold remedies for scabs, itches, and occasionally more serious complaints. In order to attract customers, these mountebanks climbed up on portable stages in the piazzas and performed slapstick comedy routines using characters and plots that would later come to constitute commedia dell'arte.

This background makes it easy to imagine the famous Doctor Graziano, a stock character in the commedia dell'arte tradition: Dressed in tight knee breeches, a ruffled doublet, and a bright-colored cloak, he mounts the scaffold and spouts learned platitudes and outrageous malapropisms. "He who is sick cannot be said to be well," he expounds in a mock-serious tone, parodying the physicians, and proves it by the analogy that "a walking man isn't dead." In posing as his Carnival doctor, Leonardo exploited this rich comic tradition. His histrionic speech to the physicians echoed the cast of characters who entertained spectators in the piazzas.

Yet the manner in which his first patient recovered made a strong impression on Fioravanti: Two stiff doses of Precipitato had caused the man to expel an astonishing amount of rubbish from his belly, curing him completely. The event was the beginning, he admits, of his "good luck" in using strong drugs to vanquish sicknesses. Precipitato was a strong drug, alright: Though nothing but a powerful emetic in small doses, mercuric oxide becomes a deadly poison in larger quantities.

Fioravanti could not have seized a better moment to try the remedy. Talk of purging the suffering body was so ubiquitous during Carnival that its significance would not have escaped an astute observer such as Fioravanti. Just as Carnival was, in the words of historian Piero Camporesi, "the suitable therapy for the infected social body"—an enormous purgative that cleansed society of "corrupt humors"—so too did medical purges rid the physical body of the rotten humors that caused sickness.

Graziano, the *commedia* doctor, was often contrasted in popular literature to Bertoldo, the wise peasant of Giulio Cesare Croce's famous pamphlet, *The Subtle Wiles of Bertoldo.* Carnival opposites, one signified empty doctrine and the other country wisdom. Rejecting school learning, Fioravanti turned to the people's wisdom. The liberating spirit of Carnival became another instrument in his toolkit of self-fashioning. Of course, Carnival did not imply nihilism, for the ritual both permitted revelry and prescribed its bounds. Carnival merely enabled Fioravanti, in the words of Rabelais scholar Mikhail Bakhtin, "to find a position permitting a look at the other side of established values, so that new bearings could be taken."

Leonardo had seen the other side. He would take his bearings from there.

8

THE NEW ASCLEPIUS

Leonardo Fioravanti was a lucky man. By chance, the first patient he treated in Palermo was a Spanish gentleman named Alejandro San Piero. His second patient, whom he identifies only as Señor Ximenes, was a member of the Spanish viceroy's court. Together, the two men knew many Spaniards who were quartered in the city. Leonardo's name got around. Soon he was being consulted in the usual range of surgeon's cases, which he would treat in the usual way: a salve to clear up a rash, a corrosive plaster to eat away swelling, or an ointment to ease pain.

Other, more serious ailments called for more dramatic interventions—and through these cases, Fioravanti would forge his new identity. In April 1549, an event occurred that made him think God's hand might be working through him. A Genoese silk merchant, Giacomo Sandese, asked Leonardo to examine his black slave, a 22-year-old man who had developed a "tumor" that Fioravanti described as resembling a thin cloth covering the eyes (evidently a cataract). "This is a strange infirmity, Master Giacomo," Leonardo said to the merchant after examining the slave. "I've never seen anything like it. How long has he been like this?"

"His eyes became covered over like this about a year ago," Sandese replied. "Before that he could see perfectly, but now he's completely blind." Gazing into the poor man's rheumy eyes, Fioravanti declared the condition incurable.

Sandese persisted. "I know of your excellency's great fame in these parts," he implored. "I beg of you, try by any means possible to restore the poor man's sight. He's a valuable slave. Spare no expense for anything you need."

With a promised reward of 150 gold scudi if he succeeded, Leonardo asked himself whether he might be able to dissolve the tumors with some sort of caustic solution. He remembered having heard that films covering the eyes could be removed that way. As he recalled in his memoir:

> I decided to try Appio Riso, an herb well known for this use. I took some of it and crushed it and applied it to the right eye, keeping it there for twenty-four hours. Then, after washing the eye, I found that it had almost completely dissolved the tumor. I put butter and cabbage leaves on it, and this cleared the film from the eye, and the slave was able to see from that eye again. I did the same with the other eye, and its vision returned as well. The master and slave were so happy about this that they soon let it be known that I had restored sight to the blind. Immediately blind people from all over the city and its environs began coming to me, and I cured many of them the same way. It wasn't long before people were comparing me to Jesus Christ, Our Redeemer, who applied mud to the eyes of the blind and restored their sight.

In other cases Fioravanti reported equally impressive results. He described the case of a 34-year-old baron afflicted with scabies so severe it kept him bedridden. Scabies is a condition usually related to poverty and poor hygiene, but during the Renaissance it attacked the rich as well, given that they lived in conditions of equal squalor. The malady is caused by an infestation of microscopic mites, which cause intense itching. Left untreated, it can spread to the entire body and become extremely painful.

So advanced was the baron's condition that Fioravanti doubted he could cure him. But a friend of the baron's urged him to try, so he mixed a liniment of litharge, or lead monoxide—this would have yielded a fairly corrosive composition—and rubbed it on the baron's body. To the astonishment of all, his symptoms began to diminish within a few days. "The whole city marveled at this," reports Leonardo, "because he had been bedridden since autumn."

LEONARDO'S VANTAGE POINT

Hoping to turn his good fortune into a position at the viceregal court, Fioravanti found a house near the Church of Santa Maria della Catena, a short distance from Palermo's marina. The location was ideally suited for building contacts with Spanish soldiers, sailors, and courtiers. From his house he could see galleys arriving in the harbor, unloading goods from distant parts of the globe. From Spain came ships laden with New World merchandise; from the Orient came exotic spices, drugs, and dyes. Leonardo learned Spanish and listened closely to conversations among soldiers and sailors about the places they had visited. He hired an alchemist to teach him the art of distillation and built a laboratory in his house, where he conducted experiments to discover new drugs. Soon, he relates, his house was filled with people seeking his counsel.

Fioravanti continued his search for the ancient empirical ways of healing. He talked to old people, barbers, apothecaries, and empirics to learn about epidemics in the area—and the healing methods used to treat them. From an 86-year-old pharmacist named Giannuccio Spatafora, "a very learned and experienced man," he learned about the quality of the airs and winds of Palermo, the medicinal plants of the countryside, and the plagues that had visited Sicily in times past. He climbed Mount Pellegrino, where he discovered herbs of marvelous virtue. Nowhere else in Italy, wrote Leonardo, can you find the palm used to make true *diapalma*—the rare unguent effective in treating sores caused by the French disease. The locals called the plant *zaffaioni*. "The true *diapalma* is made only from this plant," he observed. "The [unguent] that many pharmacists sell under the name *diapalma* has about as much in common with the true *diapalma* as a cat has with a horse."

Another old empiric taught him ways to treat wounds that were completely new to him. The man was able not only to heal patients, "but to almost raise them from the dead," Leonardo exclaimed.

As he gathered knowledge, Fioravanti's reputation as a surgeon grew. Before long, he reports, people were calling him the "new Asclepius."

THE MYSTERIOUS MALADY OF MARULLA GRECO

Emboldened, he would take on any case brought to him—even those that the physicians had "given up as dead." In April 1549, a captain in the imperial navy by the name of Matteo Greco came to visit Leonardo. His 24-year-old wife, Marulla—said to be the most beautiful woman in the city—was desperately ill. Some months back, Captain Greco recounted, Marulla had come down with a "malignant fever" that had swollen her spleen and "caused both of her legs to become horribly ulcerated," leaving her utterly debilitated. Several physicians had examined Marulla and told her the spleen would have to come out. The operation was not dangerous, they assured her—though as Fioravanti matter-of-factly notes, "none of them would do it."

In modern medical terms, Marulla had splenomegaly (also megalosplenia), or "big spleen disease." It is characterized by massive swelling of the spleen and sharp pain in the abdomen. The spleen can grow to enormous proportions—as much as 80 times its normal size—grotesquely distending the abdominal region. The most common cause of splenomegaly is malaria, endemic to southern Italy and Sicily in Leonardo's day. Splenomegaly is easily treated with antimalarial drugs. Left untreated, however, it can be a serious disease: Rapid enlargement of the spleen may result in splenic rupture, and massive splenomegaly places a heavy burden on the heart and circulatory system. Whereas a normal spleen absorbs only 5 percent of the heart's blood output, an enlarged spleen may absorb more than half. In addition, splenomegaly often causes an increase in the volume of blood plasma, which may result in anemia. It can also cause sharp pain in the abdomen and back, especially if the spleen has become so large that it puts pressure on other organs. That was evidently the case with poor Marulla. She was in such pain, Leonardo writes, that "she finally decided that she would either be cured or would die." Marulla begged her husband to find a surgeon who could perform the recommended operation.

Aware of Fioravanti's reputation, Captain Greco asked the surgeon if he had the courage to take out her spleen. Leonardo picks up the story:

> "Why, yes," I answered cheerfully, even though up until that time I'd never done anything like it. To tell the truth, even though I promised him I'd do it, I really didn't want to because I was afraid I might botch it. But I knew an old surgeon from the town of Palo in the Kingdom of Naples. He was called Andreano Zaccarello and he operated with the knife, removing cataracts and similar things, and was very expert in that profession. So I called for the old man and he hurried to my house. I asked him, "Dear Master Andriano, a strange wish has come to Captain Matteo's wife: by Hercules, she wants to have her spleen taken out! Tell me, can this be done safely?"
>
> "Of course," the old man answered. "I've done it many times."
>
> "Do you have the courage to go ahead with it now?" He said that he'd do it with me, but otherwise not. So we agreed to do it together.
>
> I went back to arrange things with the woman and her husband, then went to the authorities to give her up as dead, according to the custom. With this license, we went back one morning to the woman's house. We laid her on a table and had two servants hold her fast. Then the good old surgeon took out a razor and cut the woman's body just above the spleen, which popped out of her body like a fishing float. We quickly separated the organ from the tissue until we had it completely out, then sewed up the wound, leaving a tiny air-hole. I treated the wound with hypericon oil, powder of incense, mastic, and myrrh with sarcocolla, and made her drink water boiled with a dried apple, betony, and cardo santo. I took care of her in this way until, in just twenty-four days, she was completely healed. She went to mass at the Madonna of the Miracles, according to her obligation, and was healed and saved.

Having accomplished the unimaginable, Fioravanti created an amazing publicity stunt to advertize his surgical talents. He carried the deformed organ to the open-air merchants' arcade *(loggia de' mercanti)* in the center of the city, where it was displayed for three days. Marulla's spleen, weighing fully two pounds (the organ normally averages only about five ounces), was a marvelous sight to behold. As people passed by to view it, Leonardo must have told and retold the story of the extraordinary surgery, embroidering his exploits with each iteration until it became a mythical tale of medical heroism. "The glory of this experiment was mine," he gloated, "and because of this the people gathered about me, as to an oracle."

"CURE THOSE YOU CAN AND PRAY FOR THE REST"

An overnight celebrity, Fioravanti came to the attention of Doña Eleonora de Vega, the wife of the Spanish viceroy. The viceregina, "a true friend of the poor," was benefactor of numerous charities. She was the founder and patron of the Ospedale degli Incurabili, one of many hospitals set up to care for victims of syphilis, whose grim mortality in 16th-century Italy gave the "hospital of the incurables" its name.

One day in May 1549, Doña Eleonora summoned Fioravanti to her palace. "Señor doctor," she implored, "for the love of God, come with me to the hospital to see the patients there. Cure those you can and pray for the rest. Your favor will give me great satisfaction. I promise, in the name of Don Juan, my husband, that anything you desire from us will be granted. If it pleases you, tomorrow morning I shall take you there and we will see if it is God's pleasure that these poor souls should be healed."

Early the next morning, Leonardo walked the short distance from his house across the piazza to the Church of Santa Maria della Catena to attend Mass. Then he proceeded to the hospital to await the viceregina. When she arrived, they entered the hospital together to visit the sick. There were a great many of them, the surgeon reports, all afflicted with hideous sores. "I believe that even among the souls of hell no cries of pain are as strident as those I heard that day in the hospital," he recalled. The Viceregina said, "Señor doctor,

I know that you are a man of great knowledge. I beg you, use all of your powers to heal as many of these wretched souls as you can. Please, do this for the love of God and for the love of me."

Leonardo employed an elaborate procedure to treat the hospital patients: First he made a decoction of Lignum Sanctum boiled with herbs, honey, and wine, then administered four ounces of this medicine to every patient, morning and evening. A popular cure, Lignum Sanctum was made by boiling shavings from the wood of the guaiacum tree, which grows in the West Indies. An effective diaphoretic, the medicine supposedly caused patients to sweat the sickness out. Along with mercury, it was the standard treatment for the French pox in 16th-century Europe. Evidently the medicine did its job, for the patients began to sweat profusely. Fioravanti then gave each one his trusty purge—a dose of Precipitato with rose water. He continued this treatment for 20 days, encouraging the patients to eat well so they could endure the sweating and evacuations. By following this regimen, Fioravanti reported, 32 patients were cured and released from the hospital.

For the patients who remained, he made a preparation of arsenic sublimate, sal ammoniac, and vinegar, then applied it to their sores. Arsenic sublimate and sal ammoniac were mineral treatments that European surgeons had picked up in the 13th century from their new Arabic sources. Arsenic sublimate, for its part, was a highly effective cauterizing agent. The 14th-century Montpellier physician Arnald of Villanova, for example, found the compound capable of searing the skin "as well as fire"; it was therefore used to heal ulcers and fistulas (but proved fatal if taken internally). Sal ammoniac, or ammonium chloride, was a mild caustic agent. By Fioravanti's day, the two medicines had become valuable additions to the surgeon's technical repertoire.

Finally, Leonardo washed the sores with hot vinegar and rubbed them with ointments. By the time he finished his work, he writes, "very few perished and those that survived are still healthy. The whole city marveled at this."

Hardly had Leonardo begun to bask in his newly won fame than the viceroy moved his court to Messina and asked—or rather ordered—Fioravanti to come along. "I was forced to give up the undertaking and go with the court," he writes. "And so I left Palermo—much against my will—and went to Messina, where the Viceroy gave me a good salary and asked me to stay the year."

Relieved of the necessity to treat patients, Fioravanti threw himself into the alchemical experiments he'd begun in Palermo. It was through the fiery dreams of alchemy that he would forge his new identity.

9

THE MARVELOUS VIRTUES OF PRECIPITATO

In mastering alchemy, Leonardo became a devotee of an art whose practitioners were among the most ardent investigators of nature during the Scientific Revolution. He joined a loose-knit community of adepts who advocated various kinds of alchemy, for there was not just one alchemical school, nor just one way of practicing the art, but many.

Some alchemists were physicians. Others were artisans. Some devoted their lives—and often their material wealth—to the pursuit of a philosopher's stone that would miraculously transmute base metals into gold. Others labored over the furnace to discover new medicines by means of distillation. Some delved into esoteric doctrines. Others scoffed at such mystical excesses, preferring the more practical pursuit of discovering new procedures for making metals and chemicals.

Alchemy was practiced in the laboratory, the distillery, the court, and the kitchen. Women as well as men practiced the art. Some alchemists lived on the margins of society, while others enjoyed positions in the households of lords and princes, who sought out their skills as shortcuts to economic woes in an age of rampant inflation.

When we moderns think of alchemy, fraud almost always comes to mind. Certainly deception played a role, but there were sincere alchemists as well as cheats, successful alchemists as well as failures. Although a variety of alchemical theories were batted about in the 16th century, alchemy—as historian Bruce Moran points out—was not so much something people *believed* in as something they *did.* Virtually all alchemists manipulated various materials and substances to produce new effects. It was a manual art, not a contemplative exercise. Alchemists understood their craft as the practice of dismantling materials into their constituent parts and recombining them to make a different substance; or, when they distilled something, separating the "pure" from the "impure" parts of a substance in order to extract a more potent end product.

Did alchemists contribute to the development of modern science? Doubtlessly they added to the repertoire of chemical processes and substances. Through their experiments they refined laboratory techniques, and even their harshest critics acknowledged the alchemists' contribution to the understanding of how materials were produced. Sienese mining engineer Vannoccio Biringuccio, writing in 1540, decried goldmaking as a "vain wish and fanciful dream," yet he conceded that "this art is the origin and foundation of many other arts, wherefore it should be held in reverence and practiced."

By the same token, historians of science have begun to take more seriously the genuine interest in alchemy displayed by many of the originators of modern science. When we realize that scientists of the stature of Robert Boyle and Isaac Newton had alchemical laboratories and incorporated alchemical concepts into their cosmologies, we begin to appreciate the distance between early modern science and our own. It wasn't just charlatans who succumbed to the lure of alchemy's promise.

Like many alchemists of the period, Biringuccio distinguished between the "fanciful dream" of alchemical transmutation and the hard work of producing concrete results in the laboratory. To be an alchemist required a high level of commitment. The risks of failure were great and, in many alchemical endeavors, the chances of success were slim. An alchemist needed a certain daring, because he knew that he would be the object of derision by the scientific "establishment," which continued to regard alchemy as an illegitimate and fraudulent enterprise.

The peril of such opprobrium Leonardo Fioravanti took willingly. To him, alchemy opened the door to medical secrets never before imagined.

PLAYING WITH FIRE

Of all the alchemical medicines that Leonardo experimented with, Precipitato (mercuric oxide) fascinated him the most. Ever since his fortuitous discovery of the drug's powerful effects, additional experience had confirmed his belief that robust purges and emetics that could rid the body of toxic matter were more efficacious than the physicians' diets and regimens. Precipitato was a wonder drug that imitated the virtues of the herbal remedies that he witnessed people using to cleanse themselves naturally. The potent drug, in Leonardo's words, "is used in cases of festering pains to take out the corrupt matter from the interior parts to the exterior." Precipitato would be his panacea—the magic bullet that he would use to drive out any offending pollution and return the body to its pristine natural state.

Alchemists concocted mercuric oxide by heating mercury in a solution of nitric acid, which they called aqua fortis. Quicksilver *(argento vivo)*, or mercury, was considered to be the mother of all minerals—a "material spirit that embraces all metals," as Leonardo put it—and when it changes alchemically, its transformations are sudden, violent, and spectacular, revealing its new properties instantly, as in the Creation. Fioravanti describes the process of making Precipitato in his *Medical Caprices:*

> Take aqua fortis for parting [acid], for each three ounces mix it with two ounces of mercury (that has not been calcined with any other mineral). Put this mixture into a small bottle with a long neck that has been well sealed. Put the receptacle on the fire until the water is well desiccated and the carafe doesn't smoke any longer. When the stove has cooled down, break the bottle and you will find on the bottom a mass of material that will be red, like minium. Grind this very

fine in a mortar, so that it is almost impalpable, and this will be Precipitato.

The chemical reaction is quite impressive. Heat a solution of quicksilver with aqua fortis in a closed receptacle and a thick red vapor will rise above the surface of the solution. When the solution reaches a temperature of 350 degrees Celsius, sparkling red crystals suddenly precipitate at the bottom of the receptacle. It was just the sort of reaction that convinced the alchemists that mercury, the shape-shifting mother of all metals, transcended both solid and liquid states, both heaven and earth, life and death.

Precipitato has a thousand uses, said Leonardo. It works wonders against the French pox because it "purges the body completely." He used it to rid the body of stomach corruptions caused by eating bad food. He included it in the ointments that he made for treating chancres and wounds. He even used it to treat the falling sickness, believing that epilepsy, like so many other diseases, was caused by pollution. "The polluted stomach sends up bad vapors to the brain, causing the symptoms of the illness," he explained. That mercuric oxide should have been used as a treatment for epilepsy probably had to do with the fact that convulsions and seizures were frequent symptoms of advanced syphilis; the two diseases might thus have been confused. For surgeons, mercury was the treatment of choice for the French pox. Physicians, who preferred the guaiacum treatment, often blamed mercurial unctions for causing the disease.

Fioravanti had to use the drug with extreme caution. Like all inorganic mercury salts, mercuric oxide is extremely toxic. Because poisoning can result even from skin absorption, its use in ointments to treat chancres—a relatively common medieval practice—was not without danger. Fioravanti's usual dosage (10 to 12 grains dissolved in rose water) would have yielded a highly toxic formula if the entire amount were swallowed. However, mercuric oxide is only slightly soluble in water; if Leonardo administered a dosage composed of just the solution, leaving the undissolved solids behind, he would have given his patients a much more dilute form of the drug. The "solution in rosewater" that he prescribed would have resulted in a strong but probably not fatal purge. Furthermore, since mercuric oxide is such a powerful emetic, chances are high that the compound would be ejected by vomiting before the body could absorb it. Even so, on more than one occasion Leonardo was accused of killing his patients with his potent drugs.

In short, prescribing Precipitato was playing with fire.

LEONARDO'S PARTICULAR SECRET

Not long after he arrived in Messina, he had a chance to demonstrate the "miraculous" properties of the drug. Here's how Fioravanti tells the story:

> At the beginning of the month of July, 1549, having already cured a lot of people in Messina, I was asked to look in on a Spanish woman. She was about sixty-two years old and for about three years had been tormented by a severe stomach ailment. The poor woman was near death. She was being treated by a friend of mine, a physician from Bologna called Armeleo. Now, Armeleo was a learned and experienced man, but all the remedies he tried failed. "If you have a particular secret, Leonardo, go ahead and use it," he said. "I'll do anything necessary to expedite the cure."
>
> I proposed that we give her Precipitato. "There's no doubt that this woman's sickness is in the stomach," I explained. "Precipitato will work because it provokes vomiting and empties the stomach of offensive matter. Other medicines can't do this." Armeleo was convinced, and the next morning I gave her twelve grains of Precipitato in honey and rosewater. I went about my business and returned home to have dinner with the other boarders at my house.
>
> As I was sitting at the table, a Spanish soldier rushed in and said that if I wanted to see something incredible, I should go immediately to the woman's house. Right away I mounted my horse and rode there. When I arrived, I found

> that she had vomited an enormous quantity of putrid matter, and among the things she vomited up was a huge clump, as big as a hand, and it was alive! Staring at it, never having seen such a thing, I was stupefied. I took it to Leonardo Testa's pharmacy and left it there for the entire city to marvel at. The thing lived for two days in tepid water. The whole city talked about it and because of it I became very famous in Messina.

Fioravanti had arrived at his belief in the efficacy of Precipitato through research into the traditional healing practices of the common people of Sicily and southern Italy. He interviewed the old folks in the region because, as he put it, "I wanted to know what rules of life they followed in order to reach such an advanced age." In Palermo, he met a 98-year-old man who regularly purged himself with hellebore.

Leonardo met another man in Messina who was 104 and healthy. "Tell me," he asked the man as the two dined together one evening, "have you ever taken any medicine?"

"Never in my life," the old man replied, "although I do take some Soldanella [*Convolvulus soldanella,* or bindweed, a cathartic] in the springtime. We have lots of it around here and every time I take it, you know it makes me vomit thoroughly. It leaves my stomach so clean that I go a whole year without being sick. . . . I do this every year and it seems like a thousand years until the next spring comes when I can take it. With this and God's help I hope to stay well the entire year." A few years later, while living in Naples, Leonardo met an 87-year-old man who told him that he occasionally took white hellebore (*Veratrum album,* an emetic and cathartic) with a cooked apple, which "made him vomit and moved his bowels so that he was very well purged."

From such observations, Leonardo concluded that robust emetics and purges were good for cleansing the body of corruption. The old people of the south thought of purges not as medicine, but as "rules of life" they followed to keep themselves healthy. If regular purging was good for maintaining health, Leonardo reasoned, why shouldn't it be good for restoring health too? It was, he believed, a time-tested rule of medicine that went all the way back to the mythical "first physicians," who, observing that the animals instinctively purged themselves when they got sick, made purging a first course of action in the fight against illness.

The emphasis on purging the body of poisons that are continually being produced in it was part and parcel of the barber-surgeon's worldview that Fioravanti had absorbed during his days as an apprentice. For barber-surgeons, cleansing the body to maintain health meant not just cutting and cleaning unruly hair but also removing waste products that had built up beneath the skin, causing pathologies of various kinds. Cutting hair, paring nails, cleaning the ears, and other barbering functions were seen to serve aesthetic purposes, of course, but they were also deemed essential to maintaining health. In that sense, all hygienic practices were understood as forms of purging.

Besides drawing on his professional experience to explain disease, in identifying putrefaction as the cause of illness Fioravanti appropriated a familiar aspect of everyday life. Renaissance society's experience of festering dead bodies, rotten food, and decaying garbage was much more immediate than it is in modern developed countries, where decomposed matter is and sanitized and quarantined. Every Renaissance town and village teemed with the stench of animal and human feces on the streets, piles of decaying offal and blood outside butchers' shops, open sewers, cesspools, dung heaps, and garbage pits. The everyday experience of corruption and decay was a metaphor tailor-made to explain the mysterious onset of sickness, and it would have provided Fioravanti with a language that anyone could understand.

OF PURGATORY AND PURGING

Physicians didn't necessarily agree with Leonardo's methods. Once, while living in Messina, he was consulted in the case of a Ragusa merchant named Lazaro Scuti, who suffered from what Fioravanti identified as *"flusso epatico"* (possibly dysentery). After interviewing the patient about his medical history, the surgeon concluded that the ailment had been caused by a previous attack of the pox. He advised the man's doctor, Spanish physician Andrea Santa Croce, to give Scuti a purge. Santa Croce demurred, insisting not unreasonably that a binding remedy was needed. Leonardo recalled the contretemps this way:

> I responded, citing the text of Galen, *"fluxus fluxum curat"* [flowing cures the flux] and advancing other powerful arguments. Finally he consented to follow my method. So I gave the patient a dose of Precipitato and in a little while he began to vomit. He vomited five or six times and let go from below three more times, and with this remedy he was greatly relieved. When the doctor saw that the man was so well restored to health, he was stupefied, for it seemed to him a miracle.

Nor was this the end of the internal cleansing that poor Lazaro Scuti was made to endure. The surgeon prescribed that Scuti be purged "four or five times per day" for another ten days with a decoction of colocynth *(coloquintida)*, a wild gourd whose pulp is a drastic hydragogue cathartic. So great is the plant's purging power that large doses sometimes prompt bloody discharges and dangerous inflammation of the bowels. Fioravanti's dilute decoction of the drug would have produced milder but still dramatic effects. The regimen he inflicted on Scuti must therefore have been both painful and exhausting.

To Leonardo, however, there was nothing trifling about the corruption that resulted from the onslaught of disease. In his mind he saw a parallel between the physical threat to human health caused by bodily corruption and the moral threat to Christendom posed by heresy. Both must be attacked by extreme means. To Fioravanti, the more violent the purge, the better the cleansing. Why else would he take such a careful accounting of the number of times his patients would vomit and defecate after enduring a dose of one of his purges? The amount of foul matter expelled from the guts was to him a measure of a cure's success.

The archives yield not a scrap of information about Leonardo's sojourn in Sicily, yet we can be certain of one thing: Sicily opened his eyes not only to alchemy, but to the possibility of a theatrical style of healing that placed him front and center on a stage that featured the dramatic actions of cleansing purges—foremost amongst which were the marvelous virtues of Precipitato.

10

CHARLATAN OR WONDER WORKER?

Leonardo claimed a reputation as a wonder-working healer. Yet sometimes people's reactions even surprised him. "I really didn't know much beyond what I'd read in books," he admitted, remembering his arrival in Palermo, "so all of these experiences were new to me." Did the people really believe in him? Did his cures really work? Or do we detect in his account a charlatan's humbug?

A parallel may be drawn with the experiences of another northern traveler to the south of Italy, one not of the 16th but of the 20th century. In the mid-1930s, physician and author Carlo Levi was exiled for his antifascist political activism to a small village in Lucania, a rural province in southern Italy. It was a "land without comfort or solace, where the peasant lives out his motionless civilization on barren ground in remote poverty, and in the presence of death." To this day, the region remains unknown not only to most tourists but also to the vast majority of Italians.

In his memoir, *Christ Stopped at Eboli,* Levi describes the wonderment with which the locals regarded him. Although he had trained as a physician, he had not practiced in many years and was at first reluctant to attend to the village's sick. Yet by giving them even the simplest medical care, which the local doctors seemed incapable of providing, Levi was looked upon as some sort of miracle worker. "Their faith and hope in me were absolute and I could only wonder at them," he remembered. Even after he failed to save a man afflicted with malaria, the people pressed him to tend their "pale, thin, waxen-faced children":

> Perhaps I owed their esteem to the natural prestige of a stranger whose faraway origin makes him a sort of god, or else to their perception that, in spite of the hopelessness of his case, I had really tried to do something for the dying man and that I had looked at him first with real interest and later with genuine sorrow. I was astonished and shamed by their confidence, which was as complete as it was undeserved.

A few months later, Levi reported, "my reputation as a miracle man was growing by leaps and bounds, and patients came from remote villages to consult me."

Is it any less believable that, in the 16th century, in a part of Europe known to the Jesuits as "the other Indies" because of its geographical and cultural isolation, a foreigner such as Leonardo Fioravanti might have caused a similar reaction? Everyone, especially the physicians, must have been astonished when he not only dared to operate on Marulla Greco but also successfully removed her ruptured spleen. What a miracle it must have seemed to have saved the beautiful young woman's life! And what luck that she should turn out to be a Spanish captain's wife. Unlike Carlo Levi, whose humility was so eloquent, Fioravanti made sure the entire city knew about the operation. Of course, he omitted the salient detail that Neapolitan surgeon Andreano Zaccarello, not he, had actually performed the surgery.

Physiologically, the operation was hardly impossible. Although risky because of the danger of infection and doubtless excruciatingly painful without anesthesia, a splenectomy would not necessarily kill the patient. In the 17th century, Italian surgeon Giuseppe Zambeccari proved experimentally that the spleen is not essential to sustain life. Although the organ performs an important function in the body's immune system by storing lymphocytes that produce antibodies, surgically removing the spleen would not necessarily have been fatal.

Indeed, some historical evidence shows that splenectomies were routinely performed in premodern times. Pliny, for example, noted that because a swollen spleen impedes running, Roman athletes sometimes had the organ removed. And Benedetto Ramberti, who accompanied the Venetian ambassador to the Ottoman sultan on a journey to Istanbul in 1534, reported that Turkish surgeons splenectomized *peiks,* or couriers, to enable them to run faster.

A CURE FOR THE INCURABLE?

We have better reason to be skeptical about Fioravanti's claim to have cured the patients of Palermo's Hospital of the Incurables, who suffered from the French pox, or syphilis. Although the disease was incurable in Fioravanti's day, he may have created the illusion of effecting a cure. He was treating second- and third-generation victims of the epidemic, for whom the experience of the ailment was quite different from that of earlier generations. Although still a horrible and disfiguring scourge, syphilis was not as virulent as it had once been: Its symptoms were less severe, its period of remission longer. People began to think that the disease was, after all, curable.

For 16th-century surgeons and empirics, syphilis was thus an "opportunity disease"—an illness that an ambitious (or unscrupulous) healer could exploit for profit and renown. The physicians had little to offer in the way of a cure. They argued about whether the disease was new or ancient, whether it came from the New World or somewhere else, but they couldn't agree on a treatment. Syphilis didn't seem to fit the Galenic model, which made some wonder whether it was a disease at all. Mostly they simply shunned its victims—who, denied treatment at regular hospitals, were consigned to facilities for "incurables." Orthodox Renaissance medicine was unsuited to the French pox; more than that, it was powerless in the face of it.

Meanwhile, empirics entered the picture. Few of them seemed to doubt that the French pox was curable; all seemed to possess some surefire remedy for it. Finding a cure for the disease was the Renaissance healer's holy grail, and in the competition for cures the natural history of syphilis gave the advantage to the empiric. The painful early symptoms of the illness subside in a few weeks; secondary symptoms, which can recur six to eight weeks later, are comparatively mild. Thus the sickness "heals" spontaneously and remains latent for a period of one to twenty years. The tertiary phase of the disease, which occurs in about one-third of untreated patients, is characterized by progressively destructive lesions of the skin, mucous membranes, bones, and internal organs, eventually leading to dementia and death.

From a cultural standpoint, syphilis was a disease that favored dramatic "specifics." Although the empirics' heroic interventions may have had no more real effect on curing the pox than the regimens of Galenic medicine, unlike the latter they produced visible physiological changes. When dramatic bodily alterations (such as prolonged bouts of vomiting) were followed by relief of symptoms, sufferers naturally established a link between the medicine and the cure. Even if the "cure" was simply a spontaneous remission of the disease's symptoms, the empirics' remedies appeared more "efficacious" than the physicians' mild regimens, which did not seem to bring about any physiological changes at all. The French pox was thus perfectly suited to the medical self-fashioning of empirics, who challenged orthodox medicine with remedies that really seemed to work.

Another perfect fit was between entrepreneurial healers such as Fioravanti and the niche in the medical economy opened up by a dreaded disease that appeared to respond to a wonder drug. Guaiacum, the "holy wood" from the New World, was one such drug, and its popularity brought huge profits to the Fugger banking house, its chief European importer. Precipitato, Leonardo's powerful emetic, was another. Precipitato certainly induced dramatic results, but the "cure" was probably an illusion created by the disease's longer period of remission. The symptoms would reappear later—but only much later, and by then the famous itinerant healer would have moved on. In the historical record, only his version of the event survived.

Fioravanti relished his celebrity. Believing that he possessed the "true medicine of the first physicians"—a gift of God given first to the brute animals, and now to him—he could refute the tenets of official medicine. The act of displaying wonders such as Marulla's hypertrophied spleen in the marketplace and the "live" bolus of teaming matter miraculously ejected from the Spanish woman's belly became yet another instance of opportunistic self-fashioning.

Spectacle was crucial to the art of the itinerant healer. But there was more to it than that. The stark contrast that Fioravanti drew—and demonstrated in his healing stunts—between the physician's weak diets and empty arguments and his own rapid, reliable remedies must have struck a responsive chord in the inhabitants of the Sicilian towns where he practiced. Evidently, his methods were more deeply connected to the cultural realities of the people than official Galenic medicine.

11

AN INGENIOUS SURGERY

Leonardo's fame rested on more than violent purges. He continued to collect folk wisdom, and in Sicily he discovered the "true method" of treating wounds that would later make him famous. By chance, he became a disciple of an elderly surgeon in Messina, a Franciscan friar by the name of Matteo Guaruccio. According to Fioravanti, Fra Matteo was famous in the region for his ability to treat wounds. Like many surgeons, he had developed his own special medications for treating various injuries. One evening, while dining at Fioravanti's house, the friar offered to reveal his secret for curing wounds. "The good old man showed me how to make the three remedies that he used to treat every type of wound so divinely: a water, a powder, and an oil," Fioravanti recalled. "I refined and improved these three secrets so well that the things he was able to accomplish in one month I could do in just six days."

Attending to wounds was one of the riskiest yet most common procedures the Renaissance surgeon was called upon to perform. Wounds were a part of everyday life, both because of the dangers of manual work and because of frequent violent altercations. Falls and accidents caused by falling objects were continual in the construction industry, resulting in countless broken bones, concussions, and head wounds. The 15th-century Florentine wall builder *(muratore)* Gaspare Nadi kept a diary of his working life for half a century, recording numerous falls that laid him up for weeks—and some that almost killed him. Nadi was lucky: In the woeful hygienic conditions of the early modern workplace, open wounds invited infections that could lead to tetanus or gangrene. Without proper care, even a minor wound could be fatal.

The workplace was not nearly as dangerous as the streets, however. Italy was a violent place. Men were quick to draw daggers or swords to defend their honor. Sudden brawls, often triggered by trifling arguments, erupted with little warning, while simmering vendettas broke out into bloody warfare. Even a seemingly trivial *mentita,* or insult, sufficed to spark bloodshed. Muggings and brigandage were also threats, especially in Italy's south, where lawlessness reigned. Gangs of youths roamed towns armed with sticks, knives, and guns to uphold the honor of their neighborhoods. In Rome, where surgeons were required to inform the authorities of any wounds they treated, the archive is replete with reports of stabbings, beatings, shootings, and wounds inflicted in duels. Renaissance Italy was, as one historian writes, "a society in which violence was an easy, almost acceptable method of solving problems."

Leonardo named his new remedies Wound Powder *(polvere da ferite),* Mighty Elixir *(magno elixir),* and Blessed Oil *(oleo benedetto).* Another Messina surgeon showed him how to make an ointment to treat wounds. After months of experimenting with the recipe, Fioravanti developed a balm that he named Leonardo's Grand Liquor *(magno licore Leonardi).* "It takes almost a year to prepare," he wrote, "but it cicatrizes wounds wonderfully and is an excellent treatment for ringworm, too."

These four remedies Leonardo put to use countless times with, as he claims, "miraculous" success. What did they actually do? According to Fioravanti, each treatment had special properties and all worked together. He doesn't disclose the ingredients in Wound Powder, but the fact that he used it to stanch blood and to treat inflammation leads one to suspect that it was a powder composed of a mineral earth such as terra Lemnia or Armenian bole, which have strong astringent properties and were well-known folk remedies for wounds and venomous bites.

Mighty Elixir was a composition of herbs, spices, honey, and sugar that had been fermented and distilled three times, producing a clear, sterile, perfumed liquid of fairly strong alcoholic content. It would have been an effective antibacterial cleansing agent. Fioravanti used the elixir to relieve pain and "conserve the flesh."

Leonardo's Blessed Oil was a composition distilled from egg white and tormentil *(Tormentilla potentilla),* a plant whose leaves have strong astringent properties. Tormentil has long been used in traditional and homeopathic medicine as a styptic to stop bleeding. The oil also contained a small amount of myrrh, which has been shown to have astringent, antiseptic, and antimicrobial properties.

Grand Liquor, composed of about a dozen herbs, had as its principal ingredient hypericum *(Hypericum perforatum),* known in English as St. John's wort. St. John's wort has long been used successfully as a remedy for wounds because of its powerful astringent properties. Fioravanti claimed that the medicament "cicatrizes the wound, stanches bleeding, and promotes growth of the flesh." His claim is substantiated by scientific research, which has demonstrated that ointments composed of hypericum promote wound contraction and the regeneration of tissue at the wound site. The ruby red oil of hypericum has also been shown to have antifungal and antimicrobial properties; for that reason it is recommended in homeopathic medicine as a treatment for burns, bruises, wounds, and ringworm.

THE RENAISSANCE NOSE JOB

Thus the Bologna surgeon left Sicily armed with an arsenal of effective wound treatments. Naturally, he was anxious to try them out. "I decided to move on to Naples," he recalled, "a violent city where every day many are injured in duels and brawls." He knew that his services would be in great demand there. But first he wanted to stop off in Calabria, because he heard that some surgeons there had invented an ingenious method for repairing mutilated noses, and he was eager to learn it.

The surgeons lived in a little fishing village called Tropea. It is located on the Tyrrhenian coast, hanging on a cliff like an eagle's aerie.

Although nowadays the town is famous for its red onions and not much else, in Fioravanti's day Tropea was the home of a family of highly skilled surgeons who had perfected the art of rebuilding damaged noses by means of plastic surgery—in modern terminology, rhinoplasty. When Fioravanti arrived there in late 1549, the art was being practiced with unmatched skill by two brothers who worked together in the same house. Their names were Pietro and Paolo Vianeo.

Sicilian surgeons had begun practicing rhinoplasty in the early 15th century, but its origins have been traced as far back as the 6th century B.C.E., when it appeared in the *Susruta*—the basic text of Hindu medicine. Branca de' Branca, a Catania surgeon, practiced a technique similar to the Hindu method, which required cutting a flap of skin from the cheek and grafting it to the nose. His son Antonio is credited with abandoning the Hindu method and taking the reparative skin flap from the arm, thus leaving the face unscarred.

The technique was further developed in the early 16th century by Vincenzo Vianeo of Tropea. In the manner typical of the transmission of trade secrets, Vincenzo passed the art down to his nephew Bernardino, who in turn taught it to his sons Pietro and Paolo, the brothers whom Leonardo visited. The Vianeo brothers used the method to repair noses, lips, ears, and other facial defects. As all-around plastic surgeons, their skills were widely sought-after—partly because of the ravages of the French pox and partly because of the violent tenor of Renaissance life.

One of the most shocking symptoms of advanced syphilis was the gaping hole left in the center of the face where the disease had eaten away the flesh and cartilage of the nose. The condition, known in modern medicine as saddle-nose deformity, is caused by the collapse of the nasal bridge and is relatively common among victims of congenital syphilis. With the outbreak of the syphilis epidemic in 16th-century Europe, the syphilitic nose became a mark of shame—a visible sign of the moral and corporeal corruption that stigmatized its unfortunate victims.

Others lost their noses by more sudden means. Aristocratic violence, especially in Italy's Spanish south, was legendary. Dueling was part of the gentleman's code, and violent quarrels took place over even the most trivial violations of honor. Historian Donald Weinstein observes, "In a society obsessed by maintaining *la bella figura* and formed by a culture that glorified violence, men would constantly be on guard against insults to their honor and they would find ways to fight." Often, the "duel" was little more than a street brawl, but the weapons were the same and the stakes were just as high. When two hot-blooded cavaliers went at it with weapons drawn, rapiers flailed wildly in the air and the odds of receiving a blow to the head were high. The indignity of sacrificing a nose in a fight was compounded by the fact that the loser bore the mark of defeat for life, smack in the middle of his face.

SURGICAL ESPIONAGE

Immediately upon arriving in Tropea in November 1549, Fioravanti sought out the Vianeo brothers. Posing as a Bolognese nobleman, he explained that he had come on behalf of a relative who had lost his nose in the Battle of Serravalle, and he wanted to observe the rhinoplastic surgery so that he could tell his relative what to expect. The brothers consented to Leonardo's request. When their patients were ready, they called him in to watch the procedure. "Pretending to be horrified at the sight, I turned my face away," he writes, "but secretly I made sure I was able to see everything. I saw the whole secret from beginning to end and learned it well."

Although numerous references to the Branca family crop up in Renaissance medical literature, Fioravanti was the first to describe the method employed by the Vianeo brothers. His description is so clear it needs little comment:

> First they gave the patient a purgative. Then they took pincers and grabbed the skin in the left arm between the shoulder and the elbow and passed a large knife between the pincers and the muscle, cutting a slit in the skin. They passed a small piece of wool or linen under the skin and medicated it until the skin thickened. When it was just right, they cut the nose

> to fit the end of the little skin flap. Then they snipped the skin on the arm at one end and sewed it to the nose. They bound it there so artfully that it could not be moved in any way until the skin had grown onto the nose. When the skin flap was joined to the nose, they cut the other end from the arm. They skinned the lip of the mouth and sewed the flap of skin from the arm onto it, and medicated it until it was joined to the lip. Then they put a metal form on it, and fastened it there until the nose grew into it to the right proportions. It remained well formed but somewhat whiter than the face. It's a fine operation and an excellent experience.

One can only imagine what excruciating agony the operation must have caused. Added to the pain of the surgery was the discomfort the patient had to suffer during the prolonged healing process. The entire operation could take as long as 45 days, including 15 days during which the arm was bound to the head in a harness as the skin graft took hold. The risk of infection to the open wound must also have been high. Yet the success rate of the operation encouraged many to make the journey to Tropea: The Vianeo brothers had five patients waiting in line when Fioravanti visited them.

Those who endured the operation seem to have deemed the discomfort and inconvenience well worth it. The humanist Camillo Porzio, who underwent the procedure in 1561 to restore a nose that had been cut off in a fight with a jealous husband, admitted that he had "suffered the greatest trials" during the operation, yet he was pleased with the results, deeming his new nose "so similar to the first one that it will be difficult for those who do not know to realize that it is not the same."

The Calabrian method of rhinoplasty was one of those rare surgical secrets done by only a handful of surgeons. Long practiced with a high degree of success in the south of Italy and in Sicily, the procedure was still more than two decades removed from being taught in any university. Physicians occasionally heard about the technique from travelers who had seen it or from actual patients,

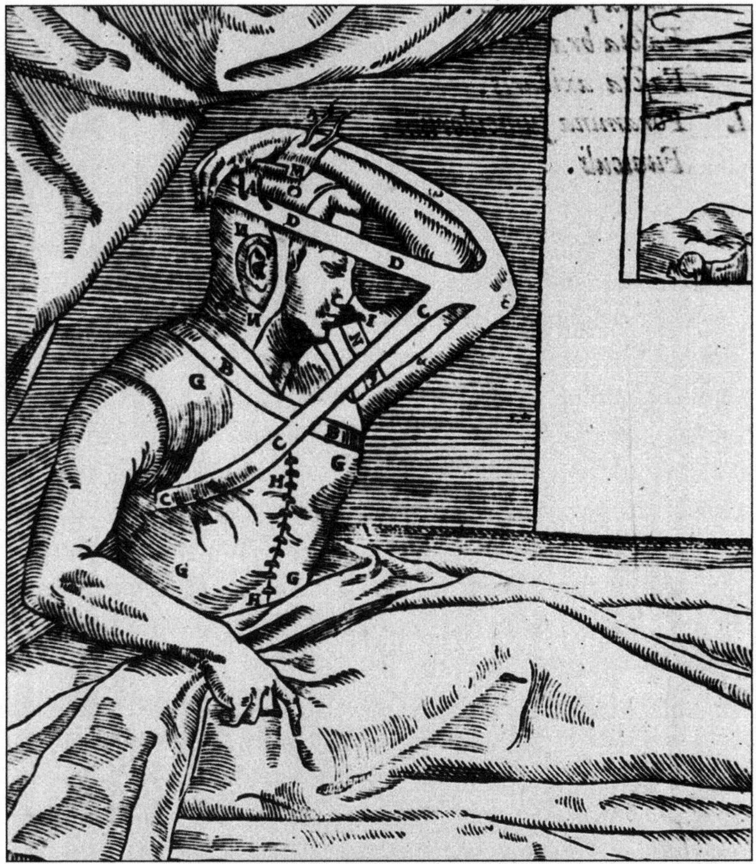

In this 1597 illustration of the Calabrian method of rhinoplasty a patient is depicted in a brace that holds the arm firmly in place while the skin flap grafts to the nose. This method could take as long as 40 days to complete.

but their customary reaction was incredulity. They could not see how a new nose could be grafted onto the vacant space where the old one once grew. The anatomist Gabriele Falloppio took it as "proven by Hippocrates" that a severed body part could not be reattached.

However, it all made perfect sense to Leonardo Fioravanti, who said that surgery was an "agriculture of the body"—or, as he put it somewhat more poetically in his *Mirror of Universal Science,* a "farming of men." Just as the farmer will bandage an injured tree and allow it to heal, or create better orchard stock by grafting a stem onto the trunk of a tree, in the same way the surgeon should assist the human body in finding its own natural path back to health. That's why doctors should attend to nature's ways—studying the habits of animals, for example, or observing the way farmers care for their orchards. As Fioravanti's doctrine suggests, often in the history of science and medicine, the trajectory toward "the modern" is tortuous and indirect.

Fioravanti said that the "new way of healing" was a gift from God that had come to him by way of the people. This kind of knowledge, he admitted, was neither rational nor theoretical. It was more cunning, a craftiness born of long experience. The ancient Greeks had a name for it—*mêtis,* which they contrasted with *sophia,* the contemplative wisdom of the philosophers. Mêtis was the kind of know-how on which mariners, warriors, and hunters relied, knowledge that equipped them to react to the moment in shifting and uncertain terrain. It is the opposite of philosophical knowledge, which is about the timeless world of Being.

To Fioravanti, the Calabrian method of rhinoplasty—rebuilding noses by means of plastic surgery—epitomized the people's wisdom, and mêtis—the trickster's art—enabled him to discover it. Disguising himself to avoid being found out as a thief stealing a trade secret, he made off with the trick with the wiliness of a fox. Mêtis, the power of cunning and deceit, always operates in disguise, and Fioravanti used it with consummate skill.

The procedure for rebuilding noses perfected by the Vianeo family demanded extreme fortitude of patients. Yet anyone who underwent the grueling procedure seemed satisfied with the results. Camillo Porzio, obviously pleased with his new nose, lamented that the procedure had not been published for the edification of more surgeons. He was convinced that the surgeon who operated on him would "for a consideration small in comparison to the great usefulness of the remedy" be persuaded to reveal his secret for publication. That, evidently, did not happen. It was left to Leonardo Fioravanti to steal the secret.

THE SECRET SPREADS

Not until the 1560s did Calabrian rhinoplasty finally reach an academic audience. Although reports of the operation had been heard in academia from time to time since early in that century, medical writers gave garbled or incoherent versions of it. Vesalius reportedly thought that the new nose was to be shaped from a muscle dug out of the forearm—an impossibility that betrays the famous anatomist's ignorance of the method.

As it happened, Leonardo Fioravanti would become the intermediary through whom knowledge of the Calabrian technique reached academic culture. Decades later, when he belatedly returned to Bologna to obtain his medical degree, he met Giulio Cesare Aranzio, a professor of surgery. Leonardo already knew Aranzio by reputation. So skillful a surgeon was he, according to Fioravanti, that "he almost brings the dead back to life when he lays hand on them." A cordial friendship developed between the two Bologna natives. Eager to share his knowledge of the Calabrian secret with Bologna's most distinguished surgery professor, Leonardo regaled his younger colleague with stories of the heroic surgeons of the south. Around the time of Fioravanti's visit, Aranzio himself began practicing rhinoplasty at Bologna.

Among Aranzio's pupils was medical student Gaspare Tagliacozzi, another Bologna native. After his graduation in 1576, Tagliacozzi began teaching anatomy at the university. At about the same time, evidently encouraged by Aranzio, he began experimenting with the Calabrian technique. By 1588 he was calling himself, rather exaggeratedly, "*narium et aurium primus reformator*—first restorer of noses and ears."

In 1597, Tagliacozzi published a Latin treatise on the subject titled *De curtorum chirurgia*. He argued that the operation was not frivolous or merely cosmetic, but was intended to "buoy up the spirits and help the mind of the afflicted." These affirmations were meant to ennoble the art of surgery, linking it to the ideology of human autonomy advanced by humanists such as Pico della Mirandola. In his *Oration on the Dignity of Man*, Pico has God tell Adam (in opposition to the view that human nature is fixed) that "you may, as the free and proud shaper of your own being, fashion yourself in the form you may prefer."

Tagliacozzi's only acknowledgment of the folk roots of rhinoplasty was to note that he intended to correct and improve upon the "haphazard methods" of the Calabrians. To give rhinoplasty an acceptable academic pedigree, he traced its origins back to the ancient Roman agricultural authors Palladius and Columella, who had written on grafting. Rhinoplasty, as Fioravanti had pointed out, was a way of grafting a new nose onto a face.

Within a few years of Tagliacozzi's death in 1597, the practice of reconstructive surgery seems to have completely died out. Except for a few isolated cases of academic surgeons attempting the procedure, Tagliacozzi's work was forgotten. With the Vianeo family extinct and few surgeons willing to risk the difficult technique, rhinoplasty fell into disuse and is not recorded again until the 18th century.

A VITAL ART ECLIPSED

How could such a promising procedure have disappeared so suddenly? Historians have ventured a number of explanations for the demise of the Calabrian method. Some have blamed the "general state of sterility" into which surgery had supposedly lapsed by the 17th century. Yet the status of surgery rose to become part of the medical school curriculum.

The most plausible explanation for the eclipse of rhinoplasty is simply that no one after the Vianeo brothers, Tagliacozzi included, was able to accomplish the difficult and painful surgery to the satisfaction of patients. Despite Tagliacozzi's claim of having "perfected" the technique, only about half a dozen instances can be documented of his having performed the operation, and these were mixed successes. Far from perfecting the method, Tagliacozzi produced results that were inferior to those of the more experienced surgeons from Tropea. The Vianeo brothers had a monopoly on this rare and demanding art, and they took it with them to the grave.

That conclusion would have pleased Leonardo Fioravanti. His allegiance to the "natural philosophy of the Calabrians"—the shepherds, empirics, midwives, and peasants of the south—was central to his medical doctrine. At the core of his method as it developed during his sojourn in the south was the belief that medicine had been born in emulation of the natural healing ways of the animals. That's why he urged a return to the pristine system of the "first physicians," who "knew no medical system, nor any method at all, they just had good judgment." Fioravanti's medical primitivism, rooted in his experiences in southern Italy and Sicily, prepared him for the more philosophical brand of naturalism that he would encounter at the next stage of his journey.

When Leonardo arrived in Naples in December 1549, he was already convinced that nature pullulated with life. This view matched the animated, pulsing nature of the Neapolitan philosophical tradition that had grown up around the ideas of Calabrian philosopher Bernardino Telesio, whom Francis Bacon dubbed "the first of the moderns." Telesio put into exacting philosophical terms a natural philosophy that Fioravanti had been blindly groping for: Nature must be understood and investigated "according to its own principles," Telesio insisted. Observation alone, not reason or authority, was the one true pathway to knowledge.

Naples would file the rough edges off Fioravanti's primitive naturalism. There he would be introduced to a community of thinkers who shared his conviction that nature in all its aspects is immediately accessible to the senses. From them Leonardo would learn a new experimental method to advance that doctrine.

12

THE MARVELS OF NAPLES

The sprawling, dilapidated Naples of today is starkly different from the city beheld by its Renaissance denizens. Once graced by elegant Spanish and Italianate palaces, the modern city lies buried beneath layers of grime and soot. Luxurious mansions that formerly housed aristocrats, princes, and ambassadors from all over Europe have become crowded tenements. Below clotheslines strung across spacious courtyards, peeling frescoes and crumbling curved stairways remind visitors of Naples's splendid past. They, along with the ever-present *scugnizzi*—street urchins who survive by petty theft—bear witness to the slow decline of Italy's south, to which Italian governments have been largely indifferent.

Naples in the 16th century, by contrast, was a brilliant metropolis that attracted merchants, bureaucrats, and nobles from throughout Italy and the Spanish realm, who came to enjoy the many privileges the Kingdom of Naples conferred on its citizens. If you were a Spaniard of means, you could live better in Naples than anywhere in Spain, especially Madrid—the dingy market town to which, in 1561, King Philip II moved his court.

Naples's grandeur owed much to its Spanish Viceroy, Don Pedro de Toledo, who administered the royal domain from 1532 until his death in 1553. A stern man seasoned by war in Germany, Don Pedro was hated by the Neapolitan nobles; before the arrival of the Spanish viceroys they had ruled with a free hand, plunging the city into a vicious cycle of feud and warfare.

Whereas elsewhere in Italy feudalism was in decay, noted Italian historian Benedetto Croce, "in the Kingdom of Naples it drew upon fresh blood." Weak and inept sovereigns had for centuries failed to discipline the bellicose big shots who bullied their way around the realm. The Holy Roman Emperor Charles V, Philip's father, sent Toledo to Naples to implement the Spanish policy of reducing the barons to the rank of subjects. According to 18th-century historian Pietro Giannone, the people welcomed Toledo, "being persuaded by his reputation that he would govern them with prudence and justice, reform the many abuses and corruptions that had crept in, and liberate them from the insolence of the nobility."

AN ELITE REBELLION

Decades of baronial infighting, the French invasion, and unrelenting pestilence had reduced the kingdom to "a miserable state," Toledo discovered. Soon after his arrival in 1532, he enacted measures to restore public order and bring the barons to heel. He forbade the carrying of arms, instituted a curfew, and tore down balconies that could harbor assassins. These actions angered the nobles, and Toledo's subsequent attempt to introduce the Inquisition gave them the pretext they needed for open rebellion. On May 11, 1547, when the edict announcing its establishment was posted, the city exploded in revolt. "To arms! To arms!" cried the mob, tearing down the proclamation. Shops were shuttered and the people, urged on by the nobility, stormed the Spanish garrison. The uprising lasted through the summer. Giannone gave this sour account of those tumultuous months:

> It was lamentable to see the city void of nobility and honest citizens, and only filled with an arrogant mob and shoals of *banditi,* who, running from place to place, committed a thousand insolences, and whoever reproved them were insulted, called traitors to their country, and forced to take arms and join them; but whoever appeared swaggering in the streets in their doublets, or arms in their hands, boasting of their willingness to die for their country, and threatening the Giant

Naples as it appeared in the late 15th century. This panoramic view, completed around 1472–73 by the Bolognese artist Francesco Pagano, depicts the entry of the Aragonese fleet after the Battle of Ischia in 1465.

of the Castle (for so they called the Viceroy) were honoured, styled patriots, and deemed worthy to be made Deputies of the City.

Hundreds were killed and arrested before the revolt was finally crushed. Giannone thought that the "tumult" of 1547 attested to Toledo's harsh but enlightened rule, whereas Croce deemed it to be "the last evidence of Neapolitan independence and political vitality." The facts on the ground support both interpretations.

Having reined in the barons, Toledo launched an ambitious program of urban renewal. To realize his vision of a modern capital, he demolished medieval buildings and razed entire neighborhoods. He expanded the city walls and rebuilt its bastions to defend against the Turks. He hired architects and engineers to construct new squares,

water supplies, and fountains. He ordered the building of hospitals and orphanages, the restoration of churches, and the construction of the wide avenue named after him, Via Toledo, which bisects the city and rises steeply toward the hill of Capodimonte. Finally, Toledo undertook the restoration of the imposing medieval fortress, Castel Nuovo, transforming it into a showcase viceregal residence.

"A PARADISE INHABITED BY DEVILS"

These building projects were in full swing in 1549, the year that Fioravanti reached the city by way of the gently curving Bay of Naples, inspiring him to describe it as "among the loveliest, most famous, and most noble cities in the world today."

None of this Renaissance splendor could mask the pervasive poverty that, then as now, was a stark reality of Neapolitan life. Just as it enticed the wealthy, Naples attracted vast numbers of destitute immigrants. Like the lava ashes it was built on, the city of 250,000 smoldered with tens of thousands of the south's poor. Behind the splendid palaces, Naples's tough neighborhoods were jam-packed with hovels housing fishermen, porters, laundresses, blacksmiths, carpenters, and herb women who lived from day to day. The dangers of pauperism and parasitism were not lost on the government. The presence of so many marginal people—beggars, vagabonds, bandits, prostitutes—was a potential threat to public order, the viceroy observed, because they are the ones who "are wont to look with favor on changes in the state, thinking that they have something to gain and nothing to lose."

A proverb coined during Angevin times—"*Napoli è un paradiso abitato da diavoli*—Naples is a paradise inhabited by devils"—juxtaposes the grandeur of the countryside with the squalidness of the city. The extremes that so marked the economic and political life of Naples were not lost on its philosophers, either. No one was more awed by the terror and wonder of the Neapolitan landscape than Bernardino Telesio, who transposed the miracle of its prodigiousness into metaphysics.

Telesio grew up in the hillside town of Cosenza, at the confluence of the Busento and Crati Rivers southwest of Naples. He studied natural philosophy at the University of Padua while Vesalius was teaching anatomy there in the 1530s. While reading Aristotle in Greek, Telesio became disgusted with Scholastic natural philosophy and resolved to formulate a view of nature that dispensed with the arbitrary categories that philosophers had imposed on it. Nature must be investigated "according to its own principles," he declared, and be allowed to "speak for itself."

Rejecting Aristotelian metaphysics, Telesio reduced the principles of his system to the active, sensible forces of heat and cold, which acted on passive matter. As polar opposites, heat and cold battle each other to gain possession of matter; from that perpetual, Heraclitean struggle arise the qualities of things as we know them. To Telesio, the universal principles of heat and cold were as real as the smoking brimstone of the Phlegraean fields outside the city walls of Naples and the icy mountain peaks of Calabria. To those who gathered at his house in Naples to discuss the composition and nature of the universe, a new world beckoned.

Although nature to Telesio was concrete and physical, it was not inert, like the mute atoms of Lucretius. Things did not arise by blind chance. Endowed with sensation and an instinct for self-preservation, nature "feels" the shapes and forms that are appropriate to it. Telesio's nature was alive, sentient, and pulsing. His natural philosophy extolled observation and strove to explain the physical world by principles discoverable in nature, not those invented by the human mind. Radically anti-Aristotelian and intensely materialistic (according to him, even the soul and knowledge itself are corporeal), Telesio's naturalism was uplifting, liberating, and dangerous: It implied that you could subject social and religious norms to the same empirical scrutiny with which you regarded nature, and that you could use nature as the standard for judging them. In the fecund soil of the south, naturalism sprouted a reform agenda, taking aim at social and religious conventions.

Reform naturalism found its cause célèbre in the trial of the radical Dominican friar Giordano Bruno. Arrested by the Venetian Inquisition in 1600 and extradited to Rome, he was tried for heresy and burned alive in the Campo Fiori. The Bruno legend—a favorite among Italian communists—portrays the Calabrian philosopher as a scientific martyr, but the legend isn't very convincing. More incriminating were his radical religious and political beliefs, above all his scheme to employ astrology and magic in a bizarre plot to establish a new universal religion. Convinced that Moses and Christ were magi, Friar Bruno believed that, as a magus himself, he would play an instrumental role in preparing the way for the new millennium. Telesio had reopened the debate about how magic works, and all hell broke loose.

THE ALLURE OF MAGIC

Magic was reborn in the Renaissance. It all started in 1466, when the humanist Marsilio Ficino acquired a manuscript containing a group of texts in Greek known collectively as *Hermes Trismegistus,* or *Thrice Great Hermes.* The Hermetic books, supposedly the repository of ancient Egyptian magic, told how the magi attracted beneficent influences from the stars by using images, talismans, and gemstones.

In 1614, English scholar Isaac Casauban would use philological methods to prove that the Hermetic texts were spurious. To the intellectuals of Fioravanti's generation, however, they exerted a talismanic power.

Hermetism found a natural home in this port city. Long before anyone in Italy had heard of *Hermes Trismegistus,* the streets of Naples had hummed with legends of magicians. The ancient Roman poet Virgil was the Neapolitans' favorite magus. The poet had lived much of his life in Naples, where he composed his great work, *The Aeneid.* Local legends told of the many clever devices Virgil had fashioned by natural magic to protect the city, including a bronze fly that drove away all flies and a bronze statue of an archer aiming an arrow at nearby Mount Vesuvius. For a long time, tradition held, the statue worked its magic to keep the mountain quiet, until one fine day a peasant, not understanding why the figure should stand there forever with its bow drawn, fired the arrow, which struck the edge of the crater, causing it to erupt.

Yet the appeal of the occult was hardly limited to Naples. Natural magic—the art of producing "marvelous" effects by manipulating nature's hidden forces—emerged in the Renaissance as Europe's most advanced research science, more promising even than the fields of astronomy and anatomy, wherein modern historians detect the origins of the Scientific Revolution. In hindsight, natural magic looks like one of the more spectacular dead ends of the history of science, but its agenda in the Renaissance was as electrifying as the search for the human genome is in ours. Natural magic promised to unveil the "secrets" of nature and enable the magus to do wonders in healing disease, improving technology, and promoting human welfare.

Dangerous and alluring, natural magic was a power for good. Used immoderately, though, it could lead one to forbidden places. Its most famous practitioner, Neapolitan magus Giambattista della Porta, was for a time the rival of Galileo. Born in 1535 to a minor Neapolitan nobleman, della Porta enjoyed a life of privilege that enabled him to indulge his passions for writing comedies and dabbling in experiments. As a precocious teenager in the 1540s, he founded an "academy of curious men" that met at the family palazzo in the fashionable Piazza Carità in the heart of Naples and at his seaside estate on the Sorrentine Peninsula.

Della Porta called his group the Academy of Secrets *(*Academia Secretorum). Its purpose? To search for "secrets of nature," whether in books or from other savants, test them by experiment, and "register only those proved true." To della Porta, nature was "an inexhaustible treasure of secrets" that could be manipulated to produce wonders: lenses to make optical illusions; invisible writing; methods to preserve fruits and vegetables through the year; tempering steel; and channeling the power of the imagination to sire multicolored horses and children that resembled gods.

The random and playful experimenting that went on at della Porta's villa among his aristocratic companions may strike modern sensibilities as so many adolescent games, yet their activities had a serious intent. Della Porta's real purpose was to demonstrate how the powers of nature could be managed and directed to beneficial ends.

Della Porta contained his zeal for natural magic within the boundaries of respectability. His younger contemporary, Tommaso Campanella, on the other hand, let his enthusiasm take him too far. The two men were as opposite in their thinking about magic as they were in their social backgrounds. The son of an illiterate, impoverished cobbler from the tiny Calabrian village of Stilo, Campanella entered the Dominican order at the age of 14. Transferred to Cosenza to complete his education, he was given a copy of Telesio's *On the Nature of Things According to Their Own Principles.* Immediately converted to Telesian naturalism, Campanella became a passionate defender of the doctrine.

Campanella moved to Naples and joined the della Porta circle, but he quickly tired of its dilettantish research. What do these aristocrats know of the crushing poverty of Calabria? he wondered. What use is magic if it cannot right these wrongs? To Campanella, della Porta's magical agenda did not go far enough because it was not a manifesto to change the world. In the spring of 1599, under the banner of natural magic and biblical prophecy, Campanella led a wretched band of libertine Dominicans, declassed noblemen, refugees, heretics, and bandits in a fantastic plot to overthrow the Spanish government in Calabria and establish a communist state—the City of the Sun—that Campanella would govern. For this reckless act, he spent the next 27 years languishing in a Naples dungeon.

The reform naturalism that propelled Giordano Bruno to heresy and Tommaso Campanella to revolution affected Leonardo Fioravanti in a completely different way. Upon arriving in Naples, he'd already played the learned doctor, devised miracle cures, and been rewarded by the astonished faces of crowds. He knew about magical tricks. Whereas Campanella believed wholeheartedly in the potential of magic to transform the world, Fioravanti was skeptical. To him, natural magic was no different than the magic he'd seen performed in piazzas by charlatans and jugglers—impressive, useful, but in the end mere tricks.

If unimpressed by magic, Leonardo was utterly persuaded by Telesio's championing of nature as the universal standard of truth. Too cynical to seriously entertain the possibility of a utopia such as Campanella's City of the Sun, he nevertheless looked back to a golden age of medicine, when empirics practiced freely and physicians had not yet monopolized the art. Like Campanella and Bruno, he had come to Naples with his eyes open wide and his mind full of wonder. In Naples, the paradise inhabited by devils, his rough ideas about nature and justice and the road to "true" medicine found a new voice.

13

AN ACADEMY OF MAGI

The universities closed their doors to Bernardino Telesio. The Cosenza philosopher's radical naturalistic metaphysics was too bold, too threatening to interests vested in the Aristotelian doctrine. Failing to obtain a chair at Padua, he returned to Cosenza in the 1540s and set up an "academy" of his own. The Accademia Cosentina—which, to this day, convenes regularly in its elegant meeting room in the Civic Library of Cosenza—became a center for the diffusion of Telesio's radical philosophy. Although his major work, *On the Nature of Things According to Their Own Principles,* was not published until 1565, his ideas were well known around Naples by the late 1540s.

A few years before Leonardo Fioravanti's 1549 move to Naples, a group of humanists and natural philosophers met to form a scientific academy there. They called their company of 27 men the Accademia Segreta, a name meaning both "Secret Academy" and "Academy of Secrets." The humanist Girolamo Ruscelli, one of its members, left a detailed description of the Segreti's activities in his book, *Secreti nuovi* (*New Secrets*, 1567). Generously supported by an unnamed "magnanimous Prince," Ruscelli reports, "Our intention was to make the most diligent inquiries and, as it were, a true anatomy of things and of the operations of nature in and of itself." They proposed to make their "true anatomies" of nature by means of experiments.

To accommodate its ambitious and novel program, the academy built a spacious house with a garden to grow the herbs they needed.

The meeting house boasted a laboratory, the Filosofia, equipped with the latest alchemical equipment; here the Segreti conducted their experiments. They hired craftsmen to assist them and recorded their results in detail. They conducted hundreds of experiments aimed at discovering new secrets in alchemy, metallurgy, and medicine. They made perfumes, dyes, and cosmetics, and tried out more than a thousand medicinal concoctions. During the Segreti's brief life span, its patrons spent 7,800 scudi on the academy—roughly three-fourths the annual salary of the Spanish viceroy.

TRIAL BY FIRE

Scientific experiments today employ a rigorous method designed to test a hypothesis about how nature works. However, that understanding of the scientific method evolved only in the 17th century. In the Renaissance, the idea of using experiments to investigate nature was entirely new and, from the standpoint of conventional science, dubious. The subjects that make up what we call science were then part of the discipline known as natural philosophy, which aimed at understanding the "ordinary course of nature"—nature as it routinely appears to the unaided senses. According to Scholastic epistemology, which governed the practice of natural philosophy in the universities, the intent of science was to explain phenomena that were already known, not to make new discoveries. Scholastic science was, as historian John Murdoch aptly described it, "natural philosophy without nature." Although Aristotle and the Scholastics who followed him maintained that the foundation of natural knowledge was sense experience, the kinds of "experiences" they had in mind were general observations such as "Heavy bodies fall" or "The sun rises in the east." Isolated, unusual, and singular events did not reveal how nature behaves "always or for the most part."

By design, experiments subvert nature, making it go "off course." Most medieval Scholastics would therefore not have placed much value on such events. According to the logic of science that prevailed in the universities, experiments could provide only distorted or misleading information about how nature works. Rather than giving reliable knowledge about how nature *normally* behaves, experiments produced results that the professors classified as "marvelous" because they did not reveal nature's true character. Metaphysical outlaws, experiments were more characteristic of alchemy and the occult sciences than what was then considered natural philosophy.

To the natural philosophers who made up the Accademia Segreta, however, experiments were the very essence of science. Their hands-on methodology was the harbinger of an entirely new way of doing natural philosophy. The experimental method, a key ingredient of the Scientific Revolution that gave birth to modern science, did not come to fruition until the 17th century. The first act in the drama of its development was played out during the Renaissance, in academies like the one Ruscelli described.

The Segreti's experiments were designed to make technological and medical improvements: discovering new ways to temper and harden iron, inventing new perfume scents, finding cures for new and old diseases. Their passionate pursuit of craft secrets confirms the insight of historian Edgar Zilsel; more than half a century ago, Zilsel argued from a Marxist perspective that the roots of the experimental scientific method lay in crafts such as glassmaking, dyeing, and metalworking, where manual work and the manipulation of natural materials were both essential and refined to a high degree. Recently historians have extended those roots to alchemy—another insight confirmed by the activities of the Segreti. Whether motivated by market pressures or the search for the philosopher's stone, alchemy and the crafts prized innovation through experimentation and "trial by fire."

The idea that artisanal and alchemical techniques might be systematically deployed to make experiments that would be validated by a community of scientists germinated in the Renaissance academies. Unlike the craft tradition, in which knowledge was passed on from individual to individual within an apprentice system, the academies favored communal learning. And in contrast to the alchemical practitioners, who were obsessed with maintaining secrecy and who clothed their secrets in obscure language, the academies favored public knowledge and recorded their work in writing for posterity. Even if that public was a circumscribed one, as it often was, the academies rejected esotericism. The academies were communities dedicated to common aims and interests. As for the Accademia Segreta, its aim was to use experiments to fulfill the promise of Telesio's metaphysics: that of making an "anatomy" of nature "according to its own principles." That natural truths might be discovered through the manipulation of materials was a radical new scientific idea.

AT THE COURT OF DON PEDRO DE TOLEDO

When Leonardo Fioravanti arrived in Naples, he bore a letter of introduction from the Sicilian viceroy Juan de Vega, and with it he gained entrée to the court of Don Pedro de Toledo, where he would soon serve as one of the Neapolitan viceroy's family surgeons. He found lodging in a house near the Castel Nuovo, in the heart of the city, close to Toledo's court, and reacquainted himself with many of the Spaniards he had met in Sicily. He set up an alchemical laboratory and stocked it with furnaces and glassware. He hired an alchemist to tutor him in the art of distillation. "Alchemists and distillers of many different nations came to my house to practice their art," he recalled, "and thus every day we discovered new things and made countless rare experiments."

Among the victims of Toledo's repression following the aristocratic revolt of 1547 had been the literary and philosophical academies, which the viceroy considered to be seedbeds of political and religious subversion. Toledo's suspicions were well founded. Many of the academies were patronized by the nobility. Proud, fiercely independent, and protective of the autonomy they enjoyed as subjects of the king of Naples, the barons chafed under the rule of the viceroys, who forced them to submit absolutely to the Spanish monarchy. The cloak of secrecy under which many of the academies operated only reinforced Toledo's misgivings. With some justification, he believed that the academicians were plotting against him.

The closing of the academies proved to be only temporary. Most of them simply ignored the ban and reopened once the situation cooled down. Informal and semiprivate, they were difficult to detect. In practice, the ban was impossible to enforce. By the time

Fioravanti settled in Naples, the academies flourished once more. Though Leonardo does not mention the "tumult of '47" in any of his published writings, so fresh was the memory of the revolt on the minds of Neapolitans that he must have known about it.

He would also have learned about the elusive Accademia Segreta—probably from Giovanni Battista d'Azzia, the Marchese della Terza. Azzia, Ruscelli's former patron, was a familiar figure in the culture of the academies. He had been a member of the Sereni, a group of citizens that met in the courtyard of the Church of Sant'Angelo a Nido, where they discussed poetry, philosophy, and astrology. Fioravanti knew a host of academicians, including the physician Giovanni Francesco Brancaleone, formerly one of Pope Paul III's physicians. Brancaleone, also a member of the Sereni, was in addition head of the short-lived Euboleans, a literary group that began meeting in 1546 and was disbanded by the viceroy a year later. The physician Donato Antonio Altomare, another of Fioravanti's acquaintances, hosted an academy at his home that discussed natural philosophy and medicine. Fioravanti was thus immersed in the culture of the Neapolitan academies.

Little surprise, then, that the resourceful improviser soon formed his own academy at his house near the Castel Nuovo. We know about the academy from a letter he wrote in 1568 from Venice to Alfonso da Rienzo, a physician in Naples, in which he describes the informal group. Fioravanti waxed nostalgic about "the sweet conversations of old that we had in Naples, when along with His Excellency the Marchese della Terza, Signor Cesare Mormino, Fra Carubino, and Signor Mario da Penna, we made all those experiments on cures for the French Disease, gout, and phthisis. And to think of all the distillations we made! Just remembering it brought me back to my academy, with all of you." Two others completed the membership in Fioravanti's nameless group: Fra Aurelio di Compagna and Antonello da Cifune, both skilled alchemists and experts in the art of "fixing silver into gold." The resemblance between Fioravanti's little academy and Ruscelli's Segreti is uncanny.

A passion for alchemy united the seven. Alchemy, they believed, was the key to unlocking nature's deepest secrets. They did experiments with distillation to find new drugs, essayed treatments for wounds and the French pox, and speculated about new instruments of warfare and defense. They conducted metallurgical experiments, including attempts to transmute changebase metals into silver and gold. Fra Carubino, Fioravanti claimed, invented a method "to transmute silver into the finest gold," and da Cifune could make 24-carat gold. Nearly 20 years later, in 1568, da Rienzo was still doing alchemical experiments using the methods he and his colleagues had developed in Leonardo's academy.

Although alchemy did not become a part of the academic curriculum until the 17th century, plenty of books were available that explained the practical as well as the recondite secrets of the art. Fioravanti himself would contribute his share of them. Some were strictly utilitarian, such as the ever popular books of secrets, which published hundreds of recipes for everything from conserving fruits through the year to making printer's ink. The most famous book of secrets was Alessio Piemontese's *Secrets of Alessio Piemontese.* But there were dozens of others. Alchemy occupied a prominent place in the books of secrets, and no serious alchemist's library would be complete without one or more of them.

RAMON LULL AND THE PHILOSOPHER'S STONE

If you were unsatisfied by mere recipes and wished to explore the esoteric principles of the alchemical arts, you could easily find books on those subjects, too. While living in Naples, Fioravanti would undoubtedly have heard of the alchemical treatises attributed to one Ramon Lull, a 13th-century Catalonian philosopher and mystic from Majorca. These writings—all spurious—circulated in Neapolitan intellectual circles, where Lull's obscure doctrines were feverishly debated.

Central to Lull's art of alchemy was the elixir, or philosopher's stone, an agent of transmutation that perfected metals and acted as a medical panacea. Lull made extravagant claims for the alchemical elixir. Using the philosopher's stone, you could transform base metals into gold, the most perfect of metals, and you could extract essences possessing heavenly qualities that could preserve the body and prolong life. The mythical Lull even had faith that alchemy could serve to convert infidels. Alchemy's "Promethean ambition" to perfect nature in all its aspects drew adepts to the art from across Europe.

Some alchemists questioned Lull's grandiose claims. Among them was Isabella Cortese. That a woman should have practiced alchemy was not in itself unusual. Cooking, distilling, and baking—all the province of women—were considered alchemical processes. However, Cortese was unusual in that she was intimately familiar with the works of Lull and other alchemical writers. In her book, *Secrets of Lady Isabella Cortese* (1561), she revealed that she had traveled widely in search of alchemical secrets and learned techniques firsthand from alchemists in Italy and Eastern Europe. Yet while she was an avid alchemical practitioner, she was contemptuous of alchemical theory. If you want to practice the art of alchemy, she warned readers, "don't follow the teachings of Geber or Ramon [Lull] or Arnaldo [Villanova] or any of the other philosophers, because their books are full of lies and riddles."

Almost without exception, the alchemical books described alchemy as the art of transmutation. That could mean almost any form of chemical technology, such as making colored glass, tinting metals to fashion jewelry, or making dyes and artists' pigments. "Many arts have issued solely from alchemy," wrote Vannoccio Biringuccio; "indeed, without it or its means it would have been impossible for them to have been discovered." Transmutation could also mean making alchemical gold, a commodity that cash-strapped princes eagerly pursued. Thus alchemists found a particularly favorable reception in the courts. In addition to the practical services they provided, alchemists by their very presence in the courts buttressed, metaphorically, the political ambitions of enthusiastic patrons.

Transmutation could also mean perfecting drugs by distillation. In Leonardo's day, alchemy's medical promise was, perhaps, its greatest appeal. Distillation—"purifying the gross from the subtle and the subtle from the gross," as Heironymus Brunschwig described it in his *Book Concerning the Art of Distillation* (1500)—was wildly popular because it promised to enable the adept to transform ordinary herbs into "quintessences" with miraculous healing powers. As historian Bruce Moran put it, "What they were all looking for was a super-medicine, an elixir or *aqua vitae* that could purify physical bodies of their impurities, rid the human body of disease, and prolong life."

The guiding spirit behind the little community of Renaissance alchemists that Fioravanti joined was, most likely, the Marchese della Terza. A powerful nobleman, he was a generous patron and one of the bright lights of the Neapolitan literati. Leonardo cultivated della Terza's patronage among others in the Neapolitan aristocracy. His patients included the Duke of Paliano, whom he treated for gout, while Cesare Mormile, a nobleman of the Porta Nova and one of those implicated in the "tumult of '47," was a member of della Terza's academy.

Before long, Fioravanti's reputation as a surgeon was impressive enough to earn him employment at the court of Don Pedro of Toledo. The viceroy's patronage—to say nothing of a wealthy clientele of gouty aristocrats—gave Leonardo the leisure he needed to pursue his passion for experiments and natural history. Freed from the burden of his regular medical practice, he explored the countryside to observe the flora, fauna, airs, and waters of the region. He investigated the spas and steam baths of Pozzuoli, Avernia, Agnano, and Baia. He smelled and tasted the waters, noting their sulfurous and mineral qualities, and interviewed the locals to determine which medicinal virtues people claimed for the spas. He distilled samples of the waters and collected the mineral salts left in the vessels. Fioravanti even claimed to have invented a way to make artificial spas that "are of much greater strength and virtue than natural baths."

The six years that Leonardo spent in Naples were among the most serene of his life. He visited villages in Campana and talked to the common people to learn about the "rules of life" that enabled them to live to a ripe old age. Their "natural" methods made a deep impression on Fioravanti, confirming what he had learned about the pure empirical medicine of the "first physicians." The old men

In this stylized illustration, alchemical solutions are heated in the furnaces at the bottom of the apparatus and distilled medicinal water is collected in the vessels at the top. Distillation was thought to produce a more potent drug.

of the countryside knew, just as the original physicians had known, that diseases arise from "indispositions" in the stomach. He became convinced that the evils that corrupt the stomach could not be persuaded to leave the body with the delicate regimens the physicians prescribed. Instead, they must be driven out. Discovering new remedies to expel bodily corruption became Fioravanti's scientific quest—and alchemy became his tool for finding them.

MIRROR OF MONSTROSITY

Sometime between 1550 and 1555, Leonardo met a Neapolitan gentleman who showed him a magical mirror. The device, the surgeon later wrote, was "made with such artifice that when a person presented himself before it to view himself, he saw come out of it more than a dozen figures, or shadows. It struck fear into those who set eyes on it. Nothing more astonishing *(mostruosa)* had ever been seen before in this art."

Who might have shown Leonardo this novel mirror that miraculously made "monstrous" multiple images appear in it? A likely candidate was the precocious Neapolitan nobleman Giambattista della Porta, whose famous book, *Natural Magic,* described a mirror nearly identical to the one witnessed by Fioravanti. Della Porta would become the Renaissance's most famous magus, although when Fioravanti resided in Naples he was only beginning his researches in the philosophical academy that he organized at his villa in Vico Equense outside Naples, coincidentally named the Secreti. Della Porta was quite the prodigy, at least in his own mind: Despite the fact that *Natural Magic* was not published until 1558, when he was 23, he claimed to have written it at the tender age of 15.

Whoever the mysterious mirror owner was, the encounter illustrates Fioravanti's acquaintance with the Neapolitan circles engaged in researching the occult sciences. Even if he was unimpressed with their magic tricks, he knew that natural magic endorsed experimentation—and that it employed the same craft techniques that he himself used. Later on, he would write an encyclopedic treatise on the trades and professions.

Natural magic provided a radical and convincing philosophical rationale for experimentation as a way to investigate nature. It relied on neither demonic nor supernatural agencies to produce its miracles; rather, it employed natural forces, applying art to improve nature. Natural magic proved to Leonardo that the occult forces of nature were accessible, and that they could be tapped to benefit the common good.

Naples proved to be the crucible in which Fioravanti transmuted his primitive naturalism into a natural philosophy. His contacts with alchemists and distillers, his encounter with natural magic, and his growing familiarity with the philosophical naturalist tradition of the south converged to form his novel view of the relationship between theory and experience that was the crux of his philosophy of science. Theory and experience were intimately linked, as he saw things, yet he left little doubt that experience was the superior of the two. Theory was like a lamp that guides experience—which otherwise would be indiscriminate and random—yet theory could not be based on speculation about things unseen. "I believe more in a little experience than in all the theories of the world taken together."

The mariner who gazes at maps but lacks experience at the tiller, Fioravanti said, will make a poor sailor indeed. Yet rare is the sailor who can keep his bearings while navigating the high seas without a chart. Until Naples, Fioravanti sailed without a chart. Alchemy showed him a new way of proceeding, guiding him, as if by lamplight, to the port that harbored the hidden secrets of nature. True philosophy, he now knew, was made not in the leisure of the study but by hard work, sweating in front of the glowing alchemical furnace.

All of these newly won certitudes—including Leonardo's assurance that he had discovered a "new way of healing" superior to all others—were about to be tested not just by fire, but by blood.

14

THE UNIVERSITY OF WAR

In *Physician,* one of the writings collected under the name of Hippocrates in the fifth century B.C.E., the aspiring surgeon is instructed to follow an army to learn the art of surgery. In times of peace, writes Hippocrates, rarely if ever, "even in a whole lifetime," does one encounter the kinds of severe wounds that one must contend with in the heat of battle.

The coldly analytic language of the Hippocratic corpus barely conceals the irony in the suggestion that warfare, whose aim is to maim and kill, should be such fine training for the surgeon, whose art is that of healing. Yet behind that counsel lies the understanding that in learning any art, whether carpentry, tennis, or playing the cello, practice alone makes perfect. The trouble is, in the education of a surgeon, the novice has to practice on people.

The moral burden of practicing on people seems to have been lost on Leonardo Fioravanti. With typical bravado, he reported that when he was a surgeon during the African campaign, he made "anatomies of living men," meaning the brutal battle wounds he encountered gave him a chance to peer inside live human bodies—and, doubtless, to poke around a bit before sewing them up. Warfare, deadlier than ever in the 16th century as a result of the augmented use of firearms, made vivisection commonplace. It must have been quite a sight for a surgeon's eyes. Based on what we can gather from Fioravanti's personal testimony, the war was to him a surgeon's school and an opportunity to hone his skills—both of surgery and of self-aggrandizement.

Despite the fact that the region's wars had ended, peace in the Mediterranean inevitably brought about a resurgence in privateering, a substitute for declared war. The Mediterranean was infested with pirates, Christian and Muslim alike. Turkish corsairs preyed on ships at sea and raided the coastal towns of Calabria and Sicily seemingly at will. Fioravanti later warned Cosimo de' Medici that "the great dog of a Turk is very powerful and seeks with great diligence to ruin our poor Christendom and put us under him," and offered the grand duke various inventions to help him defend his realm against the threat.

Booty and slaves were the pirates' quarry. Raids on merchant ships and coastal villages netted a steady supply of grain, oil, slaves, and other merchandise, transforming the lazy harbor towns of Tunis and Algiers into crowded merchant metropolises. Massive coastal slaving expeditions involving fleets of galleys scooped up thousands of captives. Those prisoners not immediately condemned to the galleys were transported to Algiers and other slaving capitals and herded into the dreaded *bagnos,* or "baths," of the slave markets.

Perhaps even more feared than the large fleets—because the threat was more imminent—were smaller, more frequent raids by petty pirates who patrolled the Sicilian and Neapolitan coasts in the hope of surprising a village and capturing a fisherman, robbing a granary, or kidnapping a few harvesters. Turkish corsairs roamed the Mediterranean until the end of the 18th century and were still remembered in the early years of the 20th, when a Sicilian woman reported, "The oldest still tell of a time in which the Turks arrived in Sicily every day . . . and the tears ran like rivers through all the houses."

DRAGUT THE DREADFUL

During the 1550s, the Turkish corsair Turghut, the most feared of the Barbary pirates, was familiar by his European name, Dragut, to every fisherman in Sicily and to every ship captain in the Mediterranean. A Greek Christian by birth, he had grown up on the

Karamanian coast of Turkey, opposite the island of Rhodes, a place where corsairs were a boy's heroes. His was the sort of rags-to-riches story that was often told about privateers. Adopted by Muslim parents, Dragut served in the Turkish fleet and honed his sailing skills. Eventually he bought a galleon and began raiding merchant ships in the Levant. His exploits gained the attention of Khair al-Din (Barbarossa), now governor general of Algiers and admiral of the Turkish fleet, who outfitted Dragut with 20 galleys and turned him loose in the Mediterranean. The reckless abandon with which Dragut carried out his attacks—usually in broad daylight, and seemingly without fear of reprisal—struck terror in the inhabitants of the coastal towns of the Kingdom of Naples. Dragut sailed the shores of southern Italy as if they were his personal hunting ground.

In March 1550, word reached Naples that Dragut had captured the North African city of Mahdiya, known to Europeans as Aphrodisium, or simply Africa. About 120 miles south of Tunis on the Barbary Coast, Mahdiya was located on an isthmus protruding about a mile into the sea. Its landward side was blocked by a defensive wall more than eight meters thick, making the city virtually impregnable. Dragut was able to take it by bribery, not by siege. With Barbarossa already installed in Tunis, the prospect of Dragut establishing a base for himself in the middle of the Mediterranean made Europeans extremely uneasy. Emperor Charles V, worried that Tunisia might be organized into a formal Ottoman state, authorized a Christian armada to take Mahdiya and expel Dragut from the western Mediterranean.

The emperor appointed the old Genoese admiral, Andrea Doria, who commanded the pope's galleys, to lead the fleet. He was aided by Don Garcia de Toledo, the Sicilian viceroy's son, who commanded the Spanish fleet, and by Don Juan de Vega, the Neapolitan viceroy's son, who led the forces of Naples. Fioravanti was appointed to accompany the expedition as personal physician to Don Garcia de Toledo. Eager to distinguish themselves in battle, dozens of aristocratic warriors likewise joined the fleet. Among them were Prince Giordano Orsini of the famous Roman family, who commanded the

Florentine fleet, and Don Luis Perez de Vargas, commander of the Spanish presidio at La Goletta.

Ships from Naples, Sicily, Malta, and Rome brought the imperial fleet to more than 40 galleys, which set sail from Naples on May 11, 1550. Although much of what characterized the chivalrous code in the Renaissance was purely imaginary, the emphasis it placed on heroism and bold deeds was real. As in Ludovico Ariosto's best-selling romance, *Orlando furioso,* the Renaissance knight was expected to display fearlessness in battle and fidelity to his lord.

Living and working among Spanish soldiers and courtiers, Fioravanti was immersed in the martial spirit that suffused court culture. The Spanish viceroys passionately cultivated the image of Ariosto's *Orlando* and its fairy-tale world. Fioravanti watched from a skeptical distance, picking up the signs that betokened the cavalier. He saw Don Quixotes everywhere, and his observations about fawning courtiers show he was nobody's fool when it came to the dynamics of courtly life. Yet he shared their motivation. If the knights could impress a prince and win favor by their military feats, then he would become a renowned warrior-surgeon. His armamentarium would be the drugs he'd invented; his battle shield would be his new way of healing wounds.

Fioravanti's "new way" of medicine was calculated to exhibit the same daring and fearlessness in the face of the enemy—in this case disease and bodily corruption—exemplified by Ariosto's Orlando. To him every ailment was an invasion of bad humors, and every cure was a martial assault on the corruptions that built up and putrefied within the body. Diseases were enemies that must be attacked head-on and violently expelled, using the medical counterparts of the arquebus and cannon: emetics and purgatives such as Dia Aromatica, Elettuario Angelico, and his trusty standby, Precipitato. Once he used Precipitato to cause a woman to discharge a great bolus of "corruption" from her stomach and carried the shapeless mass to the medical school at Salerno as a trophy, proof of the efficacy of his new way of healing. Like a knight victorious in battle, he proudly exhibited his defeated foes.

Based on a Titian portrait, this etching of Roman knight Giordano Orsini in armor, ready to engage in battle or defend his honor against an insult, echoes Fioravanti's portrayal of the captain in his Treasury of Human Life.

PRINCE ORSINI PAYS THE PRICE

Warfare is fraught with hidden dangers. So the Roman captain Giordano Orsini discovered during the siege of the city of Africa. Prince Orsini was Orlando redivivus, a swaggering, hot-tempered warrior. Titian's portrait shows a man with intense eyes and jutting jaw, his hand gripping his cudgel as though he had just been insulted.

Fioravanti recorded several instances of Orsini's short fuse. Once, when a fellow officer insulted a dinner guest, Orsini beat the officer senseless with his fists. Summoned to the scene, Leonardo found that Orsini had "hit the poor man so hard that he was bleeding from the chest and was near death." He treated the "almost dead" officer with his balm, Quintessence.

One afternoon not long after the army made camp on the Tunisian coast, Orsini and some companions were accompanying a caravan on its way to an olive orchard to collect wood. Wishing to explore the countryside, the prince and his entourage wandered off and became separated from the caravan. Catching sight of some falcons landing in a nearby thicket, Orsini turned his horse and, with his arquebus slung over his saddle, raced toward the woods.

Suddenly, out of the forest raced an African knight in a blue jubbah and turban, riding a chestnut horse and armed with a long-bladed spear. Prince Orsini turned his horse and headed back toward the caravan, but not before the Moorish knight hurled his spear, piercing Orsini's arm clear through. The prince fell from his horse and cried out for help. His companions raced to the rescue. The Moor, retreating toward the woods, turned his horse violently and raised a second spear above his head. "Wait till next time, Christian dogs!" he cried out, then disappeared into the forest.

Orsini, bleeding profusely from his arm, was brought back to camp in great pain. Fioravanti rushed to his aid. The surgeon calmly removed the spear and medicated the wound with Quintessence and Artificial Balsam, healing the wound in just five days.

Such were the acts of heroism and quick thinking that Fioravanti hoped might gain him favor at a princely court. He must have been bitterly disappointed when, nearing the crest of his fame, his patron, Don Pedro, died in 1553 during the Battle of Siena.

A SERENDIPITOUS DISCOVERY

Fioravanti's most important wartime discovery was the "true way of healing wounds." To him, it was proof of the doctrine of organic nature that he had learned in Naples. The most dramatic demonstration of the principle took place during a lull in the African campaign. One sultry day in July, soldiers in the emperor's army were encamped near Mahdiya, nervously awaiting orders to launch a final assault on the city. Fioravanti and a Spanish officer were strolling through the camp when they came upon two soldiers engaged in a heated quarrel. The men drew their swords and squared off.

Leonardo's companion tried to stop the brawl, only to receive a backhand sword blow that neatly sliced off his nose, which fell to the ground. As the astonished officer stood with his mouth agape, bleeding profusely from the face, Leonardo calmly picked up the severed nose from the dirt where it lay. "Holding it in my hand," he recalled, "I pissed on it, and having washed it off with urine, I attached it to him and sewed it on firmly, medicated it with Balsam, and bandaged it."

Though privately dubious about the outcome of his battlefield surgery, Fioravanti recalled, "when I untied it I found it was very well attached again." The grisly episode seemed to demonstrate the rule that nature, alive and sentient, "always wants to reunite its separated parts." The conclusion was simple: Wounds want to heal, and the body nourishes severed parts that have been rejoined to keep them from rotting.

As for Fioravanti's "new way" of treating wounds, he would dress the wound with one of his balms and bathe it daily in Quintessence or Artifical Balsam—waters distilled from herbal concoctions containing high concentrations of alcohol. He made extravagant claims for the curative powers of his balms. Treating gunshot wounds by cleaning them with an alcoholic tincture and letting nature take its course at least had the merit of reducing infection. Yet his "secret" was not really new. Military surgeons since the Middle Ages had followed a similar principle in treating infected wounds.

MARVELOUS HEALING BALMS

The history of medicine comprises many myths. One of its most enduring is the legend that French surgeon Ambroise Paré "liberated" surgery from the dangerous practice of cauterizing gunshot wounds with a red-hot iron. Paré himself was the originator of the legend, having published an account of it in his book, *Method of Treating Wounds Made by Arquebuses and Other Firearms* (1545). On a military campaign in Italy in 1537, he relates, he was forced to innovate. Initially, as he was taught, he used boiling oil to cauterize what were considered to be poisonous gunpowder wounds:

> But my oil ran out and I had to apply a healing salve made of egg-white, rose-oil and turpentine. The next day I slept badly, plagued by the thought that I would find the men dead whose wounds I had failed to burn, so I got up early to visit them. To my great surprise, those treated with salve felt little pain, showed no inflammation or swelling, and had passed the night rather calmly—while the ones on which seething oil had been used lay in high fever with aches, swelling and inflammation around the wound. At this, I resolved never again cruelly to burn poor people who had suffered gunshot wounds.

Paré's representation of the event was a brilliant performance—one that catapulted him to the court of King Henri II. Yet how common was the practice of cauterizing gunshot wounds in the 16th century? In other words, was "Paré's doctrine" really Paré's?

Paré's modern biographer, Joseph François Malgaigne, identified numerous contemporary Italian and German surgeons who used methods similar to the one that Paré advanced—evidence, supposedly, of the "wide diffusion of [Paré's] ideas." Yet none of the others ever cited Paré in connection with the method, nor gave him credit for its discovery—a neglect for which Malgaigne soundly rebuked them. Apparently it never occurred to Malgaigne that instead of being proof of the diffusion of Paré's ideas, the widespread use of the technique associated with the French surgeon's name in fact bears witness to the perpetuation of a traditional medieval method.

Fioravanti didn't cauterize gunshot wounds, even though, like other surgeons, he believed that they were poisonous. Yet he almost certainly never read Paré's book, nor would he have learned about Paré's "discovery" by word of mouth from other surgeons. His wound treatment was essentially the standard medieval method—one described in detail by such 14th- and 15th-century surgeons as Henri de Mondeville, Guy de Chuliac, and Heinrich von Pfolspeundt. The procedure that Paré refutes in his account of his "discovery" was in reality an innovation introduced by the Italian surgeon Giovanni de Vigo, who revived an Arabic technique in his surgical manual, *Practice of the Art of Surgery* (1514).

De Vigo's manual was widely used as a textbook in universities and hospitals, and Paré knew it well: Trained in the Hôtel Dieu, where university professors regularly lectured, he had a copy of the *Practice* with him during the campaign. But because most surgeons lacked formal training—having learned the art instead through apprenticeship to a master surgeon—the traditional medieval method was handed down orally through the generations. Most surgeons would not have known about de Vigo's innovation.

Fioravanti's practice—to clean the wound, suture it, and apply a healing balm—was essentially the standard medieval method. Why then did he claim that he had discovered a "new way" to treat wounds? His innovation was the invention of new healing balms: Mighty Elixir, Blessed Oil, and Artificial Balsam. His use of an ointment to heal wounds was tied not only to medieval surgical practice but also to a folkloric tradition whose origins are, in part, biblical. The Balm of Gilead mentioned in the Book of Jeremiah was the most famous of all unguents, and became a well-used metaphor of healing. Magical waters and wound-healing balms are common motifs in medieval folklore, and the ancient dream of a magical balm that healed wounds instantly without leaving a scar was still alive and well during the Renaissance. Cervantes turned it into a joke with Don Quixote's "Fierabrás's balm," two drops of which will heal a knight cut in half.

The ancient idea of the magical wound-healing balm—tied to the conviction that wounds caused by a new kind of weaponry demanded a new kind of balm—gave rise to an alchemical quest that Fioravanti eagerly joined. Leonardo did, after all, have a new way of healing wounds, and it was composed of four ingredients: a medieval surgical procedure, the science of alchemy, the folklore of wound-healing balms, and skills learned in the heat of battle.

SIEGE BY SAMBUCA

The city of Africa held out for four months before finally falling to the Christians. Unable to breach the city's walls by land, the generals turned to a military engineer, Antonio Ferramolino of Bergamo, for a solution. Ferramolino was familiar with the work of the ancient engineers, and he designed a siege engine mounted on galleys similar to the one built for Roman commander Marcus Claudius Marcellus at the siege of Syracuse in 211 C.E. The device, called a sambuca, or "harp," was designed to attack a city from its seaward side.

The sambuca was a gigantic ladder, carried by two ships lashed together. Protective covering over the ladder shielded the soldiers climbing the device. As the twin ships approached the fortress wall, sailors hoisted the sambuca to the requisite height using ropes attached to one of the masts. With the sambuca in place, the soldiers climbed the ladder and swarmed the wall.

So went the theory. The ancient Syracusans, however, had prepared clever measures of their own. Archimedes, the famous engineer, had arrayed a battery of catapults to stop the ships from reaching the wall. The defenders bombarded the galleys with a hail of missiles, destroying the sambuca.

Unlike Marcellus's contraption, the one designed by Ferramolino worked as planned. The siege of Africa was successful, and the town surrendered on September 10, 1550.

Fioravanti, who treated the wounded aboard a crude hospital ship, reported that the numbers killed and wounded on both sides during the siege was "stupefying." Among the casualties was Antonio Ferramolino himself, killed by a gunshot wound to the chest.

As he had so often and so daringly before, Dragut escaped capture once again. Indeed, the Christians would never catch him: He continued to maraud Mediterranean coasts until 1565, when he was killed during the Battle of Malta—a victim of the accidents of war. Assisting an engineer, he was struck on the head by a falling beam and died a few hours later.

The fall of Africa was celebrated throughout the Holy Roman Empire as a glorious victory for Christendom and a crushing defeat for the Turks. Scholars wrote learned histories of the war and published elegant Latin *éloges* to the Christian heroes who had perished in it. In reality, however, the victory was a minor one. The imperial forces managed to hold the remote promontory for a few years, but by 1554 the fortress had been abandoned.

DOCTOR AND KNIGHT

At the conclusion of the war, Fioravanti returned to Naples, where he lived for another five years. They were, by all accounts, among the happiest of his life. In the *Treasury of Human Life,* for example, he waxed nostalgic about the "marvels of Naples": its castles and monuments, the fertility of its countryside, the miraculous healing powers of its herbs. He experimented with the medicinal properties of the springs and baths around Naples and, like any tourist, visited its monasteries and churches. He continued his medical practice, gathered pupils, and gained fame for treating advanced cases of the French pox.

Contented as he was, Leonardo nevertheless decided to leave Naples. He doesn't divulge the reasons for his decision, but they are easy enough to divine. Through the vicissitudes of war he had forged close ties with Roman Prince Orsini, who convinced him that his future lay in Rome. Somewhat reluctantly, Fioravanti departed from Naples in February 1555 and moved to the Holy City, leaving his patients in the care of a disciple, Giuseppe Moletti.

The battlefield taught Leonardo many practical skills: how to reattach a nose sliced off by a sword, how to design siege engines, how to treat wounds in a "new way." He had witnessed horrific slaughter and learned to stay calm amid chaos.

Equally important, he had learned a style: that of the *cavaliere.* Many years later, when Fioravanti finally graduated in medicine from the University of Bologna, he gained that rank—and thereafter proudly displayed it alongside his title of doctor. But long before he acquired his degree, he knew that he was "*Leonardo Fioravanti, medico e cavaliere*—Leonardo Fioravanti, doctor and knight."

15

THE CARDINAL'S HOUSE

Naples was a center of the Spanish Empire, the first empire in history upon which the sun never set. Although Italians circulated within the viceregal courts, preferment was generally reserved for Spaniards. Rome, on the other hand, was the seat of Christendom, a diplomatic center the equal of Madrid or Paris, and the residence of many noble Italian families. The city was, at the same time, a vital player in the Spanish Empire and a city increasingly drawn into the orbit of Spain. Although formally an autonomous monarchy, Rome was regarded by the Spanish kings as part of their own domain. The Spanish monarchy played a direct role in Rome's political life and was its most beneficent patron of the arts and letters.

For an ambitious sort like Leonardo Fioravanti, the Holy City provided fertile ground. The years spent in the Kingdom of Naples netted contacts with Spanish and Roman aristocrats—most notably the gallant but explosive warrior Giordano Orsini, whose battle wounds Fioravanti had healed with his Artificial Balsam. The Orsini clan was a prominent noble family, and the surgeon's friendship with the young knight opened the door to the court of Cardinal Giovanni Angelo Medici (later Pope Pius IV). Leonardo must have thought he had found a trajectory to the top.

Giovanni Angelo Medici was no relation to the more famous Florentine Medici, yet in some respects the histories of the two families are similar. He and his brother, Giangiacomo, represent two different aspects of Renaissance aspiration. They were the sons of Bernardino Medici, a Milanese tax farmer. Although officially a noble family, the Medici of Milan fell on hard times in the 16th century. Bernardino, with 13 children to support, was briefly incarcerated for debt.

In many ways, his oldest son, Giangiacomo, epitomized the untrammeled ambition and thirst for glory that are so often associated with the Italian Renaissance. Nicknamed "Il Medeghino" ("The Little Medici"), Giangiacomo displayed his thuggish character early on, committing his first murder for hire at the age of 16. Banished from Milan, he took refuge in a castle on Lake Como, raised an army of hooligans, and commenced to enrich himself through terror and piracy. With an armada of seven ships and a mercenary army of 4,000, he ruled Lake Como as if it were his principality—which indeed it later became. He swore fealty to the Duke of Milan until he perceived the Sforza family declining, then switched his loyalty to the Holy Roman Emperor, who gave him the title Marchese di Marignano. By age 30 Giangiacomo Medici had risen from nothing to a prince, confirming violent behavior as a path to Renaissance fame and upward mobility.

If Il Medeghino was a condottiere of the old style, that kind of mercenary captain was fast going out of style in the late Renaissance. As states consolidated their power, governments preferred to entrust military matters to disciplined professional armies, which were more loyal and easier to control than the condottieri. "Mercenary commanders are either skilled in warfare or they are not," Machiavelli observed. "If they are, you cannot trust them, because they are anxious to advance their own greatness, either by coercing you, their employer, or by coercing others against your own wishes."

Giangiacomo's younger brother, Giovanni Angelo, chose an opposite course in life, and in some ways, his ambition was more typical of the late Renaissance. After earning a doctorate in canon law from the University of Bologna, he moved to Rome to seek his fortune. Arriving in the Holy City in December 1527, a few months after the Sack of Rome, he began his career as a notary under the papacy of Clement VIII, and remained in the papal court under Paul

III. A brilliant administrator, Giovanni Angelo received an excellent education and became an accomplished scholar. Giovanni Angelo advanced rapidly. He was made archbishop of Ragusa (Dubrovnik) in 1545, even though he had never set foot in Dalmatian territory, nor did he in Calabria, where he was "transferred" as archbishop of Cassano in 1553. He became a cardinal in 1549 and was elected pope a decade later, taking the name Pius IV.

THE PATRICIAN'S MALADY

During the years that Fioravanti lived in Rome, Medici was one of the most prominent of the 30 or so cardinals who resided in the Holy City at any given time. His court at the Palazzo Fieschi was a center of humanistic culture and political power. Medici was firmly allied to the pro-Spanish Orsini family, which his brother Giangiacomo married into. His pronounced Spanish sympathies were critical to winning Philip II's support when, in 1559, Cardinal Medici was elected pope. Fioravanti would have gained entrée into the cardinal's house via Orsini's influence, or through that of a Spanish nobleman. However he arrived, he used his newly won status as a springboard to launch his career in Rome.

Leonardo began practicing his trade among influential Romans and foreigners almost from the instant of his arrival. One of his first Roman patients was a servant of the Venetian ambassador, and within a few weeks he was treating patients in Cardinal Medici's palace. Medici, a typical Renaissance prelate, spent lavishly on the arts and letters, and his court attracted humanists and artists from throughout Italy. Fioravanti remembered treating a young Milanese sculptor who suffered from "a certain kind of *etesia,* a continuous fever that debilitates a person little by little." Another time, the painter Alessandro Oliverio, a disciple of Giovanni Bellini, was stabbed in the arm with a rapier that went completely through and into his ribs. Fioravanti treated him with Artificial Balsam and "cured the wound in just four days."

The cardinal himself may have been one of Leonardo's patients. Medici, then in his 50s, suffered from gout, a disease considered largely incurable. Gout afflicts the joints of the extremities, classically the big toe. During attacks (which flare up suddenly, often at night) the joints become swollen and excruciatingly painful. The disease is brought on by abnormally high concentrations of uric acid in the blood, causing deposits of uric salts to build up in the joints.

Of course, Renaissance doctors knew nothing about that. Under its official medical name of podagra, gout was thought to be caused by superfluous humors collecting in the joints. Healers of the era were also aware that meat- and fat-rich diets contribute to the condition, which is why gout has historically tended to afflict the upper classes. Thus it earned the nickname "patrician's malady" from the belief that the wellborn and mighty brought the disease upon themselves through their profligate lifestyle.

Cardinal Medici was said to be extremely fond of the heavy foods and pastries of his native Milan—tastes that might have precipitated his condition. Fioravanti claimed to have had great success treating gout with medicines that relieved the joint pains accompanying the disease. And perhaps they did have some effect: One of his gout remedies was still in widespread use in the late 17th century. Rumors flew that Cardinal Medici also suffered from complications "*delle cose venere,*" meaning some sort of venereal disease: Giovanni Angelo had several illegitimate children before taking orders. Possibly Fioravanti, a well-known pox doctor, treated his venereal symptoms with one of his remedies.

Promoted by Orsini and favored by Cardinal Medici, Fioravanti became known among the Roman nobility and visiting dignitaries for his unorthodox cures. In August 1555 he was called to the palace of the ambassador of Portugal to treat an ulcer "the size of a hand" in the arm of a gentleman in the ambassador's retinue. As news about his success managing the difficult cure spread, others sought out his services.

The Portuguese ambassador himself—who, like Cardinal Medici, suffered a severe case of gout—thought that Fioravanti was a godsend. The two struck up an unlikely friendship, for the ambassador turned out to be an avid collector of curiosities and secrets:

Now, this ambassador took an inordinate pleasure in secrets and things of virtuosity, and he asked me to stay around. He held me in such esteem that he asked if I would show him the secret to cure the gout. Not content merely with the recipe, he also wanted me to medicate five other patients just so he could see the true experience, and all five were healed very quickly *(con gran prestezza)*. In return, he showed me about twenty-four precious secrets in many professions, secrets of truly great worth, and wrote them down for me.

SECRETS OF THE HOUSE OF GUISE

One of Fioravanti's patients was Giovanni Francesco Carafa, the Duke of Paliano and nephew of Pope Paul IV. Through Carafa's influence the surgeon came to play a minor role in what would later be called the Carafa War—a conflict that historian Fernand Braudel calls "a turning point in western history." Named after the reigning pope, the war resulted in an alliance of the papacy with Spain, thus securing Spanish hegemony in Italy until the 1580s.

Gian Pietro Carafa, who in 1555 became Pope Paul IV, was a native of Naples. He was, in the words of historian Michael Levin, "driven by a lifelong desire to free his homeland, and indeed all of Italy, from Spanish rule." Pope Paul signed a secret pact with King Henry II of France, promising him Naples in return for military assistance against the Habsburgs. The pope declared war on Spain, excommunicated King Philip II, and invited French troops into Italy.

François de Guise, the Duke of Lorraine, commanded the French army, which arrived in Rome in December 1556. The war went badly for the pope from the start. Inexplicably, Guise delayed his advance on Naples until April of the following year. Historian Braudel attributes the delay to "political intrigue" on Guise's part, but there may be a simpler explanation. According to Fioravanti, the duke, in Rome "to prosecute the war against the king of Spain," accidentally stabbed himself in the knee while dismounting from his horse. Upon learning of his injury, Giovanni Francesco Carafa sent for Leonardo, who treated Guise's wound "to his great satisfaction and that of his entire army."

The duke, an aficionado of alchemy and an avid collector of secrets, wanted Fioravanti to demonstrate how to make the secret that he used to treat his wound. In exchange, he gave Leonardo "many secrets that the house of Guise acquired from the great doctors of France" to cure urinary disorders, gout, and other ailments. "He made me swear never to reveal the secrets to anyone," Fioravanti relates.

While Guise recuperated in Rome and exchanged secrets with Fioravanti, the Duke of Alba led a Spanish army to Rome, encamping just outside the city. Guise's delay proved costly. The pope, doubtlessly remembering the disastrous 1527 Sack of Rome, capitulated to Spain, and the peace treaty, essentially dictated by Alba, imposed a Spanish alliance on the papacy.

Whatever Leonardo accomplished in the cardinal's house endured. In 1564, six years after Fioravanti had left Rome, Battista Pelegrino wrote to him from Genoa, saying that a local bookseller had told him about his marvelous cures of an "incurable disease" in the house of Cardinal Medici—a reference, no doubt, to the French pox. The bookseller, eager to make a sale, probably inflated the account (profitably, for he sold Battista two of Fioravanti's books), but the story, remembered so long after, is a mark of Leonardo Fioravanti's lasting impact on the local scene—and a harbinger of fame to come.

16

A SURGEON IN ROME

Two different records of Leonardo's career in Rome survive: one from his own pen and the other from the archives.

Fioravanti according to Fioravanti was a miraculous healer who cured patients abandoned by the physicians.

Fioravanti according to the archives was an undistinguished surgeon.

The truth probably lies somewhere in between. Though the archival record may seem more objective, it is incomplete. Surgeons appear in the Roman archive because they were required to be licensed and because they were obligated to report to the authorities their treatment of any wound incurred as a result of accidents or violence. Surgeons seem to have taken the regulations casually—underreporting was the norm, and licensing standards were lax.

Fioravanti did not apply for a license to practice until September 1557—more than two years after he arrived in the Holy City—and he did so, it appears, only because he sought permission "to treat any surgical case in Rome as well as to give by mouth his decoction of *Lignum Sanctum*." The license he had received from the Neapolitan Protomedicato persuaded the examiners to grant him the desired permit. This was unusual, given that most other surgeons were enjoined from prescribing treatments by mouth. But the authorities must have seen promise in Leonardo's cure for the dreaded French pox.

Soon after he arrived in Rome, Fioravanti rented a house next to the Church of San Pantaleone, a few steps from the Piazza Navona, which was then still an open *campo.* The square would have looked very different in Leonardo's day than it does to the modern tourist: unpaved and without the obelisk, fountains, and Bernini statuary that now dominate the space, which were not completed until the 17th century. Its weekly market was a chaotic and crowded fair, making the piazza a focal point of Roman commercial life.

The widely circulated *Book of Vagabonds* described the Piazza Navona as a space that peddlers shared with permanent tradesmen, and where fruit vendors, ragpickers, and tinkers rubbed elbows with beggars, quacks, and fire-eaters, while contortionists, acrobats, and charlatans erected their stands and entertained the crowd. Yet it was also the site of palatial noble residences, such as the one that Antonio Sangallo designed for Cardinal Del Monte. The Orsini family owned a palace on the Piazza Navona, as did other powerful families, who shared the space with notaries, merchants, and artisans. The Church of San Giacomo degli Spagnoli was located nearby, and next to it stood the hospital for the Spanish nation in Rome. The neighborhood conveniently placed Fioravanti in proximity to prominent Italian nobility and Spanish political power.

THE MEAN STREETS OF RENAISSANCE ROME

The archives reveal a violent world. Renaissance Rome was a dangerous place, much more dangerous than the cities of the United States today. Surveying the records of the health board, a historian has calculated that 16th-century Rome, with a population one-hundredth that of today's New York, had 10 serious woundings per day and about 35 murders per year. At Rome's rate, modern New York would have 1,000 violent assaults and 10 murders per day! Renaissance tempers were hot, and it was best to be careful whom you insulted.

Leonardo found himself in the thick of these mean streets. Once he treated a vagabond who had been beaten over the head with a staff wielded by an innkeeper in the Campo Fiore. Another time he treated an Augustinian friar who had been brutally attacked in the night "by someone whose name no one would reveal." The friar had two stab wounds in his arm (one of which had fractured the humoral bone), one in his hand, and another in the left shoulder. Fioravanti also treated victims of the city's commonplace robberies, assaults, and duels, such as the porter who was attacked in the Campo Martio and stabbed in the arm.

Fioravanti recalled a particularly violent incident that occurred in the piazza in front of his house, where a goldsmith was stabbed 13 times and left for dead on the pavement. Giordano Orsini (who seems always to enter Fioravanti's life at just the right moment) happened to be walking by and had the man carried to the surgeon's house. Fioravanti sewed up the wounds and treated them with Quintessence, Balsam, and Secret Powder. "In just 16 days the man was healed and saved," Leonardo reports. This was a surgeon who never simply cured his patients—he invariably "healed and saved" them.

For only one incident during his Roman period can Fioravanti's personal account be compared with the archival record, and the disparity is striking. In October 1555, he reported to the authorities that he had treated the servant of Ricardo Mazzatosta, a prominent Roman gentleman, of a gunshot wound in the arm. The archival record of the incident is unadorned:

> 19 October 1555. Master Leonardo Fioravanti, surgeon, reported that yesterday he had treated Pompeo Pereto, a servant of Ricardo Mazzatosta, who was wounded in the arm by an object that was plunged into him during the night, without danger.

Not surprisingly, Fioravanti's account of the event in *The Treasury of Human Life* was much more dramatic. In his version, however, Mazzatosta, not his servant, was the victim. Consider Leonardo's account:

> Among the many stupendous and marvelous cures I made in Rome back then was one of Signore Ricardo Mazzatosta. It happened that one evening while he and his party were leaving

> the house of Signore Paolo Giordano Orsini, he was attacked by some of his enemies and shot in the chest by an archebus. The archebus shot had a great many little pellets, and eight of them struck him in various parts of his body. One of the pellets struck him in the forehead and penetrated the skull at the juncture of the frontal bone, and there it remained. I, along with another surgeon, master Jacomo da Perugia, was consulted in the case, and several physicians were also brought in. All the others were of the opinion that the pellet must have exited because they couldn't find it by probing the wound. I concluded, to the contrary, that, since we could not detect an exit wound, the bullet must have remained inside the skull. And so we argued back and forth. Nevertheless, in a few days, to everyone's amazement, the ball surfaced spontaneously. I cut the skin above it and quickly removed the object and treated the wound with Quintessence and Balsam, I used the same remedy for his other wounds and in just four days the man was completely healed. The whole city marveled at the cure.

Which of the two accounts is the true one? Neither, probably, tells the entire tale. The archival account is spare, factual, and official. It gives only the information that a bureaucrat needed to complete his report. It's a little hard to believe that anyone would have regarded the wound that Fioravanti describes in *The Treasury of Human Life* as being "without danger," but that is what he confidently reported to the authorities, who based their archival record on Leonardo's eyewitness account. Obviously, he wanted posterity to remember the night's events more dynamically than the record in the Roman archive. In the *Treasury,* the bland and indifferent archival description becomes a dramatic story about a heroic cure. The object that struck Pompeo—or was it Ricardo?—in the arm in the archival record turns out to have been eight arquebus pellets, one of which pierced his skull. Far from being "without danger," as the surgeon informed the authorities, his memoir states that the wound was so dangerous that several physicians and surgeons, including him, had to be consulted.

RENAISSANCE SELF-FASHIONING

Whether or not Leonardo was being truthful in his published account of the incident is, perhaps, less important than what the two reports reveal about Renaissance perceptions of the self. In describing the event in *The Treasury of Human Life*, he recast a historical occurrence for consumption by a new audience. In doing so, he purposefully refashioned his identity. Rather than the obscure surgeon who reported to the Roman authorities an unexceptional injury to a minor servant stemming from a garden-variety late-night brawl, the protagonist of the *Treasury* intervenes in a spectacular ambush of a prominent Roman gentleman and, with uncanny diagnostic skills and proven remedies, produces a cure at which "the whole city marveled." Moreover, he acted out his new identity in a much larger forum than the Criminal Tribunal's daily log labeled "Reports of Doctors and Barbers." For his printed book the audience numbered in the thousands.

When Fioravanti reported the injury to the Criminal Tribunal, he was performing as a professional. Like all surgeons, he was required to report such events or risk losing his license. By acting out his version of the events in print, on the other hand, he forged an identity that was uniquely his. In such displays, Fioravanti was expressing a different kind of selfhood than the modern, autonomous identity whose roots the 19th-century Swiss historian Jacob Burckhardt believed he had found in the Italian Renaissance. In the words of historian John Martin, it was the expression of a "performative self"—that is, a self-consciously theatrical demonstration of the individual. Although family, state, social rank, professional status, and religious institutions imposed rigorous restrictions on the exercise of individual autonomy, certain Renaissance figures were able to carve out latitude for themselves. Fioravanti crafted his through the printed word, donning a new identity of author-supersurgeon. The Renaissance self was, as Martin puts it, "something greater than the sum of one's social roles."

The impression left by *The Treasury of Human Life* is of a charismatic healer following a carefully laid plan of exploiting bold cures to advance himself in the highest circles of Roman society. From his strategic selection of a residence near the Italian and Spanish nobility to a series of dramatic cures in the home of the Portuguese ambassador, Fioravanti's brief Roman career seems calculated to attract the gaze of the powerful.

A CABAL OF DOCTORS

In his *Regimen for the Plague,* first published in 1565, Fioravanti interrupts a discussion of the causes of the plague to imagine a "dialogue with Lady Fortune." In that misogynistic age, *fortuna* was always portrayed as a fickle, irrational woman. At first glance, the chapter seems oddly out of place—until one realizes that Renaissance epidemics were among life's most hazardous and unpredictable circumstances, no matter how rationally or scientifically one explained them. They struck without warning and subsided as unpredictably as they erupted.

Leonardo played on this uncertainty in his dialogue with Lady Fortune, but his real subject—as ever—was himself:

> Your nature is always to flee from those who pursue you and to run alongside those who would flee from you. I remember that many years ago in Rome, you took notice of me and were moved to favor me, but some of the physicians were so envious of me that they tormented and oppressed me. As soon as you made it known that you favored my works, envy opposed it and persecuted me so greatly that I was almost completely wiped out. If it hadn't been for the help of the Supreme Monarch of all, I would have fallen into the precipice.

Fioravanti's troubles with physicians in Rome began in typical Renaissance fashion: with a challenge and a duel. A few weeks after he arrived in Rome, he was consulted to treat the Venetian ambassador's horse groom who had been injured in a street brawl.

Gianjacopo's wounds had been attended by a number of surgeons, including Realdo Colombo, a famous anatomist and prominent university professor, but the wounds failed to heal. Gianjacopo's condition worsened. With his experience treating wounds in the African war, Fioravanti felt confident he could cure the man. This is how he describes the episode:

> Poor Gianjacopo had been wounded in the head and in the hand. He'd been treated by a number of other surgeons, but his condition worsened as a result of the infection that took hold. The main doctor attending him was a man called Realdo Colombo. He had medicated the head wound with wine and oil and had treated the hand wound with tormentil and rose oil. After examining the man's wounds, I told Colombo that the treatment he was using needed to be changed immediately. The method he'd used to treat the head wound was all wrong, I explained, because raw oil putrefies and wine restrains the putrid matter that the oil generates. Such a treatment, I said, should never be used in these cases. His medication for the wound to the hand was also wrong, I continued. Tormentil is not good for this kind of wound, I explained, because it's hot and its oil putrefies and causes inflammation, which is very bad where the skin, flesh, nerves, and bones are injured. Thus I argued, very reasonably, that the treatment was all wrong and should never be used in such cases.
>
> Then I explained that the correct medication for these kinds of wounds is to apply comforting remedies to the injured parts in order to reduce the festering and to build up the flesh. That's the most reasonable cure, I said. Realdo responded that he thought my opinion would be an excellent one if only I could find a remedy that would bring about such effects. So I had the man taken to my house and treated him in the following way: First, I anointed the head wound with Quintessence and followed that with an application of Balsam. Realdo was surprised at this; he had never heard of such

> a cure. Then I medicated the wound with Grand Liquor and put over that a little of my secret Wound Powder. I treated the hand wound in the same way and in fourteen days both wounds were completely cured. The physicians marveled at this and the ambassador's family was very happy. However, Realdo was not pleased. It was on that very day that the envy of me began and it never went away during the entire time I was in Rome. Nevertheless, because of excellent outcome of this experience, I became very well known in Rome and many others began to seek me out.

If Leonardo was seeking publicity, he could not have chosen a more appropriate foe. Colombo—best known in the history of science for his discovery of pulmonary circulation—was one of the era's most famous anatomists. Trained as a surgeon, he earned a medical degree at Padua and succeeded Vesalius as professor of anatomy there in 1542. Three years later, Cosimo de' Medici invited Colombo to teach anatomy at Pisa, and in 1548 he moved to Rome to become a personal physician of Pope Paul III. A professor of medicine at the Sapienza, Rome's university, and a member of the inner circles of the papal court, Colombo was influential, ambitious—and dangerous.

We do not know the details behind the "conspiracy" that led to Fioravanti's departure (or, as he claimed, expulsion) from Rome. Only his account of the affair survives, and it is too sparse and one-sided to permit a full accounting. According to his version, the conspiracy originated in his public "humiliation" of Colombo. Fioravanti portrays the anatomist as a dark, lurking, offstage manipulator. In 1557, he reports, Colombo pressured a group of 12 physicians to file charges and give false testimony against him. This "cabal" of powerful, well-connected physicians included three professors, a former *protomedico,* and three papal physicians.

Not all of the doctors opposed him, however. Fioravanti relates that several witnesses came forward to testify on his behalf. Besides the surgeon Giacomo da Perugia, with whom Leonardo had often practiced, his defenders included the protomedico, Cosimo

Giacomelli, who in September 1557 had approved Leonardo's license to practice medicine in Rome. Another defender, Fioravanti claims, was Spanish anatomist Juan Valverde de Amusco, who was then teaching at the Hospital of Santo Spirito, Rome's largest. It would be surprising, however, if Valverde took Fioravanti's side in the dispute: Colombo had been Valverde's teacher at Padua, and the Spanish anatomist followed his master to Rome and served as his assistant. What might have motivated anatomist Valverde to defend Fioravanti—no friend of anatomy—is anyone's guess. Nor do we know the details of the legal proceeding against Fioravanti, or what charges were filed against him. The archives are silent on the matter.

Whatever the issue, Fioravanti came out on the losing side. *Invidia*—envy—drove him from Rome, he claimed. The physicians' jealousy of his accomplishments in the cardinal's house, Leonardo asserted, fomented the conspiracy to remove him from the scene.

In retrospect, we might hazard another guess. Fioravanti was fearless—and utterly without respect for the medical establishment. More than once he was accused of killing his patients with overdoses of his drugs. In the wake of the Gianjacopo affair, the upstart surgeon contemptuously referred to Colombo as "Palombo," meaning "dogfish" (the dogfish being a favorite anatomical subject). In the end, Leonardo later noted, "justice was done" in the matter of the conspiracy:

> The blessed Lord God, who always wants the infamous and damned to be separated from the company of the good, caused a great miracle to happen. Before a year had passed, He called Realdo Colombo and Giustiniano Finetto to him to know the truth of the affair. Both are dead and have gone to where the Lord will pass judgment on the good and evil works done in the world.

A man of vaulting ambition, Fioravanti had gone to Rome hoping to make a reputation that would propel him into a princely court. He almost succeeded—yet in the end, he had never fallen so far.

Perhaps while in the cardinal's house, where he practiced his "new way of healing" among the cultivated elite of Rome, he came to the realization that would change his life: Only by publishing his methods could he realize his aspiration of making his name immortal.

To accomplish that objective, Leonardo Fioravanti would have to go where books were made. He would have to journey to Venice.

17

A ROAD NOT TAKEN

The companionship that Leonardo struck up in Rome with the Portuguese ambassador was evidently a cordial one. It resulted not only in an exchange of secrets but also an invitation to serve the king of Portugal himself, João III. That, at least, is what Leonardo said, and we have no reason to disbelieve him. He'd already distinguished himself as a military surgeon during the African war, gained entrée to the house of one of Rome's greatest prelates, and earned a reputation among Roman nobles for his skill as a pox doctor. Why wouldn't the king of Portugal be interested in such a renowned healer?

But as he contemplated his future, Fioravanti chose a different path. Portugal would have to wait. Later, he recalled, "Besides exchanging secrets with me, the ambassador wanted me to proceed to Portugal to the court of His Majesty the King, but I decided not to go because I wanted to go to Venice to publish my works and to bring them to light in the world."

Fioravanti was turning down an offer to serve a major European monarch, deciding instead to embark on the precarious career of an author. Why would anyone choose such a risky course? What was the appeal? Not the promise of fortune, certainly: Most Renaissance authors earned very little money from their books. The practice of paying royalties to authors was still centuries away, and copyrights—or "privileges" as they were called—were usually granted to printers, not authors.

How, then, did writers earn a living?

Some authors worked as copy editors in printing houses to supplement the meager gleanings from their books. That's how Girolamo Ruscelli broke into the publishing trade when he moved to Venice in 1549 and began working as an editor in Vincenzo Valgrisi's printing house, one of Venice's largest. Fioravanti, too, would pay his dues by working as an editor before publishing his own books. His first published work was as an editor, not author, for a new release of a surgical manual by Pietro and Ludovico Rostinio, which came out in 1561.

Although employment in a printing house gave a writer greater independence than service in a court, Renaissance authors were never free of the patronage system. Almost all early modern books began with flattering dedications, often multiple dedications, to one or more prospective patrons, extolling the patron's generosity and wisdom. According to the logic of patronage, books were presented as "gifts" to wealthy princes or merchants in the hope of receiving a substantial gift in return. It was an imperfect system: Even when an author received a reward, it was often in the form of public recognition rather than cash; still, such notice might lead to further opportunities to curry favor.

THE QUEST FOR RENOWN

One reason, then, for becoming an author was the possibility of impressing a prince and getting connected to a court. That motivation was never far from Leonardo's mind, yet if the writer's career was risky, court life—where one's fortunes hinged on the whim of a prince—could be even more precarious. The author's life at least promised a modicum of independence. That was not the main reason for Leonardo's choice of a new career, however. To him, becoming an author was neither a means to get rich nor a strategy for advancement to a court, nor even a road to independence. What he really wanted was fame. Obsessed by the notion of renown, he wrote about it constantly.

There were only two ways to become famous, Fioravanti reckoned: "One is by walking the world and practicing in various and diverse regions in order to be able to serve many people; the other is by writing books that are delightful to read and that provide readers with something useful." The world was too vast (and life too short) to enable him to visit every part of it. However great his exploits might be, after death, he feared, memories of him would soon fade.

Yet the invention of printing transformed the game of celebrity in the Renaissance. The printing press enabled even obscure surgeons like Leonardo Fioravanti to become known throughout the wider world. He was a passionate advocate of the new technology. He attributed the Renaissance itself—"the reawakening of the world, which had been sleeping in ignorance"—solely to printing. The invention of the printing press, he thought, changed the course of history:

> Before the glorious art of printing came into being there were very few *literati;* and that was simply because, due to the high cost of books, no one could study who was not rich. So it happened of necessity that the poor were ignorant against their will: because of a lack of books they couldn't study, and those who studied Greek and Latin amazed everyone who didn't know letters with their eloquence and wit. The educated were truly content in those days because they were adored and revered as if they were gods.

The lessons of history were not lost on Leonardo Fioravanti. "Only those who are written up in books stay alive forever," he would later write, "and their names will never die."

He set out from Rome in late October 1558, journeying as far as Pesaro on the Adriatic coast, where he intended to catch a ship to Venice. Inexplicably, he remained there for seven long weeks. What delayed him? He seemed so eager to reach Venice, so keen to begin a new life far from the vindictiveness of the Roman physicians.

A ROMANCE IN PESARO

Her name was Paula. Leonardo mentions her just twice, in a 1568 letter to a Neapolitan friend and in another letter, dated 1567, to a physician in the court of the Duke of Urbino. In the correspondence she is referred to as his *"consorte."* The meaning is unclear. If she had been his spouse, Fioravanti and his correspondents might have called her his *moglie,* although the two terms were used interchangeably. Probably she lived with him as a sort of common-law wife. Evidently they had no children, and how long they were together is not known. Possibly he believed that settling in Venice would bring a new stability. He was now 41, and perhaps feeling the pull to live a more settled life. Although some men and women lived singly, such a situation struck most people as an anomaly or misfortune.

Not much is known about Paula. Her origins are not mentioned, nor does Fioravanti identify her family. A connection to Pesaro or some other location in the Duchy of Urbino is hinted at, but that too is uncertain. What sort of courtship (or even matrimony) they may have had is a complete mystery. Most Renaissance marriages were arranged, with the aim of making a family alliance, transferring property, or providing a secure livelihood for the bride. Of course, couples also met casually and fell in love, and marriages for love were not unknown. Still, every region of Italy had some version of the proverb *"Chi si piglia d'amore, di rabbia si lascia*—Marry for love, break up in anger." In the Renaissance, marriage was an arrangement made for the purpose of procreation, leaving little room for more sentimental feelings.

How old was Paula? What kind of personality did she have? What did she look like? We don't know. Generally, women married young during the Renaissance: The average age of marriage was around 18, and nearly all women were married by 25. For men, the average age was around 32. By that standard, Leonardo was long past the normal age for marriage. Perhaps Paula was a widow; Leonardo doesn't let on. If they did marry, the nuptials most likely took place in a private ceremony: Church weddings were not the rule in the Renaissance. But now we are in the realm of speculation. In his many books and dozens of published letters, Fioravanti says not one word about his love life. Oddly, for all that we can tell, the mysterious *"madonna Paula"* was almost incidental to his life.

IT'S ALL IN YOUR STOMACH

As he awaited passage to Venice, Leonardo probably busied himself with his writings, preparing them to present to a printer when he reached his destination. As always, he also saw patients. A chance encounter with a madwoman—"who wandered aimlessly as those who by some accident lose their minds are wont to do"—caused him to grapple with the complex problem of demonic possession. Was madness caused by natural or supernatural agency? Some people thought the woman was faking her illness; others believed she was possessed by demons.

Leonardo never considered insanity to be demonic. "Seeing the fury of the woman's madness," he writes, "I wanted to find some remedy to see if I could help her." Under the pretext of giving the woman candy, he had her take two drams of Dia Aromatica, one of his most powerful emetics. The violent fit of vomiting that ensued caused her madness to subside for a few days, but it then returned as furiously as before. He increased the dosage, giving the medicine in a rice soup, shaved her head, and massaged it with Balsam. Soon the woman quieted down and, miraculously it seemed, her insanity went away. "Madness is nothing more than a malignant quality engendered in certain secret parts of the stomach," Fioravanti confidently pronounced, "thus doing damage to the heart and head."

Pesaro was the capital of the Duchy of Urbino, a situation that gave Leonardo an opportunity to make connections in the court of the Duke of Urbino, Guidobaldo II della Rovere. This swaggering and spendthrift prince—almost an exact contemporary of Grand Duke Cosimo I de' Medici of Florence, and every bit as brash—had come to power at the age of 25. Guidobaldo spent lavishly on his court, and like every prince of the day he sought to enhance its prestige by hiring talented artists, musicians, and architects. He had his portrait painted by Titian, Venice's most famous painter, and continuously supported the artist during his reign. The burdensome taxes that he imposed to prop up his extravagant expenses led to an uprising in 1571; the duke mercilessly quashed it, earning him the nickname "Guidobaldaccio," or "Wicked Guidobaldo."

Fioravanti's connection to Guidobaldo's court was through the duke's personal physician, Giovangirolamo Gonzaga, with whom Leonardo struck up a lasting friendship. The two grew close and stayed in touch. In 1565, Leonardo learned that Gonzaga had traveled to the court of Niccolò Bernardino di Sanseverino, the Prince of Bisignano, in Calabria. Gonzaga had been sent to accompany Guidobaldo's 14-year-old daughter, Isabella della Rovere, who was to be married to the prince in a dynastic union meant to strengthen Guidobaldo's position among the Neapolitan nobility.

Poor Isabella: Hers was one of those tragic stories that so often befell women of the Italian aristocracy, who suffered the indignities of arranged marriages. Her husband, ten years her senior and a notorious womanizer, infected his young wife with syphilis, which caused her nose to become horribly ulcerated. Eventually the disease ate the cartilage in her nose, leaving her grotesquely disfigured. In her later years, separated from her husband and living in Naples, Isabella devoted her life to caring for patients in the Ospedale degli Incurabili, attending to the ulcerated sores of those afflicted with syphilis.

Some years later, Fioravanti published a letter from Gonzaga inquiring about Leonardo's health and that of Paula, his "consort." It is an intimate correspondence, reflecting a warm friendship. Gonzaga sends greetings from his mother and from his brother, Andreazzo, and includes a letter to Paula from her family at home. The chatty letter goes on to describe Duke Guidobaldo's recent attack of gout, so painful that "he cried day and night." Fortunately, Gonzaga reports, he had some of Fioravanti's medicaments on hand, and he used them to quickly cure the duke. In return, the grateful duke ordered Gonzaga to send Leonardo some gifts, including a dozen *caciocavallo* cheeses, some salt, and a box of *manna di fronde*—a rare and costly resin exuded from the leaves of the flowering ash tree. The duchess, worried more about her appearance than her husband's excruciating pain, also sends greetings, and requests more teeth whitener and some of Leonardo's Imperial Water ("fit for a prince") for rejuvenating the face.

Fioravanti evidently chose not to take advantage of his connection to Guidobaldo's court through Gonzaga, nor did he use that relationship to pursue a placement there. Turning down the offer to move to King João's court and forsaking whatever prospects he may have had in Pesaro, he fixed his eyes on Venice, the capital of the Italian printing industry.

At long last, Fioravanti's ship arrived in Pesaro. The unexpected delay meant it was now mid-December; Leonardo's new life as a Venetian writer, though deferred, beckoned brightly once more.

18

VENETIAN CURIOSITIES

"*Venezia è un pesce*—Venice is a fish"—writes a modern Venetian author of this city. The metaphor is apt, if a bit contrived. Consider the city's shape on a map. It resembles a gigantic sole being raised up from the deep by the fish line that is the narrow bridge connecting it to terra firma. If it seems, in this cartographic allegory by Tiziano Scarpa, as if Venice has swallowed the hook and is about to be pulled ashore, that's just an illusion. In reality, the city is nailed to the bottom of the lagoon on which it appears to float. Millions of wooden pilings, from two to ten meters long and up to 30 centimeters in diameter, were driven into the mud bottom of the shallow lagoon. Upon this dense overturned forest—which, over the centuries, gradually petrified in the salty water—were built the stone streets and brick houses, the canals and bridges, and the great marble palaces of Venice.

The oak forests of the Veneto region were denuded to erect this fabulous city, which in modern times the sea threatens to swallow up again. Each winter during *aqua alta,* the high-water season, the city's residents are reminded of this impending peril. As the lagoon rises ominously and much of the city becomes submerged under several inches of water, Venetians in clumsy galoshes teeter precariously on the two and a half miles of *passerelle*—elevated boardwalks supported on metal legs—that they take out from storage each year, as if in grudging celebration of the reality that separates them from the people of solid land.

Venice as it would have looked when Fioravanti lived there. The impressive six-part woodcut, measuring 1.3 x 2.8 meters (4.3 x 9.2 feet), is one of the most spectacular achievements of Renaissance printmaking.

Tiziano Scarpa's allegory, though hardly original, illustrates an important fact: Like fish, Venetians have always been partners with the sea. A maritime empire built on the strength of its navy, Venice forged an intimate relationship with the sea that, from its beginnings, determined its destiny. A city without walls, Venice relied on the lagoon to protect it from its enemies. Although the Venetian empire is no more, Venetians are no less connected to the ocean, since the sea gives the city its distinctive flavor, drawing millions of tourists each year. "Streets Full of Water. Please Advise," humorist Robert Benchley allegedly cabled his editor on arriving there.

The sea was a central part of the myth of Venice, *La Serrenisima,* "the Most Serene Republic," and its supposedly perfect form of government. The myth was celebrated annually in a ritual known as *La Sensa*. Each year on Ascension Day, the doge, high magistrates, and ambassadors boarded the *Bucintoro,* the doge's ceremonial galley, and were rowed out into the lagoon accompanied by thousands of gaily decorated gondolas and barges. When the party reached the mouth of the lagoon, the doge perched on the poop deck of the *Bucintoro* and tossed a gold ring into the sea, proclaiming, "*Desponsamus te Mare, in signum veri perpetuique dominii*—We wed you, O sea, as a sign of our true and everlasting dominion." La Sensa was the centerpiece of a carefully orchestrated spring festival that, appropriately, inaugurated the theater season.

When Leonardo Fioravanti arrived in Venice in the winter of 1558, the myth of the city thrived as never before. Setting foot on Venetian soil for the first time, he would immediately have seen evidence of the city's proud bearing. An ambitious building program proclaimed the republic's power. Most noticeable were the extensive renovations of the Piazza San Marco following Jacopo Sansovino's ambitious plan. The ducal library, Sansovino's finest work, was under construction on the redesigned piazzetta. His masterpiece, the elegant Loggetta at the base of the Campanile, had been recently completed, and a new facade for the Church of San Geminiano (demolished by Napoleon in 1807 to make way for a ballroom), directly opposite the basilica of San Marco, was being constructed. By the time of Fioravanti's arrival the architect's renovations had transformed the piazza into a showcase of the Venetian empire.

A MOST DELICIOUS STREET

Soon after his arrival, Leonardo found a house in the street adjoining the Church of San Giuliano, "on the corner near the fruit vendor's shop," not far from Piazza San Marco. The church fronted the Merceria, the busy commercial street connecting Piazza San Marco with the Rialto. Hundreds of shops lined the street, selling foodstuffs, spices, metalwork, clothing, household goods, textiles, jewelry, clocks, hats, perfume, and all manner of luxury goods.

In the late 17th century, English visitor John Evelyn described the Merceria as "one of the most delicious streets in the world for the sweetness of it, and is all the way on both sides tapestried as it were with cloth of gold, rich damasks and other silks, which the shops expose and hang before their houses on the first floor, and with that variety that for near half the year spent chiefly in this city I hardly remember to have seen the same piece twice exposed." Each day, walking back and forth from his house to almost anywhere in the city, Leonardo would have seen evidence of Venice's success as a commercial entrepôt.

Venice owed its imperial status—more imaginary than real by the mid-16th century—to its prosperous maritime empire. Commerce with the outside world brought a constant flow of commodities from all over the known world. The list of goods and natural objects in which Venetian merchants trafficked was, quite literally, wonderful: wine and grain from Puglia; emeralds and spices from India; alum from Anatolia; lapis lazuli from Persia; perfume and incense from Arabia; sarsaparilla and armadillos from the New World; velvet, damask, and satin from Alexandria; ginger, pepper, and cloves from the Orient; Peruvian balsam; Egyptian porphyry; African ebony; brocade and cloth of gold from Byzantium and Greece. All that evoked wonder became prized objects for Venetian patricians and merchants, who collected and displayed rare and exotic natural and artificial objects in curiosity cabinets, like peacocks proudly displaying their feathers—indeed, peacock feathers, too, were prized objects for collectors. Such objects would become the "curious" things of early modern science.

A PANOPLY OF APOTHECARIES

It was in the piazzas and the pharmacies, above all, where curiosities were displayed for public consumption. A capital of the European trade in pharmaceuticals, Venice had more than 50 apothecary shops in the mid-16th century—about one for every 3,000 Venetians. The pharmaceutical trade thrived on the novel and exotic raw materials that poured into the city from distant parts of the world: crocodile skins, basilisks, bezoar, turkeys, and Egyptian mummies for making mumia—a medicine prized for a fantastic variety of ailments, including migraines, paralysis, epilepsy, vertigo, earaches, coughs, flatulence, scorpion stings, incontinence, and "passions of the heart." The demand for the fashionable new drug was so great that it gave rise to a flourishing trade in counterfeit mumia made from the bodies of executed criminals.

Leonardo quickly found himself immersed in Venice's pharmaceutical culture. He was personally acquainted with more than a dozen pharmacists, many of whom manufactured and sold his remedies. He must have spent a good part of each day at the Orso (Bear) pharmacy in Santa Maria Formosa. He set up his medical practice there, and the shop's proprietor, Sabbà di Franceschi, was his partner in several business ventures. Jacomo Torellis, a gifted alchemist and distiller from Puglia, worked in Sabbà's pharmacy and manufactured Fioravanti's drugs there. Leonardo also knew Giorgio Melichio, who emigrated to Venice from Augsburg and established the Struzzo (Ostrich) pharmacy, one of the leading centers for the production of the cure-all theriac.

When Fioravanti moved to a house in the Campo di San Luca, he began manufacturing his remedies in the nearby Fenice (Phoenix) pharmacy, whose proprietor, Master Giovan Giacamo, was an enthusiastic proponent of Leonardo's methods. Leonardo lauded numerous other Venetian apothecaries, including Marco and Ippolito Fenari, proprietors of the Saracino (Saracen) pharmacy, Master Gabrielo at the Campanile (Bell), and Francesco di Bianchi at the Sperone (Ram).

During the Renaissance the pharmacies were the centers of some of the most advanced scientific research of the day. Aside from anatomical theaters, no scientific research laboratory existed at any university until the late 17th century. Experimental research went on elsewhere: in academies, for example, and in craftsmen's workshops. Apothecaries did innovative experiments in alchemy and refined the art of distillation to a sophisticated science.

Historian Paula Findlen points out that the pharmacies were Europe's first natural history museums. Practically every pharmacy was a museum in miniature. Some, such as Francesco Calzolari's shop in Verona and Ferrante Imperato's in Naples, were major tourist attractions. Besides containing an impressive assemblage of distillation equipment and a renowned collection of exotic plants and animals from America and Asia, Calzolari's pharmacy housed a famous museum whose inventory boasted such fantastical items as a chameleon, a unicorn's horn, and a bird of paradise. People went to the pharmacies to gaze upon these wondrous sights—and to debate their alleged virtues, as one would do in a natural history museum.

A 16TH-CENTURY WONDER DRUG?

The pharmacies were also theaters of scientific demonstration. The debate over ancient versus modern medicine was argued during the annual ritual of making theriac—the universal antidote of antiquity, and Renaissance humanism's wonder drug. First described by Galen, theriac, "the royal antidote of antidotes," was a rare and costly medicament thought to be a panacea. According to Galen's account, theriac was invented by Nero's physician, Andromachus, who took the ancient drug Mithridatium, removed some ingredients, added others—notably viper's flesh—and came up with the universal remedy that became known as *Theriake*. Compounded from 64 ingredients, theriac, in Findlen's words, "was designed to mirror man's physiological complexity; each ingredient corresponded to a particular part and function of the human body." In every major Italian city, the production of theriac took place in elaborate ceremonies that began in May with the capturing and killing of vipers and ended in June with the solemn rite of concocting the drug, always in public and always overseen by local health officials to ensure a genuine product.

In Venice the theriac-making rite was held each spring under the strict supervision of the Provveditori alla Sanità, or Public Health Board. The spectacles took place on the piazzas outside the pharmacy shops that were lucky enough to obtain one of the coveted licenses to make the drug. The piazza was adorned with rich damasks and busts of Hippocrates and Galen. Rows of benches held great majolica jars filled with the herbs and gums and spices that were used to make up the ancient antidote: pepper, myrrh, gum arabic, cinnamon, fennel, rose petals, iris roots, opium, amber, and various aromatic herbs from the East. On the highest bench, in the back row, arranged in a neat line, stood several dozen glass vessels containing live snakes. The principal ingredient of theriac—the one that gave the drug its potency—was the flesh of vipers killed and dissected according to a prescribed method. When all was prepared, the priors of the College of Medicine would arrive dressed in their academic robes with ermine collars to solemnly inspect the ingredients. Everything about the scene enhanced the ritual's pomp and ceremony.

Throngs of spectators gathered on the piazza to witness the slaughter of serpents and to watch colorfully costumed servants grinding and mixing herbs while chanting a work song. The rich aroma of peppers and spices filled the air. So many vipers were collected and killed to make theriac in Venice—more than 800 per month in the decades of its maximum production, all feminine, since only female serpents could be used to make the drug—that by the 17th century the species had been exterminated from the Euganean Hills outside nearby Padua, where they were traditionally collected.

Watching the production of theriac in Venice was a regular part of travelers' itineraries. John Evelyn, who visited Venice in 1645, reported seeing "the extraordinary ceremony whereof I had been curious to observe, for it is extremely pompous and worth seeing." He regarded his purchase of some "treacle," as theriac was termed, as one of his most valuable acquisitions in Venice.

Leonardo would have watched the ritual, too, and doubtless would have debated—perhaps with his friend, the pharmacist Sabbà di Franceschi—the virtues of theriac. It must have been a spirited discussion. Di Franceschi's Bear Pharmacy was a respected establishment, and he would have known about the ongoing debate over polypharmacy—the use of compound medicines made from multiple ingredients—that framed contemporary opinions about the drug. Perhaps Leonardo's friend, humanist Giovanni Battista Rasario, a distinguished scholar of Greek at the Scuola di San Marco, joined the conversation to defend the ancients. Renaissance humanists attacked the widespread medieval reliance on polypharmacy, which they considered to be a corruption by Arabic texts, and advocated a return to the "simples"—remedies derived from a single plant, animal, or mineral ingredient—supposedly favored by the ancient physicians.

For these reasons, theriac presented humanists with a particularly challenging case. On one hand, the drug was cited in authentic ancient sources, including Galen. Yet with so many ingredients, how could one guarantee that all 64 were genuine—and that none was in conflict with another? Many of the ingredients that went into making the drug—such as the famed opobalsum of antiquity, the original Balm of Gilead—were exotic and difficult to find. Inevitably, substitute ingredients became commonplace. How, then, could one distinguish true theriac from its cheaper imitations sold by charlatans?

Leonardo had a lot to say about the purported wonder drug, none of it favorable. Theriac, he thought, was the most extreme example of polypharmacy gone wild. He too advocated a return to simples—"natural medicaments unaltered by anyone, which retain all the medicinal virtues that God infused into them"—and railed against modern drugs that were "made with such a mix of things, most contrary to one another, that they end up doing more harm than good." As for his own remedies, which were as complex as any of those made by modern pharmacists, Leonardo justified them on the grounds that by manufacturing them by distillation, he was able to extract the pure virtues of the ingredients composing his drugs.

In the form of "Venice Treacle," various versions of theriac were made down through the 19th century. As late as the 1990s you could still buy a sticky, resinous substance called *teriaca* at the Golden Head Pharmacy at the foot of the Rialto bridge. It was a far cry from Renaissance theriac, of course, lacking its wondrous curative power. It was just another sort of candy the pharmacist sold, alongside the lozenges and licorice sticks that lined the shop shelves. The magic was gone.

19

THE LURE OF THE CHARLATAN

The fascination with novelty that characterized the Venetian pharmaceutical trade could also be seen in the piazzas, where charlatans performed acts of primitive commedia dell'arte and displayed natural marvels to attract customers for their medicines. Walking in the Piazza San Marco, Leonardo would have seen them every day mounting their portable scaffolds and holding forth. The piazza was an important medical marketplace, where people of all stations bought the latest nostrum.

Charlatans, too, were a standard part of the Renaissance tourist's itinerary, and Venice—notably the Piazza San Marco—swarmed with them. Fynes Moryson, an English traveler who walked from London to Naples in the late 16th century, described these marginal healers:

> Italy has a generation of empirics who frequently and by swarms go from city to city and haunt their marketplaces. They are called *montibanchi* or mounting banks or little scaffolds, and also *ciarlatani* of prating. They proclaim their wares upon these scaffolds, and to draw concourse of people they have a *zanni* or fool with a visard on his face, and sometimes a woman, to make comical sport. The people cast their handkerchiefs with money to them, and they cast them back with wares tied in them. . . . The wares they sell are commonly distilled waters and divers ointments for burning aches and

> stitches and the like, but especially for the itch and scabs, more vendible than the rest.... Many of them have some very good secrets, but generally they are all cheaters.

Cheats they may have been, but the stark contrast between the physician's sophisticated talk and the charlatan's promise of instant, surefire remedies must have struck a responsive chord in the audience gathered around the mountebank. Empirics and charlatans were more deeply connected to the people's suffering than the Galenic physicians, whose complex regimens were far removed from the rules by which most people lived. When they were sick, people wanted action, not just an intellectual understanding of the causes of their ailments.

The charlatans delivered—or, at least, they seemed to. But before looking at that side of the story, we need to ask: Who were the charlatans and what did they do?

First of all, they seemed to be everywhere. Thousands of charlatans practiced in early modern Italy. In cities large and small, they set up portable stages and performed routines to attract audiences that became the buyers of their wares. Most were itinerants, moving from town to town to sell their goods. Travel was such a central element of the charlatan's identity that rootlessness became part of the stereotype of the charlatan—and one of the many insults hurled at them.

Leonardo Fioravanti, too, confronted such attacks. When the Venetian physicians condemned him in 1568, they accused him both of endangering people with his unorthodox treatments *and* of being a vagabond.

Charlatans, however, stood out from ordinary peddlers by virtue of the novel marketing strategies they invented, many of which anticipated the modern pharmaceutical industry. They used trade names for their remedies, adopted nicknames and stage personas, printed handbills to advertise their wares, and staged comic performances to attract buyers. Charlatans cashed in on current medical fashions and invented some of their own. The proliferation of

I MARAVIGLIOSI,
ET OCCVLTI SECRETI
NATVRALI.
Tradotti di lingua Perſiana nella
noſtra lingua Italica.
*Diſpenſati da me Benedetto,
detto il Perſiano.*

*In Roma Venetia, Bologna, & in Milano,
Per Pandolfo Malateſta.* 1613.
Con licenza de' Superiori.

The Marvelous and Occult Secrets of Nature, *a booklet of secrets by "Benedetto the Persian," is typical of the many chapbooks sold by charlatans promising cures for common complaints such as nosebleeds. The chapbooks also included parlor diversions like invisible ink.*

artificial balsams, for example, opened up the floodgates for other balsams. The brand names that charlatans gave their balsams evoked the sacred *(Balsamo angelico)*, the biblical *(Balsamo Samaritano)*, the mystical *(Balsamo Arcano)*, the philosophical *(Balsamo philosofico)*, the natural world *(Balsamo solare)*, alchemical fashions *(Balsamo quintessenziale)*, distant and exotic places *(Balsamo del Perù)*, and claims of universal healing *(Balsamo universale)*.

Charlatans also adopted stage names, almost as many as their remedies: "Il Fortunato" (Lucky), "Scampamorte" (Death Defier), "Lingua d'Oro" (Golden Tongue), "Il Mangiabissi" (Snake Eater), and, reflecting reputed origins in distant parts of the world, "Il Turchetto" (Little Turk). The names were all part of creating a stage persona. The performances were no mere gimmick; they were an important part of the charlatan's identity and an essential element of his merchandising strategy. English traveler Thomas Coryat reckoned that charlatans might draw a thousand spectators around their portable stages. They performed the traditional roles of comic street theater, and their stage names reflected the characters they acted out in the piazzas: Zanni, the fool; Doctor Graziano, the swaggering Spanish captain; Pantalone, the miserly, lecherous old man; and so on.

The charlatans were among the first merchants to capitalize on growing literacy rates and use the new medium of print to market their goods. Handbills and chapbooks advertising their wares extended the charlatans' message beyond the piazza and into homes, workshops, and taverns. By printing handbills, often sprinkled with Latin words and highfalutin phrases, the charlatans attempted to link themselves with official medicine and impress the buying public.

At the same time, the charlatans distanced themselves from the world of hidebound learning by emphasizing their extensive experience and travel to distant lands. The not-so-subtle subtext of the chapbooks was that you shouldn't put yourself in the hands of a physician, whose book learning was worthless unless backed by experience. Instead, an entire world of remedies was available for anyone who wanted to heal himself.

CAVEAT EMPTOR

Did any of the charlatans' cures work? In strictly medical terms, most were not effective—but the same can be said of the remedies used by the physicians. Despite their extravagant brand names, most of the ingredients making up the charlatans' remedies were a regular part of the official pharmacopoeia. Although they ridiculed

Bernardino Mei's 1656 painting depicts an aged, bearded charlatan seated on a chair on his makeshift stage. The image of the charlatan as a suspicious fraud was beginning to take shape in the public's imagination.

doctors, the charlatans didn't propose an alternative medical system. Whether their nostrums "worked" or not depended on expectations and perceptions. A purgative that purges obviously works, though it may not cure the underlying condition that caused the ailment. Sometimes the charlatans' remedies produced dramatic physical changes—at least they did something, in contrast to the physicians' remedies, which often worked slowly or seemed to result in no change at all.

The fact that the charlatans' medicines sold so well means they must have been perceived to work. Perhaps they acted at a symbolic level, just as placebos "work" for certain conditions. Or perhaps the charlatans' nostrums were thought to work because they brought on physiological changes (such as vomiting or temporary relief of an annoying skin itch) that convinced users of their efficacy.

Nor should we overlook the sheer charisma of the charlatan. In modern medicine, the physician's costume (white coat and stethoscope hanging around the neck), manner (grave or optimistic), and language (medical terminology) are all meaningful enough to affect the outcome of a therapeutic encounter. Why should the same not have been true of the charlatan's remedies?

The charlatan's charisma is vividly captured in a painting by Sienese artist Bernardino Mei. Titled simply "The Charlatan," it depicts an aged, bearded charlatan seated on a wooden platform and surrounded by an astonished crowd of onlookers. The scene takes place in the Piazza del Campo in Siena. The view of the charlatan from below accentuates his imposing figure, while the dark, foreboding sky above him heightens the drama of the scene. On the floor of the stage stands an assortment of glass bottles and vials containing the charlatan's remedies. Beside the healer's cane is a handbill bearing the title *L'Olio de' filosofi di Straccione (Straccione's Philosophers' Oil)*, identifying both the charlatan and his remedy. On the back of his clenched hand, thrust out to the crowd, Straccione (Ragamuffin) balances a vial of his miraculous elixir. His penetrating gaze and authoritative gestures inspire wonder and fear in the crowd below, which listens, rapt, as the charlatan proclaims the powerful attributes of the potion in that little vial.

Charlatans have suffered mightily at the hands of historians of medicine. Indeed, the very word implies quackery and fraud. While the term began to take on that meaning as early as the 16th century, the legal definition of the word *ciarlatano* was quite different and did not necessarily imply fraud. Charlatans were licensed to sell their wares in the cities in which they set up shop (or rather, stage) and pitched their goods. They were fully legal medical providers, and local authorities devoted considerable effort to regulating them.

Mountebanks didn't sell just remedies; they also trafficked in natural and artificial curiosities. The charlatan Gulielmo Germerio would invite his audience to his home in Venice and show them his collection of "ten very stupendous monsters, marvelous to see, among which there are seven newborn animals, six alive and one dead, and three imbalmed female infants." The famous Venetian charlatan Leone Tartaglini's collection of curiosities was one of the largest in the city. Among the items he sold were various dragons and basilisks that he manufactured by cleverly fusing together the mummified body parts of rays and angelfishes. Curiosity can be dangerous: Caveat emptor.

A DISEASE CALLED CURIOSITY

Saint Augustine, in the fourth century, stated the traditional medieval view of curiosity, and it wasn't favorable. In the *Confessions,* the Bishop of Hippo made inquisitiveness in general the subject of a vicious polemic, thereby setting the tone for the debate over intellectual curiosity. Augustine included *curiositas* in his catalog of vices, identifying it as one of the three forms of lust *(concupiscentia)* that are the beginning of all sin (lust of the flesh, lust of the eyes, and ambition of the world). The overly curious mind exhibits a "lust to find out and know," not for any practical purpose but merely for the sake of knowing. Thanks to the "disease of curiosity" people go to watch freaks in circuses—or charlatans in the piazza. Augustine saw no essential difference between such perverse entertainments and the "empty longing and curiosity [that is] dignified by the names of learning and science."

No difference between gawking at freaks in a sideshow and making investigations in natural philosophy? "From the same motive," wrote Augustine, "men proceed to investigate the workings of nature, which is beyond our ken—things which it does no good to know and which men only want to know for the sake of knowing."

Augustine's severe judgment of intellectual curiosity, linking it with the sin of pride, the black arts, and the Fall, became conventional in medieval thought. In the Renaissance, it gave rise to such memorable characters as Doctor Faustus, who bartered his soul to the devil to satisfy his insatiable curiosity and quest for power.

Curiosity was the *primum mobile* of Renaissance science. Early modern curiosity was insatiable, never content with a single experience or object. The same passion for surprise and novelty that drove the luxury market propelled the Renaissance's devil-may-care experimentalism, like Fioravanti's outlandish experiments and his fearless surgical interventions. Whereas Augustine linked curiosity to sensual lust and human depravity, Renaissance natural philosophers saw it as being driven by wonder and the engine of discovery.

Venice was fertile ground for both the generation of wonder and the growth of experimental science. Galileo made his first telescope there, improving on a primitive device invented by a Dutch lens grinder. The craftsmen in Venice's Merceria were renowned for their precision, and the city's Arsenale—an immense shipbuilding factory—encompassed nearly all the mechanical arts, from carpentry and glassmaking to metallurgy and cannonry.

Indeed, Galileo relied on the testimony of craftsmen and employed them to build his scientific instruments. Questions that craftsmen asked about nature inspired him to penetrate nature's secrets more deeply. Venice's maritime empire and its rich craft tradition provided plentiful fuel for wonder and curiosity. The continual contact with exotic commodities—whether herbs from the New World, mechanical toys from Persia, or fake dragons and basilisks—fueled Renaissance inquisitiveness. Saint Paul's first-century C.E. admonition, "*Noli alta sapere*—Do not seek to know high things"—gave way in the Renaissance to Horace's more hopeful "*Sapere aude*—Dare to know." The transformation of curiosity in the Renaissance was a precondition of modernity.

The Bear Pharmacy, where Fioravanti's drugs were manufactured and sold, is depicted in a painting of the Piazza Santa Maria Formosa by Canaletto, and it still exists in its original 16th-century building. The shop's modern proprietors say the name comes from brutal bear-baiting contests staged on the piazza, one of early modern popular culture's best-loved recreations.

It's a picturesque, if unlikely, etymology. The names of Renaissance pharmacies were a kind of menagerie of the exotic: Phoenix, Saracen, Golden Eagle, Two Mermaids. It's anyone's guess how the shops originally got their names.

Not much evokes wonder in a modern Venetian pharmacy. You certainly won't see an alligator hanging from the ceiling, as you might have found in the Bear when Sabbà di Franceschi ran it. Instead of stuffed armadillos and miraculous healing stones, its windows now display glossy posters promoting the latest pharmaceutical fashions catering to tourists, like treatments for aching and blistered feet and antistress regimens. As an obligatory nod to the historical "authenticity" demanded by the tourist industry, modern Venetian pharmacies display "antique" majolica drug jars lined up neatly in a row, one prominently labeled *Teriaca* (theriac)—faithful replicas commissioned by the pharmaceutical companies. The transformation of the pharmacy shops was one of the consequences of the taming of the exotic in modern medicine.

Like a charlatan, Fioravanti traded on the Renaissance appetite for wonder. Yet he distinguished himself from the ordinary charlatans by gaining the charlatan's ultimate platform: the printed book. Instead of standing on the mountebank's stage, Leonardo became a pulp writer who created a series of popular books proclaiming the wonders of a remarkable doctor.

That, too, was the Venetian way.

20

A WRITER FOR THE AGES

When poet Dionigi Atanagi arrived in Venice in 1559 just a few months after Leonardo settled there, one of the first persons he would have looked up was his friend Girolamo Ruscelli. Atanagi had known Girolamo since at least 1541, when Ruscelli—an aspiring author working as a secretary to a Roman prelate—helped found the Sdegno (Scornful) academy, a literary society that included some of Rome's leading men of letters. Among the group's members was Atanagi, a novice writer. Born in 1504 into an impoverished family in Cagli, a mountain town in the Apennine foothills of the Marche region, Atanagi moved to Rome hoping to use his literary talents to win a place at a court. He was bitterly disappointed. Unable to find a patron, he slid into poverty and his health declined. Eventually he found employment as a secretary to the prelate Giovanni Guidiccioni. An accomplished poet known principally for his sonnets on the woes and miseries of Italy, Guidiccioni introduced his protégé to the Roman literary community. Even with these advantages, Atanagi lived in Rome for 25 years and managed to publish only two books. His literary career was going nowhere.

Ruscelli, who was about the same age, was likewise struggling to break into the literary world. After moving from patron to patron, composing letters for various prelates and princes, he settled in Venice in 1549 and saw his fortunes improve. He went to work as an editor in the Valgrisi publishing house, Venice's largest printing establishment. In 1552, Valgrisi published Ruscelli's edition of Boccaccio's *Decameron*. A few months later, the Giolito press printed a rival edition of the work by Ludovico Dolce, who took the occasion to ridicule Ruscelli's efforts. Ruscelli fired back with a scathing review of Dolce's translation of Ovid, touching off a famous literary feud. In the thick of the quarrel, Dolce wrote a diatribe playing on Ruscelli's reputation for dabbling in alchemy and magic:

> Everyone knows that Ruscelli is a good for nothing scoundrel, a swindler, and a cheat. He's ignorant and full of vice. Not being successful at alchemy, the pedantic profession that teaches all the learning of an ass, he has the temerity to translate Plutarch's *Lives* from Greek (of which he hasn't any more knowledge than a magpie), the Bible from Hebrew (which he knows about as well as my dog), and after a thousand ridiculous charlatan's recipes, he has lowered himself to the art of the pimp and has crammed his house with all sorts of courtesans and glad-handing prostitutes begging for the bread they can't earn by their own talents.

This duel with one of Venice's most celebrated writers propelled Ruscelli into the limelight. The literary circle Ruscelli founded, whose nucleus was the *Dubbiosi* (Dubious Ones) academy, included many of Venice's leading writers. Proximity to the Venetian printing industry enabled him to publish a succession of bestselling works in history, geography, and letters. Encouraged by his friend's success, Atanagi moved to Venice to seek his fortune as an independent writer.

Situated almost exactly halfway between Madrid and Istanbul, Venice was not only a great Renaissance commercial entrepôt but an important center of information and communication. News reaching Venice from distant parts of the world spread quickly through printed newsletters, placards, letters, and gossip. The political culture of such a compact city was easily lubricated by wagging tongues that spread the news from piazza to piazza. If you missed out on the local gossip, a visit to the Gòbbo di Rialto, a statue near the Rialto nicknamed "the hunchback," where anonymous political placards and scandalous comments were posted, would bring you up to date.

A MECCA FOR MANUSCRIPTS

It was for its more official forms of communication, above all printing, that Venice became famous in the early modern period. Venice produced more books than any other European city in the 16th century. Even when it began to lose its lead relative to other printing centers such as Paris, it far outstripped the book production of all other Italian cities combined. An estimated 500 printers produced a total of 15,000 to 17,000 titles—more than 150 per year, and possibly as many as 18 million copies over the course of the 1500s. That astonishing output made Venice a mecca for writers, who flocked to the city to work in its printing houses and shop their manuscripts, hoping to publish their own books—especially that one book that would bring them riches and fame, or gain them the favor of a prince.

The *poligrafi,* or tradesmen of the pen *(mestieri della penna),* sold words like a merchant selling cloth by the yard. Though few of them grew rich, some did become famous. The phenomenal success of satirist Pietro Aretino, who rose from poverty in provincial Arezzo to become a best-selling author, encouraged others to journey to Venice and try their hand at writing tales, poetry, letters, and burlesques, the standard fare of popular literature. Most poligrafi worked for menial wages as editors and proofreaders, a situation that at least gave them access to a printer, a necessary precondition for publishing. An exploited offshoot of the printing business, the professional author lived at the behest of the printer, without whom his profession would not have existed.

The life of the *poligrafo* was not a glamorous one: laboring long hours in dim light editing manuscripts, reading page proofs, composing trivial verses, and so on. And the profession could be surprisingly dangerous: Literary quarrels were excellent ways to fuel the sale of a book, but they occasionally turned violent. Just as his literary career was starting to take off, Atanagi got embroiled in a feud that almost cost him his life. The event bears scrutiny because, besides providing a glimpse at the seamier side of Renaissance print culture, it opened certain doors for Leonardo Fioravanti. Atanagi's misfortune was Leonardo's gain.

In 1562, a University of Padua student named Mercurio Concorreggio approached Atanagi through a mutual friend with a translation of a work on the lives of famous Romans by (as Concorreggio believed) the ancient Roman writer Gaius Plinius Caecilius Secundus, or Pliny the Younger. Concorreggio asked Atanagi to proofread his manuscript in preparation for printing. One can imagine the young student's anticipation: For his first book he had labored countless hours translating the text and ascertaining its authorship—incorrectly, as it turned out. (The text, *De viris illustribus urbis Romae—On Illustrious Men of Rome*—had in fact been penned by the fourth-century Roman writer Sextus Aurelius Victor.) It was just the kind of publication that would establish his humanist credentials and, possibly, land him a university teaching job. Atanagi, desperate for work and eager to forge a reputation for himself, agreed to edit the manuscript. Concorreggio returned to Padua to resume his studies and anxiously await the publication of his manuscript.

Ten months later the book came out. The result was not what Concorreggio expected. Instead of publishing the work under Concorreggio's name, Atanagi had published it under his own. In his dedication to the volume, Atanagi admitted that a rough draft of the work had been brought to him for correction by "a young scholar"—whose name Atanagi declined to mention "out of respect"—but he claimed to have done the greater share of the work. Not only had he "beautified" the prose and adorned it with appropriate embellishments, he had added new biographies and improved the text by including a glossary and explanatory apparatus.

Outraged by Atanagi's plagiarism, Concorreggio shot back with an angry broadside accusing the poet of stealing his work and altering it without permission.

But Concorreggio did not stop there. The irate student hired an assailant to get even with the writer. Armed with a *pistolese*—a short knife that could easily be hidden in his clothing—the assailant ambushed Atanagi and stabbed him repeatedly in the head and neck. So violent was the attack that one of the blows penetrated the skull. The attending surgeon deemed the case hopeless.

At that point Fioravanti was brought in. He arrived at Atanagi's bedside to find the poet near death. The Bologna surgeon treated the wound with Balsam, Grand Elixir, and Quintessence, and saved the man's life. (Atanagi's testimony confirms Leonardo's account of the case.) After his recovery, Atanagi called Fioravanti "an angel of paradise, sent by God to earth for the health and preservation of human life." As a result of the incident and Atanagi's glowing commentary on it, Fioravanti became a sensation among the Venetian literati. "He performs miracles in the world with his remedies," exclaimed Ruscelli.

LIFE AMONG THE POLIGRAFI

Saving Atanagi's life gave Leonardo entrée to the community of the poligrafi. He and his companions gravitated toward the printing houses, where the central interactions of print culture took place. The printing house was not just a place where books were produced—it was also a social and cultural nexus where members of the emerging republic of letters gathered to discuss literary and philosophical matters.

Fioravanti's first printer, Ludovico Avanzo, was a typical small publisher. He specialized in popular scientific literature. At his shop at the sign of the Tree in the Merceria, you could buy translations of Latin works such as della Porta's *Natural Magic* and Levinus Lemnius's *Occult Secrets of Nature,* as well as Italian works by anatomist Gabriele Falloppio and botanist Piero Mattioli. The backlist perfectly matched Fioravanti's lively prose style and novel approach to medicine.

Leonardo's first book, *Capricci medicinali (Medical Caprices),* came out in 1561. Its intent, as the title suggests, was to launch a new medical fashion in a marketplace fueled by fashions—a "new way of healing," as Leonardo put it. In the preface, he wrote:

> So that readers will not be astonished by the new way that I follow in writing about the arts of medicine and surgery, it seemed that I should advise you that I haven't followed the style of Hippocrates or Galen or Avicenna or any of the other ancient or modern authors, but followed only my own judgment and experience, which you might say is the mother of all things. Therefore, you will find nothing in this book that has not been proved by experience, nor any experiment that is not based on reason.

His novel, exotic "caprices" were meant to delight and entertain readers. They included all manner of recondite secrets: marvelous remedies, recipes for making potable gold, cosmetic formulas, and a secret to prolong human life. Exploiting the middle-class fascination with "secrets," he made alchemy—in particular, distillation—a key component of the new way of healing. He devoted an entire section of *Medical Caprices* to alchemy—"the greatest and most noble art and science that the philosophers have ever invented," in Leonardo's words. Setting himself squarely in opposition to regular doctors, he insisted that physicians must be able to make their own drugs rather than rely on pharmacists to compose them.

To advertise his newly invented remedies—which he informed readers could be bought at the Bear Pharmacy—Leonardo gave them catchy trade names such as Angelic Electuary, Magistral Syrup, Blessed Oil, and Dia Aromatica, the "fragrant goddess" that he prescribed as the first course of action against almost every ailment he encountered. Distilled drugs, whether made of herbal concoctions or mineral substances, were very much à la mode, and Fioravanti proclaimed that he was a master at the art of making them. Alchemy was the underpinning of the new way of healing—a way unknown to the doctors. "Whoever follows my lead," he confidently promised, "will do wonders."

Fioravanti's antiauthoritarian stance in *Medical Caprices* appealed to readers who were growing distrustful of established medicine. He represented himself as a man of the people, exposing frauds perpetrated by the educated classes. He assured readers that anyone willing to make the effort could learn the truth for themselves. To make the book easier to read, he shunned the "elegant" style of some writers and wrote in a "clear style" *(terso stile)* more appropriate for the unlettered.

The book was a phenomenal success. Avanzo reprinted it four times before a succession of printers picked it up, ultimately producing a total of 15 Italian editions. Translated into German, French, and English, *Medical Caprices* spread the name of Leonardo Fioravanti throughout Europe, making him the preeminent "professor of secrets" of the age. His literary career took off.

The book's success attracted the attention of other printers, including Vincenzo Valgrisi, one of Venice's leading publishers, who hired the novice author to write another medical handbook. Published in 1564, Fioravanti's *Compendio de i secreti rationali (Compendium of Rational Secrets)* proved nearly as popular as *Medical Caprices.* Encouraged by his success, he broadened his horizons. He wanted to be known not just as the author of how-to books, but as a writer for the ages.

A *MIRROR* OF ITALIAN CULTURE

In 1564, Valgrisi published Leonardo's most ambitious project, *Specchio di scientia universale (The Mirror of Universal Science),* a comprehensive treatise on the arts and professions of the day. "My work treats all the arts and their sciences, along with the sciences themselves, and includes discourses about various things, along with many new inventions discovered by me," he wrote. "I hope that they will be of great profit to the world." He intended the book for middle-class readers—especially the growing number of immigrants who, like Leonardo, were adjusting to life in the lagoon city.

The Mirror provided practical information about the changing social, economic, and political makeup of the republic. The trades were all represented, from agriculture to metallurgy and from gardening to architecture, distilling, glassblowing, and dancing. Young patricians could read Fioravanti's concise history of the "stocking clubs" *(compagnie delle calze),* the organizations that shaped the nobles' social and cultural lives until they reached the age of 25 and donned the black toga of duty. On festive occasions, these young men peacocked about in theatrical costumes decorated with elaborate badges and distinctive hosiery denoting the clubs to which they belonged. Fioravanti even gave a crash course on the myth of Venice. Whether in the form of facts about the professions or lessons on art appreciation such as descriptions of the various dances performed in theaters, *The Mirror* offered the sort of information that would have been useful to an ambitious person like himself when he first arrived in Venice clueless about Venetian mores. Even if you were a lowly German shoemaker or a barber-surgeon from Puglia with little hope of advancing in the world, *The Mirror* could open your eyes to professions open to your sons and daughters.

The Mirror of Universal Science was a work driven by religious zeal and high moral purpose. That was shown by the very manner Leonardo used to organize the book, presenting the arts in a hierarchy ranging from useful and honest to superfluous and vain. He extolled the "honest" arts such as agriculture, mining, masonry, and metallurgy as well as the learned arts of mapmaking and alchemy, while condemning anatomy (worse than butchering, which at least was done out of necessity) and the "diabolical art of dancing." The mother of all arts was agriculture, "the creation of Adam, who was ordained by the word of God saying to Adam, 'With the sweat of your brow you will earn your bread'." Then came medicine, surgery, and the military arts, all critical for survival. But as civilization advanced, many of the trades grew corrupted. Novel and fashionable professions developed. Instead of attending to necessities, humans invented frivolous arts such as "the gluttonous art of the cook," which had been the cause of so many physical maladies. The food we eat out of necessity doesn't make us sick, Leonardo pronounced, only what we eat out of desire. As a moral philosopher, his severe judgments were impelled by the austerity of the Counter-Reformation.

In *The Mirror of Universal Science,* Leonardo danced over almost every topic of interest to curious contemporaries: politics, medicine, the arts, the professions, the religious orders, women, marriage, and love—subjects, as he put it, "that everyone can delight in." Fioravanti addressed them all—even those in which he had limited expertise. He posed as a man of the world, convinced that experience, not book learning, was the foundation of art and science.

On most topics relating to social and cultural life, Leonardo's views were conventional, even if he sometimes reached them by quirky paths. He wrote an elegant little discourse on the origin of civil society, where he begins with the observation that humans, like the animals, by nature shun solitude and gather together in groups. "But the greater marvel is that all the species of terrestrial animals, as well as those of the sea and the air, created republics to rule themselves." Often their governments are supremely orderly and peaceful: Observe how the cranes fly in perfect order and appoint a guard when they sleep. Humans, emulating the animals, likewise created republics, and the republics became cities. But soon men became ambitious, and ambition led to rebellion and misrule. All over Italy, the republics were ruined and taken over by ambitious princes, all except "the most happy Venetian Republic." In Fioravanti's version of the myth of Venice, republicanism was the natural form of government, and only in Venice, of all the Italian states, did it still survive.

His views of women were equally traditional, custom-made to create good citizens. The woman's place is in the home, and her purpose is bearing and raising children. Yet Leonardo presents the feminist argument in a surprisingly favorable light. Although women should be keepers and bestowers and men should lord over over them, "the household is ill served by those who want to have such dominion that they treat women as slaves." The problem with the women of the day, he laments, is that they've been seduced by fashions and love of luxury, often to the detriment of their health, as when they whiten their skin with mercury sublimate.

RUNGS FOR SOCIAL CLIMBERS

His ideal woman was Zenobia, the ancient warrior queen of Palmyra, a woman "so remarkably virtuous," Boccaccio said, that she "rid herself of feminine weakness." The tale of Zenobia occupies a prominent section in Book Two, where it is wedged between two articles, "On the State of the World" and "On the Vain Desire for Worldly Things." Charming, witty, ostentatiously sophisticated, and full of moral teaching, the section gave Leonardo the opportunity to strut his humanist credentials and display his familiarity with ancient Greek and Roman literature. Even with its half-baked erudition, the collection of moral tales and examplars that constitutes the second book of *The Mirror of Universal Science* gave the social climbers who made up Leonardo's readership important tools for advancement.

Fioravanti's religious beliefs, at least what he reveals of them, were unquestionably orthodox: He was a champion of the Counter-Reformation. His political views were also conventional, although he had sharp words for fawning courtiers and tyrannical princes—normal barb-throwing among the poligrafi. Only in medicine and natural philosophy was he unorthodox and contrary, like a willful, unrepentant heretic. Some of the argument was posturing—part of his persona—and a method of promoting the "new way of healing."

Fioravanti was no mountebank, but in fashioning his persona he appropriated the identities of the ciarlatano, the worldly empiric, the learned doctor, and the country healer and reassembled them in books that had wide appeal. His deployment of the popular view of the body—the parallel between bodily corruption and moral and religious depravity, with the threat of heresy always drumming in the background—and the martial character of his remedies made the new way of healing alluring at a time when the world was polarized between Catholic and heretic, Christian and Turk.

Its eclecticism was a strength, too, for it appeared at a time when people felt that they had to take sides and when lay criticisms of official medicine were rife. The key elements of his practice were millennia old, but oriented to the readers of his time. Fashion is always modern. Fioravanti's new way of healing was an invention (or reinvention) that responded to 16th-century modernity.

Leonardo had a knack for anticipating his readers' tastes. Like all of his books, *The Mirror of Universal Science* belonged to the genre of "self-improvement literature," a body of writings that in the late Renaissance grew by astonishing proportions and included everything from sex handbooks to guidebooks for making polite conversation. Advice manuals not only offered practical instruction, they also gave readers examples of how to speak and act in public. "Today in the world of letters," noted a 17th-century observer, "there are so many handbooks . . . that anyone can quickly prepare himself for any occasion." *The Mirror* was a prominent addition to the genre. Widely read and imitated, it became a model for the most famous "professions" book of the Italian Renaissance, Tommaso Garzoni's massive *Piazza universale di tutte le professioni del mondo (The Universal Plaza of All the World's Professions).*

"A NEW WAY OF WRITING"

Renaissance books almost always carry multiple dedications, part of the culture of flattery that suffused the epoch. In one of the dozen dedicatory letters in Fioravanti's *Medical Caprices,* Dionigi Atanagi, in a fitting trope, imagined himself staying at home to read Fioravanti instead of going out to celebrate Carnival:

> This Carnival, when others go to see masks, balls, and parties, as they are wont to do in this season, I'm staying at home with *Medical Caprices* in my hands, reading it intently and to my great satisfaction: not only because it is a work by Your Excellency, whom I esteem with so much love, but much more, because of the excellent matters treated therein, and for the novel, quick, and safe way that you teach medicine and surgery.

Atanagi went on at some length in this vein, calling Fioravanti's book "a precious jewel" that embraced in a few pages "all that the immense volumes of Galen, Avicenna, and the other satraps of medicine could barely contain." Most of all, he praised Fioravanti's plain style of writing, which the surgeon accomplished "with so much ease and simplicity of words, without dressing itself with smooth talk and artful rhetoric, attending only to the pure expression of the matter at hand, because he wants to be understood by the common people."

In fact, Fioravanti did profess to have invented a "new way of writing, different from all other authors," in the same way that he had discovered a new way of healing that differed from the ordinary physicians' methods:

> Just as in the fish market they sell all kinds of fish—including expensive fish for rich people and less costly kinds for the poor—so that everyone can eat according to their rank and not go hungry, so it's necessary to have all sorts of writers. Some write for high and exalted minds, some for the middling sort, and some for those who don't understand very much at all. In this way there will be food for all. Therefore if my work is not for intellectuals and men of learning, nor even for those of middling quality, at least it will be for those who understand little. For they are the hungriest, and I want everyone to have some food for thought.

Books that were light, easy to read, instructive, and useful: These were the traits that Fioravanti prized.

His move to market-driven Venice was fortuitous. The lion city provided just the sort of environment that favored the bravura and showmanship that characterized his professional life. He became increasingly critical of orthodox medicine, proclaiming that the discipline had gained more from unlettered experience than from science, delighting Venetian popular culture. "The physician will study a pretty theory," he trumpeted, putting on the mask of Bertoldo. "He'll think he understands the causes of diseases and knows how to cure them, but when he encounters a difficult case, he won't have any idea how to proceed." His audience, whether in the "academy" or in his house in San Luca, is enthralled and eagerly awaits the punch line. "Then some experienced hag will come along, and with the rules of life and an enema will make the fever cease, or with some unction will make the pain go away, or with some fomentation will make the patient sleep. In so proceeding, the old hag will know more than the physician."

Vaunting empirical remedies, extolling common experience, and ridiculing the learned physicians were precisely the kinds of strategies that made Fioravanti's books—and those of his fellow poligrafi—appeal to the information-hungry new Venetians of the 16th century.

21

VENICE'S SCIENTIFIC UNDERWORLD

Leonardo's Venetian circle was both literary and scientific. His companions, including pharmacists, surgeons, distillers, alchemists, and craftsmen, made up a band of experimenters who followed the path laid out by Alessio Piemontese, the mythical professor of secrets. His circle included alchemists such as Jacomo Torellis, who had emigrated to Venice from Puglia, a region famous for making aqua vitae. A talented distiller, Torellis worked in Sabbà di Franceschi's Bear Pharmacy and was, according to Fioravanti, "one of the most expert practitioners of the art." He knew alchemists such as Decio Bellobuono, who operated a distillery in the Campo dei Frari, and Giovandomenico di Fabii, "a man of great doctrine and wisdom in the arts of natural philosophy and distillation," who invented a distilled water to nourish a tree whose leaves, when eaten daily, restored health and vigor. Leonardo knew potters, instrument makers, lens grinders, pharmacists, and glassblowers—men such as Guido Trasuntino, an organ maker and accomplished alchemist who had a rare secret for whitening silver, and the Murano glassmaker Nicolo dall'Aquila, who crafted distillation apparatus for the Venetian alchemists.

These men—workers and craftsmen, mainly—had an intimate knowledge of materials, because they worked and experimented with them every day. Jacomo Torellis was said to understand the properties of more than 2,000 plant, mineral, and animal substances. Such an impressive body of knowledge could have been gained only by close-up empirical observation. Passionately devoted to experiments, Leonardo and his companions belonged to a thriving underworld of science. In one way or another, all were professors of secrets, like Alessio Piemontese.

ALESSIO UNMASKED

As it turned out, the real Alessio had been in their midst all along. Girolamo Ruscelli, in a work published posthumously in 1567, revealed himself to be the author of Alessio's famed collection of arcana, *The Secrets of Alessio Piemontese.* In *Secreti nuovi (New Secrets),* Ruscelli disclosed that the more than 1,500 secrets revealed in those two volumes had been proven in the Academy of Secrets he founded in Naples back in the 1540s. The elaborately crafted preface to *The Secrets of Alessio Piemontese* had portrayed Alessio as a monkish and untiring seeker of secrets, but that was nothing more than fiction—a kind of joke on the learned establishment. The poligrafi were continually making up such inside jokes among themselves in an ongoing game of literary one-upmanship.

Girolamo Ruscelli was one of Leonardo's closest companions, and it's likely that Leonardo was in on his joke. They met often in each other's homes or at the Bear Pharmacy to do experiments. They distilled medicinal waters, made cosmetics, and experimented with explosives. They speculated about designs for fortresses and contrived military inventions.

Ruscelli described Leonardo's military inventions in his 1568 book, *Precetti della militia moderna (Rules for the Modern Militia).* In it Girolamo revealed that the surgeon had once showed him an ingenious life jacket that he had invented. It was made of leather stitched up to form a balloon, which could be filled with air and strapped on the chest to buoy the user above water. Another time, Leonardo showed Ruscelli an instrument with multiple guns that, when thrown aboard a ship being assaulted, would "cause unimaginable damage."

Girolamo was a valuable friend to have. A well-connected author whose social network included most of the major writers living in Venice (as well as many of its artists, publishers, and men of public affairs), he was a spirited defender of the "new way of healing" and an enthusiastic promoter of Fioravanti's books.

Although Leonardo had enemies—especially among the regular doctors—he had many Venetian friends as well. A spirit of joie de vivre prevailed among his circle of acquaintances. Whether gathering for conversation in Leonardo's rooms in San Luca or doing experiments in their "academy," Leonardo and his friends delighted in experimenting—and in debating topics such as the virtues of theriac, the cause of the French pox, the nature of occult qualities, and news of discoveries in America. Yet behind that blithe facade lay a grave seriousness of purpose: They genuinely believed they were conducting a quest for the unknown arcana of nature—and that they were about to discover secrets of vital importance for humanity.

Sixteenth-century Venice was a compact city. The entire town could be traversed on foot within minutes. Its streets bustled with men and women investigating the natural world or doing experiments to tease out some secret of nature or another. The city buzzed with the sounds of artisans in their workshops, merchants making deals, fishmongers and fruit vendors hawking their wares, and charlatans haranguing passersby. Neighborhoods spilled into neighborhoods, facilitating the easy exchange of information. Gossip was rampant.

Such informal channels of communication were essential for nurturing Renaissance experimentation, because much of what experimenters were doing in their laboratories depended on familiarity with various crafts. Surgeons, said Fioravanti, had to know about woodcarving (to make splints and crutches), blacksmithing (to make surgical tools), perfuming (to make unguents), and alchemy (to distill drugs).

Venice overflowed with shops. A walk along the busy Merceria, for example, would have taken Leonardo past the stalls of metalworkers, tailors, clockmakers, jewelers, milliners, and perfumers. In any one of them, he could have paused to watch craftsmen work and ask questions about how they plied their trades.

Experience, wrote Leonardo, using a trope repeated by countless other professors of secrets, "is the mother of all knowledge." He promised readers that in his books (unlike those of the ancients), "you will not find a single thing that has not been proved by experience, nor any experiment that is not accompanied by sound reason." The "science of experience" is accomplished only by years of travel and observation, he said: You must talk to empirics and farmers, observe animals, and visit craftsmen in their workshops to find out how things are done. In other words, "You have to have a white beard to really understand things."

THE PULL OF PUBLIC SECRETS

A proper professor of secrets always published his secrets. That paradox was a consequence of the discovery that publishing secrets could be a more effective way to earn fame than withholding them. The mythical Alessio Piemontese worried that "if the secrets be known by every man, they should no more be called secrets, but public and common"; his fame as a collector of secrets would thereby be diminished. The real Alessio, popular writer Girolamo Ruscelli, knew otherwise. Tommaso Garzoni, who first styled the professors of secrets, asserted that "professing" secrets meant publishing them. The ones that Fioravanti and his Venetian companions had discovered were revealed in his book *Compendio de i secreti rationali (Compendium of Rational Secrets),* which came out in 1564. With a dozen 16th- and 17th-century editions, it became one of his most popular books. Along with *Medical Caprices,* it placed him among the foremost professors of secrets of the day.

In his preface to the work, Leonardo observed that many books of secrets had come out lately, written by both men and women:

> There are many good and true things in them. But they are written in such a way that, even though people can read them, they still aren't satisfied with them because they are written with such brevity and without any explanation that they aren't very useful to anyone. . . . And so I've taken from many books that talk about secrets and made a compendium of all the ones that can be proven with reason and experiments.

But his book of secrets differed from the others, wrote Leonardo; it was a compendium of *rational* secrets, judiciously selected and confirmed by experiment. "In this book I'll write about all kinds of operations concerning the arts, along with their causes, and occult secrets as well, in a manner that anyone can understand."

The plain language he uses to convey complex technological processes, crafted for an audience of nonspecialists, permeates the book. Leonardo describes a *forno di riverbero* (a type of alchemical furnace) as "like an oven for making bread." Reading the *Compendium,* you can almost hear the clang of metal vessels and the tinkle of glass flasks in the alchemical laboratory.

Alchemy takes up a large section of Leonardo's book. He defines alchemy as the art of transmutation—"that is, transmuting one thing into another." By that he meant imitating how things are made in the workshop, as, for example, when the dyer makes a fast dye for wool. Such matters were open "secrets" to the craftsmen who had long practiced them, but to most Renaissance middle-class readers they were entirely new. Alchemy symbolized what experimentation could accomplish. Leonardo praised alchemy as a "divine art" but warned of the danger of using the wrong kind of alchemy. In a chapter on coloring metals gold, he carefully disassociated himself from the goldmaking kind of alchemy:

> I'm not saying that you can literally make gold and silver. I write to demonstrate the force and nobility of the art of alchemy, which I've always practiced—except for two things, which I've never searched for nor ever tried to do, nor ever want to do, and they are these: making gold and silver. So don't be surprised if I don't write about any of those things. Instead I'm going to write about a multitude of recipes to produce marvelous effects.

The *Compendium of Rational Secrets* is a rich compilation of artisanal techniques and lore. It's also completely down-to-earth and devoid of any concern with using alchemy to reach a higher reality or purpose. Leonardo's preoccupation with producing "marvelous" things—a fundamentally courtly aim—gives the book its distinctively Renaissance feel: pragmatic yet hopelessly engulfed in wonders. In that sense, his aims were consistent with those of natural magic. Both were concerned with finding ways to increase mankind's bounty by means of the secrets of nature.

Utility ruled in the *Compendium of Rational Secrets*. Through long experience in the arts, Leonardo had acquired an intimate familiarity with the pharmaceutical, metallurgical, and alchemical procedures that are so conspicuous in the work, and developed an uncanny ability to explain complex techniques in language that was concrete and tied to the familiar. Here, for example, is his recipe for making copper that resembles gold—which, in turn, can be used to fashion cheap jewelry and other objects:

> If you want to make copper the color of gold for fashioning various things, do this: Take chunks of rosette copper *(rame peloso)* that haven't ever been worked and break them up into tiny pieces; then put enough of them into a crucible to make it two-thirds full. Cover the copper with powdered calamine *(pietra gellamina)* and, over it, fill the crucible with ground glass. Put the crucible into the furnace and heat it until the mixture fuses together. Pour the metal into ingots and you'll have copper that looks just like gold.

Leonardo also revealed the secret of alloying silver and gold to soften it and make it more workable. He explained how to make metal for forging cannon; how to clean and renew brass; and how to manufacture artificial fireworks for celebrations and military offensives, including an "infernal fire" that produces "the most diabolical fire ever imagined."

Anyone interested in painting could use the *Compendium* to learn how artists make their pigments and how to mix up writing ink. Fioravanti included an entire section on beauty—not a treatise on its fundamental nature but a practical guide on how to formulate cosmetics that could beautify one's appearance. If your beard was turning gray, the *Compendium* taught you how to dye it; it also revealed how to remove unsightly spots from your face or dye your hair "Venetian blonde"—a nearly white color that "almost all the Venetian women use." He warned that some of the cosmetics in use are dangerous to the skin. "They often do the opposite of what they were intended to do, causing a lot of damage to the face." The *Compendium*, he assured readers, would teach which ones were safe.

Compendium readers encountered everything from how to distill perfumes and oils to sweeten the body to how to make glue and varnish to repair and restore furniture. Its author disclosed secrets for stocking the larder, too: instructions for grafting fruit trees and increasing the yield of the garden; tips on preserving fruits and vegetables throughout the year; and directions for making mustard, condiments, and various kinds of cheese. If 16th-century readers sought practical information—and they did—the *Compendium of Rational Secrets* was the most authoritative guidebook of its day.

MOLDING A UNIVERSAL METAL

Leonardo claimed that his companion and fellow professor of secrets Jacomo Torellis (the one who worked in the Bear Pharmacy) made the best antimony available anywhere in the world. Torelli's special knack was "preparing" the brittle, lustrous white metal—that is, reducing its ore, stibnite, to yield the "regulus of antimony," or metallic antimony.

That was no mean skill: Antimony was an important industrial material in early modern Venice. Imported from Germany in the form of stibnite cakes, antimony had a wide variety of applications. It was used by bell founders to improve the sound of bells, in the glassmaking industry to make mirrors and colored glass, by metallurgists to separate gold from silver, by type founders to make type metal, and in the cosmetic industry to make skin whiteners. Colormakers used antimony to compose a vibrant yellow pigment, while potters relied on it to glaze ceramics.

Antimony also figured prominently in the alchemical debates of the period because it could be employed to make a powerful purgative. Indeed, it was one of the most controversial chemical drugs of the Renaissance, an era when the practice of using alchemically prepared medicines polarized the medical community. On one side were the Galenists, who believed that diseases were caused by humoral imbalances and should be cured by drugs of contrary qualities. On the other side were the followers of the Swiss medical reformer Paracelsus, who argued that diseases were caused by toxins and had to be attacked and driven out by powerful agents. The debate over antimony reached a fever pitch in the 1560s in France during the so-called antimony war between the medical faculty at Montpellier, which favored chemical drugs, and Paris, which remained vehemently opposed to their use.

Professors of secrets such as Jacomo Torellis and Leonardo Fioravanti prosecuted their search for the secrets of nature fully conscious of the moral weight that attended their passion. Being a professor of secrets carried two responsibilities:

First, one had to be committed to a life of experimenting "with heart yearning more for that than for one's daily necessities," as Tommaso Garzoni put it.

Second, one was obliged to publish secrets so that others could benefit from them. That was the moral of the story of the apocryphal Alessio Piemontese, which Girolamo Ruscelli had recounted with such eloquence and good humor.

Alessio's made-up life dramatized the difference between being a professor of secrets and a mere possessor of them. Whether making regulus of antimony, inventing new ways to desalinate seawater, or coming up with techniques to manufacture cheap jewelry, the professors of secrets made utility, next to personal fame, their main goal. Of course, the early modern experimenters could not have known they were "professors of secrets" until Garzoni named them so in his 1585 book, *The Universal Plaza of All the World's Professions*. But Garzoni drew his model from a thriving tradition. When he wrote his article about the professors of secrets *(professori di segreti)*, he was really describing the scientific underworld of Renaissance Venice.

22
MATHEMATICAL MAGIC

Before publishing his first book, *Medical Caprices,* Leonardo had to prove himself to his printer, Ludovico Avanzo. This he did by redacting an annotated edition of *Compendium of Surgery,* a popular surgical manual by Pietro and Ludovico Rostinio that was first published in 1557. It was exactly the sort of editing job that a printer would give to an aspiring poligrafo. Seizing the opportunity, Fioravanti thrust himself center stage, as if preparing his imagined audience for the books that would soon appear under his own name.

The *Compendium of Surgery* that came out in 1561, "augmented and supplemented" with a separate surgical tract by Fioravanti, reads like an extended advertisement for *Medical Caprices,* which would be published that same year. On practically every page he found an occasion to recommend one of his own remedies—and his forthcoming book. For a skin ulcer, for example, he advises, "You might use Leonardo's Artificial Balsam, which he writes about in his *Medical Caprices.* It is a secret of secrets and something very stupendous and rare." Rather than merely editing the Rostinio volume, in other words, Leonardo Fioravanti made the job another exercise in self-fashioning.

Fioravanti dedicated the book to his Sicilian disciple, Giuseppe Moletti. The young mathematician, who had immigrated to Venice in 1556, was working as a humble public teacher of mathematics, but Leonardo could tell he was a rising star. In 1570 Moletti became a private tutor in the court of the Duke of Mantua, and in 1577 he was appointed to the chair of mathematics at the University of Padua.

A respected author and teacher, Moletti was a frequent guest of the famous bibliophile Gian Vincenzo Pinelli, whose enormous library, comprising 8,500 printed books and hundreds of manuscripts, was probably the largest in Italy at the time. The philosophical circle that gathered at Pinelli's residence in Padua included many of the prominent scientific and literary personalities of the day. Ruscelli was a member; so, years later, was a young Padua mathematics professor by the name of Galileo Galilei. The Republic of Venice, with its philosophical academies, its flourishing mercantile economy, its Arsenale, and its famous university, provided fertile ground for the growth of Renaissance mathematics.

In the Renaissance, perhaps for the first time since Plato, people began to comprehend that reality is mathematical. Europeans had been measuring things for centuries: time with clocks; economic value with money and double-entry bookkeeping; space with compasses, maps, and the art of perspective. But the intuition that the basic structure of the universe is mathematical is fundamentally a Platonic idea, and in the Renaissance Plato's ideas enjoyed a spectacular revival. The leading cosmologists of the day—Copernicus, Kepler, and Galileo—were all, to one degree or another, Platonists. For the Medici dukes and the condottieri who seized power in Milan, Mantua, Ferrara, and Urbino, Plato's philosophy also came in handy to legitimize the political rule of these new Renaissance princes who had climbed to the top over the ruins of failed republics. The new princes identified with the Platonic ideal of the philosopher-prince, who rules "philosophically" but absolutely.

So what happened when Renaissance Platonism's passion for mathematics was combined with the taste for wonder and surprise that infused the courts? The answer: mathematical magic.

One of Fioravanti's Venetian companions was Ettore Ausonio, a little-known alchemist and mathematician from Milan. Leonardo fawned on Ausonio, describing him as "an exceedingly rare and learned man." The Milanese mathematician, he noted, was "known by the majority of the Christian princes" for the marvelous mirrors and lenses he had invented.

Born in Milan, Ausonio graduated from the University of Padua in 1543—the very year Copernicus published his revolutionary *On the Revolutions of the Heavenly Spheres,* which postulated a heliocentric universe. Ausonio applied for a chair in mathematics at the university but was turned down in favor of another candidate. He practiced medicine in Venice for a while and was briefly the Duchess of Savoy's mathematics tutor, but he seems to have made his living principally by giving private mathematics lessons.

Ausonio's obscurity is easy to understand. Although he was a prolific author, he published nothing. His entire oeuvre consists of works on mathematics, astrology, medicine, and alchemy, scattered throughout several dozen codices preserved in the Ambrosian Library in Milan and the Florentine National Library. The manuscripts reveal a man of tremendous intellectual ambition and wide-ranging interests, but also something of a dilettante. A cosmographer, astrologer, alchemist, optical physicist, and inventor of scientific instruments, Ettore Ausonio authored works on geography, astronomy, natural magic, geometry, mechanics, perspective, poetics, mineralogy, and medicine, to say nothing of astrolabes, mirrors, clocks, and musical instruments. He began dozens of projects with enthusiasm. He finished few.

"MARVELOUS AND GREAT THINGS APPEAR"

One work that Ausonio did complete—the only one that was ever published, and posthumously at that—was his *Theorica speculi concavi sphaerici (Theory of the Concave Spherical Mirror),* which appeared in 1602 in an edition edited by Bologna astronomer Giovanni Antonio Magini. Constituting a single folio sheet, the work set out a series of geometrical theorems pertaining to the concave spherical mirror and described how the instrument could be employed as a burning mirror, as a device to produce distorting effects, or to reflect heat, cold, or sound.

Fioravanti waxed enthusiastic about Ausonio's optical experiments. In *The Mirror of Universal Science,* he reported that Ausonio's inventions impressed onlookers with their ingenuity and their capacity to produce marvelous effects:

> In the illustrious city of Venice, I saw mirrors, miraculous in their operation, that were fabricated by the great philosopher and mathematician, Ettore Ausonio of Venice, inventor of the finest mathematical instruments that have ever been seen or heard of in the world. He has made concave mirrors of impressive size in which marvelous and great things appear, which I will not describe here, since by now all the princes of the world know about them. Besides mirrors, this extraordinary man has developed so many wonderful things pertaining to mathematics that it's a miracle. . . . This mirror of his, as I said, is so amazing that anyone who sees it is stupefied. I've seen him make so many things that produce strange and stupendous visions that even if I were to try to describe all the bizarre things that I saw it would be endless and by comparison to what he has done, nothing at all.

Catoptrics, the branch of optics dealing with the formation of images by mirrors, has a rich history that stretches back to Archimedes. During the Renaissance, it was one of the subjects that made up the immense field of natural magic, which was still considered a legitimate and promising scientific discipline in Fioravanti's day. Natural magic endeavored to harness nature's occult forces to produce "marvelous" effects, like the powerful burning mirror that Archimedes used to set fire to the Roman navy besieging Syracuse.

Such effects were "marvelous" in scientific terms because they did not occur naturally, but happened only with the intervention of a magician. Optical illusions created by mirrors and lenses were among the most impressive achievements of natural magic. Although mirrors and lenses were familiar artifacts of urban life, mirrors that produced wondrous visions were novel and rare. Anamorphosis—the art of projecting distorted or "monstrous" images that become visible only when viewed through a curved mirror—was decidedly avant-garde in the 16th century.

SIGNORE DELLA PORTA'S DUTY

After Ausonio's death around 1570, his manuscripts were purchased by Moletti's patron, the book-loving Pinelli. Among the visitors to Pinelli's famous academy in Padua was the Neapolitan magus Giambattista della Porta, who in 1580 was in Venice at the behest of his patron, Cardinal d'Este. Della Porta had come with orders to construct a parabolic mirror, a task complicated by the fact that no one knew how to fashion such a device.

During his Venice sojourn, della Porta met a Servite friar named Paolo Sarpi, who happened to be a member of Pinelli's circle. Sarpi, something of an amateur scientist himself, had a special interest in optics. One of his unpublished works was a compilation of notes and observations on rainbows, mirrors, and lenses that included Ausonio's manuscript of the *Theory of the Concave Spherical Mirror.* Fra Sarpi had included Ausonio's treatise because it intrigued him so. Elaborating on the work, the friar noted that the mirror could be used as a burning mirror, as a device to project "marvelous images," and as a military tool that enabled armies "to see things in enemies' camps."

Visiting Pinelli's library in Padua one day, della Porta chanced to read Ausonio's manuscript. Sarpi must have shown it to him because Ausonio had discovered an important secret about the concave spherical mirror: Its focal point was at the "fourth part of the diameter of the mirror," or half the radius of its curvature. Della Porta needed this key piece of information in order to direct a Murano glassmaker he had contracted to fashion Cardinal d'Este's parabolic mirror.

Fioravanti noted that "all of the princely courts of the world" were filled with the sorts of mirrors, lenses, and optical devices for which Ausonio was celebrated. As the 16th-century poet Torquato Tasso remarked, illusion was the substance of court culture, and it took myriad forms, from the court buffoon's sleight of hand to acrobatic entertainment to the passion for anamorphic art. No respectable prince would allow his curiosity cabinet to lack an assortment of distorting mirrors that shifted, warped, and animated forms in a playful display of deception.

The power of mirrors to create illusions was an optical allegory of the prince's power to bend and shape the world to his will. Cardinal d'Este would have expected his charge to bring him examples of the latest "marvelous" instruments coming out of Venice. Evidently, the magus della Porta did not disappoint him.

GALILEO SOLVES A LUNAR PUZZLE

In 1593, della Porta, by now world-famous for his monumental treatise on natural magic, returned to Venice to oversee the publication of an Italian translation of his *De humana physiognomonia (Human Physiognomy).* On a visit to Pinelli's residence in Padua, della Porta met Galileo, who at 28 had just been appointed to the chair of mathematics at the University of Padua.

Galileo, the physicist and cosmologist, was the harbinger of a new mathematical and mechanical understanding of nature that would soon supplant natural magic. At the time he was just beginning the experiments on motion that would lead, nearly 40 years later, to his new physics. But that would have been difficult to foresee in 1593, when the meeting between della Porta and Galileo took place.

Galileo's approach to science was entirely new. In his use of Archimedean mechanics—essentially the science of simple machines, such as the lever and balance—he provided a model for nature that was concrete, picturable, and familiar. Abandoning the pedantic style of scholastic commentators, who always wrote in Latin, Galileo chose to write in the vernacular and made his discoveries a literary event.

Not only did Galileo advance a new kind of science, he was also the first scientific celebrity. In some measure, his celebrity status led to his trial for the heresy of defending the Copernican worldview. The trial of Galileo illustrates the fundamental incompatibility between the church's overarching claim to be the arbiter of truth in matters of physics as well as faith and Galileo's more secular view of the world that proclaimed the independence of science from theology. As he wrote in a letter to the Grand Duchess Christina of Tuscany in 1615, "The intention of the Holy Ghost is to teach us how one goes to heaven, not how the heaven goes."

That day in 1593, Galileo was intrigued by Ausonio's treatise, in particular its revelation that the concave spherical mirror might be used to make distant objects appear close. He copied the manuscript in its entirety and carefully reproduced the diagram that accompanied Ausonio's discovery.

Years later, following the publication of his sensational *Starry Messenger* in 1610, Galileo returned to Ausonio's manuscript. It contained a clue that would solve a troubling anomaly in his theory of the lunar surface. The nature of the moon's surface was a theoretical touchstone in the debate about the new cosmologies. Galileo's observations with the telescope revealed the moon's surface to be jagged with mountains and pocked with craters. The rough and opaque lunar surface that Galileo saw through his telescope conflicted sharply with the crystalline, diaphanous moon of Aristotelian-Ptolemaic cosmology. But how was Galileo to reconcile his telescopic observations with what the naked eye revealed about the moon—a glowing orb, perfect against the night sky?

Returning to Ausonio's manuscript on the concave spherical mirror, Galileo used the principles of mirror anamorphosis—producing a distorted image that becomes visible only with a special mirror—to explain how the moon, though rough and uneven, could appear perfectly spherical from Earth. Ausonio's obscure manuscript turns out to have been a crucial piece of the puzzle in the victory of the new cosmology.

One of the works that Ausonio began with trademark zeal but abandoned with typical distraction was a treatise on *The New Astrology*, a textbook to teach "easily and quickly" the principles of ancient and Copernican astronomy. Ausonio seems to have written the work in imitation of Fioravanti's books on the "new way of healing." We'll never know the full extent of that parallel, however, for the work, like so many of his projects, ends in mid-sentence.

Yet Fioravanti positively adored Ausonio, describing him as "a great philosopher" and a physician "so expert in healing that [he] not only cures the sick but almost raises the dead from their sepulchers with his divine and precious liquors." To Fioravanti, Ausonio was the ideal philosopher of natural secrets. Unconcerned with fame or fortune, he selflessly devoted himself to the search for the most arcane secrets of nature. In Leonardo's eyes, Ausonio was pure and uncorrupted, like Alessio Piemontese.

23

THE SEARCH FOR THE PHILOSOPHER'S STONE

Besides being a wizard at making magical mirrors, Ettore Ausonio was an avid alchemist. As a follower of the alchemical doctrine of the mythical Ramon Lull, he wrote voluminously on the subject and struggled to develop a comprehensive cosmology based on alchemical theory. Ausonio came up with a sort of 16th-century Grand Unified Theory that strove to unite matter and all the forces of nature into a single universal whole.

No one doubted that the recondite alchemical doctrine attributed to the 13th-century philosopher and mystic Ramon Lull was genuine. Lull, a Franciscan friar from Majorca, was famous for having devised a system for acquiring universal knowledge that he claimed was infallible because it was based on the actual structure of reality. He used his complex "Art" in debates with Muslim clerics during a bizarre mission to convert the infidels of Tunis in 1293. The local sultan, having gotten wind of Lull's audacious act, ordered the friar expelled.

Emboldened, Lull returned to Africa in 1307, landing in the town of Bougie, or Béjaïa, in present-day northern Algeria. There Lull appeared in the central square and cried out, "The Christian religion is true, holy, and acceptable to God; but the Saracen religion is false, and this I'm prepared to prove." The town *mufdi* saved Lull from a mob threatening to stone him to death. Jailed and then expelled from the country, Lull nevertheless returned to Tunis in 1314. After that he disappears from history. Most scholars agree that he died in 1316 at the age of 84, either in Tunis or on a ship back to Majorca.

The first of the many alchemical works attributed to the Majorcan friar appeared in 1332. By the end of the century, a full-blown legend about Lull the alchemist had taken shape. According to Ausonio's version of the myth, Lull learned the art of alchemy from Arnald of Villanova, a native of Valencia and one of the most famous physicians of his age. In reality, like so much of the medieval alchemical corpus, the alchemical writings ascribed to Lull—more than a hundred books in all—were forged, as were those attributed to Arnald.

Fioravanti probably encountered Lull's works for the first time in Naples, a thriving center of Lullist alchemy, but it was Ausonio who awakened him to the search for the philosopher's stone.

Lull's doctrine was the alchemical expression of the age-old dream of prolonging human life. The theory had first been elaborated by the 14th-century Franciscan friar John of Rupescissa. Born around 1310 near Aurillac in southern France, Friar John was also a prophet who had visions that came to him recurrently in dreams. The visions convinced him that the end of the world was at hand—and that an army of "evangelical men" would be needed to combat the forces of the Antichrist. John believed these spiritual soldiers could be fortified in their battle by a "heavenly" medicine, or alchemical quintessence, that would give them the strength necessary to withstand apocalyptic tribulations.

In elaborating his theory of the quintessence, Friar John reasoned that none of the four elements can serve the purpose of preserving the body because they are themselves subject to decay. Therefore, one must seek something that bears the same relation to the four bodily humors as the heavens bear to the four elements. This "fifth element," or quintessence (so called after the fifth element of which the heavens are composed) turned out to be the spirit of wine—that is, alcohol produced through multiple distillations of wine. The medicine reputedly had the miraculous faculty of preserving matter from corruption and curing diseases characterized by corruption of the whole body, such as plague. John's *Consideration of the Quintessence,* written a few years after the Black Death, gave rise to a radical new pharmacology based on the idea that distillation could perfect the medicinal virtues of any drug.

Arnald of Villanova, a follower of John of Rupescissa, was an accomplished distiller. However, according to the legend of Lull the alchemist, Arnald lacked a theoretical understanding of the art. This Lull provided with his theory of the elixir—the elusive universal remedy that was the centerpiece of his doctrine. In traditional alchemy, the elixir, or philosopher's stone, was the agent of metallic transmutation, thought capable of converting any base metal into gold, the most perfect of metals. Extended to the field of medicine, the elixir was the agent that could perfect the corruptible part of matter and transform the body into perfect health. It was manufactured by distillation, the art of separating the pure from the impure, the perfect from the imperfect.

Auschwitz survivor Primo Levi, an industrial chemist as well as an author, said that distillation is a "philosophic" art. In his memoir, *The Periodic Table,* Levi wrote that "Distilling is beautiful" because it gives you time to think about other things while contemplating the changes taking place in your apparatus:

> [I]t involves a metamorphosis from liquid to vapor (invisible), and from this once again to liquid; but in this double journey, up and down, purity is attained, an ambiguous and fascinating condition, which starts with chemistry and goes very far. . . . [W]hen you set about distilling, you acquire the consciousness of repeating a ritual consecrated by the centuries, almost a religious act, in which from imperfect material you obtain the essence, the *usia,* the spirit, and in the first place alcohol, which gladdens the spirit and warms the heart.

That is what distilling was for Ettore Ausonio as well: a slow, silent, philosophic art that penetrated nature's deepest secrets. Watching his alembic drip, drip, dripping its essence in a process that took days and nights, Ausonio reflected on the cosmic meaning of the separation of purity from impurity. In the prolonged ritual of that alchemical process, the metamorphosis of the human soul could be traced, reproduced, and comprehended.

LA PIETRA FILOSOFALE

Lull's doctrine of the elixir was an epiphany to Fioravanti. Its dramatic opposition of purity and corruption provided the cosmological view of sickness and health he had been seeking, while its emphasis on "philosophical purgation" seemed to validate the rules of life he had learned from the old men of the south.

Shifting his interests from practical alchemy to an attempt to comprehend the complex theory underlying the art, Leonardo became a disciple not only of Ausonio but (as he believed) of the Majorcan philosopher Ramon Lull. If until this point he had regarded distillation as merely a practical tool to make new drugs, now he saw it as the track that would lead to the discovery of the philosopher's stone.

The question that underlay Fioravanti's new way of healing was one for which everyone wanted an answer: Is it possible to find a single remedy to cure all diseases? Since Fioravanti's success depended upon his panaceas, it's not surprising that he answered the question in the affirmative. All diseases arise from a single cause, he explained: the indisposition of the stomach. Therefore, he concluded, all diseases can be cured by driving out the bad humors that corrupt the stomach. Medicines made with his philosopher's stone *(pietra filosofale)*, he claimed, had the ability to attract bodily corruptions and expel them. A powerful emetic distilled from Roman vitriol, mercury, and other substances, the philosopher's stone was a key ingredient of many of his drugs. Like the alchemical stone, it was the catalyst that transformed an inert herbal mixture into a potent drug.

Leonardo was not claiming that he had discovered *the* philosopher's stone—the one sought by alchemical philosophers since antiquity. Rather, his was a trade name that he had invented by analogy with alchemy. Fioravanti had made an important discovery, alright, but it had little to do with the esoteric mysteries of alchemy.

What he had stumbled across was, however, just as valuable: the use of brand names that captured the mood of the times.

Still, Leonardo's theory of the origin of disease had radical implications. It amounted to the claim that the doctrine of the four humors was the Great Lie of the physicians. The humoral theory enabled the physicians to sustain the orthodox view that proper treatment must be based on an understanding of the subtle physiological differences among patients—the kind of theoretical understanding, that is, that would be available only to academically trained doctors. But if all illnesses stemmed from a single cause, then all could be cured by a single medicine, regardless of the patient's individual humoral complexion. This newer theory perfectly matched the marketplace's demand for fast, cheap cures.

Fioravanti was not necessarily insincere in espousing alchemical cures. He fervently believed not only in making drugs alchemically, but also in the possibility of using alchemy to transform sickness into health, just as it was possible to transmute base metals into silver and gold. "The art of alchemy can be done similarly on human bodies," he wrote, "with the intention of transmuting one complexion into another, and of fortifying and invigorating nature."

Fioravanti's "alchemy of the human body" was based on an analogy with the process for transmuting metals, following the six alchemical stages of preparation, calcination, solution, congelation, fixation, and projection. Each step required the use of one or more of Fioravanti's drugs to complete the process. Thus in the first stage, *preparatione,* the body is prepared to be transmuted "from a bad complexion into one of good temperament" by the use of Leonardo's soothing syrups. In the second stage, *calcinatione,* the body is desiccated of superfluous humidity with sudorific, or sweat-inducing, drugs. Then, because desiccation leaves the blood "almost frozen in the veins," the *solutione* stage applies various electuaries, or medicinal lozenges such as theriac or Artificial Balsam, to dissolve the blood and prepare it for *congelatione.* In this fourth stage of human alchemy, rich food, confections, and Quintessence are prescribed to retain the humors that have been purified. This readies the body for the *fissatione* stage, using Fioravanti's oil-of-vitriol composition, which ensures that the process will remain fixed and "not go up in smoke." Now the body is ready for the final stage, *proiettione,* which projects the qualities of gold, silver, mercury, tin, copper, or lead onto the body, depending on the type of disease being treated.

There is no evidence that Fioravanti ever administered this fantastic alchemical regimen to any of his patients. Indeed, it is one of the few procedures whose effectiveness he did not document. Leonardo's "alchemy of the human body" therefore seems to have been employed mainly as a kind of metaphor signifying a series of successive therapeutic stages. Or perhaps it was only a theory, invented to legitimize his methods by imbedding them in a fashionable and complex scientific doctrine.

Whether real, theoretical, or metaphorical, such "caprices" were precisely the sort of novel techniques by which Leonardo aligned himself with the new, and modish, alchemical medicine.

24

A STAR IS BORN

Leonardo's meteoric rise in the cultural world of Venice was unusual. Within a little over a year, he had become a favorite of the literati; by the end of his first decade in the city, he was the center of an alternative medical movement—his much vaunted "new way of healing." From all over Italy, people wrote asking for cures and lavishing praise on his miraculous healing powers. Why were refined poligrafi attracted to this seemingly uncultivated empiric? And how are we to account for his appeal among ordinary and cultivated Venetians alike?

For one thing, Fioravanti simply charmed them. Contemporaries describe him as a socialite who entertained guests at his house in San Luca with "great flattery and courtesy." More important, the poligrafi regarded him as the quintessential philosopher of natural secrets. Plain-spoken, irreverent, and vulgar when it served him, yet savvy, experienced, and shrewd, he was like the folk hero Bertoldo—in fact, he was a model for Croce's famous character.

Part of Leonardo's charm derived from his "picaresque" character. Indeed, to the poligrafi he must have seemed like a real-life *pícaro*—a literary type celebrated in Spanish novels such as *La vida de Lazarillo de Tormes (The Life of Lazarillo de Tormes),* the original (and widely imitated) picaresque novel published in the 1550s.

Italy had its own literature of roguery (the so-called *letteratura furfantesca*), which was hugely popular among the literati. Romantic legends about beggars—ever present in daily life—made them out as clever tricksters and free-spirited vagabonds, tied to no city. Choosing their home in any nation they liked, they seemed to be true citizens of the world. As historian Fernand Braudel wrote, "Italy was completely overrun with delinquents, vagabonds and beggars, all characters destined for literary fame."

One can only imagine the stories Leonardo must have told his Venetian companions about his adventures: He teemed with tales about showing up the learned doctors—such as his public rebuke in Rome of famous anatomist Realdo Colombo for his ignorance of surgery—and performing daring surgical interventions, such as his extraction of the swollen spleen from the beautiful Marulla Greco. No doubt he also regaled his listeners with war stories and accounts of marvelous folk cures he'd witnessed, such as the time an old Spanish woman in Naples used a strange herb to cure a gentleman of the clap when all the doctors had given up on him. He may even have told them about the time an old woman fooled him by passing off some Tribiano wine as her urine sample.

Fioravanti's medical doctrine was also fashionable because he presented it as a return to a pristine golden age when humans were close to nature. His therapeutic system stemmed from the natural way of healing, he claimed, a method discovered by the earliest physicians. To the poligrafi he was a champion of experience who demonstrated the value of sagacity and good judgment as opposed to the empty doctrines of the authorities. They saw in his medical system an approach similar to their own in literature and ethics. Just like Leonardo, they railed against hypocrisy and extolled a life of simple virtue.

Leonardo's rejection of Galenic therapeutics in favor of more aggressive tactics won the sympathy of the poligrafi for esthetic reasons, too. He always said that his cures were done with *prestezza*—that is, so quickly and so effortlessly they seemed natural. Prestezza, denoting spontaneity and rapidity of execution, became a hallmark of 16th-century Venetian painting. Jacopo Robusti, known as Tintoretto, was the acknowledged master of prestezza in painting. His uncommon success stemmed largely from his strategy of tackling several commissions at once—and painting each one quickly. His ability to complete large, complex paintings in a matter of weeks rather than months or years was legendary. For Tintoretto, prestezza was not merely an esthetic trait; it was an economic strategy and the secret of his artistic freedom.

Critics attacked Tintoretto's unorthodox methods, saying his paintings were carelessly executed or that he painted solely for money. But the poligrafi loved his work. Why? Because they were driven by the same market forces as he was. They recognized in Tintoretto's paintings three goals they aimed for in their own compositions: spontaneity, improvisation, and versatility, which they insisted demonstrated an artist's virtuosity and distinguished his art (and indeed *all* art) from mere mechanical work. Artistic productions that displayed prestezza were truer than those weighted down by erudition, they believed. In elevating prestezza to an aesthetic ideal, the poligrafi promoted an artistic identity that contrasted with the courtly model represented by writers such as Castiglione, Vasari, and Aretino.

For these reasons, the prestezza of the new way of healing resonated with Venetian literary and artistic tastes. The seemingly miraculous prestezza of Leonardo's cures and the equally miraculous ease with which they could be learned were the two traits of Fioravanti's medical system that contemporary writers most often extolled. Dionigi Atanagi thought that his remedies—"so quick, easy, and certain"—bore no relation to those of ordinary empirics; instead, in his eyes, they were the inventions of a "most rational professor of the art." And Girolamo Ruscelli, for his part, proclaimed Fioravanti's Artificial Balsam a treatment that cured gunshot wounds "with extraordinary quickness" *(con grandissima prestezza).*

IT'S UNDERSTOOD

Charismatic as Leonardo may have been, that wasn't all that beguiled the Venetians. He had "It."

What is It? In the words of cultural historian Joseph Roach, It is "a certain quality, easy to perceive but hard to define, possessed by abnormally interesting people." We usually think of It as a quality possessed by performers and modern celebrities. Some actors and a few artists have It. Andy Warhol had It; Norman Rockwell did not—but then, he didn't need It.

In Fioravanti's day, certain courtiers and princes had It. The Venetian courtesan Veronica Franco certainly did. She was Venice's most famous "honest courtesan" *(cortigiana onesta)*—the kind of high-class prostitute who, in the words of historian Margaret Rosenthal, "satisfied her society's need for a refined, sexualized version of the aristocratic woman," as opposed to the common prostitute *(cortigiana di lume),* who satisfied her society's need for sex.

Well-educated and a gifted conversationalist, Franco was also a celebrated writer who penned erotic verses, sonnets, and "familiar letters" to prominent literary figures. Famous for her beauty, wit, and sexual prowess, she was the most renowned courtesan of the Renaissance. Tintoretto did her portrait. Franco even had a tryst with the young Henri III of Valois, who visited Venice in the summer of 1574 on his way to Paris to claim his crown as King of France.

Yet as a result of her celebrity, Franco was vulnerable to rivals and adversaries who resented her social stature and political influence. In 1580, she was summoned before the Inquisition to respond to anonymous charges of having performed heretical incantations in her house. Although Franco was exonerated of the charges, her reputation suffered irreparable damage. Impoverished by the plague years of 1575–77, she was living at age 36 in the neighborhood of the Church of San Samuele, a section of Venice that was home to countless destitute prostitutes. Her death at 45 ended a life of glamour and wealth that was perilously balanced against the threat of danger and loss. She personified the contradictory elements that Joseph Roach describes as essential to having It:

> "It" is the power of apparently effortless embodiment of contradictory qualities simultaneously: strength *and* vulnerability, innocence *and* experience, and singularity *and* typicality among them. The possessor of It keeps a precarious balance

between such mutually exclusive alternatives, suspended at the tipping point like a tightrope dancer on one foot; and the empathetic tension of waiting for the apparently inevitable fall makes for breathless spectatorship.

So it was with Leonardo Fioravanti. He projected in his writings a fragile equipoise between roguery and puritanical morality, between the innocent provincial surgeon and the experienced, world-wise empiric, between the insider and the outsider. He touted a scientific methodology that he labeled "the theory of experience," an unstable balancing of long-contested domains. And he promoted himself as the discoverer of a "new way of medicine"—which, in reality, was the most ancient medicine of all, having been invented by the "first physicians" of old.

A STELLAR SURGEON

Unlike Veronica Franco, Leonardo was not a frequent guest in the houses of highbrow Venetian patrons. But then, he didn't have to be. The rise of print culture enabled him to become, in effect, Europe's first medical celebrity and the largely self-invented focus of an alternative medical movement. Four centuries before an obscure South African surgeon by the name of Christiaan Barnard became a household name by performing the first human heart transplant, Leonardo Fioravanti emerged as a Renaissance medical celebrity with books such as *Medical Caprices,* which introduced his "new way of healing" to an admiring public, and *The Mirror of Universal Science,* which entertained middle-class Italians and educated newly arrived Venetians in how to become a citizen of the city. The printed book spread his renown. Students and faculty at the medical school in Padua debated his doctrines, while pharmacists as far away as London sold his drugs.

Historian Daniel Boorstin famously defined a celebrity as "a person who is known for his well-knownness." Whatever their true accomplishments, modern celebrities are, in effect, media creations, more often than not the product of what Boorstin called "pseudo-events"—events such as press conferences and photo ops, which exist purely for the purpose of being reported. Fashioning an image is all-important, and in the modern context it is largely the product of press agents and other cultural mediators.

Can the same be said of celebrity creation in the 16th century? In other words, did Leonardo, too, have his "handlers"?

Regrettably, we may never know the answers to those questions. The archival record does not unveil the mechanisms by which Leonardo constructed his celebrity status. We do know enough, however, to make some reasonable conjectures.

Clever as Leonardo was, it doesn't seem possible that he catapulted himself to prominence on his own. A foreigner, he knew little about the city. The media culture then developing around the printing press was unfamiliar to him. Arriving in Venice in December 1558, he was anonymous and alone—that is, until his chance encounter with the wounded poet Atanagi. Without help from printers and popular writers, Leonardo might never have become the celebrity he so quickly did.

His companion, the humanist and popular writer Ruscelli, was instrumental to Leonardo's self-fashioning as a celebrity. Ruscelli was as close to being a patron as Fioravanti ever had in Venice. Ruscelli knew all the major writers in Venice and enjoyed close connections with the printing industry, partly because he belonged to the fashionable Accademia Venetiana—or, as it was better known, the Accademia della Fama (Fame).

Founded in 1557 by Venetian patrician Federigo Badoer, this exclusive society met every day for discussions in the vestibule of the new Marciana Library. At its height, the Fama numbered about a hundred members and included prominent philosophers, musicians, artists, and writers. Its secretary, Bernardo Tasso, was paid the phenomenal salary of 200 ducats a year—one reason why, perhaps, the academy went bankrupt within just a few years.

In 1561, already thousands of ducats in debt, the society was suppressed by the government and Badoer was imprisoned. Despite the scandal, the Fama had opened doors for many aspiring artists

This portrait of Fioravanti by the celebrated Venetian illustrator Niccolò Nelli is dated 1566 but was not published until 1582, when it appeared in the Sessa edition of Fioravanti's Tesoro della vita humana.

and intellectuals. If you were a writer or artist of note in Venice, you could expect to be a member of the Fama.

Another member of the Fama was Leonardo's former pupil, Giuseppe Moletti, who had likewise carved out a place in Venetian cultural circles. Moletti knew Leonardo from the old days in Sicily, when the surgeon accomplished wonders with the knife and startled the doctors with his blunt and outspoken manner. A close friend of the prominent patrician Nicolò Zen, Moletti would have been an important connection for Leonardo.

With the help of printers and friends among the poligrafo community, Leonardo crafted an image of himself as a pícaro—a world-wise empiric whose distrust of the doctors made him appeal to readers who were themselves skeptical about mainstream medicine. A correspondent from Pieve, in northern Italy, having failed to find a cure from a local doctor, wrote to Leonardo: "To me you are someone divine *(un'huomo divino),* for I have never before seen remedies that cure like yours." Another patient rhapsodized that Leonardo was "like Apollo, or even Prince Hippocrates." Even physicians reported being prepared, in the words of a doctor in Istria, to "throw all the books in my study into the fire" after learning his methods.

THE IMAGE MASTER

Becoming a celebrity depends on crafting a public image, and in this regard Fioravanti was a genius. He used the prefaces and dedications to his books (multiple dedications for every book) not so much to gain patronage as to associate himself with princes, patricians, and leading cultural figures—and to hone his public image as a crafty and potent healer. Spectacular episodes of conflict—such as the alleged "conspiracy" that drove him from Rome and the one that would soon cause him trouble in Venice—lent an aura of sensationalism to his life story.

Sociologist Chris Rojek, in his book *Celebrity,* brands this type of public career massage "staged celebrity"—in other words, "calculated technologies and strategies of performance and self projection designed to achieve a status of monumentality in public culture." Even in the 16th century, Fioravanti understood the value of the media in shaping public opinion. By exploiting the possibilities of early modern printing, he fashioned a persona as a celebrity healer.

When Leonardo decided to have his portrait done for display in his books, he commissioned prominent Venetian engraver Niccolò Nelli to do the work. Nelli, who specialized in book illustration, had drawn portraits of Ruscelli, Atanagi, and other popular writers. Nelli's portrait captures Leonardo as a rugged, battle-scarred empiricist. Clad in a plain artisan's blouse and coat, he wears a full beard and close-cropped hair. His penetrating gaze, sharpened by experience, looks the viewer straight in the eye.

By choosing to focus on his subject's eyes—wily, active, and alert—the artist conveys the idea that true knowledge is gained from observation, for the eyes symbolize sensory (that is to say, empirical) knowledge. That's why Federico Cesi, an idealistic young Roman nobleman, chose the sharp-eyed lynx as the emblem for his Accademia dei Lincei (Academy of Lynxes), the experimental academy he founded in Rome in 1603. The lynx symbolized the academy's purpose: to investigate nature *cum propris oculis* (with one's own eyes), rejecting reliance on the authority of the ancients.

One of the paradoxes of being a celebrity professor of secrets, as "Alessio Piemontese" famously noted, is that the mechanisms of celebrity—revelation and publicity—are the very ones that rob secrets of the aura of their mystery. A secret intrigues only when it's unknown, yet the professor of secrets found fame only by revealing his.

The same holds true when it comes to Leonardo's professed disdain for the physicians: Even as he voiced contempt for orthodox medicine, he was powerless to resist his fascination with—and longing to join—the establishment he so vigorously condemned.

In the final analysis, he mistook celebrity for fame. By contrast with celebrity, fame implies a reputation that transcends its immediate cultural context. Fame is linked with posterity, whereas celebrity is bound to a specific culture and time. Celebrity is therefore more likely to be superficial and capricious.

Leonardo Fioravanti strove for everlasting fame. What he got instead was a brief shining moment of celebrity.

25

THE MEDICAL ENTREPRENEUR

Renaissance Venice was a school for entrepreneurialism. The city's industries, traditionally tightly controlled by guilds, were being cracked open by adventurous entrepreneurs willing to risk their capital. Technological innovations made investment in industry highly profitable, attracting large numbers of foreigners with the promise of easy profits. So many newcomers became involved in wool and silk manufacturing that in 1558 the Senate, fearing the textile industries would be taken over by outsiders, decreed that only "original citizens" could trade in woolen and silk fabrics. Native Venetians were just as ambitious; they exuded the self-confidence and daring that have been hailed as quintessentially Renaissance traits ever since Burckhardt's classic *Civilization of the Renaissance in Italy.*

No Italian, perhaps, had a stronger sense of self than Leonardo Fioravanti. He arrived in Venice licking the wounds inflicted on him by the physicians' "cabal" that drove him from Rome. A foreigner in a strange city, he had no contacts and no friends. Yet within a few years he had developed a successful medical practice, which he ran out of the Bear and Phoenix Pharmacies, and he was a celebrated author, a favorite of the Venetian literati.

Entrepreneurialism was not new to Venice, but Fioravanti emblematized a new kind of capitalist. He was a businessman of the medical stripe, inventing new ways of selling remedies and exploiting the metaphors of sickness and health to create novel commercial ventures.

THE DAWN OF MAIL-ORDER MARKETING

Typical of Leonardo's innovative methods for expanding his influence was the mail-order medical business he launched while living in Rome. The Portuguese ambassador first suggested the idea:

> The ambassador couldn't get enough of seeing me work my cures, and with his help, every day I medicated diverse sick people various in cities of the world without even seeing them. It was enough that they wrote to me describing the nature of their illness; nothing more. I would send them advice along with the most important secret remedies pertaining to their cases. Thus in every city of Italy, and even outside Italy, I continued to medicate countless sick people, and they always turned out with happy successes.

The mail-order doctor: what a clever way of responding to the changing medical marketplace! Though medical consultation by mail would become commonplace by the 18th century, the notion and the practice were new in Leonardo's day. Indeed, he may have been the first to employ it over an extended period of time. He was looking for original and different ways to market his "new way of healing." The piazzas swarmed with itinerant healers competing with one another and with regular doctors. Charlatans in bright costumes pitched their wares and acted out comedies. Tooth pullers set up temporary shop in the squares and hung out banners advertising their services. Snake handlers on portable scaffolds waved serpents in the air like broadswords, and frightening people into buying their supposedly infallible antidotes. Herb women set up stalls and offered potions for whatever ailed you.

The brisk demand for medical services in early modern European cities—be it in Venice, London, or Seville—fanned competition among rival healers. To succeed, Fioravanti had to stay a jump ahead. His mail-order business was designed to appeal to a fresh audience: not ordinary urban dwellers strolling through the piazza, but literate professionals who might become buyers and readers of his books.

Among the myriad healers swarming the piazzas in Renaissance Italy, the snake handler (sanpaolaro) *was surely one of the strangest and most dramatic. This print, from a portfolio of drawings on the humble trades, depicts one performing in a Bologna piazza.*

The mail-order practice that Leonardo inaugurated in Rome thrived in Venice. Originally, the business may have been intended to enhance his income, but Leonardo quickly saw its potential to publicize the "new way of healing." Surely that was what spurred him to publish a selection of symptom letters in *The Treasury of Human Life* (1570). People wrote in from all over Italy (and some from Europe), inquiring about his remedies or testifying to their miraculous results (see page 224). Assuming the selection he published is representative of the entire correspondence, the mail-order business was most active from 1565 to 1568, a four-year period that coincides with the publication of three of Fioravanti's most popular books. Out of "a very great quantity of letters," Leonardo reports, he published "a few" as proof of his doctrine. With the letters before them, he explained, readers could learn from the experience of others and take heart, so that they might heal themselves:

> For those who read the letters will hear about wonderful cases that have been communicated to me by various persons and will understand the many sicknesses that have been cured with our remedies; so that with the help of these things people will themselves become experts, and many that suffer from various infirmities will make up their minds to go ahead and cure them with our medicaments, which are so easy to make and so profitable to use that it's something marvelous. Now, I don't want you just to believe me, but instead, credit the many testimonies that you'll find in the following letters. And if someone should be stricken by similar infirmities, in imitation of these others, he can have the courage to cure himself with our instructions, even if they find themselves in distant countries, as many have and continue to do.

Leonardo was correct: The cases are wonderful. Filippo Arcioni, the chamberlain of the Bishop of Troia (Puglia), for one, wrote from Rome to tell Leonardo about being cured of a "vile sickness" with a dose of Dia Aromatica, which the surgeon had recommended. Arcioni's doctors had dismissed Fioravanti's counsel, warning their patient that he would not last ten days if he followed the prescribed course, but he forged ahead anyway. With Fioravanti's letter and a copy of *Medical Caprices* in hand, he went to his pharmacist to have the Dia Aromatica prepared. After a light dinner, Arcioni took the dose advised. This is what happened next:

> As I was speaking with the Monsignor, I suddenly began to feel queasy and the whole castle seemed to turn upside-down. Suddenly, I was overtaken by a bout of vomiting so strong that I threw up my meal and along with it about ten pounds of choler and phlegm. Among other things, I threw up a worm with a hairy head, as long as a palm and a half, which was something marvelous. Immediately I began to feel better.

In reply, Leonardo tells Arcioni that he is pleased with the results. At the distant patient's request, he encloses a vial of Quintessence, for which Arcioni had paid (in advance) 12 ducats.

IT'S ALL IN THE EDITING

Fioravanti's manner of presenting the correspondence was strategic as well. Rather than organizing the letters chronologically, he arranged them to frame a narrative about the superiority of his "new way of healing." The first several exchanges tell stories of hidebound physicians standing in the way of rational treatment. In the opening letter, Lazaro Palatino reported from Imola that he took his copy of *Medical Caprices* to his pharmacist in order to have an electuary (lozenge) prepared. There he met two physicians who rudely confiscated the book and prescribed a different treatment altogether. Following their advice, Palatino watched his condition worsen. When he showed the physicians the letter in which Leonardo advised a contrary method of treatment, the physicians scorned it, saying it went against Avicenna's orders. Luckily, wrote Palatino, he opted to follow Leonardo's method instead—and was fully cured.

After Palatino's letter comes one from Tommaso Lucchese, who, writing from Rome in 1564, upbraided the "malicious" Roman physicians for driving Leonardo from the city. "If you would only return," he implored, "the gentlemen of Rome would erect a statue

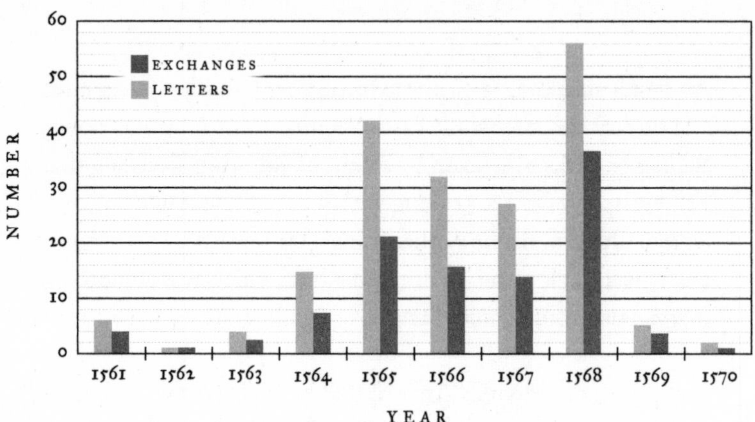

The graph shows the number of letters and exchanges of correspondence from Italy and parts of Europe published in the Tesoro della vita humana *(1570). It appears that Fioravanti's mail-order business was most active when he published his three most popular books.*

of you in Campidoglio," referring to the monumental civic piazza that was being constructed on the Capitoline Hill after a design by Michelangelo. "As for returning to Rome," Fioravanti wrote in reply, "I've never given it a moment's thought because I want to stay in Venice to print all of my books before my life is finished."

In a letter dated 13 February 1565, one Giovandomenico Zavaglione reported from Naples that Leonardo was so greatly missed there that Zavaglione and some of his friends had resolved to raise funds to persuade the surgeon to return to the city and become one of its physicians. Fioravanti declined the offer—and its princely salary of 200 ducats per year—but sent copies of his books to be sold at Marco di Maria's bookshop.

The letters continued in this adulatory vein.

Hercole Romani described a visit to Rome during which all his friends were talking about *Medical Caprices.* He noted that *The Mirror of Universal Science,* which had just come out, was being read and discussed all over town.

Pietro Jacopo Petruccio, writing from Pesaro in 1567, proudly recounted owning five of Leonardo's books, which he consulted regularly and used to treat illnesses among members of his household. "I showed your *Medical Caprices* to some physicians and they recommended against your counsel. They told me that I should be prepared to depart from this world if I used your remedies." Nevertheless, against the advice of his doctors, he decided to go ahead and treat himself with Leonardo's remedy. The predictable result: complete success. "Everywhere I go," wrote Petruccio, "in palaces, shops, and courts, I hear of your fame."

Not all doctors, it seems, were backward-looking. The collection includes letters from pharmacists, surgeons, and physicians who reported outstanding results using Leonardo's medicaments. Giovanni di Agnolo, a Tivoli pharmacist who manufactured Fioravanti's drugs, wrote in 1565 to describe the wonderful outcomes he had achieved with them. Recently, he related, a notary had visited his shop for a bad case of colic. "Without consulting the doctors," di Agnolo administered a dose of Dia Aromatica, which healed the notary instantly. He also treated his own mother—who had been laid up with catarrh and was "in a bad way"—by anointing her stomach with Elixir Vitae and Balsam, according to Leonardo's instructions. "Now she is so much better off that our physicians say they think that the spirit of Asclepius must have been resurrected in you."

A letter from physician Bartolomeo Carrero revealed that Fioravanti had visited the town of San Vito in the Friuli in 1565. "Since you left I've made countless stupendous and rare cures using your methods," Carrero wrote in gratitude. "I've cured more patients in these past five months than I'd accomplished in the previous two years."

Even the professors were discussing and debating the "new way," according to Leonardo's correspondents. Giovanni Bruccii, a pharmacist from Pisa, stated that the literati and university students debated his doctrines every day. He was doing a brisk business selling Fioravanti's remedies, he wrote, while Leonardo's books had sold out in bookstores. "I promise you that nowadays your books are studied more than those of Aristotle, and worthily, too, because they contain nothing but the truth," wrote Bruccii. Fioravanti replied, "If you follow our way, every day you'll work great wonders and will acquire much fame."

If the letters are any indication, passionate disciples of Leonardo and his doctrines were all over Italy. Cola Riguzzo, a 60-year-old medical doctor and Franciscan friar from the south of Italy, wrote that, having experimented with Leonardo's methods, he was now ready to cast the works of Galen, Avicenna, and Hippocrates into the fire. So convinced by the "new way" was Fra Cola that he wanted to rush to Venice to be with Leonardo, "to have you teach me so that I might all the more have the honor of being your disciple," promising to "follow no other doctrine than yours."

From Vicenza, physician Prudentio Bellobuono asked Fioravanti to teach his son Propertio his doctrines, and in 1566, Johannes Kromer, a German medical student at the University of Padua, wrote proudly that he had defended Fioravanti's remedies in a public dispute against six other scholars—and, as proof, he had cured one of their servants. According to Kromer, the students positively raved about Fioravanti.

HAM-AND-EGG COPAYMENTS

Although many of the letters were from professional medical workers, most came from individuals seeking Fioravanti's help. In return, they sent payments, either in money or in kind. Paolo Zanotto of Parma sent some cheese and 200 eggs in recompense for a cure of his wife's stomach pains.

Rarely did Fioravanti refuse treatment. An exception arose when Paolo Sandrini of the village of Roccabianca, near Parma, sent two hams and six sausages along with a request for a remedy to cure his cousin's disorder; sadly, Leonardo wrote in reply, the ailment was "totally incurable." In another letter, he informed the physician Giovanni Ornaro, who also lived near Parma, that he could not send any eyewash because he had recently shipped his entire supply to England.

What are we to make of these testimonials, with their over-the-top praise of Fioravanti and their hyperbolic style? Doubtless some of the language can be attributed to the period's deliberately obsequious and flattering epistolary conventions. Also, the letters were selected to delineate a persona and confirm the truth of the "new way of healing."

Could they all be merely fakes? Forgeries crafted by the masterly hand of Fioravanti himself? That would be the way of the charlatan. But the detailed descriptions they contain of places and people, as well as the presence of events and personalities that can be independently verified, lends veracity to the letters—at least to a point. Certainly, Leonardo selected the letters in such a way as to present a certain narrative, and he probably edited them as well.

As always, Fioravanti was in control.

26

AMBITION AND GLORY

Fioravanti's mail-order medical business supplemented his income and advertised his practice, but it was hardly his sole entrepreneurial venture. In 1560, he became involved in a scheme that he thought would make him rich. His partner in the venture was pharmacist Sabbà di Franceschi, owner of the Bear Pharmacy. Between them, they devised an ambitious plan to revive the Istrian city of Pola (Pula), whose population had been devastated in the 15th century by war and disease.

Pola, an ancient city on the Adriatic coast in present-day Croatia—in the Renaissance, about a day's sail from Venice—was a favorite resort for the Roman emperors. Julius Caesar built an immense coliseum seating more than 20,000 in the heart of the city, and Augustus transformed the sleepy port town into an impressive imperial outpost. A possession of the Venetian empire since the early 13th century, Pola struggled to survive disease, famine, and a succession of attacks by Turkish pirates. Just as the city's population began to recover from the disasters of the 15th century, however, the plague of 1527 struck, reducing Pola's population of 4,000 to less than 500. As a final blow, in 1550 a blight killed off the territory's olive orchards. By the time the two partners Fioravanti and Franceschi learned about Pola, the town was nearly abandoned. Its shops closed, its houses vacant and derelict, its streets overgrown with weeds, Pola teetered on the verge of becoming a ghost town.

Venice had made several attempts to recolonize Pola in the first half of the 16th century. Because Pola owed Venice an annual tribute of 2,000 pounds of olive oil, the economic impact of its decline was significant. Every bid to resuscitate it had failed, however, and the odds were dim that renewed efforts would succeed. Nevertheless, in 1560 Fioravanti and Franceschi, together with a third partner, engineer Giovanni Antonio all'Occha, appeared before the Reclamation Commission with a scheme to revive Pola "without any public expense whatsoever."

The plan was premised on the idea that Pola's misfortunes stemmed from its corrupt air, which had been fouled by a succession of plagues, continual warfare, and the decline of agriculture. The theory was essentially an extension of Fioravanti's doctrine of corruption as the cause of disease. Extreme mortality, such as that experienced at Pola, he reasoned, makes death "hang in the air." The fields go barren for lack of cultivation; poisonous animals and plants take over, making human habitation dangerous; and the desolation of the land taints the air. "But when the terrain is well cultivated and rid of such noxious things, the air becomes good again." Therefore, repopulating the city and restoring the region's agriculture, Leonardo argued, would purify the contaminated air and lead to Pola's rebirth.

To accomplish this, the three entrepreneurs proposed that the Senate grant a concession to any family that would migrate to Pola and permanently settle there. In return, the settlers would be exempt from taxation for 20 years. They would be allowed to take over abandoned houses and property; own the surrounding woods, lakes, and pastures in common; and hold two annual fairs to sell agricultural products. After remaining in Pola for 20 years, the settlers and their families would be granted title to the property they had taken over.

The trio promised that their Pola project would "purify the air, make the springs gush with water, promulgate new, useful, and necessary devices for agriculture, and send many farmers with new methods to settle there." In their request, the three entrepreneurs made vague promises to "freely disclose and put into true effect our secret to make this place habitable." As recompense for organizing

Though Pola's poverty and decay is shown as picturesque in this copperplate based on a 1782 sketch, Fioravanti and his followers found the city a squalid ruin desperately in need of renewal.

the expedition, Fioravanti, Franceschi, and all'Occha requested 4 percent of the wealth produced by the revived city.

The Reclamation Commission forwarded Fioravanti's proposal to the Senate, recommending its approval. The commission supported the scheme because it was an inexpensive way to revitalize a formerly productive city and because it promised to provide an outlet for the growing number of foreign immigrants in Venice. The Senate approved the plan; then, in a broadsheet posted throughout the city, it published a call for settlers. In 1563 all'Occha surveyed the region around Pola and gave the Senate a detailed report on the region's cultivated and uncultivated lands. Vincenzo all'Acqua, a fourth partner, was enlisted in the project to lead the band of colonists and oversee the venture.

Several dozen families, mostly Neapolitan and Cypriot immigrants, emigrated to Istria (the region around Pola). Fioravanti visited Pola in 1565 and reported that "the city is more beautiful than ever and has perfect air. It's the very health of infinite numbers who go there to live, because they all are made rich." Pola's population was renewed, he declared, the houses were repaired, and agriculture was flourishing. All in all, he claimed, the project was a phenomenal success.

AN ILL-FATED VENTURE

Behind this cheerful story lay a dreary reality. The Pola project, it seems, ran into difficulties from the start. The small number of local nobility who still lived there viewed the settlers as a threat to their power. The local inhabitants resented the colonists, who came with newfangled agricultural schemes and conspired to take away their land. According to complaints by Pola's suspicious residents, the pioneers brought with them a "novel" kind of agriculture. The details are murky; perhaps they adhered to a body of techniques based on Telesio's radical naturalism, supported by Fioravanti's theory of disease, and backed by experiments that the amateur agronomists did in Fioravanti's informal academy.

The growing tension between the Polese and the pioneers came to a head in 1565, when a local nobleman attacked all'Acqua in the town's central piazza and bludgeoned him to death. According to a complaint filed by all'Acqua's distraught widow and mother, Vincenzo had quarreled with a certain Hieronimo Candolmesi and a group of thugs, who "beat him on the head and mortally wounded him." Other settlers, they charged, had been attacked as well. As a result, "everyone who plans to go and live there is frightened away."

It seems unlikely that Fioravanti would have profited much from his Istrian venture. Like the other colonization schemes that came before and after, his plan to revive Pola, evidently, was a failure.

Indeed, his grandiose rhetoric notwithstanding, Fioravanti probably did not get rich from any of his business ventures. Although his books sold well in bookstores all over Italy, the lack of an efficient distribution system would have prevented him from making much money from writing. And whereas his mail-order medical business spread his fame, a few hams and sausages and some sacks of grain would not have enabled him to purchase property. Apparently he never owned a house, renting rooms wherever he lived.

But perhaps, after all, fame *was* the point. To Fioravanti, as to many of his contemporaries, the world was a stage and he an actor performing a role, the script for which he wrote himself. The task at hand was to give a convincing performance—and thereby establish

Fioravanti's business partner, the engineer Giovanni Antonio all'Occha, made this map of Pola's arable lands, lakes, springs, rivers, forests, and seaports after an extensive survey of the area. The city of Pola is located in the port at the bottom right of the map.

a reputation. In the words of historian Erik Ringmar, "fame was the entrepreneurial coin in which the real profits were counted." True to the thespian spirit of the age, Leonardo wanted more than anything else to succeed at the art of self-promotion. In that sense, it didn't matter if the Pola project failed. He could make it a success by proclaiming it such in his essay "Discourse on the City of Pola," which he published in his book *Regimen for the Plague* (1565). To that extent, the aims of the Renaissance entrepreneur and those of the courtier were the same: The stages on which they played were strewn with hazards. On both, image was everything.

THE PROFESSOR OF SECRETS AND THE PRINCE

If Leonardo's Pola venture was a plank in his platform to be regarded as a Venetian, it was a spectacular failure. In some respects, he seemed terribly out of place there. A child of Bologna in the Papal States, seasoned in Naples and a world dominated by princely courts, he aimed higher than the vulgar world of commerce, where he was reduced to selling his books and remedies while fending off attacks from physicians. He aspired to greater heights: To join the court of some worthy prince, he believed, would befit a man of his talents.

The protocol for being welcomed into a court required that a prospective client offer a gift to his hoped-for patron. Gift exchange, according to historian Mario Biagioli, was "the logic of patronage." Renaissance Italian princes were showered with inventions, instruments, exotic plants and animals, trick mirrors, "curious" artifacts, and works of art and literature—all gifts of social climbers jockeying for places at the court. One of the most famous scientific tributes of the late Renaissance was Galileo's dedication of the four satellites of Jupiter, which he had discovered with a telescope, to Cosimo II de' Medici, the Grand Duke of Tusçany. Galileo named the moons the Medicean Stars after Cosimo and his three brothers. Galileo's rewards were more down-to-earth: The grand duke gave the astronomer a place at his court and a stipend of 1,000 scudi.

Like Galileo, Fioravanti was building his arsenal of gifts to offer a prince. Even as he prepared his books for publication, he had set his sights on grander targets and was enacting a plan to achieve his goal. We can follow the trail of his brief career as an inventor through the patent applications he sent to the Senate for consideration. In 1560 the Senate approved his petition for a patent on a novel design for an unsinkable ship. In 1565 he received patents for both a new method to process oil for lamps and a new technique to make soap—discoveries he made, presumably, in his "academy."

The poligrafo Girolamo Ruscelli provides further insight on Leonardo's inventions. The two men met often at Leonardo's house in San Luca to carry out alchemical experiments. They distilled medicinal waters, made cosmetics, and experimented with explosives.

They speculated about designs for fortresses and contrived military inventions—among them a brutal mechanism to cripple the horses of an attacking cavalry, which Ruscelli described in his book on the military arts.

In keeping with Leonardo's temerity, he chose Italy's most powerful prince, Cosimo I de' Medici, the Grand Duke of Tuscany, as the one to whom he would offer his secrets. It was widely known that Cosimo was fascinated by secrets and eager to hear about new inventions. A pragmatic, modernizing prince on the lookout for the latest scientific discoveries that would help him make medical, industrial, and military improvements, Cosimo had built an alchemical laboratory, or *fonderia,* in the ducal palace. He was an avid experimenter who worked alongside the distillers in the palace laboratory, and he invented an oil for muscle spasms that was said to be very effective. The alchemical activity at the palace was so constant that nearby residents complained of the *"bacchanalia"* of noise echoing from the laboratory.

As was customary, Leonardo first showed his inventions to Cosimo's agent in Venice, Piero Gelido. Either intrigued by Fioravanti's devices or merely obligated by politeness, Gelido promised that he would contact the grand duke.

Leonardo waited for several weeks. No word came from Florence. Finally, growing impatient and wondering whether Gelido had ever written the promised letter, he decided to write directly to the grand duke. His letter, dated 2 November 1560 and written in his own carefully drawn hand, is preserved in the Florentine state archive:

Most Illustrious and Excellent Duke,

Having spoken to your Lord Ambassador in Venice about various important and necessary things, but not being certain whether word of our conversations had reached you, I take the liberty to introduce myself, your most affectionate and loyal servant Leonardo Fioravanti of Bologna, doctor of medicine and surgery. I write to inform Your Excellency that I have traveled to various and diverse countries and have ploughed the seas to many places, and by these efforts have learned many things in order thereby to be able to be useful to princes and other great and honored persons. Thus, with the help of God, I've found many things not ever heard of by anyone in the world. First, I have found a medicine that the whole world has searched for, but found only by me, a medicine that will cure every infirmity that can affect the human body of whatever complexion. I've also found the true treatment for wounds, which heals every sort of wound quickly and miraculously. I have found a way to make a ship that cannot be lost at sea in any way, because it cannot be upended nor penetrated nor sunk. I can also build a castle to mount on top of the ship in order to defend it against all enemy ships; and I have designed an ingenious device with which the said castle can be defended against infinite galleys that might attack it. I've also discovered a sort of pitch that, when coated on a ship's hull, will make it go exceedingly fast. What is truly marvelous is that I have invented a simple device that can put to rout two hundred cavalrymen and their horses. I have also discovered, not far from Your Excellency, a place where nature has made an impregnable hidden fortress. All these things are necessary for a great prince, because the great Turkish dog is very powerful and seeks with all diligence to ruin our poor Christendom and put us under him. I shall reveal all these secrets to you, to your great satisfaction, if you will only invite me to your court.

Your most humble and faithful servant,
Leonardo Fioravanti of Bologna

Cosimo's reply to this rather fanciful set of proposals was polite but noncommittal. He complimented the petitioner for his "extraordinary virtue," but informed him that instead of promises, he would prefer to see actions. Cosimo evaluated dozens of petitioners with dozens of projects each year. "I would like not just to hear about things," he answered through his agent in Venice, "but to see proofs."

CLASSICAL SHOCK AND AWE

Rather than interpreting Cosimo's response as rejection, Fioravanti saw the opening he desired. He sent more letters promising new secrets, including a gadget to enable an army to defend itself against an attack by as many as 50,000 cavalry. The device, modeled on the ancient caltrop mentioned by the Roman writer Vegetius, was fashioned out of four pointed metal spikes welded together in the shape of a star: when cast into the ground, it rested on three spikes, with the fourth always projecting upward. The Romans used the caltrop to stymie charges by cavalry or chariot.

Leonardo could also promise a fantastic jumping cannon, a small bronze cannon surrounded by about 30 miniature cannon *(archibuggetti)* that, when thrown aboard a ship, would invariably land upright and fire a cannonball into the ship's deck, simultaneously spraying bullets in all directions—a sort of Renaissance grenade. He showed Cosimo's agent some sketches of his designs and talked vaguely about his claim to have discovered "a fort made completely by nature" somewhere in the Tuscan hills. In another letter, he promised to renew the city of Pisa, whose harbors had silted in and whose trade had declined. He proposed to develop a resort and market center on the shores of an unidentified lake in Tuscany and make it "a second Venice" without any expense to the duke.

Cultivating an image as an engineer and inventor came easy to Fioravanti. A devotee of natural magic, an experimenter, and a brash opportunist, he also had a famous surname. Almost exactly a century earlier, a Bolognese engineer and architect by the name of Aristotele Fioravanti, "the second Aristotle," had become world-famous for his spectacular engineering feats. As the communal engineer for Bologna in the service of Giovanni II Bentivoglio, he moved the tower of Santa Maria del Tempio a distance of some 20 meters and built the Palazzo del Podestà in the center of the city. In 1471, he transported the Vatican obelisk for Pope Paul II. In 1475, Aristotele went to Moscow at the invitation of Ivan III, where he designed the Kremlin and the Assumption Cathedral, two of medieval Russia's most important buildings. Whether or not Leonardo was related to Aristotele Fioravanti, it would have been tempting to appropriate the name of such a visionary engineer.

Leonardo waited impatiently for several months. In May 1561, when he felt he could wait no longer, he made the journey to Florence with the hope of meeting Cosimo and demonstrating his secrets. But the grand duke was at his villa in Poggio, so Fioravanti was turned away.

Dejected, he returned to Venice and penned a final letter to Cosimo, complaining that he had, at considerable expense, left his affairs in Venice and traveled to Florence, only to discover that the grand duke was absent. Yet he was "more inflamed than ever" to be Cosimo's loyal servant. If only the grand duke would invite him to Florence, Leonardo promised, Pisa would become "the most miraculous and stupendous city of Europe."

Finally, in June 1561, in a last, desperate attempt to gain Cosimo's favor, Fioravanti sent the grand duke a handwritten tract, *Discourse on the Five Things I Propose to Your Excellency,* summarizing his inventions. In the most eloquent and mannerly voice he could muster, he elaborated on the "natural fortress" that he had discovered at some undisclosed location in Tuscany. He also detailed his unsinkable ship, the mechanical cannon that would destroy enemy vessels at sea, the pitch that would defend the hull of a ship against any sea animal, and his new and improved caltrop that would defend an army against a cavalry force of 50,000 horses.

Two months later, Leonardo dedicated his first book, *Medical Secrets* (later retitled *Medical Caprices*), to Cosimo. In the dedication, he noted that three endowments constitute true happiness: fear of God, good health, and prosperity. Similarly, a prince must possess three attributes to govern well: reverence, justice, and a united populace. Leonardo promised that his book would provide Cosimo, the "most fortunate of all princes," the key to a successful reign. The grand duke politely thanked the surgeon for his "ingenious work" *(operetta ingeniosa)* but never offered him a place at court.

Unwilling to surrender his ambition, Leonardo shopped his wares around. In 1561 he sent his proposals to Alfonso II d'Este, the Duke of Ferrara. He repackaged *Medical Secrets* as *Medical Caprices* and dedicated it to Alfonso. Recycling the dedication he had written to Cosimo, Fioravanti wrote that all princes should seek four things: to receive God's grace, to rule a large realm, to be loved by the people, and to have a healthy body. Alfonso was fortunate to possess all four, Fioravanti noted; to secure his continued health, he proudly presented the duke this "new way of healing."

As far as we know, Alfonso never answered Leonardo's letters—nor did he respond to the dedication of *Medical Caprices.*

SEISMIC RIGHTEOUSNESS

It seemed like divine justice to Leonardo Fioravanti when a series of violent earthquakes struck Ferrara in November 1570, killing hundreds and causing massive destruction. The letter he wrote to Alfonso afterward, expressing his "great sadness and sorrow" over the city's ruin, oozes with irony and sarcasm. Such terrible events did not happen by chance, Leonardo bluntly informed the hapless duke; they were God's punishment for wickedness. Alfonso's court had been a place of dazzling splendor, Leonardo acknowledged: A typical Renaissance prince, the duke had lavished his patronage on poets, artists, musicians, and humanists. Yet to sustain the magnificent show, Leonardo clucked, the duke had imposed oppressive taxes, monopolies on grain and salt, and cruel game laws. Worse, Ferrara had become "a Sodom and Gomorrah of public sodomy."

Plainly, the earthquakes signaled God's wrath. And the cause of "the rotten state of Ferrara"? The duke had listened to the wrong advisers:

> And so My Illustrious Lord, I've taken it upon myself to make these things known to you, because I am certain that as a Christian and Catholic prince you will turn to God for help and counsel, and will remedy all these things, so that our Lord

> God will calm his anger and return your city to its pristine state, as he did to the city of Nineveh. And if it is Your Illustrious Lordship's wish, after all this has come to pass I'll show you the true way to quickly restore and augment the city.

In writing to Alfonso, Fioravanti played a new role: that of biblical prophet, a modern-day Jonah admonishing the Duke of Ferrara to drive the flatterers from his court and return the city to its "pristine state." Marshaling all the moral indignation the role required, he chastised the duke for filling his court with freeloaders who sought only personal gain. How unfortunate that the duke had not accepted Leonardo into the court when he had the chance nine years before.

Alfonso did not respond.

Fioravanti's political philosophy, which he sketched out in *The Mirror of Universal Science,* was hardened by his disappointments with princes. In one chapter, "On the Rule of Princes," he decried the tyranny that modern-day rulers wield over "the poor vassals" who submit to them:

> I hear the whole world crying out for change! All the people are rising up because they cannot tolerate being so miserably oppressed any longer. All over Europe nowadays the people bear tribulations they can no longer suffer. . . . O what a great pity to see the miseries of people who willing put themselves in the hands of princes and then are so miserably treated.

He complained that too many princes give themselves over to flatterers who make them "see black for white." They forget their true responsibilities, which are the same as those of physicians: to care for their subjects with compassion and love. How different are modern princes, Leonardo lamented, from the ancient Roman rulers such as Octavian, who loved his subjects and treated them with justice and clemency. "The only exceptions are those that are governed under the flying lion," he wrote, referring to Venice, "people truly happy to live under such a glorious standard."

Fioravanti discerned other parallels between politics and medicine. His entire worldview was centered on the body, and for him the human body sustained a particular view of society. He believed that the cause of Italy's moral and political decline was an internal pollution that began in the courts and spread throughout the commonwealth. The pollution was caused by vainglory, which infects the court and turns princes and courtiers into parasites sucking the lifeblood from the body politic. Just as the "bad quality of the stomach" spreads its contagion to the body's organs, so corrupt rulers and their fawning courtiers ruined the body politic.

The cure? As in medicine, so in politics: Rid the body politic of corrupt ministers, then restore it with virtue and justice.

True to form, Fioravanti had much to say about the art of the courtier, despite lacking experience as one. The courtier's art is "the most laborious and desperate art that the world has ever seen," he wrote. Because princes "want only to be praised by their officers and ministers," rarely does one find men of talent in the court. A prince would rather have a good cook in his kitchen than a brave captain to defend his fortress, and "is more content to be toasted by simpletons than by sages, and so, being a little slothful himself, quickly finishes off his provisions." The court, he wrote, is like "a sign that only shows a thing's image, which never comes into reality." Dissimulation is the courtier's fine art:

> The measure by which fortune distributes merits and demerits to a courtier is not reason but opinion, because in the court more than anywhere else, water burns without fire, the knife cuts without steel, the candle lights without a flame, and the mill grinds without water. By this I mean that many times in the court fortune runs away from those who seek her and runs head-on into those who try to flee from her.

Fioravanti blamed his disappointment on bad princes and the wicked advisers who led them astray. In reality, he lacked the central virtue of the courtier: prudence. He was too confrontational, too volatile, too caught up in the pursuit of glory more characteristic of a prince. As Leonardo unabashedly confessed to Cosimo de' Medici, he wanted his inventions "to bring me immortal fame in the world."

In the end he went the Venetian way, casting his pearls before swine: The rare secrets with which he had once tried to entice princes he published for all the world to read in his *Mirror of Universal Science.*

27

A CONSPIRACY OF DOCTORS

Fioravanti fared well in Venice. Although he never landed a position in a princely court, he built a stable medical practice that served patients from all walks of life—noblemen, merchants, and commoners. He was a successful writer, and his books popularized his methods throughout Europe. His patent drugs, which were available not only in Venice but also in pharmacies in Naples, Rome, Milan, and London, became a standard part of the pharmacist's stock. In 1562 he moved from San Giuliano to the "new houses" in San Luca, just around the corner from the palazzo Grimani, a neighborhood where many poligrafi lived.

Yet for all Leonardo's success, he was practicing illegally. His attempts to obtain a license from the Venetian Public Health Board (Provveditori alla Sanità) were unsuccessful. He was able to operate openly as a surgeon, treating wounds and other external ailments, but legally he could not prescribe drugs taken orally. That created a problem, for his nostrums, which he used to treat all of his patients, were the foundation of his "new way of healing." Without them, Leonardo Fioravanti was no different than an ordinary surgeon. And that was exactly the way the medical authorities wanted to keep it: They had no intention of allowing him to invade the territory of the physicians.

The earliest record of Leonardo's attempts to obtain a license to practice "physical medicine"—that is, to dispense drugs to be taken orally—appears in a petition of October 1563 to the Dieci

Savi (literally, "Ten Sages"), which functioned as an appellate court. In the document Fioravanti appeals a decision by the health board denying him the right "to medicate *in fisica.*" The court denied the petition, and Fioravanti's litigation with the health board continued on and off for several more years. Although archival documents show that he was granted a license to "medicate," this must have been a permit to practice surgery.

The health board's central concern was guarding the border that divided physicians from surgeons and other practitioners. The principle was simple: The qualification for being a physician was a university medical degree, and only physicians could legally prescribe drugs. Yet, like all boundaries, the one that separated physicians from other healers was permeable. Unlicensed practitioners operated in Venice and other Italian cities without much trouble from the authorities. Fioravanti himself quietly treated patients at the Bear and Phoenix Pharmacies. Besides physicians and surgeons, unlettered empirics of all kinds set up shop and competed for patients—some legally, others not.

It was a surprisingly specialized group of medical providers, including experts in treating cataracts, fractures, abcesses, hernias, and bladder stones. Barbers bled patients and pulled teeth, while midwives assisted at childbirth. Charlatans crowded the Piazza San Marco to hawk their secrets, while distillers produced a steady supply of medicinal waters. And how many were there like the blind Elena Crusichi—named "La Draga" after one of the spirits inside her—who could touch a shred of a sick person's clothing and tell immediately what the illness was? A strangely delusional woman who occasionally disintegrated into multiple personalities, La Draga could also ascertain whether a child had been consumed by a demon—and, if so, there she conveniently stood, ready and able to drive the demon out.

Tasked with controlling this swarm of practitioners was the Public Health Board, which authorized the College of Physicians (the physicians' guild) to examine and certify the degrees and competencies of physicians and surgeons. The health board made membership in the college compulsory for all physicians. Although empirics were likewise required to register with the health board, large numbers of itinerant practitioners made their rounds of the piazzas and moved on without notice.

Finding and prosecuting offenders would have been extremely difficult. From 1545 to 1560 only ten empirics were prosecuted for operating without a license—a lackluster enforcement record that the College of Physicians found less and less tolerable. In 1567, the college finally pressured the health board to give it the authority to license practitioners, rather than merely consulting the college for its opinions about qualifications. Under the new provisions, failure to obtain a license from the College of Physicians carried a sentence of 18 months tied to an oar in a galley.

Not surprisingly, Leonardo was swept up in the crackdown. He stood apart from the crowd of miscellaneous healers who operated in the marketplace. For starters, he was more vocal than others in his criticism of the establishment. Other empirics resented the power of the physicians just as much, but it was one thing to sell potions in the piazza while cracking crude jokes about the physicians and quite another to expose the fallacies of medicine in the popular press. Fioravanti was a widely revered popular healer, hence a serious economic threat. Reportedly, students and professors at the Padua medical college even debated his doctrine—a sure sign that the doctors took him seriously. The problem was, he not only looked like an empiric, he spoke for empirics to an increasingly skeptical public.

A THOROUGHLY MODERN MEDICINE MAN

Fioravanti's "new way of healing" was contrived to take advantage of early modern Italy's rapidly changing medical marketplace. Intense competition favored specialization and novelty; to succeed, it was essential to find a niche. Fioravanti's "new way" was tailor-made for the fashion-driven medical economy. Hellebore, calomel (mercurous chloride), and Roman vitriol (copper sulfate)—all powerful emetics and purges—were ingredients in several of his drugs. But he relied above all on Precipitato, or mercuric oxide. Usually given with sweetened rose water, it was his supreme weapon against bodily corruption. Precipitato looms large and dangerous in his arsenal of drugs, like a loaded arquebus. In the struggle between sickness and health that Leonardo waged, therapeutic intervention necessarily took on heroic dimensions.

Fioravanti's claim that his therapeutic system was a return to the natural way of healing struck a responsive chord—moral decline from a golden age being a prominent motif in Venetian thought and letters. Not only that, but imaginary scenarios of ideal societies were immensely popular among middle-class readers. With his promise to drive out bad humors and restore the body to its pristine state of perfect health, Fioravanti appropriated these primitivist themes and put them to work as marketing ploys.

Did Leonardo's therapy really work? Could it have accomplished any of the cures he claimed for it? Did it make patients feel better? His patients often reported vomiting worms and other "putrid matter"—and feeling much relieved in the wake of their ordeal. Stomach and intestinal parasites were a common malady in early modern Europe, where spoiled and undercooked meat and poor hygiene made the human body a stew pot of microbes and worms. For some of these conditions, emetics and purgatives probably gave some relief. The ejection of vermin and foul-smelling material from the body also gave empirical evidence of Fioravanti's theory that the sick body abounds with corruptions. Purging episodes identified a specific cause of a disordered, incomprehensible physiological state, brought relief, and seemingly restored the body to order. Insofar as health may be defined as a condition of mental and physiological well-being, Fioravanti's treatments created the illusion, at least, of having brought about a cure.

Some historians have characterized such methods as "popular Galenism." Yet that depiction obscures the real sources of the popular healer's power. Leonardo wasn't selling debased versions of Galenic drugs; he was promoting an alternative kind of medicine, and that is how his clients saw it. This wasn't trickled-down Galenism or proto-homeopathy; it was all-out war on the corruptions that debilitated the body. This accounts, perhaps, for his rather shocking willingness to experiment on patients with apparent disregard for the possible consequences—administering poisons as a regular part of therapy, for example.

Leonardo Fioravanti believed that disease was a dangerous enemy that needed to be attacked with extreme remedies. Historian Gianna Pomata points out that patients tended to view illness as "something that moves inside the body"—that "something" being not the limpid humoral imbalances of Galenic medicine, but foul corruptions and rotten matter that swelled and collected in abscesses, pustules, and seeping boils. Fioravanti wanted to attack corruptions at their source—the stomach—and drive them out. One reason why he became such a famous healer was that his methods jibed with the average person's conception of his or her own body. Then as now, people wanted results; regimens that produced no physiological changes—like those advanced by the physicians—were easy targets for unorthodox healers.

FROM ACCUSED TO ACCREDITED

The "conspiracy of the doctors" came to a head in March 1568, when a group of physicians denounced Fioravanti to the College of Physicians for malpractice, accusing him of using poisons and killing his patients. Then Fioravanti made an amazing turnaround. He returned to Bologna—evidently for the first time since leaving the city 20 years before—and applied for doctorates in arts and medicine. Even more amazing is that the University of Bologna awarded him the degrees.

On its face, it seems implausible that Fioravanti could have made a quick jaunt to Bologna and, without taking a single university course, picked up a medical degree. The Venetian physicians were certainly incredulous—and said as much in a protest they filed with the University of Bologna. Yet there is no question of the legality of the degrees. Records of the award of the two degrees are kept in the Bologna state archive, and his medical degree is recorded in full in the archives of the Venetian Public Health Board. How could a candidate with so little formal university training have earned a doctor's degree from Renaissance Italy's preeminent medical college?

The system by which the doctorate was conferred in 16th-century Bologna did not, in fact, require matriculation. When a person applied for a degree, a series of subjects, or *puncta,* were presented to the candidate to argue before the university community. The process did not involve a rigorous examination of a person's overall knowledge, but rather a speech on a point already known in advance—and for which a candidate would have had ample time to prepare, most likely with the help of a tutor or one of his promoters. The degree-granting process favored those with skills of declamation and persuasion—precisely the talents Leonardo had honed throughout his long career.

In seeking the degree, Fioravanti could apply either as a native Bolognese and pay full fees, or as a foreigner and pay smaller fees. One advantage of applying as a native was that it qualified an applicant for membership in the College of Medicine if approved by a vote of its members. Initially, Leonardo applied as a foreigner to avoid paying the higher costs, for he was not interested in becoming a member of the medical college. The next day, however, he changed his mind. He decided to apply as a native—probably after learning that graduates of the medical college obtained the title of Count of the Sacred Lateran Palace (Comites Palatii Lateranensis), a palatine knighthood.

This privilege stemmed from the historic occasion in 1530 when Charles V was crowned Holy Roman Emperor in Bologna by Pope Clement VII. Wishing to leave a lasting token of the occasion, Charles granted the college a special concession to grant its graduates the title. Though purely an honorific—it conferred no special privileges and had no political import—the knighthood must have seemed auspicious to Leonardo. He intended to make his way as an author, not as an academic, so the prospect of displaying such an exalted title on the frontispieces of his books and in his letters to patients must have been irresistible. The faculty granted his request on the condition that he pay the remaining fees within a year and promise not to apply for admission to the medical college.

Early modern academic culture was highly ceremonial. The traditional rites of graduation were performed with much pomp and solemnity. Before applying for the degree, Leonardo had to produce two respected citizens of Bologna who would certify that he was a good Christian and of sound moral character. Then, before the academic examination, he had to appear before the Vicar General of the Archbishop to swear the Physician's Oath, which was required of medical school graduates by a bull of Pius V promulgated in 1566. The bull decreed that no physician should receive the doctorate unless he first took an oath not to treat a sick person for longer than three days without having the patient confess his sins to a proper confessor. Having sworn the Physician's Oath as prescribed by the church, Leonardo was ready for the formalities of the academic examination, a process that would take two days.

On March 28, 1568—the eve of his examination—he had to appear before the prior of the college, along with two sponsors or "promoters" from each of the colleges to which he had applied for degrees. Accompanying Leonardo from the arts faculty were two philosophy professors, Antonio Francesco Fabbio and Domenico Bonfigli. From the College of Medicine, his promoters were Fabrizio Garzoni, a distinguished professor of theoretical medicine, and Lattanzio Benacci, who taught astronomy and medicine. During the interview the Prior presented Leonardo with the puncta in arts and medicine that he would be required to argue.

The next day, accompanied by his promoters in full academic regalia, Leonardo proceeded to the Basilica of San Petronio in the heart of the city to appear before the Archdeacon, Tommaso Campeggi, and the assembled doctors of the university in order to present his *recitatio,* or declamation on the puncta given to him the day before. According to the regulations of the university, he was supposed to undergo two examinations: one in private, testing his knowledge of medical texts, which would have been conducted by his promoters, and another in public, a more formal event in which the candidate made his declamation. Only the latter is mentioned in the archival record, an indication of the high esteem that academics placed on the candidate's ability to syllogize on the fine points of medicine.

THE KEEPER OF SECRETS STEPS FROM THE SHADOWS

Leonardo must have impressed his examiners. The committee unanimously judged him "suitable and adequate" for promotion to the degree.

Following the vote, his promoters solemnly presented him with the symbols of his academic investiture: a book, a doctoral cap, and a gold ring. Then, bowing his head and placing his hand on the symbolic sword of the palatine knighthood, Leonardo would have heard the archdeacon intone: "*Miles strenuus esto!*—Behold the agile knight!" Suddenly, the professor of secrets became a doctor and knight.

The archives do not reveal which puncta Fioravanti argued before the professors. Evidence from his account of the events suggests that one of them may have been a personal favorite: Can one remedy cure all diseases? He certainly had an answer for that one—and doubtless a fine speech, too.

In April 1568, Leonardo returned triumphantly to Venice, where, he announced to an admiring public, "I hope to live and die." As a certified physician, a writer with a growing reputation, and the focus of what amounted to an alternative medical movement, he had reason to be satisfied. Finally he had conquered the doctors—by becoming one of them.

With his degree officially registered in the rolls of the Venetian College of Physicians, Fioravanti could now practice the "new way of healing" legally. His reputation extended throughout Italy and Europe. Just as they had in Sicily, doctors from small towns such as Sulmona and Ronciglione were calling him the "new Asclepius." Praise came in less overt forms as well, as when an impostor posed as the Duke of Urbino's ambassador to attempt extracting some secrets from Leonardo.

Although a group of disgruntled physicians sent an angry letter to the University of Bologna protesting his newly acquired doctorate (in it they managed to call Fioravanti a peddler and a murderer), there was nothing they could do—legally, at least—to stop him from practicing medicine in Venice.

28

LEONARDO THE CHAMELEON

Fioravanti immediately set out to refashion a new identity—not as a surgeon or empiric, but as a physician championing "true medicine," the ancient art of Akron of Agrigento, which had supposedly been corrupted by the cancer of Galenism. The result was his fifth book, *The Treasury of Human Life,* published in 1570 by the Heirs of Melchiore Sessa, one of Venice's most prominent printing firms. Like all of his books, the work targeted a popular as well as a professional readership. In it he exchanged the image of the rugged empiric for that of *dottore e cavaliere,* doctor and knight.

The Treasury of Human Life opens with a series of dedications to distinguished literary and scientific figures. The dedications were not the usual bids for patronage; instead they were intended to place Leonardo among the most learned men of the day. The dedicatees include the eminent Udinese physician Luigi Luigini, who had recently published a three-volume compilation of treatises on the French pox; Girolamo Capodivacca, a renowned medical professor at Padua; and Ulisse Aldrovandi, a famous naturalist from Bologna. A dozen lesser-known physicians, artists, distillers, and surgeons likewise earned amention—among them Leonardo's disciple Giovanpaolo de Guglielmo of Pizzo, a village in Calabria, "who follows my doctrine in every way and has argued for it in Naples, Padua, Venice, and many other places, where he has acquired great fame."

At the head of this parade of illustrious personages emerges a shiny new image of Fioravanti. The new Leonardo is no longer the battle-scarred surgeon of *Medical Caprices,* but a distinguished physician and graduate of the "sacrosanct" college of arts of the University of Bologna, whose faculty he applauds in two lengthy dedications. Moreover, he boasted, by virtue of earning his medical degree from Bologna, he had qualified to become a physician, a knight, a member of the Bologna College of Physicians, and the equal of any of the doctors who had persecuted him.

A new identity required a new portrait. Instead of using the engraving done in 1566 for the *Compendium of Rational Secrets,* which portrayed Fioravanti as a savvy, world-wise surgeon, the new image was that of a much older man—although, in reality, he was only four years older. In the new portrait, a profile view, he appears as a seasoned scholar-traveler and gentleman. The lynx eyes of the earlier portrait have grown tired, the hair has thinned, and age lines score the face. Leonardo wears a formal robe with a broad collar; around his neck we see a crucifix on a heavy chain. The crucifix, prominently displayed and turned toward the viewer, is part of the ceremonial regalia of his status as a count palatine. (Although the clerical tonsure that he sports in the portrait was not required of members of the Order of the Golden Spur, with which palatine knights were affiliated, Fioravanti wore it as a sign of piety.) The profile view, consistently used in commemorative medals, is intended to ennoble him.

Overall, Leonardo's portrait in *The Treasury of Human Life* is meant to portray the man's suffering and grief, his long experience, and his piety—or does that proud chin denote righteousness instead? "Leonardo Fioravanti Cavaliere," reads the caption. Most Bologna doctors didn't bother to mention the knighthood that went with their degrees, but Fioravanti exhibited his proudly. It was an essential part of his new persona because it captured, symbolically, the manner in which he had superseded the physicians: not only in knowledge and experience but also in honor and glory.

Then comes a jubilant introduction of the new Leonardo. Following the example of ancient philosophers who roamed the globe seeking knowledge, he wrote:

> Many years ago, I too, in imitation of them, departed from my sweet native land, Bologna, and began to walk the earth and plough the seas, visiting many cities and provinces, practicing with various qualities of persons, and medicating men and women afflicted with various sorts of infirmities. . . . All these things I did for no other purpose than to rid myself of the ignorance that enveloped me.

His pilgrimage concluded, he promised the reader to "show the whole truth of medicine and surgery, just as I did in Palermo, Messina, Naples, Rome, and Venice." Despite persecution and calumny, he writes, "The truth of my doctrine now shines throughout Europe."

The Treasury of Human Life tells the story of a man's climb out of dark ignorance and into the clear light of truth. Besides its medical treasures, the book contained the treasury of Leonardo's life: The autobiography of a playful empiric who made comic fools of the physicians, then trumped them all simply by "going out into the world" and listening to the voices of the common people—midwives, old women, craftsmen, surgeons. It was the tale of a simple man who shows the world that the wisdom of the vineyard and the piazza outshines the artificial erudition of the schools.

A trope? Of course. It combined the themes from folklore and popular literature that together made up the figure of the wandering empiric—the professor of secrets. *The Treasury of Human Life* is, essentially, a picaresque narrative. Leonardo would have been familiar with the genre through his contacts with Spanish soldiers and officials in Naples. The original picaresque tale, generally acknowledged to have founded the genre, was the Spanish novel *La vida de Lazarillo de Tormes* (The Life of Lazarillo de Tormes), which was published in 1554, while Leonardo was living in Naples. The novel, whose author is unknown, tells the story of a boy named Lazarillo, the son of an impoverished miller, who climbs out of poverty and wanders the world, surviving by his cunning. Given away by his mother to a wily blind beggar, who employs the boy as a guide, Lazarillo begins his education in the school of hard knocks. About

This portrait, by an unknown illustrator, first appeared in Fioravanti's Tesoro della vita humana *(Venice, 1570). A profile view, the portrait captures Fioravanti as a wise and experienced sage of medicine, a complete reversal of the previous image of him as a battle-worn surgeon.*

the only thing Lazarillo inherits from the beggar is this piece of advice: "A blind man's boy needs to know a trick more than the Devil." Eventually Lazarillo runs away and takes to the road, serving one miserly and dishonest master after another. Only by deceit and trickery is he able to get by.

Laced with savage attacks on the social injustices of the day, *Lazarillo de Tormes* became a favorite of soldiers and the talk of Spanish society. It spawned scores of yarns about the pícaro—the rogue who lives by his wits. While living in Naples, besides hearing stories about *pícaros,* Leonardo would have seen dispossessed *scugnizzi* (street urchins) who, for better or worse, embodied the picaresque in real life. Conquered and overcome by society at every turn, the pícaro is defeated at a superficial level, but his victory is that he has the last word: He tells his story.

Like a picaresque novel, *The Treasury of Human Life* depicts the nonfictional adventures of a trickster in a decadent world of fraudulent and conniving doctors who hide behind their pretentious degrees and sham theories. Like a pícaro, Leonardo "goes out into the world" to seek his fortune, making his way by cunning and, when necessary, deceit. He passes himself off as a learned doctor in Palermo and uses deception to steal the secret of rhinoplasty. Beaten down at every turn by "conspiracies of the doctors," he turns the tables on the physicians by returning to Bologna and (by trickery?) gaining his medical degree.

Indeed, picaresque elements are present in stories sprinkled throughout Fioravanti's books. A good fellow *(buon compagno)* uses a ruse to steal some sausages from a hostler (the picaresque hero is always motivated by hunger); a peasant plays a trick on a doctor by bringing in a jar of mule's urine for analysis.

And what about Fioravanti's own cures? Were they tricks, too? In the end, triumphantly, Leonardo the pícaro lives to tell the tale.

THE MAN WITH THE SAVVY SHOE BUCKLES

The fictional life of Alessio Piemontese was another element that went into the creation of the topos of the peripatetic empiric. So too were the real-life adventures of 16th-century Swiss alchemist and medical reformer Theophrastus Bombastus von Hohenheim, who called himself Paracelsus. He had at least two things in common with Leonardo Fioravanti: He was a former military surgeon, and he was contemptuous of the physicians. "My shoebuckles are more learned than your Galen and Avicenna and my beard has more experience than all your high colleges," he proclaimed.

With Paracelsus, the figure of the professor of secrets shades into that of the magus, bringing to mind a contemporary, Georg Helmstetter of Worms, whose legendary passion for secrets and the occult sciences transformed him into the folk hero—and villain—Doctor Faustus. One wonders: How much did the trope shape Renaissance reality? Was life an imitation of art?

The picaresque travel narrative served another end, too. Fioravanti deployed it to demonstrate the central tenet of his scientific philosophy: Experience trounces book learning. Distrust of formal learning was, of course, the rallying cry of the empiric, but Fioravanti's skepticism went deeper. He vigorously defended the empirics against the charge of not knowing the causes of diseases. "Why should they?" he spat back, "I don't know a single doctor who treats causes." Unseen causes, such as Galenic humors, are beyond the knowledge of the physician, he declared:

> As for me, I've never seen anyone treat a cause, but I've certainly treated and have seen others treat the disease, which is the effect. For the cause is always first and the effect follows. So if the cause is never cured, but only the effect is, why should we bother to know about this damned cause when it's never cured? To treat a wound you have to know what's important to the wound, not why the man was wounded.

Episodes of conflict punctuate the *Treasury:* the war in Africa, Leonardo's feud with the physicians, the near-mortal wounding of Dionigi Atanagi—and, above all, the struggle between disease and the healer. To Fioravanti, disease was a threatening *male* (in Italian, both "evil" and "sickness"), and the healer was a soldier waging war against bodily corruption. The entire narrative is framed as a succession of cures, some arrived at by chance, others by conjecture. Often they were cases that baffled the physicians. Some were heroic, as in his treatments of battle wounds; some were miraculous, as in his removal of Marulla's spleen; all were noteworthy. In the war between the empirics and the physicians, the travel narrative was a political document championing experience and sagacity over the entrenched learning of the schools.

VENETIAN YEARS

Leonardo's Venetian years are a blur of novel and daring cures. As in Rome, the physicians grew jealous of him. "My adversaries tried in every way to prohibit me from using my marvelous cures and remedies," he recalled. *Invidia* (envy) had been the root of his troubles. He considered himself an expert on envy; he published a little discourse on the subject in his *Mirror of Universal Science.* The narrative's climax is his victory over the doctors, when he returns to Bologna, "my motherland and *mater studiorum,*" where "the masters, besides giving me the grade of doctor, made me a Count and Knight with the highest authority." The *Treasury* concludes with a lengthy list of his remedies, from Dia Aromatica to Wound Powder, which any physician or surgeon could use with the same astounding effects. But just in case someone might try to match him, he cautioned, "I'll reserve some remedies for myself in order to have a few secrets of my own."

After the autobiography come the testimonials. In a sampling of more than 80 letters that make up the third part of the *Treasury,* he let his correspondents speak for him. Patients wrote to seek his counsel. Physicians and pharmacists reported the amazing cures they had witnessed using his remedies. Alchemists inquired about the virtues of regulus of antimony or the elixir vitae (elixir of life). Some wrote to tell him they had converted to his system, others simply to let him know how famous he was in their part of the world.

Although the letters seem intended mainly to present Fioravanti's public persona, occasionally they provide real insights into the private Leonardo. A letter to Alfonso da Rienzo, for example, which he sent a few weeks after returning from Bologna, reveals the newly degreed physician in one of his most reflective moments. (It is, curiously, the only place in his oeuvre where he bares his interior self.)

Da Rienzo, one of Fioravanti's Neapolitan disciples, had written to tell his teacher that he was continuing to practice alchemy according to the master's instructions. Leonardo was pleased:

> Death being common to all men, we should not marvel at it; yet surely we should lament that it carries away with it the lovely flower of our works and that so much of our effort remains unfinished. However, we should be content to dedicate ourselves to our work until the very end, so that our descendants will be able to take notice of us and the body and our fame not die together. I promise you my dear Alfonso that I shall never tire of reading and writing books and doing experiments, and every day I shall distill various compositions, never resting, so that one day men will find themselves happier than they are today.... We all depart from the world as equals, leaving behind everything that we own: our possessions, our fame, and our shame.... I want above all to leave behind an honored memory.

Leonardo Fioravanti was as obsessed with fame as any of historian Jacob Burckhardt's great Renaissance characters. To him, the desire to notch a memorable achievement was, as Burckhardt put it, "something dæmonic." Yet his was not the same pursuit of personal glory that Burckhardt saw as the hallmark of Renaissance individualism. Rather, Leonardo was preoccupied with the reputation of his "school." He wanted the "new way of healing" to live on after his death, and his name along with it. In putting on his new mask—that of the learned empiric defending the ancient ways of the "first physicians" against the teachers of "false medicine"—Fioravanti was able to trace his pedigree back to the original discoverers of medicine and to identify with the ancient healers who had been persecuted and abused. The physicians may have called him a charlatan, but, he was quick to respond, the real quacks were those "with little practice and a whiff of Galen."

Toward the end of *The Treasury of Human Life,* Fioravanti writes about "the author's secret of secrets, with which you can cure all physical infirmities and heal pains immediately." To the reader's disappointment, it turns out to be not the recipe for the universal panacea but an admonition to "draw near to" nature and receive its truths as one would receive the Sacraments:

> I've spent many years investigating novel things and have had experiences of human bodies never brought to light in ancient times. Our ancient predecessors were never able to find the path that leads to true and certain remedies, but instead followed another, longer and darker path. . . . Whoever wishes to know great and high things must cast off the sciences and draw near to experience and nature, the masters of all creation. In so doing, he will learn things as important as this high and mighty secret, never seen or heard of by anyone before me.

Leonardo Fioravanti had reached the pinnacle of his fame. He was, he told da Rienzo, "the happiest man on earth" because he'd found "three things that few in the world possess, namely, I'm not jealous of anyone, I'm content with the station that I'm in, and by God's grace I have health."

Seemingly contented, Leonardo might have remained in Venice for the rest of his life. Yet he did not. Instead, he left Venice with as little regret as he had earlier departed Bologna, Palermo, Naples, and Rome. The next time we hear of him it will be 1573, and Fioravanti will be stewing in a Milanese jail.

29

LIFE AND ART

Did the relentless pressure from the physicians drive him away? Or did he simply grow restless? Did he want to explore new parts of the world? Historical records do not reveal why Leonardo decided to leave Venice. For all his praise of the "Most Serene Republic," one senses that he was not a republican at heart. Yet his bitter comments about the courts after being spurned by Cosimo de' Medici make it difficult to imagine that he relished the courtier's life. Perhaps, with the publication of his *Surgery* in 1570, Fioravanti felt that he had completed his medical oeuvre. (In fact, he would publish one more book, but not until a decade had passed.) After all, the book contained his definitive statement of the science for which he was best known.

The Surgery reveals Leonardo in a philosophical frame of mind. In it he reflects on the origins of medicine, expounds on the importance of alchemy, presents a passionate critique of anatomy, and writes thoughtfully about the Hippocratic corpus. He struggles to define the relation between theory and experience. Both are important, he concludes, yet we cure by experience, so experience outweighs learning. It alone leads to the quality most important to the surgeon: good judgment.

That said, surgery is both an art and a science—a "mixture of science and practice." After all, a surgeon is no mere cobbler. Both work with skin, but there's a world of difference between live human skin and leather. "If a cobbler tears an old boot or shoe," Leonardo wrote, "he can replace it at little cost; but if a surgeon who lacks knowledge injures or kills a man there's no way he can repair it." Only science can provide the knowledge the surgeon needs to understand the living body.

The surgeon must follow the rhythms of the body's response to injury, he continues. The surgeon is a "minister of nature"; his role is not to cut, but to help nature repair the body. Leonardo advised surgeons to be "imitators of nature in medicating wounds and scars and not become experts at dismembering the living and dead." To follow the law of nature, he continues, surgeons must imitate farmers; surgery is like a "farming of men." For example, "When a farmer comes upon a tree with a torn branch or with its top broken off from the wind or rain, he immediately puts the branch back in its proper place, ties it up, bandages it, and supports it with a wooden brace, and in this way lets nature do its work." The surgeon should do the same by uniting the separated parts of a wound with sutures and bandages and assisting nature in the healing process with fortifying medicines such as Quintessence and Artificial Balsam.

Too often, Leonardo thinks, surgeons work in opposition to nature. They have been seduced by anatomy, which he considers to be "a great and profound subtlety of wit, a delightful art, good to know how to talk about in the company of others," but extremely dangerous for the surgeon. That's because anatomy teaches only about dead bodies, treating the living corpus as though it were an inert contraption. "I'm not satisfied that the anatomist just shows me muscles," he writes. "I also require that he tell me what kind of illnesses are caused by disorders of the muscles and what kind of remedies I can use to cure them." How can you really understand the eye just by dissecting it, when to do so neglects it as the cause of so many ruined households and republics? The eye made Paris fall in love with Helen, causing the destruction of Troy. If Eve's ear hadn't heard the serpent speaking to her, would she have eaten the forbidden fruit? And how often does what comes from the mouth cause us trouble! "These are things that the anatomist has never seen or considered." The human body is more than the sum of its parts.

His message to the anatomist is clear: Don't just show me the body's parts; tell me *why* it exists and show me *how* to cure it. If you can't do that, what use is your science to the doctor? Anatomy brings out the worst instincts in people, transforming surgeons into butchers and observers into gawking spectators.

Leonardo's outrage was genuine, yet one wonders whether his hostility toward anatomy might have had another cause: competition over medical showmanship. Public anatomical dissections drew large crowds, often in the hundreds. Among the throng might be fishmongers, shoemakers, tailors, and other townspeople as well as students and professors, who crowded into anatomical theaters and other public spaces to witness the spectacles. Musical performances and rich academic regalia heightened the theatricality of the occasion.

Leonardo resented the competition from the anatomists. Although he wasn't a charlatan in the precise sense of the term—he didn't perform on a makeshift stage in the piazza—he thrived on being the center of attention. People came to him in droves and were spellbound by his feats as a healer. He relished his role as a theatrical wonder worker and his ability to galvanize people. To Tommaso Garzoni, he was "the glorious Fioravanti, the man of new miracles."

In this medical marketplace, Fioravanti and the anatomists were rivals for viewership. A man as conscious of his public image as Leonardo could not help resenting anyone who stole his thunder.

That in itself may provide a clue to his decision to leave Venice. Already in his mid-50s and at the height of his power and influence, he may have concluded that changes were afoot that would revolutionize the medical world, transforming surgery into an abstract science and making the empirical healer obsolete. He had seen surgery begin to shift from a craft to a learned profession and had loudly protested the manner in which anatomy was altering the surgeon's trade.

In a 1568 letter to his Neapolitan friend Alfonso da Rienzo, Leonardo professed that he was "the happiest man on earth." Yet the letter betrays a mental state bordering on depression. The Venetian way of life, with its crass commercialism (from which he so richly benefited), seems no longer to have suited Leonardo. Whatever the reasons for his departure from his "glorious Venice," the last record of his lengthy stay there is dated 1571, in dedications of new editions of his *Rational Secrets* and *The Mirror of Universal Sciences*, which Giovanni Sessa printed that year.

LETTER FROM A MILANESE JAIL

The next time he turns up is in a document from the Milan state archive. It is a letter, in Leonardo's own careful hand, dated 22 April 1573 and addressed to the protophysician (Niccolo Boldoni) and the viceroy of justice. The letter, we learn, was written from the city jail, where the angry surgeon had been locked up on charges filed against him by the College of Physicians. He was seething in outrage at his humiliation. There he was, a legitimate doctor with degrees like any other, thrown in a prison cell like a common criminal.

How long he had been in Milan by this time we cannot tell, but it was long enough, evidently, to have made an impression on the local doctors. From his jail cell, he complained that he had endured eight days of examination by the College of Physicians, which accused him of poisoning "two or three" of his patients. However, Leonardo insisted, the real reason for his incarceration was "pure and simple envy." If the physicians had to account for the patients who died in their hands, he protested, "they'd all be in prison and would be forbidden from practicing medicine."

Insulted and humiliated, determined to retrieve his good name, Leonardo threw down the gauntlet: "Let there be consigned to me alone twenty or twenty-five sick people with diverse ailments, and an equal number with the same infirmities to all the physicians of Milan. If I don't cure my patients quicker and better than they do theirs, I'm willing to be banished forever from this city." Did the College of Physicians call his bluff? It hardly seems likely.

As usual, he was engaging in pure theater. He must have known that the authorities would never accept the challenge. Evidently the protophysician, loath to risk embarrassment, decided the prudent course of action was to release the prisoner. In any event, Leonardo was set free.

The Boldoni letter is all the more extraordinary in light of the adventures of Modena empiric Jacopo Coppa, the subject of a 1609 novella by Celio Malespini. According to Malespini's tale, which may have had some basis in fact, Coppa found himself down on his luck. The College of Physicians had forbidden him to practice medicine in Florence. He had a wife in Bologna to support. He was about to seek his fortune elsewhere when he befriended a gentleman of the ducal court, who arranged an audience with the Grand Duke, Cosimo de' Medici.

When Coppa explained his predicament, Cosimo smiled benevolently and asked how he might help the empiric. "I would like you to give me twenty-five patients with illnesses that the physicians here could not heal," Coppa replied, "and if I can't quickly cure them, let me be not only undeserving of your good grace, but be thrown out of your city and banished from your happy realm. But if I should restore them to health, let me be allowed, with the same entitlements that they have, to practice my art of medicine freely in your dominion."

Cosimo consented to Coppa's request. When the empiric not only cured the incurable but gave the grand duchess a secret to make her teeth "as white as heaven's clouds," he was showered with gifts and became a wealthy man.

In real life, Jacopo Coppa was a notorious charlatan of the 1540s. Known as "Il Modenese," he was, like Fioravanti, a restless vagabond who traveled often and frequently battled with physicians. Coppa was in Naples in 1542. A few years later he turned up in Venice, where he quarreled acrimoniously with the College of Physicians over the right to sell his secret electuary. Petitioning the health board, he asserted that the physicians of Venice were "malicious and biased" and urged the authorities to seek opinions from physicians in Padua and Bologna. Under pressure from Coppa's influential patron—noblewoman Catarina Barbaro—the health board granted him permission to dispense his secrets. After that, Coppa disappears from the historical record until being reincarnated in Malespini's novel.

Arriving in Venice in 1558, Fioravanti had almost certainly heard of the famous Modena empiric. Possibly he had also gotten wind of stories of his victory over the Florentine College of Physicians. Coppa's oratory skills were impressive, and he demonstrated them regularly in the Piazza San Marco, decked out in a gold-fringed velvet baldachin and standing on a makeshift stage covered with an elegant carpet. Like Fioravanti, he boasted wonder drugs, including his *Elettuario mirabile* (Marvelous Electuary), a half-almond portion of which would "comfort the brain, cheer the heart, drive away sadness or melancholy, purify the blood, fortify the limbs, and cure all infirmities of the womb."

Did Fioravanti model his challenge to the Milanese physicians on the real life of Jacopo Coppa? Or did Malespini, writing early in the 17th century, base his tale about the fictional Coppa on rumors of Leonardo's run-ins in Milan? In other words, did art imitate life, or life art? It's hard to tell. Yet the similarities between the two stories are so close that coincidence seems out of the question. "Dueling charlatans"—whether competing with one each other in the piazza or challenging the medical authorities in the courts—were not an uncommon feature of urban life in Renaissance Italy. And even though he wasn't a typical mountebank, Leonardo Fioravanti could easily imitate the self-aggrandizing, theatrical style of the charlatan. Indeed, the pursuit of fame demanded it.

Meanwhile, never abandoning his dream of entering a court, Fioravanti turned his gaze toward Spain. In 1576 he contacted the viceroy of Naples through his agent and reminded him of the service he had rendered to King Philip's father, Holy Roman Emperor Charles V, "on land and sea" during the African war. He offered to do the same for Philip, the agent reported, "without any pay, curing the sick and wounded if Your Majesty would do him the favor of granting him the title of Protomedico and Provider of Health in

Italy without obligation to demonstrate his title and degrees to any college or Protomedico of any city."

Although Philip did not grant this audacious request, he did invite the surgeon to the court to demonstrate his cures. Leonardo eagerly accepted the offer.

30

IN THE COURT OF THE CATHOLIC KING

The Duchy of Milan was within the Spanish political sphere, enabling Leonardo to cultivate contacts with Spanish soldiers and officials. He renewed friendships he'd made in Naples and, as elsewhere, gathered around him a circle of alchemists and natural philosophers.

Milan was just a stopover on his way to a new destination, however. Now he had his eye on the court of King Philip II of Spain. His service to the Spanish crown as a military surgeon during the African war, his reputation as a healer, his pro-Spanish sympathies—all worked to his advantage. His books circulated in Spain, too: Four of them were on the shelves of King Philip's private library at El Escorial. A partial translation into Spanish of *Medical Caprices* made in 1562 suggests that Leonardo's ideas were well known in Spanish medical circles.

In the spring of 1575, rumors of the return of the plague were heard in Milan. Fifty people reportedly had died of the disease in Trent, and from there it had spread south to Mantua. In July, the pestilence broke out for real in Venice, and by February of the following year more than 3,500 deaths had been reported. The contagion subsided over the winter but returned with a fury in the spring. In April, cases were reported in Venice; by midsummer the sickness had spread to Padua, Verona, and other cities in northern Italy.

In July 1576, the plague struck Milan. Giambattista Casale, a local carpenter, kept a diary that narrated the long months of the epidemic. "The plague began suddenly in the Ortolani quarter," he recorded. "Everyone said that it had been brought by certain renegade Christians who came from Turkey. . . . It took such firm hold that people dropped like flies." Some people blamed soldiers returning from the battle of Lepanto for bringing the disease. Rumors circulated of *untori*—plague spreaders—who out of sheer malice went about touching walls, gates, and streets with artificial unguents that spread the disease.

The epidemic raged for more than a year before finally subsiding in November 1577. In Milan the plague of 1576–77 was remembered as the "plague of San Carlo" after Cardinal-Archbishop Carlo Borromeo, who managed charitable relief during the epidemic and enforced stern sanitary regulations. Many contemporaries, including carpenter Casale, believed that the processions and prayers decreed by Borromeo had propitiated God, leading to the termination of the epidemic.

Whether or not the threat of the plague prompted Fioravanti to leave Milan we cannot say. Certainly he had plenty of advance warning of its coming. All we know is that he was absent from Italy during those cruel months. By the time the sickness reached Milan, he had already moved on to Madrid.

THE FILTHIEST CITY IN ALL OF SPAIN

When Philip II decided to move his court from Toledo to Madrid in 1561, the latter city was a sleepy market town of 16,000. Reestablishing the court transformed the provincial town. By the time Fioravanti arrived in 1576, Madrid's population had mushroomed to 45,000.

Judging by contemporary accounts, it was not a pleasant place to live. The development of the city's infrastructure could not keep pace with its explosive growth. Visitors frequently complained about its filthy streets and stinking latrines. Lamberto Wyts, a Dutch traveler in the 1570s, wrote, "I find the city of Madrid to be the filthiest in all of Spain. In all of the streets there are great *servidores,* as they call them, which are big urinals full of piss and shit that are emptied into the streets, giving off an unimaginable and vile stench."

Despite such complaints, courtiers and those who trailed after them flocked to the city. Philip, a generous patron, ruled the largest empire in Europe, and the court in Madrid was its hub. Even if it was a filthy stink hole, to contemporaries in Catholic Europe, Madrid was the center of the world.

The journey from Milan to Madrid would have taken Fioravanti a month—three weeks by land and sea to Barcelona, then another week by coach or horse to Madrid. The long trek would have given him plenty of time to contemplate what he had gleaned about Spain from his informants in Naples, Rome, and Milan. The royal court in Madrid was alive with scientific activity. King Philip, fascinated by the discoveries of the day, spent lavishly on scientific enterprises.

His motives were political and economic rather than purely intellectual. As ruler of the world's largest empire, he needed science and technology to realize his "grand strategy" of world dominion. To that end, he patronized royal institutions for the advancement of science and financed voyages of scientific discovery. Motivated by a desire to optimize the economic potential of his vast American possessions, the king solicited information about the geography and natural history of the New World. In 1570 he commissioned one of his court physicians, Francisco Hernández, to make an extensive survey of the medicinal plants of the Americas, and ordered his Portuguese viceroy of India to gather information about the medicinal plants of that region. The next year he appointed Juan López de Velasco to the newly created post of cosmographer-chronicler of the Indies, instructing him to compile maps, cosmographic tables, records of tides and eclipses, and a natural history of the Indies, making the Spanish royal court a center of news and research about America. In addition, Philip developed extensive botanical gardens at his royal palaces in Aranjuez and Madrid, where species from distant parts of the empire were collected and cultivated.

Since the beginning of the 16th century, Spain had been a center for the study of navigation and cosmography—subjects of immediate practical interest in maintaining its overseas empire. The Casa de Contratación (House of Trade) in Seville, founded by the Catholic monarchs in 1503, was charged with training pilots in the art and theory of navigation. English navigator Stephen Borough, who visited the Casa in 1558, so admired the union of theory and practice taught there that he lobbied for the founding of a similar institution in England. In 1582 Philip founded an Academy of Mathematics at Madrid, where courses on military engineering, navigation, and architecture were taught.

Historians have sometimes portrayed Philip II as an intransigent obstacle to new scientific ideas. In reality, from the standpoint of scientific patronage he was one of Europe's most enlightened monarchs. Indeed, Spain under Philip II ushered in modern, state-sponsored "big science."

As an international center of news and research about the Indies, Philip's court gave Leonardo opportunities to talk with people who had journeyed to the New World. His informants were sometimes reliable, sometimes sketchy. From a Corsican sailor, for example, he learned about the Peruvian Indians and their customs: their ships and weaponry, their supposedly bellicose nature, their wars with a barbarous tribe "whose men dressed in lions' skins." The sailor told him about an island inhabited by apelike creatures with yard-long penises who threw stones and feared fire, like satyrs. From a Peruvian Indian he learned firsthand about a bird with feathers of a dozen colors, about magical stones, about an herb called *bacaza* that glows in the dark and enables one to foretell the future, and about a marvelous fountain in the distant reaches of Peru whose water turns the skin perfectly white.

What was an American Indian doing in King Philip's court? In fact, Indians and mestizos were fairly common in early modern Spain. Some arrived in the service of Spanish hidalgos; others were shipped to Spain as slaves. Some were caciques sent by their villages to request a favor from the king; others had been sent by their families to be educated at one of the universities. Some returned to the Americas; others stayed in Spain. Nothing else is known about the Indian that Fioravanti met in Philip's court. Possibly he was one of those caciques who occasionally came to pursue their prerogatives, or perhaps he was a captive brought to the court as a curiosity piece and put on display as a symbol of the king's personal empire.

BOTANICA EXOTICA

In a Seville bookshop, Leonardo discovered Nicolás Monardes's *Medicinal History of the Things Brought from the New World*, one of the most important scientific treatises of the 16th century. Monardes—a respected Seville physician and a prosperous trader in transatlantic commodities—had a medical degree from Alcalá de Henares, a leading European center of medical research. He was, in the words of historian Marcy Norton, "the first humanist-trained university doctor to systematically consider American materia medica, a dramatic reversal of the hostility humanist-inclined botanists and physicians had shown to New World substances until that point." Strictly an armchair traveler, Monardes learned about American plants and animals from merchants returning to Seville, at that time a center of Spanish trade with the New World. He also kept an herb garden in which he cultivated plants from the Americas.

Monardes's book of New World flora captivated Leonardo. So enamored of its plants was the surgeon that he copied out and translated into Italian lengthy passages from the Spanish author, then published them in his own book, *Of Physic,* which chronicled his journey to Spain. He described exotic plants such as chile, sarsaparilla, *guacatane,* a shrub used as a treatment for hemorrhoids, and *mechoacan,* a powerful purgative from Peru. Monardes also wrote detailed reports of his experiments with the American plants. He acquired some resin of the caraña tree *(Protium caranna)* and, preparing it in the Indian manner, found it to be extremely effective in treating superficial wounds. Tobacco, whose medicinal virtues Monardes praised to the skies, fascinated Leonardo. Having concocted a distilled water from the herb, he marveled at its healing properties. "Everyone should use tobacco," he advised, "because it's an herb that God has revealed to our century for the health of mankind."

In *Of Physic,* Leonardo implies that he met Monardes personally: Concerning *tacamahaca,* a balsamic resin obtained from a Venezuelan poplar, he writes, "I saw more of this with Doctor Monardes." Such an encounter seems quite possible. Fioravanti's name was well known in Spain; on his visit to Seville, where Monardes lived, he might naturally have visited the aging botanist. To Leonardo, Monardes was "the most famous physician in all of Spain." His announcement of the Spanish doctor's "joyful news from the New World"—as Monardes's English translator later characterized it—was among the earliest revelations in Italian of Monardes's important book.

Regrettably, Monardes's significance for the history of science has been overshadowed by the grand narrative of the Scientific Revolution that governs the history of early modern science. That story places mathematics and the physical sciences at the forefront of a dramatic overthrow of the dominant Aristotelian-Ptolemaic cosmology. The canonical version of the Scientific Revolution is the triumph of reason and enlightenment over dark ignorance and religious bigotry—a history in the "elegiac mode," as one historian described it.

In that story the Copernican revolution takes center stage, yet for most people of the time it was a revolution of little import. Until the 17th century, when the trial of Galileo made Copernicanism the focus of a public spectacle, debates over the new cosmology were confined mainly to small circles of mathematicians and astronomers. A leading modern authority on Copernicus has been able to identify only ten avowed Copernicans from 1543 to 1600. Nor did the new cosmology seem to offer any significant advantages to those who brought the science of astronomy down to earth in the form of astrological forecasts and nativities. As long as people could buy their almanacs, what did they care whether it was Ptolemy's or Copernicus's mathematics that astrologers employed in making them?

To the majority of 16th-century Europeans, the real scientific revolution was not the revelation of a novel arrangement of the heavens but the discovery of new worlds on earth. Daily life was transformed by the exchanges with America. With the introduction of new foodstuffs, diets changed; new fashions, such as smoking tobacco, took off. Many of the modern world's most important food plants—like maize, squashes, tomatoes—originated in the New World. It's impossible to imagine Italian cuisine without the tomato, yet Italians lived for millennia without it. And who can conceive of Spanish-American food without chilies, eastern European dishes without paprika, or English and German dinners without the potato, all New World plants? Think of how impoverished our dessert-rich palates would be without *tlixochitl*—Nahuatl for what the Spaniards called "vanilla."

The assimilation of tobacco and chocolate into European culture provides a perfect example of how the discovery of the New World transformed everyday life. When they first encountered tobacco and cacao (as the Spanish translated the Nahuatl word *cacauatl*), Europeans associated both items with heathen rituals, for in the New World they were primarily consumed in sacred settings. But Europeans could not long resist the stimulating and narcotic effects of the two products. As tobacco and chocolate consumption grew throughout the 17th century, their uses shifted from medicinal to social and domestic settings. Europeans became accustomed to the stimulating effects of tobacco and the bitter taste of cacao. Tobacco was cherished for providing folk with a respite from their labors—and an occasion to enjoy the company of others. Chocolate was prized as an antidote to fatigue and melancholy.

By the end of the 17th century, chocolate consumption had spread beyond the elite to the public spaces of the city. In 1685, city officials in Madrid reported that "there was hardly to be found a street without one, two, or even three stands making and selling chocolate." Meanwhile, tobacco smoking became commonplace in social settings such as taverns and weddings.

So ubiquitous were tobacco and chocolate in early modern Europe, writes Marcy Norton, that their incorporation into daily life contributed to the secularization of European culture. The routine consumption of tobacco and chocolate stripped these formerly sacred products of their mystical connotations and made them a normal part of secular culture. In creating a monopoly on the trade in tobacco and chocolate, the state became a guarantor of the consumption of "vice" goods. "Spain was like a funnel for the Americas," Norton writes, channeling return migrants, Indians and mestizos, new drugs, and exotic plants and animals to the Old World.

Spain served as a conduit for a phenomenal number of other New World drugs, transforming the European pharmacopoeia. In terms of the sheer quantity of new drugs introduced into the marketplace, the early modern period would probably not be surpassed until the explosive growth of the chemical pharmaceutical industry in the 20th century. Well stocked with dried specimens of exotic plants and animals from all over the world, apothecary shops were like public museums, displaying strange objects from distant lands for a curious and admiring public. From a pharmacy you could purchase everything from guaiac wood (to treat syphilis) to exotic dried fish (to stock curiosity cabinets) to bezoar stones (to counteract poisoning). Many pharmacists amassed impressive natural history collections, and collectors relied heavily on the apothecary shops for natural curiosities.

Many of the new drugs helped cure new diseases, like syphilis, which also came from the New World. The impact of the French pox upon everyday life went far beyond its victims. The pox ruined lives—but made profits for merchants and doctors, and sharpened medical debates. The sudden appearance of a new and virulent illness that did not seem to fit the Galenic framework profoundly challenged traditional medicine. The pox tested the limits of classical medicine, proving that the ancients did not have all the answers. More than any other event in early modern Europe, the syphilis epidemic undermined the traditional paradigm about the nature and causation of disease. As these examples demonstrate, measured by its impact on everyday life, the discovery of the New World far surpassed the design of a new cosmos.

"THINGS OF STUPENDOUS WONDER"

Science, too, was transformed by the geographical discoveries. News from the Indies generated intense interest among the "new philosophers," as the members of the emerging community of experimental scientists styled themselves. Thanks to the printing press, the New World discoveries became widely known—and thus a part of public discourse. Reports of objects that explorers and navigators brought back from the New World traveled swiftly in the correspondence of naturalists and physicians. Monardes's *Medicinal History of the New World*—translated into English in 1577 with the whimsical title *Joyful News out of the New Found World*—played a key role in disseminating knowledge in Europe of the American plants. The book was a phenomenal success: Twenty-five editions of the work in six languages were published before the end of the 16th century, and 14 more appeared in the 17th.

The intense interest in the geography and natural history of the New World, which reverberated in the scientific community, contributed to the emergence of a new conception of the aims and methods of science: the idea of science as a hunt for the secrets of nature. The search for secrets in unknown regions of nature appears as a theme in Renaissance scientific literature with striking regularity. At the end of the 16th century, French historian Louis Le Roy sounded giddy as he contemplated the marvels of the new age:

> All the mysteries of God and secrets of nature are not discovered at one time. . . . How many have been first known and found out in this age? I say, new lands, new seas, new forms of men, manners, laws, and customs; new diseases, and new remedies; new ways of the heavens and of the oceans, never before found out, and new stars seen? Yea, and how many remain to be known by our posterity? That which is now hidden, with time will come to light; and our successors will wonder that we were ignorant of them.

As late as the mid-17th century, English virtuoso Joseph Glanvill still envisioned the opening up of an "America of secrets and an unknown Peru of nature." Like the New World, nature loomed before investigators as uncharted territory.

Another consequence of the debates sparked by the discovery of the New World was the emergence of a new conception of human nature and, with that, a new science: comparative ethnology. As collectors of massive amounts of data about the people and societies of the New World, the Spaniards were among the first Europeans to face questions of ethnology, the uniformity and diversity of races, and the like. Strange cultural practices like smoking tobacco and consuming bitter, frothy chocolate drinks "were often the flash-points for cultural authorities in the New World and the Old World who sought to define the boundaries separating Christian and idolatrous, European and Amerindian, and civilized and barbarian," notes historian Marcy Norton. "The result of the encounter was a far-reaching change in the understanding of human societies," writes historian Anthony Pagden, "a change from a description of cultures in terms of a human nature thought to be constant over time and space to a wider anthropological and historical relativism."

Leonardo Fioravanti would never have stated it that way, but he too was conscious of the far-reaching changes that had taken place as a result of the European encounter with America. He could barely contain his enthusiasm when discussing the resplendent variety of the novelties found there. "To discourse about matters of the Indies is like a chaos that one can never find a way out of," he wrote. "For the regions are so vast, the people of such varied customs, the animals so different, the climate so productive of things of stupendous wonder, the land so luxuriant in fantastic herbs and trees unknown to us, and the minerals so completely different from ours, that it is almost impossible to put into words."

Leonardo's experience in the Spanish royal court made a deep impression on him. His contact with sailors and adventurers who had visited the New World convinced him—if he needed convincing—that the ancients were wrong about many things. Reading Monardes's book and conversing with Native Americans also persuaded him that Amerindians were more in touch with nature than supposedly more "civilized" Europeans. That immediacy enabled New World shamans to make discoveries that eluded the Italian physicians, whose senses were corrupted by theory. "The Indians have discovered medicines in simples and don't ever use compound medicines like we do," he observed. Maybe they didn't know "true medicine," as did he, but they had discovered an elemental truth that confirmed the correctness of his new way of healing.

31

MASTERS OF FIRE

King Philip II of Spain has always been a controversial figure. Even during his own lifetime he was attacked for cruelty and religious fanaticism, while being praised as a wise and prudent monarch. To contemporaries in the Catholic world, whether in Italy, Spain, or Germany, he was the "Most Catholic King" of Europe. Protestants in northern Europe, however, saw an entirely different Philip. William of Orange, leader of the Dutch revolt against Spanish rule, saw the king as a monster in league with the devil. The Spanish Inquisition and Philip II together became the emblem of Spain's moral depravity in the so-called Black Legend that northern European Protestants constructed about Spain in the 16th and 17th centuries. The propaganda war was fueled by Fray Bartolomé de Las Casas's polemical tract, *A Brief Account of the Destruction of the Indies* (1552), a record of Spain's brutal treatment of the Indians. Other nations, most notably England, were equally guilty of the faults that Protestants blamed on Spain, but they had better propaganda machines and therefore won the battle of words.

During the 18th-century Enlightenment, Philip came to represent tyranny, obscurantism, and intolerance—an image that would persist for more than a century. To the American historian Walter Prescott, Philip II, whose biography Prescott published in 1855, was evil incarnate, a king who "nurtured schemes of mad ambition" and denied Spain the opportunity to join the modern world.

After his death, Philip's defenders tried to rescue his reputation from the stain of tyranny and religious fanaticism that the originators of the Black Legend left in their wake. The 17th-century Spanish chronicler Baltasar Porreño, in his eulogistic *Words and Deeds of King Philip II* (1628), portrayed Philip as a second Solomon whose prudence and pure Catholic faith kept him free from all types of superstition. In one of his stories about the king, Porreño tells how Philip ordered the publication of an astrologer's prognostication for 1579 because its dire predictions had not come to pass. The king "wanted to demonstrate the vanity of the author and to admonish and embarrass him," Porreño writes, in order to expose the futility of astrology.

The truth about King Philip lies somewhere in between the extremes. Porreño's hagiographical account notwithstanding, Philip was intensely curious about the occult sciences—though whether or not that made him "superstitious" is debatable. Like most monarchs of the day, he turned to experts for astrological advice on foreign and domestic policy. Although his curiosity may have been more restrained than that of his nephew, the Holy Roman Emperor Rudolf II, whose court at Prague was a haven for astrologers and natural magicians, Philip consulted astrologers as he did other ministers, sometimes taking their advice, sometimes not. Such an attitude was not exceptional among contemporary rulers, nor does it suggest the influenced of "superstition." German astronomer Johannes Kepler, whose discovery of the three basic laws of planetary motion ranks him among the greatest astronomers of all time, was a passionate adept of astrology and one of Rudolf II's leading advisers.

Philip was also a devotee of alchemy. Like many Renaissance princes, he valued alchemy as a practical science that might be used to increase the wealth, health, and well-being of the realm. Chronically short of money to finance his empire, he sought an alchemical remedy for his financial problems. Before long, foreigners learned of Philip's fondess for alchemy and began venturing to Madrid in the hope of securing the king's patronage. In 1569, the Roman adept Marco Antonio Bufale offered Philip his alchemical secret to transmute base metals into gold—but, he complained, he had been kept waiting for three months without ever hearing whether the king was interested.

Probably he wasn't. Philip's confidence in making precious metals alchemically had been shaken by the results of experiments conducted under his supervision in the early 1560s. Time and again he would turn away alchemists with similar promises. Yet he never lost faith in alchemy altogether.

ALCHEMICAL CLIQUE

By 1570 or so the king had his eye on a different kind of philosopher's stone: the one that might serve as a panacea. His health had never been good, and it had deteriorated in the 1560s, when he suffered his first attacks of gout. But it was not just his own health that worried him. The infante Fernando, the male heir to the throne, was also unwell, as were other members of the royal family. Attending to the physical health of the royal family became urgent state business.

Philip's belief in the possibility of obtaining a universal medicine was fueled by his interest in what he and his contemporaries believed were the alchemical doctrines of Ramon Lull. King Philip was a passionate adherent of Lull's philosophy. Although we do not know exactly when his curiosity about Lull's doctrines originated, by 1576 he had assembled a sizable collection of Lull's books in the library at El Escorial. By 1580, he was consulting with Majorcan scholar Juan Seguí about establishing colleges dedicated to Lullist philosophy throughout the kingdom. It's unclear whether the king saw Lull's doctrine as the key to universal knowledge, as a means of converting infidels, or as a source of the secret to the philosopher's stone. What is known is that by the 1570s, his court was a center of Lullist philosophical activity.

Philip vigorously promoted the manufacture of Lullian quintessences. Although he had grown skeptical of goldmaking, he retained his faith in the medicinal potential of alchemy. In 1564 he established a distillation laboratory at the royal palace in Aranjuez and appointed a Fleming, Francis Holbeeck, as royal distiller. A few years later, a Neapolitan, Giovanni Vincenzo Forte, was invited to the court and provided a house and distillation laboratory in the Royal Garden. In 1572, Philip had a distillation laboratory built at the royal palace to manufacture quintessences. Not long after, Italian alchemists and distillers, particularly from the Kingdom of Naples (one of Europe's leading centers of Lullism) began migrating to the court.

Fioravanti quickly joined the alchemical community at the royal court. He encountered numerous Italians and soon gathered a circle of devoted followers. The group met weekly to discuss their alchemical experiments, he reports, and to talk about "the true medicine and surgery"—doubtless meaning Fioravanti's "new way of healing." Leonardo identifies Bolognese surgeon Giovanni Angelo Santini as *mio creato,* meaning his servant or laboratory assistant. This *"alchimista terribilissimo"* was so adept at making drugs that Fioravanti compared him to the greatest alchemists of all time: Ramon Lull, John of Rupescissa, and Paracelsus. He described another Italian disciple, Agostino Bravo, as *"un hombre diabolico"* because of his familiarity with alchemical furnaces. "He knows more about fire than all the devils in hell," enthused Leonardo.

Two Spaniards rounded out Leonardo's alchemical circle. One was Juan Cornejo, a physician from Córdoba and one of the hypochondriac king's legion of doctors. Some years later, Cornejo wrote a treatise on making potable gold entirely of plant substances that supposedly relieved the king's gout with such success that Cornejo dedicated the printed version of the work to the pope. The second Spaniard—physician and alchemist Juan Fernández—had offered his services to the king as early as 1572, when Philip's royal secretary, Antonio Gracián, reported that, after years of labor and considerable expense, the alchemist had "discovered the secret" for transmuting base metals into gold. The king was skeptical of the claim. "I have always regarded this as a hoax," Philip replied. Even so, he asked Gracián not to send the man away, but to put the alchemist to work and report back "when he has brought it to completion, which I am sure he never will." The letter from Gracián and the king's reply have been interpreted to indicate Philip's hostility toward alchemy, yet the fact that Fernández was still practicing alchemy in the court in 1576 and was active in Fioravanti's circle suggests otherwise.

WORKING WONDERS WITH "BARBARIC" TOBACCO

Leonardo's encounter with the exotic plants and minerals from the New World steered his alchemical research in new directions. One of the plants he encountered in Spain was tobacco. From reading Monardes, Leonardo learned that the Indians used the leaves of the plant to treat headaches, chest pains, and stomach disorders. They inhaled the smoke of tobacco to expel the chest material from asthmatics and ingested its juice to expel worms. They used it when taking a long journey, placing a plug of tobacco under their tongue to stanch hunger and thirst. Tobacco was almost a panacea: It was used to treat toothache, skin diseases, swelling, and uterine ailments. Monardes had even devoted a section of his treatise to the veterinary uses of tobacco.

As a surgeon, Leonardo was intrigued by tobacco's potential to treat wounds and ulcers. Monardes noted that the Indians made an ointment of pulverized tobacco leaves and used it to cure venomous bites and to treat the wounds caused by poisonous arrows. Applied to ulcers on the feet and other parts of the body, he wrote, "it works wonders." Leonardo was determined to investigate further, using alchemical means to perfect tobacco's curative virtues.

Where Leonardo obtained the tobacco he used in his experiments is a mystery. The plant wasn't widely available in Europe, even in Iberia, before the end of the 16th century. Most of the tobacco cultivated in Spain, Monardes tells us, was grown as an ornamental plant to decorate gardens. According to import-tax records, less than 3,000 pounds of the stuff entered Spain through Seville in the early 1590s. Very few 16th-century Europeans smoked tobacco—a practice associated with the "barbaric" Indians of the New World—although after 1700, the number of smokers and people taking tobacco as snuff rapidly multiplied. When Fioravanti was in Spain, tobacco was found mainly in pharmacies, since it was used as a medicinal, or it was obtained from someone who grew it in a garden. Monardes, who cultivated tobacco plants in his herb garden in Seville, was one possible source.

Fioravanti experimented on tobacco continuously for several months, certain that it had curative powers. In one trial, he took whole tobacco plants and ground them up in a mortar to make a thick paste, covered it with horse dung, and let it ferment for 30 days. Then he added some aqua vitae and distilled the mixture to produce a translucent liquid, leaving behind a lumpy, blackened residue. Blended with just enough oil of brimstone to give it a sharp taste, a mere spoonful of the essence, he claimed, cured fevers. Used as an ointment, it healed wounds instantly without leaving a scar.

The process that Fioravanti describes was similar to making *picietl,* a Mayan drug composed of pulverized tobacco mixed with lime to enhance its narcotic affect. The difference was that, by extracting the drug's essence through distillation, he adapted the Mayan practice to European technology. Leonardo marveled that God, in his wisdom, had given knowledge of the herb's healing power to "savage" Indians, revealing it to Christians only in the 1500s. What other mysteries, he wondered, had the Almighty been keeping from us for all these millennia? What other secrets of nature awaited imminent discovery?

32

THE CHARLATAN'S TRIAL

Fioravanti's account of his experiences in Spain—as in all of his writings—contains a certain amount of hyperbole. *Of Physic* is a characteristic example of his supreme skill at self-fashioning. His glowing account of his sojourn in Spain contains almost no hint of conflict or distress. For all that we can tell from reading the work, he was accepted in Philip's court as the prophet of a new art of healing.

But why should Spain have differed from any other place he lived? Wherever Leonardo went, he ran afoul of the medical establishment and made enemies of powerful men. Behind the rosy facade of his recollection of events in Madrid lies a darker story—one filled with court intrigue. Despite the royal family's enthusiasm for distilled essences, alchemists were not received with universal approval. Foreigners who arrived in Madrid touting obscure Lullian doctrines and newfangled ways of making drugs drew the ire of powerful court physicians. Inevitably, Fioravanti, one of the most prominent foreign alchemists in Philip's court, got snared in their net.

That side of the story is told in a manuscript in the British Library, evidently unknown to previous biographers. The manuscript, written in a formal, legalistic Castilian (and thus probably composed by a scribe or civil lawyer), contains Fioravanti's plea to the Spanish Royal Protomedicato, answering the charge of practicing medicine illegally.

Behind the affair lay powerful enemies and accusations of heinous crimes. Leonardo stood accused of having poisoned a servant of one of the king's courtiers with his cures. The man who would judge him was Prince Carlos's personal physician, Don Diego Olivares, a sworn enemy of the alchemists. Intensely jealous of these interlopers who had gained the king's favor, Olivares aimed to rid the court of foreigners, who "sneak in through the back door and leave through the front." If Fioravanti had been able to brush off such accusations with bravado and bold challenges before, this time around he was in real trouble.

The Real Tribunal del Protomedicato, or Royal Protomedicato, the court that tried Fioravanti, was the main legal body overseeing the medical professions in the Spanish Empire. The tribunal's reach extended to all Spanish territories, from Madrid to Mexico and from the Kingdom of Naples to the Duchy of Milan. Its function was to examine and license all medical practitioners in the realm, be they physicians, surgeons, or apothecaries. Its purpose was to ensure the quality of medical care and to root out dangerous and untrained practitioners. Established throughout the Spanish Empire, the Royal Protomedicato was the first worldwide system of medical regulation.

Leonardo faced five charges. The first was that, not having a license from the Protomedicato, he had been practicing medicine illegally. The law strictly forbade unlicensed practitioners and imposed stiff fines for infractions. The penalty for practicing without a license was 6,000 maravedís—roughly the equivalent of six months' wages for a skilled pressman.

In the second place, as Fioravanti tells it, "I am charged with making harmful cures with my medicaments, and with using lethal drugs to poison Tristan de la Torre's servant." We possess few clues to de la Torre's identity, but we do know that he was a well-connected member of the court.

The third accusation alleged that Leonardo lacked the proper academic titles to practice medicine in Spain. According to Castilian law, only those who had graduated from one of the three Castilian universities—Valladolid, Salamanca, or Alcalá—were authorized to practice medicine in the Kingdom of Castile. In addition, they had to pass an examination administered by the Protomedicato.

Fourth, Fioravanti was accused of making drugs in his home and using them to treat patients. Castilian law prohibited anyone but pharmacists from making and selling drugs.

The last charge accused him, rather ambiguously, of practicing surgery "against the precepts of the authorities."

Fioravanti's appeal, in Spanish, was addressed to Ramón Martín, the court attorney who had been appointed to prosecute the case, and to Olivares, the Royal Protomedico. Olivares must have seen the death of Tristan de la Torre's servant as an opportunity to rid himself of the most famous foreign alchemist in Philip's court. By discrediting Fioravanti's "new way of healing," he could disgrace all of the alchemists.

Fioravanti countered the charges with a spirited defense—on one hand pleading ignorance of the laws, on the other hand arguing that even if he had broken the law, he had done so for the good of the realm. After all, he asserted, the new way of healing was superior to the methods practiced by the Spanish physicians.

Leonardo opened his defense with a startling claim. "In response to the accusations made against me by Señor Martín, I say that the contrary is true of every one of them," he pronounced. "I say further that His Majesty's court should acquit me of each and every one of the charges and set me free and allow me to practice freely anywhere in this realm where I may be called." As for having violated the laws against practicing medicine without a license, "I knew nothing of these laws. If I broke any law, it's because I'm a foreigner newly arrived in these parts and I'm not familiar with the laws of the land."

Leonardo was being disingenuous. Having lived in Naples and Milan, he had plenty of experience with the Spanish system of medical regulation. It's impossible to believe that he would not have assumed that similar laws applied in Spain, as they did everywhere in Spanish Italy. Perhaps he felt that his proximity to the court would protect him. If so, he was mistaken. His plea that he was an inexperienced foreigner fell on deaf ears.

Fioravanti responded to the remaining charges in his customary way: He went on the attack, boldly proclaiming his methods superior to those of the Spanish physicians, because his were the ways of nature. "If Tristan's servant died while in my care, it wasn't because of the way I treated him but because of his grave and mortal illness, and because afterward he was treated by other doctors who didn't understand his sickness and applied remedies contrary to mine."

He then continued in a theological vein:

> Death is natural. To die and to cure are in God's hands, not the hands of doctors or in the power of medicines. If it were not so, men wouldn't even recognize God as our Lord but would consider themselves as Gods on earth. Being mortal, it's necessary that men die when their hour comes. God does his will. People die every day, and the doctors who treat them shouldn't be blamed. To believe otherwise is contrary to the Holy Catholic Faith.

As for his titles, he could truthfully say that his degrees came from one of Europe's most respected medical schools—even if it was Italian and not Castilian. "When you consider that I have the titles of Doctor in Physic and Surgery from universities as famous as Bologna and Naples," he argued, "naturally I didn't think it would be necessary to have any other license. I've been practicing with these degrees for more than forty years, all the while doing good works for the poor, for the love of God, so why would such a license be necessary? If I erred, I erred out of ignorance, not knowing the law."

The court rejoined that, because Fioravanti was ignorant of Latin, his degrees could not possibly be legitimate. He didn't claim to know Latin, Leonardo responded. Besides, "Speaking in Latin is no proof that you know medicine or how to heal." Every revered authority had written in his own mother tongue: Hippocrates and Galen in Greek, Avicenna in Arabic, and so on. "For medicine originates not in books but in experience," Leonardo explained, "which various authors later wrote down in their own language and not in Latin. Afterward their books were translated from Arabic and Greek into Latin, because in those times the Latin language was more common and universal."

Warming to his topic, Fioravanti went on:

> Truthfully, I haven't studied Latin to know medicine because I didn't have to. Although it's true that medicine can't be understood without knowing philosophy, it doesn't follow from this that you can't be a philosopher without knowing Latin. For, philosophy is nothing but knowing the operations of nature by natural reason and with this knowledge understanding the causes of things, which can certainly be understood without knowing Latin. Did the first philosophers learn philosophy from Latin books? Did they learn it in the university? Of course not. And so the professors of those colleges, having witnessed my doctrine and intelligence, with that experience—which is after all the mother of all wisdom in this profession—conceded to me these titles and privileges, which, as I said, are certain and true and legal.

As to the accusation that he made medicines in his own house, contrary to the law forbidding anyone but pharmacists from making drugs, Leonardo defiantly stood his ground. "I confess to the charge," he asserted, and extended his defense with an audacious discourse on the superiority of the new way of healing, pitting himself squarely against the "Arabists" who dominated Spanish medicine:

> The true method of healing, whether in medicine or surgery, is the one that I have written about in my books. My method is founded upon the true doctrine of Hippocrates, which Avicenna understood poorly. But the moderns, such as Ramon Lull, Arnald of Villanova, Abacue the Jew, Paracelsus, Cornelius Celsus, and Philip Ulstadius, understood it well and used the same methods. As Your Excellency knows, Hippocrates writes, *estrema mala morba, extremis medicamentis sunt curanda*

> (extreme remedies are to be employed when treating extreme sicknesses). This proposition is the foundation of my doctrine, but it has been badly practiced by Avicenna's followers, since grave sicknesses and diseases engendered from bad qualities have to be cured with strong medicines, not by ordinary weak medicines.

Feet firmly planted in the Lullist alchemical tradition, Fioravanti proceeded to launch an attack on the Spanish physicians and apothecaries, accusing them of using obsolete methods and outdated equipment to make their remedies. As always, he dwelled on bodily pollution. In a lengthy digression on the therapeutics of cleansing, he argued that illnesses are engendered by impurities that collect in the stomach, which expels them to the rest of the body, causing many different kinds of sickness. Therefore, it stands to reason that the cure is to drive these pollutions from the body, and the most natural and efficient way to do that is through the windpipe—that is, by vomiting rather than purging. "This was the method I followed in treating Tristan's servant, as I do in treating all of my patients," Leonardo explained. "But the poor lad was too far gone when I arrived at the scene. I did all I could for him but the doctors who came after me refused to follow my instructions."

The same applies to remedies: They too must be free of corruption. Defending himself against the charge of having made his own medicines at home rather than purchasing them from the pharmacists, Fioravanti explained that he had done so because he had to distill his medicaments in glass vessels, not in the metal alembics used by Spanish apothecaries. "My medicines are free of the bad effects of the distilled waters that are corrupted and rotten because they aren't extracted in glass vessels. The alembics they use here exhale the incorruptible and substantial spirits and absorb the corrosive quality of the metal and therefore become corrupted and putrefy."

Because his drugs were perfectly distilled, Leonardo contended, "They take on the occult properties of nature much better than those made by any other method" and thus are better able to resolve peccant humors. The Spanish apothecaries didn't understand the process of distillation, he alleged. Besides, he'd been invited to the court specifically to conduct experiments with his medicaments that might benefit His Majesty's royal army and navy. "Since I didn't find any of the medicaments that I needed here, nor anyone who knew how to make them," he explained, "I had to make them myself in order to do the experiments ordered by the king."

Regarding the charge of treating his patients with poisons, Leonardo declared it baseless. "In fact, the contrary is true, for experience shows that my medicines are antidotes, not poisons. They defend the body from the poison that comes from wounds caused by iron projectiles by driving out the venom, as is proved by the experiments that I made in His Majesty's court." He went on to explain, in alchemical terms, how his methods extracted "incorruptible spirits," which "vivify and conserve the human body by an occult property of nature."

The final charge against him—that he had practiced surgery "against the precepts of the authorities"—Leonardo rejected with equal indignation, arguing that his methods "conform to nature and natural reason, which is something that the physicians and surgeons ought to attend to more." Escalating his attack, he condemned physicians for their reliance on diet and surgeons for failing to observe the basic rule of surgery, which is to "consolidate and join" the wound.

Leonardo concluded his defense with a strangely out-of-place disquisition on the therapeutic power of human blood. Citing as his authority "Abacue the Jew" (Abacue *hebreo*), whom he claimed to quote from a book discovered in the library of King Edward of England, he explained:

> This book, which King Edward guarded as sacred and divine, treated the quintessence of human blood. It says that a dead man dismembered is worth more for human health than ten thousand living men, and other animals have this same effect. The more our medicines approach the nature and quality of man, the more effective they will be. For this reason my new

> way of healing, both in medicine and surgery, and the medicines made by these methods, are certain and true and rational and proved by experience.

The "sacred book" that Leonardo referred to was, evidently, one of the alchemical tracts Lull supposedly gave King Edward III. According to the legend that had grown up around Lull, Edward invited him to England to make gold from base metals, which the English king promised he would then use to finance a crusade. Lull kept his part of the bargain. Edward did not, instead taking up arms against the French. Disconsolate, Lull departed without revealing his secrets.

Leonardo probably learned this legend from Ettore Ausonio, who had recorded his version of it in a manuscript now in the Ambrosian Library in Milan. The mysterious Abacue *hebreo* appears nowhere in Ausonio's manuscript, but that would not have kept Ausonio from elaborating on the legend in private conversations with Fioravanti. Ausonio proved almost inexhaustibly inventive when it came to embellishing the legend of Ramon Lull—even to the point of fabricating a supposed relationship with Arnald of Villanova, who was known to have written about the quintessence of human blood.

The medicinal use of human body parts, including blood, fascinated Leonardo—as it did many of his contemporaries. He wrote about it at length in a chapter in *Of Physic,* where he characterized human fat as "warm, penetrating, and soothing and when used as an ointment is of great value where the body has hardened and the sinews are tight." You can also distill a water from the human liver, a mere half a dram of which, when drunk every morning for a month, cures those whose liver is half-rotted. Leonardo made extravagant claims for his "quintessence of human blood, with which, given as a drink to a person who had all but given up the ghost, is suddenly brought back to life."

These bizarre ideas about the body were hardly confined to Leonardo Fioravanti. To people of the Renaissance, the human body—even a dead one—was considered positively useful.

"THE LIVING ARE SUCH DIABOLICAL LIARS"

What did the authorities make of Fioravanti's rambling, occasionally incoherent defense? His castigation of the state of Spanish medicine and surgery cannot have bolstered his case. Nor could his defiant stance have won favor among the members of the Protomedicato. We are left wondering whether he was in full control of his faculties, or whether his megalomania had finally gotten the best of him.

The outcome of the proceeding is not known. Whatever trial records existed were destroyed in a fire that consumed the Protomedicato's archives during the Spanish Civil War. Yet it is difficult to believe that the court gave Leonardo permission to, as he impertinently demanded, "practice my method freely anywhere in the realm." Olivares's avowed aim was to rid the court of foreign alchemists. Surely he would have slapped Fioravanti with a heavy fine and used his influence to make him unwelcome at the court. In any case, not long after the trial, Leonardo left Madrid and returned to Naples.

Fioravanti omits the trial from *Of Physic*, uncharacteristically passing up a golden opportunity to lay out his own version of the affair. The only hint of trouble is limned in a letter that appears at book's end, almost as an afterthought. The curious missive—hilarious in some places, strangely delusional in others—is addressed to the illustrious Señor Olivares, Protomedico of His Catholic Majesty, who is now for many days dead, greetings from Doctor Fioravanti:

> Illustrious Señor, I have come to understand how Your Worship is now dead and passed on to the other life and gone straight to heaven. It weighs heavily upon me that, not having taken your mule with you, it must have been a lot of work getting up there, because you've got such a big belly and you're short of breath, and you haven't eaten in a long time. And now what will you do, Your Worship, you who took so much money from the poor (and you'll have to account for that before God), and the person you gave it to doesn't have it anymore because he gave it to the Church of Santa Maria in Calle Atocha, and you can't make it rise to heaven because

> it's too heavy. I understand that President Covarubia and his doctor, Giovanni Boscaino, are up there too, and that you also met Doctor Ortega (who left without saying a word to his friends), and an Italian doctor, my *compadre,* a very learned man, Doctor Decio Bellobuono, and others who know how to speak Latin very well and will speak it with Your Worship. I believe that you've found Judge Montenegro up there too. The two of you can make a yoke and receive hand in hand all of those who go up there, because I can point out more than fifty in the court who within forty years will all go up to heaven. Doctor Corneyo de Cordoba will go up there too, but I'd like to ask him to wait for me a little while so that many of us who are friends may go together. And I wish it might be soon, so that I can leave behind this wicked world, where men are burdened by such travail, especially at the court, where Your Worship gave out sentences. Well, don't be surprised if I talk to the dead because the living are such diabolical liars that no one can talk to them. . . . With this I conclude by commending your soul to God, and since Doctor Valles will be going up there soon, I'll send my letter with him. Vale.

In point of fact Olivares did not die until 1585—three years after the composition of this bizarre letter.

Fioravanti's humiliation was a triumph for Olivares—and an ignominious defeat for the proponents of alchemical medicine. When King Philip invited the Neapolitan alchemist Giovanni Vincenzo Forte to the court in 1579, the alchemist's efforts were continually thwarted by the court physicians. Although the king had specifically directed Forte to "prepare quintessences according to the practice of Ramon Lull for the health of the human body," Olivares stood in his way, accusing the Italian of being an impostor out to drain the resources of the crown. Two years after his appointment, Forte complained to Cardinal Granvelle, one of the king's ministers, that the court physicians blocked him at every turn, keeping him from accomplishing anything. Clearly,

Olivares—whom Fioravanti dubbed "barrel belly" for his corpulent physique—knew how to throw his weight around.

Though Olivares could claim a temporary victory, the pendulum swung back in favor of the alchemists. Francisco Valles, the king's most trusted physician and a passionate devotee of alchemical medicine, was appointed protomedico, a post that he held until his death in 1592. Valles vigorously promoted Philip's design to manufacture the quintessences described by Ramon Lull. Later, he was given the honorific title *Destilador de Su Majestad* (His Majesty's Distiller).

In 1585, when Philip began the construction of an immense distillation laboratory at his royal retreat in El Escorial, Forte was assigned to oversee its construction. The centerpiece of the laboratory was a gigantic *torre filosofal* (philosophical tower), a still more than 20 feet high that could produc 200 pounds of medicinal waters per day. From Protestant Europe, Catholic scientists came to Madrid to escape religious persecution and to continue their research at the *Real Botica* (Royal Pharmacy), the greatest pharmaceutical laboratory in the world. If you were interested in the spagyric arts, Philip's court was the place to be.

Fioravanti had been on top of the world. Never had he risen so high—nor fallen so far. Defiant to the end, he must have hoped that news of his humiliation in King Philip's court would never be disseminated.

And for several centuries, it was not.

33

"IL MIO SACCO È VUOTO"

Leaving Philip's court, Leonardo must have been bitterly disappointed. He had gone to Spain as the prophet of a new way of healing, only to be humiliated once again by the medical authorities. Having lost another battle with his oldest adversaries, he returned to Italy in 1577 and settled in Naples, where he composed his final work, *Della fisica.*

Like his other books, it is idiosyncratic. The best way to translate its title into English is to use the archaic "physic," which carried the dual meaning of 1) the art and science of learned medicine, and 2) a cathartic or purge. Alternately pessimistic and ebullient, combative and reconciled to defeat, *Of Physic* has an almost manic-depressive character. It is the last literary gasp of an aged man. *"Il mio sacco è vuoto,"* he wrote dejectedly: "My sack is empty."

Of Physic was also Fioravanti's most systematic philosophical work. He marshaled all his literary strength to represent himself as a beacon of hard-won wisdom. He recycled the portrait of himself from *The Treasury of Human Life,* which had depicted him as a timeworn sage, redeploying it to serve a new purpose: Placed in the frontispiece opposite a dedication to King Philip II of Spain, the picture now represented Fioravanti as a new Aristotle advising a new Alexander. In every way, *Of Physic* was carefully crafted to stand as an authoritative *scientific* statement of the "new way of healing."

The book opens with a discourse on the creation of the universe and humankind. A simplified and conventional natural philosophy typical of the Renaissance, it contains no surprises. Man, Leonardo writes, composed of the four elements, is part of the earth and all that surrounds it. The constitution of elements in the human body, in the form of humors (blood, phlegm, choler, and black bile), determines an individual's physical complexion. This was a Galenic doctrine on which all medical authorities agreed. Thus, Leonardo explains, if one humor—choler, say, which corresponds to the element air—predominates in a man, his material and psychological temperament will match the essence of that humor: cold and dry. Such a person will always be more comfortable living in the mountains, "where the air is purest," whereas those whose humoral composition is more watery live better near the sea and are the best swimmers. The humors that flow through the blood and congregate in the organs determine a person's complexion—a concept that gave Renaissance physicians a credible scientific explanation of individual physical and psychological traits.

So far, nothing could have been more orthodox. Indeed, we can almost see Leonardo struggling to portray himself as the most orthodox of physicians.

Then he abruptly departs from Galen's doctrine and asserts that all diseases stem from one of two causes: either the bad quality *(mala qualità)* and indisposition of the stomach, or the "alteration and putrefaction" of the blood. By reducing all diseases to one of two types—each a form of corruption—Fioravanti established a theoretical justification for his new way of healing, a method dominated by purgatives, emetics, and other strong drugs. Get rid of the corruption and you get rid of the disease, he asserts, and the best way to get rid of corruption is to attack it and drive it out. That required potent drugs, not weak diets. On this point, Fioravanti's doctrine—though it contained much that was traditional—represented the new way of healing as an alternative, counter-Galenic system.

Of Physic was a work of natural philosophy as well as medicine. Because it was being offered to a king, it had to address subjects worthy of regal attention. Fioravanti insists that the physician, who cures diseases internally, must be a natural philosopher in order to understand the subtle correspondences between the human body and the material world. He continues the discussion of the human body with a discourse on the senses: how to preserve them and how to cure defects of sensation such as failing eyesight, speech abnormalities, and hearing disabilities. A section on botany quickly turns to the New World plants that so fascinated him. He describes the experiments he made with tobacco, *caragna,* and other New World products and reports things he heard from sailors, navigators, cosmographers, and Indian informants. Natural history was important to Fioravanti because he insisted that the new way of healing was "according to the order of nature," helping nature bring about a cure.

Fioravanti then turns to the preparation of his patent drugs, all made by distillation, a technique that was central to his new way of healing. He says he has a secret remedy divulged only to his closest disciples, "because I didn't want to cast pearls before wild boars." To heighten the suspense, he reveals the secret remedy in a simple cipher, using the phrase, *"Ailibarim angam ni arepo te aitneirepse ad raf redev ilocarim la odnom."* The key to the cipher is to read each word backward, yielding *"Mirabilia Magna in opera et esperientia da far veder miracoli al mondo*—a great marvel in works and experience to make miracles be seen in the world."

For moderns accustomed to printing, the code is easy to unscramble. But early modern readers, less familiar with the written word, might well have puzzled over the phrase—and felt a rush of excitement on deciphering it. The code was not too easy to crack, yet neither was it too hard. Fioravanti was a deft reader of his audience.

Then follows a lengthy discourse on cosmography, which in the Renaissance included not just geography but also the physical nature, customs, and conditions of life in various regions of the world. Knowing cosmography was important for *medical* reasons as well. Though physicians agreed on the importance of environment in maintaining health and treating disease (the "airs, waters and places" of Hippocratic doctrine were fixtures of every physician's training), Fioravanti's idea of environment extended to the culture and the mood of a place. An inveterate reader of the "histories of the things of the world," he clipped long excerpts from various natural and political histories, including Olaus Magnus, Diodorus Siculus, and an anonymous Spanish manuscript on "monstrosities."

He had a special fondness for a story by Iambulus, the author of a narrative preserved in Diodorus's *Library of World History* (ca. 60–30 B.C.E.) and reprinted in the 16th century by Venetian humanist Giovanni Ramusio in his popular *Navigations and Voyages*. The narrative retraces a fantastic journey that one Iambulus, a merchant from Syria, supposedly made through Ethiopia to a happy Island of the Sun—a utopian communist state where property, women, and children were held in common, clothing was made from reeds, and the land supplied everyone's wants. The Sun-Islanders are ruled by a king whom everyone willingly obeys. They live simply and frugally, are versed in all branches of knowledge, and live long lives.

It's easy to see why the saga of Iambulus enthralled Leonardo. With his keen eye for what would appeal to readers, he knew that utopian themes were popular literary pulp—especially when they portrayed societies that lived in a simple state of nature, uncorrupted by civilization. Resentment of the status quo pervaded 16th-century Italian culture. In Italy as well as in northern Europe, evangelists decried clerical abuses and urged a return to a religion of simple piety and moral purity. A feeling of despair that nothing would ever change gave rise to the urge to create imaginary worlds whose qualities outshone those of the real one.

The tale of Iambulus seemed tailor-made for Fioravanti. Its basic theme was that the ideal condition of humanity lies in a simple state of nature, which supplies all human wants. The Island of the Sun was like the folkloric Land of Cockayne—a peasant's earthly paradise.

Fioravanti's New World informants, including navigators, merchants, a Corsican sailor, and a Peruvian Indian whom he met in Philip's court, were, he thought, more reliable than historians. But like so many of his contemporaries, he was fascinated by the marvelous: Many a tall tale is told in *Of Physic*. Renaissance readers would not have dismissed the yarns he gleaned from the cosmographies, because it was generally understood that nature loves to exhibit marvels and play jokes. "These truly are things that nature induces to surprise the people of the world," wrote Leonardo. Yet one cannot help wondering if that Indian—he with the stories of magical plants and prodigious penises—wasn't playing a joke on Fioravanti. It wouldn't have been the first time a native had fooled an anthropologist—nor would it be the last.

ALCHEMY TO ISOLATE THE SPIRIT

Above all, however, alchemy drives *Of Physic,* just as it propelled all of Fioravanti's scientific research. To Leonardo, alchemy was the science of sciences. Like so many Renaissance alchemists, he was fascinated by the search for the philosopher's stone, and he was convinced that in Spain he had found the secret of making it. Alchemy was the rage all over Europe, and Leonardo did not intend to be left out. While in northern Europe Paracelsus was the dominant figure in the movement, Fioravanti's style of alchemy harked directly back to the 14th-century tradition of distilling quintessences—a way of purifying medicines, of separating the pharmaceutical "spirit" from the murky concoctions that constituted Renaissance drugs.

What happened to Fioravanti in the years between his departure from Spain and the publication of *Of Physic* is a mystery. He may have returned to Italy by way of Rome, for in October 1577, he wrote from there to Grand Duke Francesco de' Medici in a last, desperate attempt to gain the Medici family's favor. Included in the letter is a *memorial,* or memorandum, promising to reveal "a secret with which you can very quickly extract a lot of money from your state of Tuscany each year, without levying any heavy taxes or raising any kind of rancor against you."

The secret?

It was an arcane natural magical technique for finding hidden treasure. The notion that the countryside concealed buried treasure may strike modern readers as a Renaissance delusion. Yet in the absence of deposit banking, the possibility of finding buried treasure was no chimera. In a world governed by chance, discovering hidden treasure seemed to be a real possibility. Did he offer a divining rod, like so many cunning men employed for the purpose, or was it a more philosophical technique, such as English mathematician John Dee's design to use the laws of sympathy and antipathy to find hidden treasure? Whatever it was, Fioravanti was confident enough in the secret to offer it to the grand duke, asking for only a 6 percent return on any treasure that turned up. As far as we know, Francesco never responded.

Leonardo must have returned briefly to Venice in 1577 or 1578, because there he addressed a dedication, dated 1578, to Count Giovanni Angusuola of Milan in a new edition of *The Mirror of Universal Science*. He then journeyed to Naples—where, he claims, he completed a new book entitled *The Twelve Secret Remedies of the Glorious Annunziata of Naples*. Fioravanti described the work as a *compendietto* (little compendium) of 12 secrets, but no record of its publication exists. The title must have refered to the Santissima Annunziata church in Naples, the site of a hospital founded in 1318 by the Confraternity of the Repentants to care for the poor and for prostitutes. Leonardo likewise reported that he was planning to publish books on cosmography and comets; neither ever appeared.

Repeatedly he foretold his impending death. "With this [work] I can say Amen forever, because my sack is empty," he wrote in *Of Physic*. Two years later, in the 1583 edition of *The Mirror of Universal Science*, he declared, "this will be the end of my labors," and bade his readers "*buena noche por siempre*—good night forever." Yet the date of his death is unknown. He is usually said to have died on September 4, 1588, but the basis of that claim is unclear. Possibly historians confused him with Valerio Fioravanti, a medical professor at the University of Bologna who died on September 5 of that year. At any rate, careful searches of the death records in the Venetian and Bolognese state archive failed to turn up any notice of his death. Obviously, many people died without leaving a trace in the archive, so we may never know the date of Fioravanti's demise.

"HE WHO LIVES WELL DIES WELL"

There is evidence that he was still living in 1594, when a new edition of his *Regimen for the Plague* was published in Venice. The new edition contains material not found in earlier editions, including references to his experiences in Spain. Fioravanti's last words in print are contained in the new material added to the book, including a "Discourse on the Art of Dying Well," a subject that weighed heavily on his mind. "He who lives well dies well," he mused, "and he who lives badly dies badly." He was resigned to death: He writes repeatedly, even expectantly of it in his last works.

Did Leonardo die well? We don't really know, but as an alchemical adept who conducted hundreds if not thousands of alchemic experiments, frequently in open vessels and often lasting many hours, even days, he would have exposed himself to a lifetime of highly toxic chemicals. He made use of a variety of metallic and nonmetallic ingredients, including sulfuric and nitric acid, mercury, copper, tin, lead, antimony, and arsenic. Like other alchemists, he probably tasted his chemical products to test them. There's no telling how much Precipitato he made, but it must have been a lot, given that it was the heavy artillery piece of his medicinal arsenal. As a result, he must have exposed himself to substantial amounts of highly volatile mercury vapors. Prolonged exposure to heavy metal vapors may, in fact, account for the instability, paranoia, and depression that he exhibited in his last writings.

If that was the case, he wouldn't have been the first alchemist to endanger life and limb by his experiments. Medieval English alchemist George Ripley noted that alchemists risked "Poisoning themselves and losing their sight, With odors, smokes, and watching up by nights." And in the 17th century Edmund Dickinson warned that alchemists suffer many misfortunes as a result of their hazardous experiments, including severe headaches, paralysis, loss of sight, consumption, and dizziness. In a supreme irony, just as he was accused of having killed so many of his patients, Leonardo's dangerous alchemical quest may have killed *him*.

He was obsessed with how posterity would assess his legacy. "Only those who discover new and useful things deserve to be remembered forever," he wrote, and he was confident that he would be remembered. Yet contemporaries do not record any mention of his death. Was he so forgotten (or ignored) that no one noticed or cared? Whatever the reason, his life history contains a fitting symmetry: Having concealed his first 30 years, he disappears into the mist of the past without leaving a trace.

34
THE JUDGMENT OF HISTORY

"I've spent forty years roaming the world, searching for the *Magna Medicina,*" Leonardo wrote toward the end of his life. We don't know whether he ever found the "Great Medicine" he was looking for. The cynicism of his last works suggests that he felt dejected and unappreciated. He likened himself to "a preacher in the desert, because few believe in my words and doctrine."

History is not generous in the way it remembers the personalities of the past, and the further back in time we go, the less it remembers about them. Those whom we classify as "major" historical figures are usually the ones about whom the archive retains the most information, or they are the ones that historians, for reasons embedded in their own times, have selected as having done the most to get us where we are.

In the 1940s, British historian Herbert Butterfield termed this tendency to read the present into the past as "the Whig interpretation of history." Nowhere has such anachronism been more evident than in the history of science and medicine.

Was Vesalius more important than Fioravanti? It depends upon whom you ask. To the modern scientist and to most historians, the answer is easy. Of course Vesalius was, because in his work we can trace the origins of modern medicine. Fioravanti, on the other hand, is one of history's dead ends. But if you could ask the question of an ordinary Venetian of the 1570s, you would probably get a different answer. "Vesalius?" he might ask, puzzled. "Wasn't he the one who taught at Padua a few years back? No, I don't know much about him. I think he wrote some books in Latin. I don't read Latin, haven't any need to. But, ah yes, Fioravanti, the great Fioravanti. He's the one who invented the glorious Balsam and the wonder-working Quintessence."

Would an ordinary Venetian have thought that Vesalius was the harbinger of medicine's future? Not likely. But the ordinary Venetian would certainly have heard of Leonardo Fioravanti. To the ordinary Venetian of the 1570s, he might have seemed the future of medicine.

For several centuries, Leonardo continued to be remembered: through his books, which were excerpted, compiled, abridged, and translated into several languages, and above all through his remedies, some of which were still being used in the 19th century. (See Appendix.) Forty-five Italian reprints of Fioravanti's works appeared between 1582, when he published his last book, and the end of the 17th century—an average of more than four per decade. His works enjoyed a robust production in translation, too, including English, French, and German editions. Between 1561, when he published his first book, and 1682, more than 83 editions of his works appeared, an average of about six per decade for 140 years. The last Fioravanti edition that I have been able to discover was printed in Naples in 1720. His books are found in private, monastic, university, courtly, and public libraries throughout Europe, from Wolfenbüttel to Madrid and from Naples to London.

Fioravanti's drugs continued to be used in Italy down through the 18th century. He enjoyed an especially good reputation during the heyday of chemical medicine in the 17th and 18th centuries. Though not a Paracelsian, he became a favorite among the followers of the Swiss medical reformer. The 17th-century Neapolitan iatrochemist (chemical physician) Giuseppe Donzelli praised the virtues of Fioravanti's medicines, singling out in particular his preparation of lapis lazuli. To this impassioned devotee of chemical drugs, Fioravanti was

> . . . the most expert empiric, who prescribed *Pietra lazuli* to provoke vomiting, liberating many quartain fevers. He calcined it for malignant fevers and extinguished it in the finest *aqua vitae* (which he says dissolves it miraculously), and used this solution to liberate many maladies, almost miraculously curing ulcers, even malign ones. He also extracted an oil from this stone, with which he miraculously induced sleep and brought rest, and used it to anoint the body to cure inflamation of the blood vessels and the pains of gout.

Fioravanti's drugs appeared in official pharmacopoeias from the 16th until the 18th century. Pope Innocent XI recommended Leonardo's balsam, and the 17th-century biologist Marcello Malpighi reported that in 1686 it was still being sold at the Canaletto pharmacy in Venice under the garbled name of *balsamo del famoso Cavaliere Fasciotti.* According to medical historian Gian Antonio Brambilla, Fioravanti's medicines were still found in Italian pharmacies as late as the 1780s, widely used as treatments for ulcers and wounds.

His drugs also enjoyed widespread use outside of Italy. The *Electuarium Leonardo Fioravanti* for the plague, for example, appears in Hanover's *Official Pharmacopia* published in 1631. As early as 1568, Fioravanti was sending his remedies to England, and enough Londoners sought his drugs to enable apothecary John Hester to make a good living preparing and selling them at his pharmacy in Paul's Wharf. Hester translated Fioravanti's writings into English and modeled his book, *Pearl of Practice,* on Fioravanti's writing style. Hester's successor at the Paul's Wharf pharmacy, James Forester, likewise made Fioravanti's drugs and reported a sizable Continental market for Hester's secrets.

After his controversial visit to Spain in the 1570s, Fioravanti became widely known in the Hispanic world. Several of his works were translated into Castilian and his drugs were widely used. Fray Antonio Castell, a pharmacist at the Benedictine monastery at Monserrat, recommended Fioravanti's compositions in his pharmaceutical manual, *Theoria y Pratica* (1592). His secrets were even brought to the New World—a turn of events that doubtless would have pleased the old surgeon. A document in the Archivo de Indias in Seville confirms that in 1603, three of his books (in Italian) were included in a bookseller's shipment to be sold in Mexico. In the 18th century, Guatemalan physician Cristobal de Hincapié Meléndez y Mayer published a book of medical recipes in Latin and Spanish for use in his practice in New Spain. Among the secrets that Hincapié recorded in his weighty tome was a recipe for Fioravanti's Life-Extending Water, a reference to his aqua vitae.

Fioravanti was frequently cited in the medical literature in the centuries after his death. Roman physician Pietro Castelli named him as an expert on emetics in his authoritative *Emetica* (1634), while in London, the Dutch emigré physician Turquet de Mayerne made extensive notations on Fioravanti's books and copied out numerous recipes in his medical notebooks.

Fioravanti's writings also provided ammunition for the 17th-century assault on Galenic physiology. The splenectomy he performed with the surgeon Zaccarello was widely cited, and his dramatic account of the operation in *The Treasury of Human Life* played a role in renewing interest in splenectomy among anatomists. In the 16th and 17th centuries, despite heated academic debate over the function of the spleen, almost nothing was introduced to change the Galenic account, which held that the organ was needed to sustain life. Not until 1657 did English physician George Thomson perform an experimental splenectomy specifically to test the Galenic theory. By successfully extracting the spleen from a dog, Thomson demonstrated that an animal could live without the organ. Of course, Fioravanti had already proved that more than a century before.

PROPHET OF MAGIC BULLETS

Although Fioravanti occupies a lesser rank than Vesalius in standard histories of medicine, in one important respect he pointed the way to the modern. He promoted the idea that a dose can be found for every sickness and that medicine can combat illness. This directly contravened the idea that had long prevailed in premodern medicine: that disease is an imbalance of humors, and that physiological "balance" is the key to health. All that official medicine had to offer a sick person was a prolonged and complex regimen to readjust the bodily humors. But Fioravanti and other Renaissance empirics offered quick and easy solutions that you could buy "over the counter," so to speak. Humoral medicine retained its hold among regular practitioners, but in public opinion, patients were passive no more. The Enlightenment dream that health is something that money can buy was born in the Renaissance.

Fioravanti and the empirics were helped by, and in turn contributed to, the long march of secularization, which conferred a greater value upon physical health in the here and now as opposed to setting store in salvation in the afterlife. Medical entrepreneurs such as Fioravanti capitalized on the growing tendency to resort to self-medication.

Presciently, Fioravanti recognized some basic secrets of the art of advertising: using brand names, publicizing remedies in print rather than face-to-face, and publishing personal testimonies from patients. His remedies were among the first brand-name medicinal products. Through his books consumers were instructed about a range of over-the-counter medicines. In addition, his "new way of healing" appealed to prevailing fashions—even if it was condemned by the regular doctors. If his campaign was radical, it was radical chic.

Fioravanti's martial therapeutic style—widely imitated by marginalized healers—eventually won out and became the dominant ideology of modern medicine. Of course, neither Precipitato nor any of his other wonder drugs became medicine's "magic bullet," and the idea of bodily pollution as the universal origin of disease would be discarded. Instead, the 19th-century discovery that infectious diseases were caused by specific pathogens—and that they could be cured by specific drug therapies—pointed the way to modern medicine. The germ theory of disease, first formulated by microbiologist Louis Pasteur, ushered in a dramatic "therapeutic revolution," forever changing the way we treat and think about diseases. Yet the similarities between Fioravanti's mode of therapy and the modern therapeutic model are unmistakable. Like the modern doctor, he insisted that the only rational therapy must be aimed at the agent causing the disease. And, he thought, it was possible to find a counter-agent that could eradicate that cause and expel it from the body.

The closest drug we have in modern medicine to Fioravanti's panacea, Precipitato, is penicillin, discovered by microbiologist Alexander Fleming in 1928. Penicillin led to the eradication of the causes of many infectious diseases—and, coincidentally, to an entirely new set of expectations about therapy. Ironically, in light of Fioravanti's effort to cure the French pox, the original magic bullet—Salvarsan, a chemical drug used to cure syphilis—was discovered in 1908 by German microbiologist Paul Erlich. The age of heroic medical conquerors that Erlich's discovery inaugurated was chronicled by Paul de Kruif in his 1926 book, *The Microbe Hunters.* De Kruif's unforgettable but oddly inaccurate portrait of Erlich makes him out to be a figure not unlike Fioravanti: defiant and unorthodox, exacting in his experiments, and a proponent of what were then considered to be "outrageous thoughts" about disease pathology. Not since the legend of Ambroise Paré as the discoverer of the modern method of treating gunshot wounds has there been a more effective example of mythmaking in the history of medicine.

The infectious-disease model of illness—the idea of disease as an alien invasion that must be conquered—became a model for all diseases, and it radically altered attitudes and expectations about illness. Even though the model is inappropriate for chronic illnesses, we continue to regard all diseases in terms of the "penicillin mode"—as entitities that can be cured rather than being cared for or simply having to be waited out. The model flourished during the Cold War era, when military metaphors were compelling, just as Fioravanti's model resonated in Counter-Reformation Italy, when a religious "cold war" coexisted with the appearance of a host of new infectious diseases such as syphilis, typhus, and plague. In both periods, healing became a battle against an alien "enemy," and a parallel was drawn between enemy foes and the causes of diseases.

We now are waging a "war" on cancer and a "war" on AIDS, while to Fioravanti's generation corruption was the compelling metaphor of the day. The notion of a dose to cure every ailment would never have occurred to the Bologna professors, and that is why many of them concluded that Leonardo and his ilk were charlatans. Fioravanti identified disease as a corruption of the body that had to be driven out, just as exorcists of the time drove out the demons that had invaded the body.

In today's medicine, *curing* has replaced *caring* as the dominant ideology of modern, technology-driven medicine. Fioravanti, the Paul Erlich of his time, had the same ambition, but his dream did not come true for more than two centuries. Ironically, as chronic illnesses became society's most intractable medical problem, the military metaphor seems less compelling, and the model that Fioravanti fought so hard to defeat is becoming more relevant than ever.

RIPPLES BEYOND THE MEDICAL REALM

Fioravanti's influence extended beyond medicine as well. Not long after his death, his persona entered popular culture as a symbol of antiauthoritarianism. The Bolognese humorist and pamphleteer Giulio Cesare Croce, whose name was synonymous with the debunking of established norms, found in Fioravanti's writings the inspiration for Bertoldo's improbable miracles.

That Fioravanti's name and doctrine resonated in popular culture can also be witnessed in the bizarre case of Costantino Saccardino, a Roman distiller and sometime court jester who, along with his son and two accomplices, was arrested in Bologna in 1622 and charged with heresy. The four conspirators were accused of having desecrated the city's sacred statues by affixing to them blasphemous placards carrying vague threats against the political and religious authorities. Saccardino scorned the Holy Scripture as a book full of lies and false prophecies. He ridiculed indulgences, called the Virgin a whore, denied that the pope had any spiritual power, and maintained that religion was a lie perpetrated by priests and politicians.

Saccardino had a notable reputation as a healer. He was the author of a medical tract with the pompous title *The Truth of Various Things*. Saccardino railed against the "idle modern physicians who flee from experimental labors and attend only to learning soothing logical formulas and rhetorical discourses so that they can pretend to give reasons for big, invisible, impalpable, and incomprehensible thing. . . . which can't ever be seen or known." How different are modern physicians from the wise philosophers of the "good old days" who, "full of love and charity, used to visit the languishing sick and disinterestedly bring them medical relief made by their own hands. . . . They didn't debate all the time the way physicians do nowadays, so that often the poor patient succumbs before the bickering and dies in their very presence."

Where did Saccardino get these outlandish ideas? Although the alchemical doctrines of the Paracelsians are evident in his tract, his main inspiration was Fioravanti, from whom Saccardino borrowed heavily. Embracing Leonardo's doctrine that the cause of all diseases was the "bad qualities and intemperance of the stomach," he converted it into a radical political ideology. From his trial records, we learn that Saccardino wandered from city to city proselytizing among artisans and teaching that religion—especially the notion of hell—was idiotic. "You're baboons if you believe it," he would say. "Princes want us to believe it, because they want to do as they please. But now, at last, the whole dovecote has opened its eyes."

It was but one of Saccardino's many borrowings from Fioravanti, who, in *The Mirror of Universal Science,* had written, concerning the ancient physicians:

> In those days they got people to believe whatever they wanted, because there was a great shortage of books then, and whenever anyone could discourse even a little about *bus* or about *bas* he was revered as a prophet, and whatever he said was believed. But ever since the blessed printing press came into being, books have multiplied so that anyone can study, especially because the majority of them are published in our mother tongue. And thus the kittens have opened their eyes.

Saccardino took the short step that Fioravanti prudently avoided, transposing the metaphor from the sphere of medicine to that of religion and politics. The crude lies of religion, he was saying, kept people in check, just as Fioravanti had asserted that the lies of the physicians endangered people's health and kept the physicians on top.

In 1622 Saccardino and his co-conspirators were hanged in the public square before a great crowd. Their bodies were then burned—the Inquisition's customary method of purging society of incorrigible heretics.

Being associated with libertines such as Croce and Saccardino did nothing to boost Fioravanti's reputation. Those associations enabled 19th-century medical historians to construct a scornful image of him. Whereas a century earlier historians of medicine had cited Leonardo Fioravanti as a respected authority on surgery, now he became the very archetype of the charlatan. In the 1840s, for instance, Italian medical historian Salvatore De Renzi stated that Fioravanti was "one of the most celebrated secretists and charlatans produced in sixteenth-century Italy." De Renzi quoted the much respected French *Biographie Médicale,* which, in an article on Fioravanti, asserted that the Bologna surgeon

> was a man of ridiculous vanity, always speaking grandiloquently, lying in the most impudent manner and shamelessly spewing out pompous panegyrics about his arcane secrets, among which one is still quite famous, i.e., the balm that is named after him. Every century medicine seems to be dishonored by one of these audacious charlatans, who, until this very day, though devoid of any true knowledge, deceive the vulgar by the art of dazzling and capture the public's confidence.

That view prevailed into the 20th century. In his 1922 volume on the history of medical charlatanism, Andrea Corsini labeled Fioravanti "a clever man with the soul and temperament of a charlatan."

Thus his reputation as a brash, antiauthoritarian reformer helped mold the modern image of Fioravanti as a charlatan. During the 19th century, and for much of the 20th as well, the history of medicine—written mainly by physicians—was deployed as an instrument in the ongoing professionalization of the field. The elaborately constructed "war against charlatanism" was an integral part of the medical profession's strategy to preserve the domain of medicine for specialists.

The medical profession demanded that modern medicine become a rational, scientific, and progressive discipline. Fioravanti's brand of medicine—vaunting empirics, praising the wisdom of the people, and exposing the "lies" of the doctors—ran counter to that image. That kind of history needs heroes and villains: heroes to reconfirm the truth of modern medicine and the inevitability of its triumph, villains to underscore the magnitude of the victory. Fioravanti's doctrine was deployed as a political instrument, just as surely as it had been in the hands of Costantino Saccardino.

THE JUDGMENT OF HISTORY

Was Fioravanti a charlatan, as he has so often been depicted? Again, the answer depends on who is being asked. "Charlatan" is a relative and politically weighted term. In the 16th century, the word carried an entirely different meaning from today. Among the many legal forms of medical practice was that of the ciarlatano, whence stems our term "charlatan." In 16th-century Italian, the term meant neither "quack" nor "fraud." Rather, it referred to the wandering empirics who sold medicines in the public squares by attracting crowds with their comic and musical performances. This new medical profession—the product of the commercial revolution and a fashion-driven marketplace—was one of the many that Tommaso Garzoni included in his authoritative guide, *The Universal Plaza of All the World's Professions.*

By contemporary standards, Fioravanti demonstrably was not a charlatan. He never mounted the mountebank's stage and never took part in the comic routines that were the hallmark of the charlatan's craft. He was a surgeon—and, by all accounts, a good one. He always considered himself a doctor and by every contemporary measure was one. He had a medical degree from the University of

Bologna, one of Italy's most respected medical colleges. If he was a charlatan, his stage was not in the piazza but in the printing house. To many physicians he may have been a fraud, but to him the real quacks were the doctors with their highfalutin Galenic theories.

So who was right—Leonardo or his critics?

Despite his unorthodox doctrine, his flamboyant public persona, and his larger-than-life portrayal of his adventures, there's no question that in some important ways Fioravanti's approach to exploring and understanding nature looked forward to the Scientific Revolution rather than backward to the age of Scholastic natural philosophy. For one thing, his untrammeled curiosity and naive sense of wonder about the marvelous properties of things put him at odds with the medieval tradition. The Scholastics didn't have much appreciation for the so-called marvels of nature. They thought that merely accepting something as marvelous—by which they meant anything seemingly inexplicable—represented a failure of the intellect. If anything seemed marvelous, they deemed it their task to explain it away. By contrast, the Renaissance natural philosophers, in the words of historians Lorraine Daston and Katharine Park, "rehabilitated wonders as useful objects of philosophical reflection." The Renaissance experimenters realized that wonder is the engine of curiosity and that curiosity is the origin of scientific discovery.

Leonardo's curiosity about nature's wonders wasn't the only thing that set him apart from the medieval scientific tradition. Also novel was his passion for experimentation. He consulted with craftsmen, farmers, surgeons, pharmacists, glassmakers, and the old men of the south to find out how they solved problems, and he recorded his observations in compendious books of experiments. It would not have occurred to most medieval natural philosophers to investigate nature by talking to farmers or visiting artisans' workshops. For the Renaissance experimenters, though, experience of the world was vastly more important than arguments about it. When Paracelsus said "My shoebuckles are more learned than your Galen and Avicenna," he meant that his shoe buckles had seen more, because they had tramped the world.

Several close parallels link Leonardo Fioravanti and the Elizabethan professor of secrets Hugh Plat, one of the London experimenters who form the centerpiece of Deborah Harkness's 2007 book, *The Jewel House.* The son of a wealthy London merchant, Plat dedicated his leisured life to experiments in agriculture, horticulture, and alchemy. Like Fioravanti, Plat attained his greatest impact through print. His works, published from 1592 to 1644, filled a niche in the market for books that furnished utilitarian knowledge to a rising middle class. Plat was intimately familiar with the Continental literature of experiments, including Fioravanti's works, which he knew through John Hester's translations. Through both Hester, an ardent disciple of Fioravanti, and Plat, a follower of Hester, Fioravanti's writings had a profound impact upon Elizabethan science.

The differences between the approaches of the two experimenters are equally instructive. Whereas Plat passionately advocated using science to improve the material well-being of the commonwealth, Fioravanti was mostly preoccupied with fame—and, of course, with his own self-image. Plat was propelled by the ethics of what historian Ayesha Mukherjee has termed "dearth science"—using science and technology to increase plenty in a country where scarcity was pervasive. Leonardo, on the other hand, was more concerned with how posterity would judge him. "The true end of all our private labors and studies ought to be the beginning of the public and common good of our country," Plat wrote. He was an inveterate "projector," with schemes for addressing practically every dearth problem of the day, from making cheap candles to brewing beer without using expensive hops, and from feeding fowl and preserving meat to, improbably, making a chafing dish that would heat food without fuel. Leonardo's schemes—from daring surgical interventions to writing books—were meant to cement his own personal everlasting fame.

How to explain the profound differences between the two Renaissance experimenters? One explanation is the dominance of the courtly tradition in Renaissance Italy. Another is the absence of a picaresque tradition in Elizabethan culture. Fioravanti, living in a universe dominated by princely courts, was driven by the ethics of honor rather than altruism or duty to country. To him, status was more important than practical utility. Plat, on the other hand, was conditioned by utilitarian, Protestant values, and he had little interest in curiosities of no practical import. Even when he admitted "novelties" into his experimental books, he characterized them, almost apologetically, as being useful "philosophical work." Significantly, Plat tossed Fioravanti's writings into the bin with the "magical crew" that included della Porta and the Renaissance magi.

Such attitudes left little room for the picaresque. To Protestants, the trickster was not to be lionized but condemned. After all, trickery was the devil's art. By contrast, the picaresque was a formative influence on Fioravanti. The pícaro—in the form of the trickster—had a long career in Renaissance Italian literature: Stories about tricksters *(beffatori)* had been in currency at least since Boccaccio. Even a scientist as "serious" as the astronomer Galileo deployed it. In his writings, Leonardo continually represented himself as a trickster, in part to entertain readers, but equally to claim that knowledge can be won through trickery. He used it to pass himself off as a learned doctor in Palermo and to steal the secret of rhinoplasty from the Vianeo brothers. Beaten down at every turn by "conspiracies of the doctors," he turned the trick on the physicians by returning to Bologna and (by trickery, I think) gaining his medical degree.

My friend Andrea Carlino was right: Fioravanti was a trucco, a trick. Picaresque elements are present in stories sprinkled throughout his oeuvre, and it is through his stories—not his doctrines—that he represented himself to his public.

epilogue

TRACES

As I wrote this book, Andrea Carlino's shrewd observation kept coming back to me. Have I succeeded in tricking Fioravanti into giving up his secrets? It's difficult to say. The professor of secrets divulges only those confidences that he wants the public—and posterity—to know. Rarely does he give them all up: The paradox of "professing" secrets, as Alessio Piemontese feared, is that secrets, once revealed, become public knowledge. Only as secrets do they retain their aura—and hence their pricelessness. Yet only by revealing them can one redeem their value in the marketplace.

Leonardo confessed that he had held back some secrets "in order to have a few secrets of my own." We can be fairly certain he meant that in a broader sense than just squirreling away a few favored remedies. He kept plenty of secrets, personal and otherwise: It was the way of the professor of secrets. I hope that I have managed to bare some of his secrets, but I still have doubts that I, or anyone else, could ever plumb his soul.

I have made no claims for Leonardo Fioravanti's original contributions to modern science. My purpose has not been to portray him as one of the moderns. Instead, I wanted to depict him in his own milieu, not the narrow space that historians have created to accommodate the supposed precursors of modern science. Leonardo and his companions don't fit that mold. In our terms, he was not a modern—nor did he claim to be. Instead, he said, he had come into the world to reveal to humankind the long-lost ancient medicine of the "first physicians," which existed before there were scientists.

No surprise, then, that historians of science have found figures such as Leonardo Fioravanti difficult to handle. Today we tend to remember the Scientific Revolution as a coherent, cataclysmic, once-and-for-all event that ushered in modern science. Our preference for a neat story and our focus on "great men" rather than communities of adepts makes it easy to leave out the stinky alchemists' laboratories, the clanking artisans' workshops, the broken glass, the exploding test tubes, the experiments gone wrong: in short, the messiness that made up Leonardo's world of science.

But real science isn't tidy; why, then, should its history have been?

The professors of secrets thought they could learn to understand the world by tinkering with the things around them. They had inherited a scientific worldview—composed of Aristotelian physics, Galenic medicine, and the opinions of the Scholastic commentators—that made no sense to them. Yet they had no theoretical system to replace those worn models. And so they looked for a new route that might lead them to discovering the "secrets of nature."

They found it in experiments.

The naive, haphazard way of going about experimenting that characterized the scientific life of the professors of secrets seems strangely alien to modern sensibilities. They had no hypothesis to test, no theory to verify. They carried out experiments simply out of curiosity—and for the sheer joy of it. Dilettantish, impatient, and open to almost every kind of seemingly outlandish claim, they conducted thousands of experiments willy-nilly, on every conceivable subject. No wonder that the Leonardo Fioravantis of Renaissance science have been so readily tossed into the intellectual waste bin labeled "Dead Ends."

For, in tracing the origins of modern science and medicine, how can we take seriously someone such as Fioravanti, who so passionately opposed anatomical dissection, a practice universally regarded by historians as heralding the beginning of modern medicine? By the same token, how can we discard from our view of science's past anyone who so avidly delved into experimentation, universally regarded by historians as one of the building blocks of modern science?

The lesson? Science developed by fits and starts. There was no straight-line trajectory to the "modern world."

It is worth remembering Leonardo Fioravanti and his companions in Venice, Palermo, Naples, Milan, Madrid, and all those other places where he stayed, because in remembering them, we are constantly reminded of another side of the scientific story. Though messier than the grand narrative of the Scientific Revolution, their stories are as much a part of the real world of Renaissance science as are the portraits of revolutionary thinkers. In crafting new narratives of the origins of modern science, we do not have to choose between Vesalius and Fioravanti, between Galileo and della Porta. We need them all.

By chance, while in Geneva to give a lecture a few summers ago, I had the good fortune to meet Andrea's colleague Micheline Louis-Courvoisier, who, with Vincent Barras and Séverine Pilloud, is constructing an extensive database of patients' letters to the famous Swiss physician Samuel Tissot (1728–1797), located in the city archive of Lausanne. Tissot wrote a popular medical self-help tract, *Avis au peuple sur la santé (Health Advice for the People),* which went through many editions. Like Fioravanti two centuries earlier, Tissot ran a flourishing mail-order medical business. More than a thousand patients, representing a wide cross-section of society, wrote to Tissot asking for his medical advice. When the database is completed, it will be one of the most important documentary sources for the history of early modern medicine.

When I mentioned the name of Fioravanti, Micheline gave me a look of immediate recognition. *"Le baume de Fioravanti,"* she said without any pause. My amazement must have been visible. "It is mentioned in several letters to Tissot in the Lausanne archive," she explained. Could Fioravanti's remedies have been so widely known in 18th-century France and Switzerland that they appeared in the correspondence of this renowned authority on domestic medicine? Micheline offered to check her database for Fioravanti.

The very next day, this e-mail arrived from Micheline:

Dear Bill,

When I returned to Lausanne yesterday, I looked for Fioravanti in our database and found four references to him.

The first reference appears in a letter of 1774, written by "lieutenant Roussy" concerning a pain in the leg that he had suffered for some twenty years. He had consulted a number of physicians and surgeons, and mentions the application of the *baume de Fioravanti,* which seems to have made the pain worse.

The second reference is found in a letter of 1768, concerning the Prince of Hesse-Kassel, who suffered from a painful discharge of pus from an ear. The *baume de Fioravanti* was applied, but we have no other details of what transpired.

The third reference is contained in a letter of Monsieur Ernest, forty-three years old, dated 1776, a coach-maker and saddler, who suffered from the pains of rheumatism for seven years. We know that he used the *baume de Fioravanti,* but no mention is made of what its effect might have been.

The fourth reference is found in an undated letter written by an unknown author, probably a healer, in reference to an anonymous thirty-four-year-old woman who suffered from headaches and, possibly, a rheumatoid humor. The *baume de Fioravanti* was applied and the author of the letter relates that it did not bring relief to the patient's satisfaction. What seems interesting about the case is that the *baume de Fioravanti* seems to have been prescribed by common healers, which makes me think that it belonged to a therapeutical arsenal that was familiar to eighteenth-century physicians and surgeons.

These are some evidences of the traces of Fioravanti, which I hope you will find useful.

Cordially,
Micheline

How many other traces of the charlatan, or supposed charlatan, lie hidden in letters, books, and archives, or in places just as unlikely and surprising? And what of those other curious Renaissance investigators of nature even more obscure than "Fioravanti of the miracles": Vincenzo Cantone, Ettore Ausonio, Isabella Cortese, the alchemist Jacomo Torellis (who understood the properties of 2,000 substances), Agostino Bravo (the *hombre diabolico* of Leonardo's Spanish days), or countless other alchemists, naturalists, and professors of secrets who made up the scientific underworld of the Renaissance?

Though their voices are mute to history, Leonardo Fioravanti spoke for them—and in remembering them he has brought us all closer to the lost world of Renaissance science.

ACKNOWLEDGMENTS

My thanks to:

Andrea Carlino for the clue that got it started.

Harvard University's Center for Italian Renaissance Studies at the Villa I Tatti, Florence, for a fellowship that gave me a year to begin the project, and the Tattiani with whom I shared that memorable year.

For financial support, the National Endowment for the Humanities (grant no. RH-21205-94), the National Science Foundation (grant no. SBR-9321061), the Lila Wallace–Reader's Digest Fund, and the Renaissance Society of America.

My colleagues in the History Department at New Mexico State University, where I first tried out a few of the sections of the book, especially Liz Horodowich and Marsha Weisiger, who read chapters and offered helpful critiques.

Librarians and archivists, too many to name, in Las Cruces, Washington, London, Venice, Florence, Rome, Milan, Modena, Palermo, Naples, Madrid, Seville, Simancas, Salamanca, and Valencia.

My friend and longtime running partner David Taylor listened to and critiqued countless ideas, some that appear in the book and many that never made it in, and expertly scanned the images.

Dwight Pitcaithley, my colleague and cycling buddy, also read portions of the manuscript and patiently let me air ideas during long rides in the Mesilla Valley.

A special thanks to John Nieto-Philips for countless memorable conversations about this book and many other matters, and for a friendship of incalculable value.

In Florence, Lorenz Boeninger was my steadfast friend and most skeptical critic, who generously put me up on many occasions and listened to me talk about Fioravanti.

My good friend Victor Navarro Brotóns taught me most of what I know about the history of early modern Spanish science and shared countless hours of memorable companionship in Valencia, Godella, and Gorga.

I am deeply grateful to a number of other friends and colleagues with whom I shared ideas and companionship during the writing of this book. Without their comments, hospitality, and interest, I doubt that I would have gotten far on the project. I would like to mention, in particular, Douglas Biow, Andrea Carolino, David Gentilcore, María Luz López Terrada, Miguel López Pérez, Mar Rey Bueno, Bruce Moran, and, in Venice, for their warm friendship, Susanna Voltarel and Nino Gianquinto.

I want to thank my incredible agent, Sandy Dijkstra, for her confidence in the project, and all the wonderful people at the Sandra Dijkstra Literary Agency. I also owe thanks to my editors, Lisa Thomas and John Paine, for helping me shape a sprawling manuscript into a book, and my text editor, Allan Fallow, for his careful reading of the text. Lynx-eyed copy editor Judith Klein saved me from numerous errors in the Notes and Bibliography.

Final thanks to:

My grandson Miguelito, too young to have a clue why, and Leslye, for him. Above all, Elba Serrano, for reasons that only we know, and for some that we probably don't.

S. Elena, Venice, Valencia, and Las Cruces, 2003-2009

APPENDIX

Catalog of Editions and Translations of Leonardo Fioravanti's Books

Secreti medicinali
Venice: Avanzo, 1561

Capricci medicinali
Venice: Avanzo, 1561
Venice: Avanzo, 1564
Venice: Avanzo, 1565
Venice: Avanzo, 1568
Venice: Avanzo, 1573
Venice: Sessa, 1582
Venice: Bonibelli, 1595
Venice: Spineda, 1602
Venice: Gallina, 1617
Venice: Spineda, 1629
Venice: Cestaro, 1647
Venice: Mortali, 1665
Venice: Mortali, 1670
Venice: Zattoni, 1680
Venice: Stefano Civiti, 1680
Bologna: n.p.

Compendio de i secreti rationali
Venice: Valgrisi, 1564
Venice: Ravenoldo, 1566
Venice: Sessa, 1571
Venice: Cornetti, 1591
Torino: Eredi di Bevilacqua, 1580
Venice: Sessa, 1581
Torino: Tarino, 1592
Venice: Salicato, 1596
Venice: Bonibelli, 1597
Venice: Miloco, 1620
Venice: Imberti, 1640
Venice: Conzatti, 1660
Venice: Prodotti, 1675

La cirugia
Venice: Sessa, 1570
Venice: Sessa, 1582
Venice: Bonibelli, 1595
Venice: Spineda, 1610
Venice: Spineda, 1630
Venice: Zattoni, 1678
Venice, Zattoni: 1679

Della fisica
Venice: Sessa, 1582
Venice: Spineda, 1603
Venice: Spineda, 1629
Venice: Sessa, 1632
Venice: Zattoni, 1678

Del Reggimento della peste
Venice: Ravenoldo, 1565
Venice: Sessa, 1571
Venice: Sessa, 1594
Venice: Spineda, 1626
Venice: Zattoni, 1680
Naples: 1720

Dello Specchio di scientia universale
Venice: Valgrisi, 1564
Venice: Ravenoldo, 1567
Venice: Sessa, 1572
Venice: Sessa, 1583
Venice: Spineda, 1603
Venice: Valentini, 1624
Venice: Sessa, 1633
Venice: Conzatti, 1660

Venice: Zattoni, 1678
Venice: Zattoni, 1679

Il Tesoro della vita humana
Venice: Sessa, 1570
Venice: Brigna, 1573
Venice: Sessa, 1582
Venice: Spineda, 1603
Venice: Spineda, 1629
Venice: Brigna, 1673
Venice: Zattoni, 1678
Venice: Sessa, 1682

Pietro and Lodovico Rostinio, *Compendio di tutta la cirugia (edited by Fioravanti and including his Discorsi... sopra la chirugia, con la dichiaratione di molte cose necessarie da sapere, non piu scritte in tale modo)*
Venice: Avanzo, 1561
Venice: Avanzo, 1568
Venice: Simbeni, 1588
Venice: Spineda, 1607
Venice: Spineda, 1630
Venice: Brigna, 1677

Scelta di diversi capitoli importantissimi alla cirugia, estratti dalle opere dell' eccellentissimo dottor, & cavaliere, m. Leonardo Fioravanti
Venice: Ravenoldo, 1568

Giovanni de Vigo, *La pratica universale in cirugia . . . Et di nuovo aggiuntivi molti capitoli estratti dalle opere dell'eccellentissimo dottor . . . Leonardo Fioravanti*
Venice: Bonelli, 1576
Venice: Zopponi, 1581
Venice: Imberti, 1584
Venice: Imberti, 1598
77 Italian editions

TRANSLATIONS

English:

A compendium of the rationall secretes, of the worthie knight and moste excellent doctour of phisicke and chirurgerie, Leonardo Phiorauante Bolognese. Translated by John Hester.
London: John Kingston, 1582

A Joyfull Jewell. Contayning . . . orders, preservatives . . . for the Plague. Translated by Thomas Hill (edited by John Hester).
London, 1579

A Short discours of the excellent doctour and knight, maister Leonardo Phioravanti Bolognese uppon chirurgerie. Translated by John Hester.
London: Thomas East, 1580
London: Edward Allde, 1626 (Augmented by Richard Booth)

An exact collection of the choicest and more rare experiments and secrets in physick and chirurgery . . . of Leonard Phioravant. Translated by John Hester.
London: G. Dawson, 1653

The pearle of practise, or practisers pearle, for phisicke and chirurgerie, found out by J. H. (a spagericke or distiller) amongst the learned observations and prooved practises of many expert men in both faculties. Edited and translated by John Hester.
London: R. Field, 1594

Three exact pieces of Leonard Phioravant Knight, and Doctor in Physick, viz. his Rationall secrets, and Chirurgery, reviewed and revived. Translated by John Hester.
London: G. Dawson, 1652

French:

Les Caprices touchant la medicine. Translated by Claude Rocard.
Paris: Cavellat, 1586

Miroir universel des arts et sciences. Translated by Gabriel Chapuys.
Paris: Cavellat, 1584
Paris: Cavellat, 1586
Paris: Cavellat, 1598

German:

Compendium oder Ausszug der Secreten, Gehaymnissen und verborgenen Künsten
Darmstadt: Johann Leinhosen, 1624

Corona; oder, Kron der Arztney
Frankfurt a. M.: Nicolaus Hoffmann, 1604
Frankfurt a. M: Anthoni Hummen, 1618

Physica, das ist experientz unnd Naturkündigung
Frankfurt a. M.: Nicolaus Hoffmann, 1604
Frankfurt a. M.: Anthoni Hummen, 1618
16 translations
93 total editions

NOTES

The notes are keyed to the text by page number and phrase or quotation in the text. Citations are by author and short title. Full citations will be found in the Bibliography.

Prologue: Experience and Memory

7 in the Piazza del Duomo: Latuada, *Descrizione,* 1737, vol. 2, p. 187. On the office of the *Protofisico* (also called the Protomedico), see Gentilcore, "All that Pertains to Medicine"; and idem, *Healers and Healing,* chap. 2.

8 "Seeing that I've cured": ASM, Autografi, Medici, Carpetta 215; published in Dall'Osso, "Due lettere."

9 a saint, a prophet, and a necromancer: Fioravanti, *Della fisica,* p. 235.

9 a reputation that would shadow him: To the 17th-century French philosopher René Descartes, Fioravanti was "nothing but an Italian charlatan" *(n'a esté qu'un charlatan italien)*: Mersenne, *Correspondence,* vol. 8, p. 211 (letter of 15 November 1638).

10 "Fioravanti of the miracles": Garzoni, *Piazza universale,* pp. 327, 752.

10 His martial therapeutics: Golub, *Limits of Medicine.*

10 desperate to be healed: Young, *Medical Messiahs;* Porter, *Health for Sale.*

Chapter 1: *Mia Dolce Patria*

14 The lament: Dante, *Purgatorio,* Canto VI, lines 76-78:
Ahi serva Italia, di dolore ostello,
nave sanza nocchiere in gran tempesta,
non donna di provincie, ma bordello!

14 "So now, left lifeless": Machiavelli, *The Prince,* p. 134.

15 "a fantasy, a dream": Ruggiero, "Renaissance Dreaming," p. 1.

15 "breaking through": Quoted in Pullan, *History of Early Renaissance Italy,* p. 167.

15 "opened the way for the return of the Muses": Boccaccio, "Life of Dante," p. 15.

16 In 1278: Martines, *Power and Imagination,* pp. 18, 130.

16 He ruled until his death in 1463: Ady, *Bentivoglio of Bologna,* p. 36.

16 "not among the more resplendent": MacKenney, *Renaissances,* p. 74.

17 "clay and rough-wooden Bologna": Clarke, "Magnificence and the City," p. 400.

18 the University of Bologna rose: Simeoni, *Storia dell' Università di Bologna.*

18 "Military Revolution": Parker, *Military Revolution.*

19 Gravediggers reported: Knecht, *Renaissance Warrior,* p. 77.
19 "most presumptuous pox": Erasmus, *Colloquies,* vol. 1, pp. 401, 405.
20 Another, more widespread outbreak: Corradi, *Annali,* pp. 395-98.
20 In his colorful history: Zinsser, *Rats, Lice, and History,* p. 180.
20 "War, plague, famine": Pietro Aretino, quoted in Grendler, *Critics,* p. 10.
20 On the top of her head: Niccoli, *Prophecy,* pp. 51-52.
21 "calamity-stricken Italy": Niccoli, *Prophecy,* p. 55.

Chapter 2: The Empire of Disease
22 Great Medicine: Fioravanti, *Della fisica,* p. 136.
22 his baptismal record: The document is in Bologna's Archepiscopal Library; a copy is in Biblioteca Archiginnasio, MS B.853, Battesimi, f. 76.
23 "relief following severe pain": Cardano, *Book of My Life,* p. 22.
24 During the epidemic: The epidemic is described by Cosmacini, *Storia della medicina,* pp. 101-102.
24 The leper: Brody, *Disease of the Soul;* Richards, *Medieval Leper.*
25 "There's nothing you can do": Strozzi, *Selected Letters,* pp. 73, 173.
25 "God's great scourge": Borgarucci, *Trattato di peste,* p. 13.
25 "The principal and most powerful cause": Fioravanti, *Reggimento,* pp. 12r-v.
26 proceed "in some occult way": Borgarucci, *Trattato di peste,* p. 13.
26 "For God has ordained": Mercurio, *De gli errori populari,* pp. 3r-4r, 114v.
27 Renaissance theory of contagion: Although 16th-century authorities believed that plague and typhus were contagious, in fact neither disease is. Typhus is passed by body lice, while bubonic plague is a disease of rats *(Rattus rattus)* that incidentally affects humans via the rat flea *(Xenopsylla cheopis),* which spreads the bacillus *(Yersinia pestis)* to humans.
27 Such "lower" groups: Calvi, *Histories,* pp. 52-53.
28 "It was provided": Daciano, *Trattato di peste,* pp. 21-26.
29 "all the houses abandoned": Lancellotti, *Cronica,* vol. 2, p. 270.
29 hundreds of thousands of victims: Estimates of plague fatalities are from Valerio Rinieri's manuscript chronicle, *Diario,* f. 9, and Corradi, *Annali,* vol. 1, p. 397; population figures are from Belletini, *La popolazione di Bologna.*
29 "the spots appeared": Fracastoro, *De contagione,* pp. 101-103; Massa, *De febre pestilentialis,* quoted in Corradi, *Annali,* vol. 4, p. 413.
30 unusually cold and wet year: The chronicler Giovanni Francesco Negri reported that in 1527 the weather was rainy and cold from the beginning of May until the end of August (*Annali di Bologna,* vol. 7, p. 211v), while Lancellotti noted that the severe weather conditions caused widespread crop failure and famine (*Cronica,* p. 278).
30 infamous Sack of Rome: Chastel, *Sack of Rome,* p. 27.
30 "commenced to steal chickens": Amaseo, *Diarii udinesi,* p. 294.
31 Some died in the streets: Corradi, *Annali,* vol. 1, p. 417.
31 he recalled the strict measures: Rosa, *Medicina e salute pubblica a Bologna.*
31 "very extreme": Amaseo, *Diarii udinesi,* vol. 2, p. 295.
32 "The remedy they found": Fioravanti, *Reggimento,* pp. 20r-v.
32 veneration of the Madonna del Soccorso: Fanti and Roversi, *Il santuario,* pp. 30-31.
33 the image is solemnly conveyed: Terpstra, "Confraternities," pp. 143-74.
33 "If what was done at the end": Fioravanti, *Reggimento,* p. 20v.
33 "medicating with deeds": Fioravanti, *Tesoro,* p. 3v.

Chapter 3: Medical Bologna
34 a world-famous institution of learning: On Bologna University in the Middle Ages, see Rashdall, *Universities,* vol. 1, pp. 87-268; Sorbelli, *Storia dell' Università di Bologna;* and Simeoni, *Storia dell' Università di Bologna.*
34 human dissection in a classroom: Park, "Criminal and Saintly Body."
34 Its faculty boasted: On Ghini, see Findlen, *Possessing Nature,* p. 166; on Corti, see Siraisi, *Avicenna,* pp. 188-90.
35 the learned physician's bible: Siraisi, *Avicenna.*
35 Skepticism about the value: Siraisi, *Avicenna,* p. 67n.
35 Relentless attacks by Renaissance moderns: French, *Medicine before Science,* pp. 134-38.
35 Rather than acquiring: On the medical curriculum, see French, *Medicine before Science.*

36 The celebrated Bologna professor: French, *Medicine before Science,* p. 102. His opponent was Gentile da Foligno.
36 "to make the ancients": French, *Medicine before Science,* p. 107.
36 Even on matters: Siraisi, *Taddeo Alderotti,* p. 262.
36 "a rigorous mental discipline": Siraisi, *Taddeo Alderotti,* p. 303.
37 dozens of doctors: Pomata, *Contracting a Cure,* p. 56.
37 The therapy was designed: For a summary of humoral theory, see Siraisi, *Medieval and Early Renaissance Medicine,* pp. 104-106. In addition, see French, *Canonical Medicine.*
38 Seasonal bloodlettings: Pomata, *Contracting a Cure,* p. 65.
38 Theirs were the hands: Green, "Women's Medical Practice."
38 A 1568 list of shops: Pomata, *Contracting a Cure,* p. 56.
39 The *norcini:* Gentilcore, *Medical Charlatanism,* pp. 181-188.
39 Others specialized in treating cataracts: Park, "Stones, Bones, and Hernias."
39 Charlatans and other remedy peddlers: Gentilcore, *Medical Charlatanism,* pp. 181-88.
39 We know that he did not graduate: The matriculation records for the period when Fioravanti would have been a student—the late 1530s through the 1540s—do not survive. Nor is he mentioned in the *Notitia Doctorum,* the official list of doctorates granted.
40 He knew some Latin: He made this admission in his testimony to the protomedico in Madrid; see chap. 32.
40 "everything I studied at Bologna": Fioravanti, *Tesoro,* p. 113v.

Chapter 4: Leonardo and the Anatomists
41 Andreas Vesalius arrived in Bologna: O'Malley, *Andreas Vesalius,* pp. 98-100.
42 To heighten the drama: Ferrari, "Public Anatomy Lessons." Ferrari suggests that the theatrical flavor of the anatomy demonstrations was in response to concerns about the decline in the number of foreign students attending the university.
42 "I certainly don't see": Quoted in Siraisi, *Avicenna,* p. 192 (slightly modified). On Corti, see DBI, vol. 29, pp. 794-96.
42 "we proceeded to the demonstration": Eriksson, *Andreas Vesalius' First Public Anatomy,* p. 55.
43 More than 200 spectators: On the public anatomies at Bologna, see Ferrari, "Public Anatomy Lessons." For descriptions of the crowds typically present at the demonstrations, see Klestinec, "History of Anatomy Theaters."
43 University statutes governing the subjects: Martinotti, *L'insegnamento dell'anatomia;* Carlino, *Books of the Body.*
43 burial in a Christian cemetery: For similar rites and practices in Rome and Padua, see Carlino, *Books of the Body,* pp. 98-115; and Park, *Secrets of Women,* pp. 211-14.
45 "Here Galen is wrong": Eriksson, *Andreas Vesalius' First Public Anatomy,* p. 273.
45 "pitiless and cruel": Fioravanti, *Specchio,* pp. 51v-52v.
45 "When I saw an anatomy done": Fioravanti, *Cirugia,* p. 54v. Fioravanti continues his diatribe against anatomy in *Cirugia,* pp. 129-31, and *Specchio,* pp. 42v-46.
46 "They just grope around": Fioravanti, *Specchio,* p. 44v.
46 "contrary to the order of nature": Fioravanti, *Cirugia,* p. 130r
47 "We see that dogs": Fioravanti, *Specchio,* p. 45v; *Cirugia,* p. 130r.
47 "The difficulty": Carlino, *Books of the Body,* p. 229.

Chapter 5: The Education of a Surgeon
48 As we know from contemporary observers: Boccaccio, *Decameron,* p. 51.
49 They inspected pharmaceuticals: On the regulation of medical practice in Bologna, see Pomata, *Contracting a Cure;* and Rosa, *Medicina e salute pubblica.*
49 "in those matters": D'Amato, *Prattica nuova,* p. 7.
49 The cornerstone of Renaissance therapeutics: Edelstein, "Dietetics."
49 The rule was repeatedly enforced: Cavallo, *Artisans of the Body,* pp. 21-27.
50 surgeons usually learned their craft: Cavallo, *Artisans of the Body,* pp. 136-56.
51 "a barber's practice": ASB, Codici Miniati, 100, Statuti della società dei barbieri, 1556-1713 (bobina 61), 13 (statute of 1556). In addition, see Pomata, "Barbieri e comari," p. 166.
51 "barbers are also useful": Garzoni, *Piazza universale,* pp. 1375-76.
51 "clean, gracious, modest": Magni, *Discorsi,* p. 5.
52 All were considered: Cavallo, *Artisans of the Body,* pp. 38-49. On hygiene and cleanliness in the Italian Renaissance, see Biow, *Culture of Cleanliness.*

52 Much safer, he counseled: Magni, *Discorsi*, pp. 9-10.
52 Menial as their professional status: Pomata, *Contracting a Cure*, p. 66.
52 Because the blood was capable: Pomata, "Barbieri e comari," p. 168; Siraisi, *Medieval and Early Renaissance Medicine*, pp. 139-41.
53 Besides drawing fluids out of the body: Cavallo, *Artisans of the Body*, p. 54.
53 "The art of the barber is very necessary": Fioravanti, *Specchio*, p. 65v.
54 Eventually surgery would become: Rosa, *Medicina e salute pubblica*, pp. 21-22.
54 "the sciences of medicine and surgery": Fioravanti, *Capricci medicinali*, p. 32r.
56 "It was done because": Fioravanti, *Capricci medicinali*, p. 32r.

Chapter 6: The Road of Experience
57 "Many years have passed": Fioravanti, *Tesoro*, p. 17v.
57 "If ever there was a year": Muzzi, *Annali*, vol. 6, p. 510.
57 He was following the example: Fioravanti, *Tesoro*, 1.
58 "[Y]ou must go walking the world": Fioravanti, *Capricci medicinali*, p. 254v.
58 Traveling by coach: Allegra, "Il viaggio," p. 37. Maczak, *Travel*.
58 "ate with the chickens": Fioravanti, *Specchio*, p. 50r.
58 "walked the world and ploughed the seas": Fioravanti, *Tesoro*, p. 1r.
60 The approximately 150-mile journey: Fynes Moryson, traveling by foot from Genoa to Milan in November 1594, was able to cover about 20 miles per day (*Itinerary*, vol. 1, p. 353). The distance from Bologna to Genoa is a little over 150 miles or about 240 kilometers. Allegra ("Il viaggio") estimates that early modern travelers could average 25 kilometers per day.
60 As the retinue entered the city: Fioravanti recollects Philip's entry into Genoa in *Tesoro*, p. 18, but the details are taken from Calvete de Estrella's memoir of Philip's grand tour, *El felicissimo viaje*, vol. 1, pp. 35-50. In addition, see Kamen, *Philip of Spain*, pp. 35-48.

Chapter 7: The Carnival Doctor
62 "Even though in those days": Fioravanti, *Capricci medicinali*, p. 108v.
62 The empiricists: Edelstein, "Empiricism."
63 "Nature gave the animals": Fioravanti, *Capricci medicinali*, pp. 29v-30v.
63 "I believe that this was the time": Fioravanti, *Secreti medicinali*, chap. 34, p. 26. Akron of Agrigento is mentioned in *Capricci*, pp. 33v, 108v. On the disputes among sects, see *Capricci medicinali*, p. 33v.
64 "most fertile kingdom of Sicily": Fioravanti's account of his sojourn in Sicily is in *Tesoro*, pp. 18-49.
65 "I stayed for many days": Fioravanti, *Tesoro*, p. 18r.
65 Carnival took place: For my account of Carnival, I rely on a number of studies, including Ruggiero, *Binding Passions*, pp. 3-23; Muir, *Civic Ritual*, pp. 158-60; and Bakhtin, *Rabelais*, pp. 196-277.
65 "When word got out": Fioravanti, *Tesoro*, pp. 18r-v.
65 "Precipitato": Mattioli, *I discorsi*, p. 694.
66 "Most excellent doctors": Fioravanti, *Tesoro*, p. 18v.
67 ballad singer and pamphleteer Giulio Cesare Croce: A poor shoemaker's son, Croce was born in 1550 in the village of Persiceto, a few miles from Bologna. Orphaned at the age of seven and adopted by an uncle, he went to work in the family's forge. Somehow he learned to read and write, and at the age of 18 moved to Bologna to begin a long career as a popular singer and writer. He wrote more than 400 songs, books, pamphlets, and mock prognostications, including his most famous, *The Subtle Wiles of Bertoldo*, a novel whose protagonist was the deformed but shrewd peasant Bertoldo, the Lombard King Alboino's court buffoon. See Camporesi, *La maschera di Bertholdo;* Guerrini, *Vita e opere*.
67 "Take the foolishness of a buffoon": The "Marvelous Secrets of Medicine" are from Croce's pamphlet, *Secreti di medicina*.
67 The Italian *ciarlatano:* On the origins of the word "ciarlatano," see Malkiel, "Italian *ciarlatano* and Its Romance Offshoots." In addition, see Gentilcore, *Medical Charlatanism*, pp. 54-55.
67 In order to attract customers: Garzoni, *Piazza universale*, pp. 740-41. For the commedia dell'arte, see Lea, *Italian Popular Comedy;* Henke, "Italian Mountebank"; and Katritzky, "Marketing Medicine."
68 "the suitable therapy for the infected social body": Camporesi, *La maschera di Bertholdo*, p. 187.

68 The liberating spirit of Carnival: On self-fashioning, see Greenblatt, *Renaissance Self-Fashioning.*
68 "to find a position": Bahktin, *Rabelais,* p. 272.

Chapter 8: The New Asclepius

69 "This is a strange infirmity": The case is described in Fioravanti, *Tesoro,* pp. 23v-24v.
70 "I decided to try Appio Riso": The identity of Appio Riso, Fioravanti's cure for cataracts (*Tesoro,* p. 23), is uncertain but was probably the *Apium risum* identified by the English herbalist John Gerard as Pasque Flower (*Herball,* pp. 385-86). The plant would appear to be *Anemone pulsatilla,* which contemporaries report was used as an ointment for eye inflammations. The oldest uses of pulsatilla were, in fact, for the relief of amaurosis (temporary blindness), cataract, and opacity of the cornea. The tincture is still widely used as a homeopathic remedy.
71 "The whole city marveled": Fioravanti, *Tesoro,* p. 21r.
71 "learned and experienced man": Fioravanti, *Reggimento,* pp. 20v-21r.
71 "The true *diapalma*": Fioravanti, *Capricci medicinali,* p. 146.
72 the "new Asclepius": Fioravanti, *Tesoro,* p. 22r.
73 " 'Why, yes,' I answered": Fioravanti, *Tesoro,* pp. 25v-26v.
74 An overnight celebrity: Fioravanti, *Tesoro,* p. 29r.
74 *Ospedale degli Incurabili*: On the *incurabili* hospitals, see Henderson, *Renaissance Hospital,* pp. 97-101.
74 "Señor doctor": Fioravanti, *Tesoro,* p. 29.
75 A popular cure: Munger, "Guaiacum."
75 Arnald of Villanova: McVaugh, "Chemical Medicine," p. 245, quoting Bruno of Longoburgo. The technique of sublimation, like distillation, was introduced into Western medicine in the 13th century from Arabic sources.
75 "The whole city marveled": Fioravanti, *Tesoro,* pp. 29v-30.
76 "I was forced": Fioravanti, *Tesoro,* p. 30r.

Chapter 9: The Marvelous Virtues of Precipitato

77 In mastering alchemy: Moran, *Distilling Knowledge,* p. 9.
77 Certainly deception played a role: Nummedal, "Problem of Fraud."
78 something they *did:* Moran, *Distilling Knowledge,* p. 6.
78 "vain wish and fanciful dream": Biringuccio, *Pirotechnia,* pp. 35, 337.
78 When we realize: Principe, *Aspiring Adept;* Dobbs, *Foundations.* William Newman is currently undertaking a full evaluation of Newton's alchemy.
79 Of all the alchemical medicines: Fioravanti, *Tesoro,* p. 19. Fioravanti gives a recipe for making the drug in *Capricci medicinali,* p. 156.
79 Precipitato was a wonder drug: The use of precipitato as a purge was also endorsed by Mattioli, *Discorsi,* pp. 694-95.
79 Precipitato would be his panacea: Fioravanti, *Capricci medicinali,* p. 156r.
79 "Take aqua fortis": Fioravanti, *Capricci medicinali,* pp. 156r-v.
80 He even used it to treat the falling sickness: On the perceived relation between epilepsy and syphilis, see Temkin, *Falling Sickness,* pp. 187-88.
80 "The polluted stomach": Fioravanti, *Capricci medicinali,* pp. 156r-v.
80 Fioravanti's usual dosage: Fioravanti normally prescribed 10 to 12 grains of Precipitato in honey or rose water (according to the alchemist Van Helmont, a grain was "the six hundreth part of an ounce," or approximately 0.06 ounce). Thus, Fioravanti's dosage would have been about 0.6 ounce, or about 17 grams. The average lethal dose for inorganic mercury salts is about 1 gram. Such a toxic compound would have killed patients unless administered in a more dilute form.
81 "At the beginning": Fioravanti, *Tesoro,* pp. 32r-v.
82 "I wanted to know": Fioravanti, *Capricci medicinali,* p. 53r.
82 "Never in my life": Fioravanti, *Capricci medicinali,* pp. 53v-54r.
82 "made him vomit": Fioravanti, *Capricci medicinali,* pp. 54r-v.
83 For barber-surgeons, cleansing the body: Cavallo, *Artisans of the Body,* pp. 38-41.
84 "I responded": Fioravanti, *Tesoro,* pp. 36r-v.
84 The surgeon prescribed: Gerard says of coloquintida: "[The] operation of purging it worketh so violently, that it doth not onely draw forth flegme and choler marvelous speedily, and in very great quantitie: but oftentimes fetcheth forth blood and bloody excrements, by shaving

the guts, and opening the ends of the meseraicall veines." Gerard recommends that it "is not to be used rashly." *Herball,* p. 915.

84 So great is the plant's purging power: Wood and Bache, *Dispensatory of the United States,* 13th ed., p. 326.

Chapter 10: Charlatan or Wonder Worker?

86 "I really didn't know much": Fioravanti, *Tesoro,* p. 18r.

87 "Perhaps I owed their esteem": Levi, *Christ Stopped at Eboli,* pp. 38-39, 219.

87 Is it any less believable: Prosperi, "Otras Indias"; Selwyn, *Paradise Inhabited by Devils.*

88 Pliny, for example, noted: Plinius Gaius Secondus, *Natural History* XI; 80 (vol. 3, p. 561); Ramberti, *Delle cose degli Turchi,* p. 245. This was also reported by Nicolas de Nicolay, who traveled to Istanbul with the French Embassy in 1555.

88 People began to think: The physician Girolamo Fracastoro, whose poem *Syphilis* gave the sickness its name, noted that "although the contagion is still flourishing today, it seems to have changed its character since those earliest periods of its appearance." Arrizabalaga et al., *Great Pox,* p. 231.

89 Guaiacum, the "Holy Wood": Munger, "Guaiacum."

Chapter 11: An Ingenious Surgery

91 "The good old man": Fioravanti, *Tesoro,* pp. 46r-v.

91 Falls and accidents: Goldthwaite, *Building of Renaissance Florence,* p. 296.

92 Sudden brawls: Muir, *Mad Blood Stirring;* Arnold, "Violence and Warfare." Public insults were so worrisome to the Venetian state that it created a special tribunal, the *Esecutori contra bestemmia,* to control it: Horodowich, *Language and Statecraft.*

92 "a society in which violence": Davidson, "Armed Band," p. 411.

92 "It takes almost a year": Fioravanti, *Capricci medicinali,* p. 47.

92 the ingredients in Wound Powder: In 1549, Fioravanti used Armenian Bole to treat a snake handler who, while hunting in the hills near Milazzo, was bitten in the hand by a viper. *Tesoro,* p. 38.

93 Grand Liquor: An extensive literature on hypericum confirms its analgesic and astringent activity; Gerard includes a recipe in his *Herball,* p. 541.

94 the syphilitic nose: One of the earliest names given to the disease was *passio turpis saturnina* (because it distorts the facial features), an appellation that appears in the literature as early as 1502, when the modern history of the disease was less than a decade old. Quétel, *History,* p. 21.

95 "In a society obsessed": Weinstein, *Captain's Concubine,* p. 149.

95 The indignity of sacrificing a nose: On dueling in early modern Europe, see Kiernan, *The Duel.*

95 "First they gave the patient a purgative": Fioravanti, *Tesoro,* pp. 47r-v.

96 The humanist Camillo Porzio: Gnudi and Webster, *Gaspare Tagliacozzi,* p. 118.

97 "proven by Hippocrates": Gnudi and Webster, *Gaspare Tagliacozzi,* p. 124.

97 "farming of men": Fioravanti, *Speccio,* p. 18v.

98 It is the opposite of philosophical knowledge: The contrast between *mêtis* and *sophia* is the subject of Detienne and Vernant, *Cunning Intelligence.*

98 "for a consideration": Gnudi and Webster, *Gaspare Tagliacozzi,* pp. 118-19.

99 "he almost brings the dead back to life": Fioravanti, *Specchio,* p. b6.

99 Around the time of Fioravanti's visit: The Polish physician Wojciech Oczko, a student at Bologna 1565-69, reported that Aranzio began experimenting with rhinoplasty around the time of Fioravanti's visit to Bologna (Gnudi and Webster, *Gaspare Tagliacozzi,* p. 133).

100 "you may": Gilman, *Making the Body Beautiful,* p. 70.

100 Far from perfecting the method: The anatomist Girolamo Mercuriale saw two of Tagliacozzi's patients and reported that the end result was "not so similar that a deception is not detected" (Gnudi and Webster, *Gaspare Tagliacozzi,* p. 135).

101 "first physicians": Fioravanti, *Capricci medicinali,* p. 31r.

101 "first of the moderns": Van Deusen, "Place of Telesio," p. 417.

Chapter 12: The Marvels of Naples

102 the slow decline of Italy's south: For a penetrating analysis of modern Italian views of the Mezzogiorno, see Dickie, *Darkest Italy.*

102 Naples in the 16th century: Enrico Bacco's *Descrittione del Regno di Napoli,* published in 1671, captures the city's Renaissance radiance: Gardiner, trans., *Naples: An Early Guide.*
103 "it drew upon fresh blood": Croce, *History of the Kingdom of Naples,* p. 60.
103 "being persuaded by his reputation": Giannone, *Civil History,* vol. 2, p. 526.
103 "It was lamentable to see": Giannone, *Civil History,* vol. 2, p. 562 (slightly modified).
104 Giannone thought: Giannone, *Civil History,* vol. 2, p. 562.
104 Croce deemed it: Croce, *History of the Kingdom of Naples,* p. 113.
105 "among the loveliest": Fioravanti, *Tesoro,* p. 71. On Toledo's urban reforms, see Giannone, *Civil History,* vol. 2, pp. 542-44; Strazzulo, *Edilizia,* pp. 3-26; and Pane, "Pietro di Toledo." On Neapolitan culture under Toledo, see Élias de Tejada, *Napoli Spagnola,* vol. 2.
106 A proverb coined during Angevin times: Marino, "Economic Idylls," p. 216.
106 Nature must be investigated "according to its own principles": Van Deusen, "Place of Telesio"; Copenhaver and Schmitt, *Renaissance Philosophy,* pp. 309-14.
107 naturalism sprouted a reform agenda: Spruit, "Telesio's Reform."
107 Reform naturalism found its cause célèbre: Foa, *Bruno;* Rowland, *Bruno.*
107 *Hermes Trismegistus:* Yates, *Bruno and the Hermetic Tradition.*
108 The ancient Roman poet Virgil: Comparetti, *Vergil in the Middle Ages;* Spargo, *Virgil the Necromancer.*
109 Della Porta called his group: Della Porta mentions his academy in the preface to *Magia naturalis* (English trans., *Natural Magick*).
109 Della Porta's real purpose: Eamon, *Science and the Secrets,* chap. 6.
109 His younger contemporary: Headley, *Tommaso Campanella;* Blanchet, *Campanella.*
109 Campanella moved to Naples: Eamon, "Natural Magic and Utopia."

Chapter 13: An Academy of Magi

111 Although his major work: On Telesio's natural philosophy, see Fiorentino, *Bernardino Telesio.* On the history of the Accademia Cosentina, see De Seta, *L'accademia Cosentina.* An important reference work on the Italian academies is Maylender, *Storia delle accademie d'Italia.* In addition, see Cochrane, "Renaissance Academies"; and Eamon, "Court, Academy, and Printing House."
111 They called their company: For the Accademia Segreta described by Ruscelli, see Eamon and Paheau, "Accademia Segreta."
112 Scholastic science was: Murdoch, "Analytical Character." In addition, see Smith, "Knowing Things Inside Out."
112 Isolated, unusual, and singular events: Dear, *Discipline and Experience,* pp. 5-6, 12-13.
113 Their passionate pursuit of craft secrets: Zilsel, "Sociological Roots"; Rossi, *Philosophy;* Smith, *Body of the Artisan.*
114 "Alchemists and distillers of many different nations": Fioravanti's Neapolitan circle and his "academy" are described in *Tesoro,* pp. 50v, 234v.
115 We know about the academy: Fioravanti's letter to Da Rienzo is in *Tesoro,* pp. 234-36, and his reference to the alchemist Cifune is from *La cirugia,* p. 165. He recounts his Neapolitan years in *Tesoro,* pp. 50-73.
116 Some were strictly utilitarian: On books of secrets, see Eamon, *Science and the Secrets.*
116 These writings—all spurious: Pereira, *Alchemical Corpus.*
116 Central to Lull's art: Pereira, "Teorie dell'elixir."
117 Alchemy's "Promethean ambition": Newman, *Promethean Ambitions.*
117 "don't follow the teachings of Geber": Cortese, *I Secreti.*
117 "Many arts have issued": Biringuccio, *Pirotechnia,* p. 337.
118 "What they were all looking for": Moran, *Distilling Knowledge,* p. 11.
120 "made with such artifice": Fioravanti, *Specchio,* p. 55.
120 A likely candidate: Della Porta described a mirror similar to the one that Fioravanti mentions in *Natural Magick,* pp. 356-57.
121 "I believe more": Fioravanti, *Capricci medicinali,* p. 32v.

Chapter 14: The University of War

122 In *Physician*: Hippocrates, *Physician,* vol. 8, p. 315.
122 "anatomies of living men": Fioravanti, *Cirugia,* p. 139v.
123 Turkish corsairs preyed on ships: Tenenti, *Piracy.*
123 "the great dog of a Turk": Fioravanti, letter to Cosimo de' Medici, 2 November 1560, ASF, Mediceo del Principato, f. 487, c. 11.

123 Those prisoners not immediately condemned: The *bagnos* of Tunis are graphically described by Morgan, *Complete History,* p. 292.
123 "The oldest still tell": On captives, see Davis, "Counting European Slaves," p. 124.
123 the Turkish corsair Turghut: On Dragut's career, in addition to Braudel, *The Mediterranean* (vol. 2, p. 755), I follow the series of articles by Monchicourt, "L'insécurité en Méditerranée"; "Episodes de la carrière tunisienne de Dragut," parts I and II; and "Dragut, amiral turc." I also consulted Salazar, *Historia.* For the Turkish side, see Khalifa, *History,* p. 79.
124 Emperor Charles V, worried: My descriptions of the city and siege of Africa are from Adriani and Adriani, *Istoria;* Manfroni, *Storia della marina italiana,* vol 3*;* Guglielmotti, *La guerra dei pirate;* Salazar, *Historia;* Calvete de Estrella, *El felicissimo viaje;* and Fioravanti's own account in *Tesoro,* pp. 60v-67r. He remembered the war as having taken place in 1550, a year from its actual date in 1551, and I have adjusted the chronology accordingly.
125 Once he used Precipitato: Fioravanti, *Tesoro,* pp. 49-50; for similar accounts, see pp. 103, 159.
127 "hit the poor man": Fioravanti, *Secreti rationali,* p. 58.
127 Suddenly, out of the forest: Salazar, *Historia,* p. 61. Fioravanti's account is in *Tesoro,* p. 21.
128 "Holding it in my hand": Fioravanti, *Tesoro,* p. 64.
128 As for Fioravanti's "new way": Modern formulas for "Balsamum Fioraventi" contain higher concentrations of alcohol. In February 1778, John Adams, the future U.S. President, aboard a ship bound for France, recorded in his diary that the ship's surgeon prescribed for him "a phial of *Balsamum Fioravanti,* for an inflammation in my eyes, which seems to be very good for them." Adams continued: "It is very much compounded; it is very subtle and penetrating. Pour a few drops into the palms of your hands, rub it over the palm and the fingers, and then hold the insides of your hands before your eyes, and the steam which evaporates enters the eyes, and works them clear." *Works,* vol. 3, p. 103.
129 "But my oil ran out": Ambroise Paré, *Method of Treating Wounds Made by Arquebuses and Other Firearms,* quoted in Porter, *Greatest Benefit,* p. 188. Malgaigne, *Surgery and Ambroise Paré,* embellishes the myth (here quoting p. 263). A more accurate version of Paré's place in the history of gunshot-wound treatment is in De Vries, "Military Surgical Practice."
130 The ancient idea: For references to the folklore of wound balms, see Thompson, *Motif-Index,* D1240 (vol. 1, p. 46). For background on ancient and medieval balsams, see Truitt, "Virtues of Balm." Cervantes's joke about "Fierabrás's balm" is in *Don Quixote,* I:10, p. 72. "Fierabrás" is usually thought to refer to a legendary Saracen who appears in several *chansons de geste,* but it seems intriguingly possible that the name might have been a corruption or play on the name Fioravanti, who was known in Spain as Fieravanti, pronounced Fierabanti in Castilian.
131 Unable to breach: Ferramolino had worked for the Spanish crown in Sicily for more than 20 years, where he oversaw the construction of the massive wall surrounding the city of Palermo, the fortifications of Messina, and a series of guard towers around the coastline of the island. His career is detailed in Hoppen, "Military Engineers"; Di Giovanni, *Le fortificazioni di Palermo.* In addition, see Tadini, "Notizie."
131 Archimedes, the famous engineer: Kern, *Ancient Siege Warfare,* p. 262.
131 the numbers killed and wounded: Fioravanti, *Tesoro,* p. 67; Prudencio de Sandoval estimated the casualties to be more than 500 dead and 1,000 wounded on the Christian side and more than 950 dead and "a multitude injured" on the Turkish side: *History of Charles Vth,* p. 430.
132 The fall of Africa was celebrated: Horatio Nucula, a scholar from Umbria, thought the war to be so significant that he penned a treatise of more than 300 pages detailing the Christian victory. Cornelius Scepper (one of Charles V's secretaries), also wrote a paean to the emperor's conquests in Africa, *Rerum à Carolo V in Africa bello gestarum Commentarii* (1554).
132 by 1554 the fortress had been abandoned: Braudel, *Mediterranean,* vol. 2, p. 910.
132 At the conclusion of the war: Fioravanti, *Tesoro,* pp. 67v-73r.
132 Somewhat reluctantly, Fioravanti departed: *Tesoro,* p. 73r.

Chapter 15: The Cardinal's House
134 Rome, on the other hand: Partner, *Renaissance Rome.* For the Spanish presence, see Dandelet, *Spanish Rome.*
134 Giovanni Angelo Medici: The portraits of Cardinal Medici and his brother are based on Pastor, *History of the Popes,* vol. 15, chap. 2.
135 "Mercenary commanders": Machiavelli, *The Prince,* p. 78.
136 Leonardo began practicing: Fioravanti's account of his experience in Rome and his conflict

with the physicians at the papal court are from *Tesoro,* pp. 73-80; *Specchio,* pp. 199r-v; and *Capricci medicinali,* pp. 80v-81.

136 the painter Alessandro Oliverio: Fioravanti, *Tesoro,* p. 75r. Oliverio was born in Bergamo around 1500. He worked as a *garzone,* or helper, in the studio of Alviso Serafin as well as that of Palma Vecchio (1480?–1528), a leading painter of the Italian Renaissance in Venice. See Armstrong, "Alessandro Oliverio"; Benezit, *Dictionnaire,* vol. 10, p. 360. Benezit says that he died "after 1544"; thus the event recorded by Fioravanti extends his recorded lifetime by about ten years.

137 Gout afflicts the joints: Porter and Rousseau, *Gout.*

137 Cardinal Medici was said: Pastor, *History of the Popes,* vol. 15, p. 88.

137 One of his gout remedies: Donzelli, "lapis lazuli," in *Teatro,* p. 44.

137 his venereal symptoms: Pastor, *History of the Popes,* vol. 15, p. 75.

137 an ulcer "the size of a hand": Fioravanti, *Tesoro,* pp. 76r-77r.

138 "Now, this ambassador": Fioravanti, *Tesoro,* p. 77v. For the large literature on aristocratic collecting, see Eamon, "Appearance, Artifice, Reality." I have not been able to identify this Portuguese ambassador to the papal court. He would have served between the terms of Pedro Mascarenhas (1539–1554?), who, after serving as ambassador to Rome, was appointed viceroy of Goa, the capital of the Portuguese possessions in Asia, and Lourenço Pires de Távora, who served as ambassador to Rome from 1559 to 1562.

138 "a turning point in western history": Braudel, *Mediterranean,* vol. 2, p. 941.

138 "driven by a lifelong desire": Levin, *Agents of Empire,* p. 64.

139 "He made me swear": Fioravanti, *Tesoro,* pp. 78v-79r. I am grateful to Professor Carole Putko for information about the Guise family and about François de Guise in particular (personal correspondence).

139 Battista Pelegrino wrote to him: Fioravanti, *Tesoro,* p. 121.

Chapter 16: A Surgeon in Rome

140 Fioravanti did not apply: Fioravanti's license to practice in Rome, dated 27 September 1557, is recorded in the Roman archives, ASR, Camerale II, Sanità, f. 20v.

141 The widely circulated *Book of Vagabonds: Camporesi, Libro dei vagabondi,* p. ci.

141 Yet it was also the site: Gregorovius, *Storia della città di Roma,* vol. 3, p. 300.

141 Renaissance Rome was a dangerous place: Blastenbrei, *Kriminalität.* As a reference point, Ciudad Juárez, Mexico, often regarded as the world's deadliest city, had approximately 3,000 murders in 2009, an average of 8 or so per day.

142 "In just 16 days": Fioravanti, *Tesoro,* pp. 75r-v.

142 For only one incident: Archival notices of Fioravanti's treatments of wounds in Rome include ASR, Tribunale del Governatore, b. 6/2, 14v (15 November 1555); and ASR, Tribunale del Governatore, b. 6 (31 March 1556).

142 "19 October 1555": ASR, Tribunale del Governatore, 9v (6 June 1555).

142 "Among the many stupendous": Fioravanti, *Tesoro,* p. 78v.

144 In such displays: Burckhardt, *Civilization of the Renaissance,* pp. 225ff. In Burckhardt's classic formulation, the Renaissance "first gave the highest development to individuality, and then led the individual to the most zealous and thorough study of himself in all forms and under all conditions." Burckhardt's idea that "the ban laid upon human personality was dissolved" in the Renaissance has been the most controversial part of his thesis, and though his interpretation of the Renaissance has been demolished in virtually all of its aspects, it continues to inform scholarly discussion. The term "Renaissance self-fashioning" is borrowed from Greenblatt, *Renaissance Self-Fashioning.*

144 expression of a "performative self": Martin, "Myth of Renaissance Individualism," pp. 214-18; idem, *Myths of Renaissance Individualism,* pp. 35-6.

144 "something greater than the sum": Martin, "Inventing Sincerity," p. 1340.

145 "Your nature is always to flee": Fioravanti, *Reggimento,* p. 66-67.

146 "Poor Gianjacopo had been wounded": Fioravanti, *Tesoro,* pp. 73r-74r.

147 This "cabal" of powerful . . . physicians: Fioravanti, *Specchio,* pp. 199r-v, and *Capricci medicinali,* pp. 80v-81r. Giustiniano Finetto, a professor of medicine at the Sapienza, is mentioned in *Specchio,* p. 220v and *Capricci medicinali,* pp. 42v, 81.

147 Not all of the doctors opposed him: ASR, Camerale II, Sanità, f. 20v (27 September 1557). On Giacomelli, see Palmer, "Medicine at the Papal Court," p. 55.

148 Spanish anatomist Juan Valverde: Guerra, "Juan de Valverde."

148 What might have motivated: At the time of Fioravanti's dispute with Colombo, Valverde was still embroiled in a quarrel with the celebrated anatomist Andreas Vesalius over a book he'd published in Spanish the year before. Valverde's book, *Historia de la composición del cuerpo humano* (Rome 1556), was an important contribution to anatomy, but because he made the unfortunate choice of basing his illustrations on Vesalius's *De fabrica,* the Flemish anatomist accused him of plagiarizing. The criticism was not entirely fair. In fact, Valverde made numerous improvements on *De fabrica,* specifically pointing out ten errors in Vesalius's work and disagreeing with Vesalius in more than 30 instances.
148 *Invidia*—envy—drove him from Rome: Fioravanti's account of his conflict with the Roman physicians are from *Tesoro,* pp. 73-80; *Specchio,* pp. 199r-v; and *Capriccio medicinali,* pp. 80v-81r. I was unable to find an account of any formal charge against him in the Roman archives.
148 "The blessed Lord God": Fioravanti, *Capricci medicinali,* p. 80v.

Chapter 17: A Road Not Taken
150 The companionship: Fioravanti, *Tesoro,* pp. 77r-v.
150 "Besides exchanging secrets": Fioravanti, *Tesoro,* p. 77v.
150 The practice of paying royalties: Witcombe, *Copyright.*
151 Although employment in a printing house: On literary life in early modern Venice, see Di Filippo Bareggi, *Il mestiere di scrivere;* Grendler, *Critics.*
151 According to the logic of patronage: Richardson, *Printing.*
151 Even when an author received: De Vivo, *Information,* p. 218.
151 "One is by walking the world": Fioravanti, *Tesoro,* p. 213v.
152 "Before the glorious art": Fioravanti, *Specchio,* pp. 61v-62r.
152 "Only those who are written up": Fioravanti, *Reggimento,* p. 70r.
152 Inexplicably, he remained there: Fioravanti blamed the weather, but 50 days seems excessive. *Tesoro,* p. 82r.
152 Leonardo mentions her: Both letters are published in the *Tesoro.* In a letter to his Neapolitan friend Pascarello da Chiusune (14 May 1568), Fioravanti mentions that he and Paula are both glad to hear of Pascarello's improved health (from *paralisia,* p. 237v). Paula is also mentioned in a letter of 5 May 1566 from Giovangirolamo Gonzaga. In his reply (17 May), Fioravanti comments that a box of letters from Paula, along with some other goods, had been dispatched to Pesaro, presumably for her family. Paula is also mentioned in a letter of Giovandomenico Zavaglione of Naples, 4 September 1565 (p. 164v). In addition, see Camporesi, *Camminare il mondo,* pp. 216, 234, 250.
153 Evidently they had no children: Letter from Giovandomenico Zavaglione, 4 September 1565 (*Tesoro,* 164v) mentions that Fioravanti had no children.
153 *"Chi si piglia d'amore":* Martines, *Strong Words,* p. 228.
153 The average age of marriage: Cohen and Cohen, *Daily Life,* p. 202; Muir, *Civic Ritual,* p. 33.
153 Church weddings were not the rule: Muir, *Civic Ritual,* pp. 32-33.
154 "Seeing the fury of the woman's madness": Fioravanti, *Capricci medicinali,* p. 72v. Dia Aromatica was essentially a spiced powder laced with Fioravanti's *pietra filosofale,* a powerful emetic that ressembled Precipitato in its composition and effects.
154 "Madness is nothing more than": Fioravanti, *Tesoro,* p. 181v.
154 Guidobaldo spent lavishly: Fontana, "Duke Guidobaldo II."
155 Poor Isabella: Conelli, "Ecclesiastical Patronage."
155 Gonzaga sends greetings: Giovangirolamo Gonzaga to Fioravanti, 5 May 1566. *Tesoro,* pp. 155v-156v. The recipe for *Acqua imperiale* occurs in *Secreti rationali,* p. 130v.

Chapter 18: Venetian Curiosities
157 *"Venezia è un pesce"*: Scarpa, *Venezia è un pesce.*
159 The myth was celebrated annually: Muir, *Civic Ritual,* pp. 119-34.
160 An ambitious building program: A contemporary description of Venice is in Sansovino, *Venetia,* p. 501. Regarding Venetian architecture and the buildings in the Piazza S. Marco, I rely on Howard, *Architectural History;* and Goy, *Venice.* Regarding Sansovino, I rely on Howard, *Jacopo Sansovino.*
160 "on the corner": Fioravanti, *Tesoro,* p. 83r.
160 The church fronted the Merceria: On the Merceria, MacKenney, *Tradesmen,* pp. 106-107.
160 "one of the most delicious streets": Evelyn, *Diary,* p. 160 (spelling modernized).
161 All that evoked wonder: Daston, "Moral Economy." In addition, see the essays in Smith and

Findlen, eds., *Merchants & Marvels.* On conspicuous consumption in the Renaissance, see Jardine, *Worldly Goods;* and Goldthwaite, *Wealth and the Demand for Art.*

161 A capital of the European trade: Palmer, "Pharmacy."

161 The pharmaceutical trade thrived: The wares of a typical, well-stocked Venetian pharmacy are described in Borgarucci, *La fabrica de gli spetiali.*

161 The demand for the fashionable new drug: Dannenfeldt, "Egyptian Mumia."

161 He set up his medical practice there: ASV, Sant'Uffizi, b. 23.

162 Jacomo Torellis: Fioravanti, *Cirugia,* p. 26v.

162 Leonardo lauded: Fioravanti, *Specchio,* pp. 110v-112v.

162 Calzolari's pharmacy housed: Findlen, *Possessing Nature,* pp. 65-66; Tergolina-Sislanzoni-Brasco, "Francesco Calzolari."

163 According to Galen's account: Watson, *Theriac and Mithridatium,* p. 45.

163 "was designed to mirror": Findlen, *Possessing Nature,* p. 241.

163 In every major Italian city: Olmi, "Farmacopea antica."

164 So many vipers: Stössl, *Lo spettacolo,* pp. 17-18.

164 "the extraordinary ceremony": Evelyn, *Diary and Correspondance,* vol. 1, p. 225.

164 Renaissance humanists: On the humanist debate over polypharmacy, see Siraisi, *Avicenna,* pp. 66-76.

165 "made with such a mix of things": *Specchio,* pp. 35v-36v.

Chapter 19: The Lure of the Charlatan

166 Walking in the Piazza San Marco: An essential work on healers, placing the *ciarlatani* (charlatans) in context, is Gentilcore, *Healers and Healing,* especially pp. 96-124. On the origins of commedia dell'arte in charlatans' performances, see Henke, *Performance.*

166 "Italy has a generation of empirics": Moryson, *Itinerary,* pp. 424-25 (spelling and punctuation modernized).

167 Thousands of charlatans: The most authoritative study of Italian charlatans is Gentilcore, *Medical Charlatanism.* Gentilcore's exhaustive research in archives across Italy turned up more than a thousand charlatans practicing in Italy between 1550 and 1800. His database is available online at www.data-archive.ac.uk.

167 Most were itinerants: Gentilcore, *Medical Charlatanism,* p. 300. On peddlers, see Fontaine, *History of Pedlars.*

168 The brand names: Gentilcore, *Medical Charlatanism,* pp. 242-43.

169 English traveler Thomas Coryat: Coryat, *Coryats Crudities,* quoted in Gentilcore, *Medical Charlatanism,* p. 310

169 The charlatans were among the first: Eamon, *Science and the Secrets,* pp. 239-44.

169 Although they ridiculed doctors: Gentilcore, *Medical Charlatanism,* p. 353.

171 Perhaps they acted at a symbolic level: Moerman and Jonas, "Deconstructing the Placebo Effect."

171 In modern medicine: Gracely, "Charisma."

172 The famous Venetian charlatan: Findlen, "Inventing Nature."

172 "From the same motive": Augustine, *Confessions,* p. 246.

173 Saint Paul's first-century C.E. admonition: Ginzburg, "High and Low."

Chapter 20: A Writer for the Ages

175 Born in 1504: On the Atanagi family, see Saffiotti and Mastrullo, *E il signor duca ne rise di buona maniera.*

176 Ruscelli fired back: On the controversy, see Richardson, *Print Culture,* pp. 112-14.

176 "Everyone knows": Quoted in Trovato, *Con ogni diligenza corretto,* p. 241.

176 Situated almost exactly halfway: Burke, "Early Modern Venice."

176 If you missed out: On gossip, see Horodowich, "Gossiping Tongue."

177 Venice produced more books: Grendler, *Roman Inquisition,* pp. 5-6.

177 The *poligrafi:* Grendler, *Critics.* Other important studies of the Venetian poligrafi include Di Filippo Bareggi, *Il mestiere di scrivere*; Quondam, " 'Mercanzia d'onore' "; and Trovato, *Con ogni diligenza corretto.*

178 The result was not what Concorreggio expected: Atanagi, *Libro de gli Huomini Illustri.*

178 Outraged by Atanagi's plagiarism: Concorreggio, *Risposte.* The quarrel is treated in detail in Paitoni, *Biblioteca degli autori antichi,* vol. 4, pp. 240-42.

179 "an angel of paradise": Atanagi's paean to Fioravanti is in Atanagi, *Le rime di diversi nobili.*

179 "He performs miracles": Ruscelli, *Precetti della militia moderna,* p. 58.
179 The backlist perfectly matched: On print culture, see Eisenstein, *The Printing Press*. For information on Venetian printers I rely on Pastorello, *Tipografi, editori, librai.*
179 Leonardo's first book: Although the *Capricci medicinali* was the first book that Fioravanti published under his own name, he made his authorial debut with an edition of Pietro and Lodovico Rostinio's *Compendio di tutta la cirugia,* to which he added a brief treatise on surgery.
180 "So that readers": Fioravanti, *Capricci medicinali,* p. a8r-v.
180 "Whoever follows my lead": Fioravanti, *Capricci medicinali,* pp. b1, 177v, 85.
181 "My work treats all the arts": Fioravanti, *Specchio,* p. 4r.
181 Fioravanti's concise history: Fioravanti, *Specchio,* pp. 41r-v.
182 a crash course on the myth of Venice: Fioravanti's rather personal and typically eccentric version of the myth of Venice is in *Specchio,* pp. 145-46, 241.
183 "But the greater marvel": Fioravanti, *Specchio,* pp. 145-v.
183 "the household is ill served": Fioravanti, *Specchio,* p. 219. Fioravanti's views of women are in *Specchio,* pp. 218-22.
183 a woman "so remarkably virtuous": Fioravanti's treatment of the story of Zenobia is on pp. 167-76 of *The Mirror.* For the myth of Zenobia, see Boccaccio, *Famous Women,* pp. 427-29. Leonardo actually copied the story almost verbatim from the *Epistolas familiares (Familiar Letters)* of the Spanish friar Antonio de Guevara, making a number of editorial changes to render the text more readable to his popular audience. Cherchi, "Leonardo Fioravanti e Antonio Guevara."
184-85 the genre of "self-improvement literature": Bell, *How to Do It.*
185 "Today in the world of letters": Quoted in Dooley, "Printing and Entrepreneurialism," pp. 565-66.
185 Tommaso Garzoni's massive *Piazza universale:* Martin, "Imaginary Piazza."
186 "This Carnival, when others go": Fioravanti, *Capricci medicinali,* dedication.
186 "Just as in the fish market": Fioravanti, *Secreti medicinali,* p. 176v.
186 "The physician will study": Fioravanti, *Capricci medicinali,* pp. 107v-108.

Chapter 21: Venice's Scientific Underworld

188 "one of the most expert practitioners": Fioravanti, *Capricci medicinali,* p. 178.
188 "a man of great doctrine": Fioravanti, *Specchio,* p. b7r.
188 Jacomo Torellis was said to understand: Fioravanti, *Cirugia,* p. 26v.
189 "cause unimaginable damage": Ruscelli, *Precetti della militia moderna,* pp. 58-59.
190 Surgeons, said Fioravanti: *Compendio,* p. 38v.
191 "you will not find": Fioravanti, *Capricci medicinali,* p. a8.
191 "You have to have a white beard": Fioravanti, *Tesoro,* p. 3r.
191 The mythical Alessio Piemontese worried: Alessio, *Secretes,* preface.
191 "There are many": Fioravanti, *Compendio,* pp. 1r-v.
192 "In this book": Fioravanti, *Compendio,* p. 79r.
192 "like an oven for making bread": *Compendio,* p. 75v.
192 He defines alchemy: Fioravanti, *Compendio,* pp. 75r-v.
192 "I'm not saying": Fioravanti, *Compendio,* p. 81.
193 "If you want to make copper": Fioravanti, *Compendio,* p. 90. "Rosette copper," or *rame peloso,* are the crusts of copper skimmed off baths of refined metal as it solidifies and sold in cakes; it was usually imported from Germany. See Biringuccio, *Pirotechnia,* p. 72. The process that Fioravanti describes would result in an inexpensive calamine brass.
193 Leonardo also revealed the secret: Fioravanti, *Compendio,* pp. 87, 100, 90v, 112v, 117v.
193 Anyone interested in painting: Fioravanti, *Compendio,* p. 110.
194 "Venetian blonde": Fioravanti, *Compendio,* p. 126v.
194 "They often do": Fioravanti, *Compendio,* p. 118v.
194 Leonardo claimed: Fioravanti, *Cirugia,* p. 26v.
194 That was no mean skill: By antimony, the alchemists and metallurgists usually meant antimony sulfide, or stibnite (Sb_2S_3).
194 Colormakers used antimony: Ember, "Incredible Colors." The process of smelting antimony is described by Agricola, *De re metallica,* p. 428.
194 Antimony also figured prominently: McCallum, *Antimony,* pp.18-19; Debus, *French Paracelsians,* especially pp. 93-97. Fioravanti and his group probably learned about the medicinal uses of antimony from Mattioli's commentary on Dioscorides' work on material medica (pp. 682-84).
195 "with heart yearning": Garzoni, *Piazza universale,* p. 324.

Chapter 22: Mathematical Magic

196 This he did by redacting: Rostinio and Rostinio, *Compendio di tutta la cirugia.*
196 Fioravanti dedicated the book: On Moletti, see Laird, *Unfinished Mechanics;* and Favaro, "Amici e corrispondenti."
197-98 "an exceedingly rare and learned man": Fioravanti, *Specchio,* p. b7v. References to Ausonio are scattered throughout Fioravanti's books, all leaving the impression that Fioravanti revered the Milanese polymath.
198 "known by the majority": Fioravanti, *Specchio,* p. 83v.
198 His entire oeuvre: Ausonio's principal work is the unpublished *Trattato sopra l'arte dell'alchimia,* now in the Biblioteca Ambrosiana, Milan, Q 118 Sup.
198 Constituting a single folio: Ausonio's research on catoptrics is detailed in Dupré, "Mathematical Instruments"; and idem, "Dioptrics."
199 "In the illustrious city of Venice": Fioravanti, *Specchio,* p. 55v.
200 After Ausonio's death: Gian Vincenzo Pinelli's famous library in Padua was purchased by Cardinal Charles Borromeo and later formed the nucleus of the Ambrosiana Library in Milan.
200 Visiting Pinelli's library: Della Porta described Ausonio's mirrors (without crediting him) in the second edition of his famous work *Magia Nathralis,* which came out in 1589, p. 362ff.
201 No respectable prince would allow his curiosity cabinet: For the significance of wonders and distorting mirrors in the courts, see Daston and Park, *Wonders,* pp. 100-108.
202 "The intention of the Holy Ghost": Galilei, "Letter to the Grand Duchess Christina," in *Discoveries and Opinions,* p. 189.
202 One of the works: Ausonio's manual for teaching astronomy, *Astrologia nova,* is contained in the Biblioteca Ambrosiana, Milan, MS Ambrosiana R 105 Sup.
203 "a great philosopher": Fioravanti, *Cirugia,* p. a4.

Chapter 23: The Search for the Philosopher's Stone

204 As a follower: Pereira, *Alchemical Corpus,* pp. 48-49; idem, "Lullian Alchemy."
205 By the end of the century: Pereira, "La leggenda." Lull's complex thought may be approached conveniently through Bonner, *Doctor Illuminatus.* In addition, see Yates, "Art of Ramon Lull."
205 The theory had first been elaborated: Lerner, *Feast of Saint Abraham,* pp. 73-88.
205 John believed: DeVun, "Human Heaven." John's theories are also treated by Thorndike, HMES, vol. 3, pp. 347-69; and Halleux, "Les ouvrages alchimiques."
206 Extended to the field of medicine: The major pseudo-Lullian alchemical text, the *Testamentum,* has recently been edited by Pereira and Spaggiari, *Il "Testamentum."* For the doctrine of the elixir, see Pereira, "Un tesoro inestimabile"; and idem, "Teorie dell'elixir."
206 "[I]t involves a metamorphosis": Levi, *Periodic Table,* pp. 57-58.
207 All diseases arise: Fioravanti, *Capricci medicinali,* p. 182.
208 "The art of alchemy can be done": Fioravanti, *Capricci medicinali,* pp. 182-88.

Chapter 24: A Star Is Born

210 "great flattery and courtesy": Fioravanti, *Tesoro,* p. 181.
210 Italy had its own literature: Camporesi, *Libro dei vagabondi.*
211 "Italy was completely overrun": Braudel, *The Mediterranean,* vol. 2, p. 743. Braudel notes that, to the authorities, it seemed that beggars, gypsies, and bravoes were everywhere: In 1545, more than 6,000 "from many nations" were said to have beleaguered the city.
211 He may even have told: Fioravanti, *Capricci medicinali,* p. 41v.
212 "a certain quality": Roach, *It,* p. 1.
213 The Venetian courtesan: Rosenthal, *Honest Courtesan,* p. 11.
213 "satisfied her society's need": Rosenthal, *Honest Courtesan,* p. 60.
213 Franco even had a tryst: Rosenthal, *Honest Courtesan,* pp. 102-103; Horodowich, *Language and Statecraft,* pp. 199-200.
213 Her death at 45: Rosenthal, *Honest Courtesan,* p. 86.
213 " 'It' is the power": Roach, *It,* p. 8.
214 Historian Daniel Boorstin: Boorstin, *Image,* p. 57.
214 "pseudo-events": Boorstin, *Image,* p. 9.
215 Founded in 1557: Rose, "Accademia Venetiana."
217 "To me you are someone divine": Fioravanti, *Tesoro,* p. 172v.
217 "like Apollo": Fioravanti, *Tesoro,* p. 159v.

217 "throw all the books": Fioravanti, *Tesoro,* p. 148.
217 "staged celebrity": Rojek, *Celebrity,* p. 121.
217 When Leonardo decided: Nelli was active in Venice from 1563 until 1572.
218 Accademia dei Lincei: Freedberg, *Eye of the Lynx,* p. 66.

Chapter 25: The Medical Entrepreneur
219 So many newcomers: Mozzato, "Production of Woollens," p. 89.
220 "The ambassador couldn't get": Fioravanti, *Tesoro,* p. 77v.
220 Though medical consultation by mail: Porter and Porter, *Patient's Progress.*
220 The piazzas swarmed: Gentilcore, *Medical Charlatanism,* pp. 174-80
222 "For those who read": Fioravanti, *Tesoro,* p. 96v.
223 "As I was speaking": Fioravanti, *Tesoro,* p. 103v.
223 In the opening letter: Fioravanti, *Tesoro,* pp. 97r-98v.
224 "As for returning to Rome": Fioravanti, *Tesoro,* p. 100r.
224 Hercole Romani described: Fioravanti, *Tesoro,* p. 105v.
225 "I showed your *Medical Caprices*": Fioravanti, *Tesoro,* pp. 198r-v.
225 "Without consulting the doctors": Fioravanti, *Tesoro,* p. 107v.
225 "Since you left": Fioravanti, *Tesoro,* p. 165v.
225 "I promise you": Fioravanti, *Tesoro,* pp. 139r-140v.
226 "to have you teach me": *Tesoro,* pp. 151r-v.
226 From Vicenza, physician Prudentio Bellobuono: Fioravanti, *Tesoro,* p. 146v.
226 According to Kromer: Fioravanti, *Tesoro,* p. 182v.
226 Paolo Zanotto of Parma: Fioravanti, *Tesoro,* p. 180.
226 the ailment was "totally incurable": Fioravanti, *Tesoro,* p. 230.
226 In another letter: Fioravanti, *Tesoro,* p. 227v.

Chapter 26: Ambition and Glory
228 Its shops closed: Benussi, *Pola,* p. 387, estimates Pola's population in 1554 at 590 inhabitants.
229 Venice had made several attempts: Benussi, *Pola,* pp. 393-98.
229 "without any public expense": Fioravanti's petition to the Provveditori sopra Beni Inculti is in ASV, Senato, Mar, Reg. 35, Filza 22.
229 "But when the terrain": Fioravanti, *Reggimento,* pp. 59v-60v.
229 To accomplish this: Fioravanti's petitions to the Senate are in ASV, Senato, Mar, Reg. 35, ff. 36r, 145r.
229 "purify the air": ASV, Senato, Mar, Reg. 35; Benussi, *Pola,* p. 396.
230 The Senate approved the plan: *Le essentione e franchezze.* The broadsheet is in the Biblioteca Marciana in Venice.
230 In 1563 all'Occha surveyed: Giovanni Antonio all'Occha's report to the Senate is in the Museo Correr, Venice (MCV, Cod. Cicogna 2547, c. 7r-v). His map of Pola is also in the Museo Correr (MCV, Ms. P.D.849.C).
230 "the city is more beautiful than ever": Fioravanti, *Tesoro,* p. 148. Fioravanti reported that in 1571 colonists were still going to Pola under his plan (*Reggimento,* p. 56).
231 According to a complaint: The petition of Vincenzo all'Aqua's widow is in MCV, Cod. Cicogna 2547, c. 9-10. Conditions in Pola are also described in a *suplica* (petition) of Sabastian Bravi, MCV, Cod. Cicogna, 2547, c. 8r-v. Local reactions to the settlement venture are described by Benussi, *Pola,* p. 397.
232 "fame was the entrepreneurial coin": Ringmar, *Mechanics of Modernity,* p. 70.
232 "Discourse on the City of Pola": Fioravanti, *Reggimento,* pp. 58-60.
233 "logic of patronage": Biagioli, *Galileo Courtier,* p. 36. In addition, see Findlen, "Economy of Scientific Exchange."
233 In 1565 he received patents: ASV, Senato, Terra, Reg. 45, c. 200v.
234 a brutal mechanism: Ruscelli, *Precetti di militia moderna,* pp. 57v-59r.
234 It was widely known: On alchemical research in the Medici court, see in particular Butters, *Triumph of Vulcan,* vol. 1, chap. 14. In addition, see Lensi Orlandi, *Cosimo e Francesco d'Medici;* Berti, *Principe dello studiolo.* During Cosimo's reign, Florence became a center of Paracelsian research: Galluzzi, "Motivi Paracelsiana"; Covoni, *Don Antonio de' Medici.*
234 The alchemical activity at the palace: Butters, *Triumph of Vulcan,* p. 247.
234 "Most Illustrious and Excellent Duke": ASF, Mediceo del Principato, f. 487, c. 11r-v (edited and abbreviated).

235 Cosimo's reply: Fioravanti's letters to Cosimo I de' Medici are in the Florentine State Archive (Archivio di Stato), and include: ASF, Mediceo del Principato, f. 487, c. 11r-v (2 November 1560); f. 487, c. 371 (14 December 1560); f. 488, c. 460r-v (6 May 1561); f. 488a, c. 1071 (21 June 1561); f. 489, c. 7 (2 July 1561). Secretarial copies of Cosimo's replies to Fioravanti and through his agent Piero Gelido are in: ASF, Mediceo del Principato, Registri, v. 213, c. 60; v. 214, c. 41 and 45; v. 216, c. 13v-14r and c. 43v.

236 The device: Vegetius describes the tribulus in *De re militari* (Vegetius, *Epitome*), 3.24, p. 105. Fioravanti's version of the device is depicted in Ruscelli, *Precetti,* 59. Fioravanti offered the device to Cosimo in a letter of 14 December 1560 (ASF, Mediceo del Principato, f. 487, c. 371).

236 Almost exactly a century earlier: Aristotele Fioravanti's career and reputation are treated in Oechslin, "La fama di Aristotele Fioravanti"; and Beltrami, *Vita.*

237 "more inflamed than ever": ASF, Mediceo del Principato, f. 488, c. 460r-v (6 May 1561).

237 *Discourse on the Five Things*: 21 June 1561, ASF, Mediceo del Principato, f. 488a, c. 1071.

237-38 The grand duke politely thanked: ASF, Mediceo del Principato, Registri, v. 216, c. 43v (Cosimo I to Fioravanti, 29 August 1561).

238 "And so My Illustrious Lord": ASMo, Archivio per materie, Medici, b. 19 (95). Published in part by Dall'Osso, "Due lettere."

239 "I hear the whole world crying out": Fioravanti, *Specchio,* p. 141r.

239 "The only exceptions": Fioravanti, *Specchio,* p. 141r.

240 "The measure by which": Fioravanti, *Specchio,* pp. 95-96.

Chapter 27: A Conspiracy of Doctors

242 His patent drugs: Several of Fioravanti's drugs are included in Prospero Borgarucci's *La fabrica de gli spetiali* (Venice, 1567), a standard pharmaceutical manual.

242 In 1562 he moved: Fioravanti locates his address in Venice in a letter to the Duke of Ferrara (15 August 1562), Modena, Biblioteca Estense, Fondo Estense, 1844 (Beta 1, 5, 2), where he notes that he was then living *"in vinetia a san lucca nelle case nove al no. 27."*

242 The earliest record: ASV, X poi XX Savi, b. 24. The ruling, dated January 1567, was in reference to the Sanità's ruling *"in data 23 ottobre 1563."*

243 The court denied the petition: In *Tesoro* (1570), Fioravanti writes that his litigation had gone on "continuously" for two years (p. 83). His Venetian license is recorded in ASV, Giustizia Vecchia, b. 49, reg. 79.

243 Besides physicians and surgeons: Medical specialists in the Renaissance are treated in Park, "Medicine and Magic"; and idem, "Stones, Bones and Hernias." On the *sanpaolini* (or *sanpaolari*), see Eamon, *Science and the Secrets,* chap. 7; Gentilcore, *Healers and Healing,* chap. 4; and Park, "Country Medicine."

243 And how many were there: "La Draga" is discussed by Ruggiero, *Binding Passions,* pp. 149-52; and Milani, *Antiche pratiche.*

244 From 1545 to 1560 only ten empirics were prosecuted: Laughran, *The Body,* p. 172.

245 Fioravanti's claim: Fioravanti, *Della fisica,* pp. 29-30; Levin, *Myth of the Golden Age.*

245 Some historians: Brockliss and Jones, *Medical World,* pp. 273-83.

246 Historian Gianna Pomata: Pomata, *Contracting a Cure,* pp. 129-39.

246 The "conspiracy of the doctors": Fioravanti, *Tesoro,* p. 83v.

246 He returned to Bologna: It is impossible to determine on the basis of existing documents when Fioravanti traveled to Bologna and how long he was there to obtain the degree. The only possible clue is that he wrote a letter from Venice dated 18 October 1567, and again from Venice, six months later, on 14 April 1568. We cannot account for the time between the two letters.

246 The Venetian physicians: ASB, Studio Bolognese, 217, c. 155v.

246 Records of the award: The documents relating to his Bologna medical degree are in ASB, Studio Bolognese, 193, Liber Actorum Utriusque Collegii, c. 311r, c. 314r, and c. 314v. As the documents make clear, he completed the required examinations on 28-29 March 1568. His promotors in arts were professors Antonio Fabbio and Dominico Bonfiolo (medicine); and Lactantius de Benatiis and Fabrizio Garzoni (arts). Gabriele Beate oversaw the examination. Fioravanti's account of the event is in *Reggimento,* p. 69v; and *Tesoro,* p. 83v. Fioravanti's degree was registered with the Venetian Health Board on 4 May 1568 (ASV, Provveditori alla Sanita, b. 731, 55v-58v).

246 The system by which: Rashdall, *Universities,* vol. 1, pp. 224-31.

247 The process did not involve: Fioravanti hired Gabriele Beate, a professor of logic, philosophy, and medicine at the university, as a private tutor to help him prepare for the examination. *Tesoro,* p. 232.
247 In seeking the degree: Gentili, "Leonardo Fioravanti," p. 24; Gnudi and Webster, *Gaspare Tagliacozzi*, p. 50.
247 Initially, Leonardo applied: Gentili, "Leonardo Fioravanti," pp. 27-31.
247 This privilege stemmed: Selden, *Titles,* pp. 314-20.
247 The faculty granted his request: ASB, Studio Bolognese, 193, Liber Actorum Utriusque Collegii, c. 311r, 314r-v.
247 Before applying for the degree: Realio Reali and Michele Moratti are named as his character witnesses in ASB, Studio Bolognese, 193, Liber Actorum Utriusque Collegii, c. 311r.
248 The bull decreed: The bull, Cum Infirmitas, was issued at Rome and Bologna in 1566. Gnudi and Webster, *Gaspare Tagliacozzi,* pp. 55-56.
248 During the interview: ASB, Studio Bolognese, 127, Libro Segreto (Collegio di Medicina ed Arti), c. 149v.
248 The next day: ASV, Provveditori alla Sanità, Reg. 731, c. 55v-58v, a copy of Fioravanti's degree registered with the Venetian Health Board.
248 "suitable and adequate": "Quem pro idoneo et sufficienti omnes doctores unanimes amiserunt," Gentili, "Leonardo Fioravanti," p. 22.
249 *"Miles strenuus esto!"*: Gentili, "Leonardo Fioravanti," p. 40.
249 "I hope to live and die.": Fioravanti, *Tesoro,* p. 83.
249 Praise came in less overt forms: Fioravanti, *Tesoro,* pp. 1-2.
249 Although a group of disgruntled physicians: ASB, Studio Bolognese, 217, c. 155.

Chapter 28: Leonardo the Chameleon

250 "who follows my doctrine": Fioravanti, *Tesoro,* p. b4v.
252 "Many years ago": Fioravanti, *Tesoro,* pp. 1-2.
253 "A blind man's boy": Hesse and Williams, eds., *Lazarillo de Tormes,* p. 8: *"Necio, aprende, que el mozo del ciego un punto ha de saber mas que el diablo."*
254 A good fellow: Fioravanti, *Specchio,* chap. 19; Fioravanti, *Capriccio medicinali,* pp. 42v-43.
254 "My shoebuckles": Paracelsus, *Selected Writings,* 79.
255 Georg Helmstetter of Worms: On the Faust legend, see Baron, *Doctor Faustus.*
255 "As for me": Fioravanti, *Secreti medicinali,* p. 26.
256 "My adversaries tried in every way": Fioravanti, *Tesoro,* pp. 83r-v.
257 "Death being common": Fioravanti, *Tesoro,* pp. 234-36.
257 "something dæmonic": Burckhardt, *Civilization of the Renaissance,* p. 115.
257 "with little practice": Fioravanti, *Capricci medicinali,* p. 225.
258 "I've spent many years": Fioravanti, *Tesoro,* p. 295.
258 "the happiest man on earth": Fioravanti, *Tesoro,* p. 235r.

Chapter 29: Life and Art

259 After all, the book contained: The last records of Fioravanti's Venetian period are in dedications of new editions of two of his books: *In Specchio* (Venice, 1572) the dedication is dated 1571; and in the *Compendio* (Venice, 1571). Possibly, he remained in Venice until 1573 to oversee a new edition of his *Capricci medicinali* that came out that year, although there is no document to verify it.
259 He struggles to define: Fioravanti, *Cirugia,* p. 4r.
260 "If a cobbler tears an old boot": Fioravanti, *Cirugia,* p. 7v.
260 "minister of nature": Fioravanti, *Cirugia,* p. 9r; or, as he puts it in the *Specchio,* the surgeon "is nothing other than a helper of nature" (*non è altro se non un'adiutorio di natura*, p. 18r).
260 "imitators of nature": Fioravanti, *Specchio,* p. 16r.
260 "farming of men": Fioravanti, *Specchio,* p. 16r.
260 "When a farmer comes upon a tree": Fioravanti, *Cirugia,* pp. 8v-9r.
260 "a great and profound subtlety": Fioravanti, *Cirugia,* p. 141v.
260 "I'm not satisfied": Fioravanti, *Cirugia,* p. 135r.
261 "These are things": Fioravanti, *Cirugia,* p. 149r.
261 Public anatomical dissections: Klestinec, "History of Anatomy Theaters," p. 407.
261 "the glorious Fioravanti": Garzoni, *La piazza universale,* pp. 327, 752.
261 He had seen surgery begin to shift: Cavallo, *Artisans of the Body,* pp. 31-32.

262 It is a letter: ASMi, Autografi, Medici, Carpetta 215, fasc. 15. The letter was published by Dall'Osso, "Due lettere."
263 The Boldoni letter: Malespini, "Prodezze medicinali di Iacopo Coppa fatte nella Città di Fiorenza." ("Medical Exploits of Jacopo Coppa in the City of Florence"), in *Ducento novelle*, pp. 299r-301v.
263 In real life, Jacopo Coppa was: Gentilcore, *Medical Charlatanism*, pp. 302-306.
264 "Dueling charlatans": Gentilcore, *Medical Charlatanism*, pp. 146-47, 169-70.
264 In 1576 he contacted the viceroy: Archivo General de Simancas, Estado, leg. 1065, fol. 99.

Chapter 30: In the Court of the Catholic King

266 A partial translation into Spanish: The translation, in manuscript, includes Fioravanti's commentary on the panacea. It was made in 1562 by an unidentified author and is found in the Biblioteca Nacional, Madrid, ms. 6.149, f. 193. (I thank Miguel López for alerting me to this manuscript and transcribing it for me.) The inventory of Philip's library at El Escorial, containing several of Fioravanti's publications, is published in Andrés, ed., *Documentos*, vol. VII.
266 Fifty people reportedly had died: Corradi, *Annali*, vol. 1, pp. 493-4.
267 "The plague began suddenly": Marcora, "Diario di Giambattista Casale," pp. 290-91.
267 Rumors circulated of *untori:* Carmichael, "Last Past Plague," p. 147; La Cava, *Peste di S. Carlo*, pp. 103-105.
267 "plague of San Carlo": La Cava, *Peste di S. Carlo*, pp. 151-71.
267 By the time Fioravanti arrived: My estimate for Madrid's population in the mid-1570s is based on a simple extrapolation from Alvar Ezquerra's figures in *El nacimiento*.
267 "I find the city of Madrid": Alvar Ezquerra, *Felipe II*, pp. 62-74.
268 King Philip, fascinated: Portuondo, *Secret Science;* Goodman, *Power and Penury*.
268 As ruler: Parker, *Grand Strategy*.
268 In 1570 he commissioned one of his court physicians: Selections from Hernández's manuscripts have been published in *Mexican Treasury*. See also López Piñero and Pardo Tomás, *La influencia de Francisco Hernández*.
268 In addition, Philip developed: The current state of scholarship on science in early modern Spain is summarized in Cañizares-Esguerra, "Iberian Science." Representative new scholarship may be found in Navarro Brotòns and Eamon, eds., *Beyond the Black Legend*. In addition, see Barrera-Osorio, *Experiencing Nature*.
269 What was an American Indian: Fioravanti reports on his conversation with a Corsican sailor in *Della fisica*, pp. 304ff.; and on his conversations with a Peruvian Indian on pp. 302-304. For information about Indians in 16th-century Spain, I am grateful to Professor Berta Ares of the Escuela de Estudios Hispanoamericanos in Seville (personal communication) and Thomas Abercrombie of New York University (personal communication).
270 In a Seville bookshop: The book was originally published in three separate parts. The first appeared in 1565, and three parts were published together in one volume in 1574. The title that Fioravanti encountered was actually *Primero y Segunda y Tercera Partes de la Historia Medicinal de las Cosas que se traen de nuestras Indias Occidentales que serven en Medicina* (Sevilla, 1574). Monardes's treatise has been published in a facsmile edition with an introduction by J. M. López Piñero (Madrid, 1992). Important studies of the introduction of New World plants into Europe include: López Piñero and López Terrada, *La influencia española;* López Terrada and Pardo Tomás, *Las primeras noticias*.
270 Monardes—a respected Seville physician: Guerra, *Nicolás Bautista Monardes;* Rodríguez Marín, *Verdadera biografía*.
270 "the first humanist-trained university doctor": Norton, *Sacred Gifts*, p. 110.
270 he copied out and translated: Fioravanti, *Della fisica*, pp. 345-59.
270 He acquired some resin: Fioravanti, *Della fisica*, p. 58.
271 "Everyone should use tobacco": Fioravanti, *Della fisica*, p. 58.
271 "I saw more of this": Fioravanti, *Della fisica*, p. 61.
271 "the most famous physician": Fioravanti, *Della fisica*, p. 57.
271 In that story: Daston, "History of Science."
272 "there was hardly to be found": Norton, *Sacred Gifts*, p. 165.
273 "Spain was like a funnel": Norton, *Sacred Gifts*, pp. 171, 255.
273 In terms of the sheer quantity: Guerra, "Drugs from the Indies."
274 the idea of science as a hunt: Eamon, "Science as a Hunt."
274 "All the mysteries": Le Roy, *Interchangeable Course*, p. 127v.

274 "America of secrets": Glanvill, *Vanity of Dogmatizing,* p. 178.
275 "were often the flashpoints": Norton, *Sacred Gifts,* p. 129.
275 "a change from a description": Padgen, *Fall of Natural Man,* p. 1.
275 "To discourse about matters of the Indies": Fioravanti, *Della fisica,* p. 357.
276 "The Indians have discovered": Fioravanti, *Della fisica,* p. 358.

Chapter 31: Masters of Fire

277 King Philip II of Spain: On the historical image of Philip II, see Kamen, *Imagining Spain;* and Kagan, *Clio & the Crown.*
277 To the American historian: Kagan, "Prescott's Paradigm."
278 "wanted to demonstrate": Porreño, *Dichos y hechos,* p. 92.
278 Like most monarchs of the day: Goodman, *Power and Penury,* pp. 8-9.
278 Like many Renaissance princes: Rodríguez Marín, *Felipe II y la alquimia;* Ruiz, "Los alquimistas de Felipe II."
278 Chronically short of money: Goodman, *Power and Penury,* p. 12; Rodríguez Marín, *Felipe II y la alquimia,* pp. 17ff.
278 In 1569, the Roman adept: Puerto Sarmiento, "La panacea aurea," p. 116.
279 Philip's belief: On Lull, see chap. 23.
279 by 1576 he had assembled a sizable collection: López Pérez, "Algunos rasgos," p. 349; idem, *Asclepio renovado,* p. 119.
279 By 1580, he was consulting: Goodman, *Power and Penury,* p. 10.
279 What is known: Puerto Sarmiento and Folch Jou, "Los manuscritos alquímicos"; Taylor, "Architecture and Magic."
279 Philip vigorously promoted: Rey Bueno, *Los señores del fuego.*
280 The group met weekly: Fioravanti, *Della fisica,* p. 362.
280 Leonardo identifies Bolognese surgeon: Fioravanti, *Della fisica,* pp. 172, 362.
280 "He knows more about fire": Fioravanti, *Della fisica,* p. 372.
280 Cornejo wrote a treatise: Cornejo, *Discurso.*
280 "I have always regarded this": Goodman, *Power and Penury,* p. 13.
281 According to import-tax records: Norton, *Sacred Gifts,* p. 142.
282 *picietl,* a Mayan drug: Norton, *Sacred Gifts,* p. 20.

Chapter 32: The Charlatan's Trial

283 That side of the story is told: BL, Add. MS 28,353, ff. 57-61. I have published a complete transcription of the manuscript, in Spanish, in "The Charlatan's Trial." Unless otherwise noted, all references to the proceedings are to this source.
284 "sneak in through the back door": The original reads: *"entran por la manga y salen por el cabezón"* (literally, "come in through the sleeve and go out through the big head"), quoted in Rey Bueno, *Los señores del fuego,* p. 53. The phrase comes from an ancient Castilian adoption ceremony, by which an illegitimate child passed through the wide sleeve of a shift and emerged through the collar, to be adopted into the family. It was applied to favorites who assumed authority by virtue of a patronage relationship.
284 The Real Tribunal del Protomedicato: Tate Lanning, *Royal Protomedicato;* Campos Díez, *Real Tribunal.* The regulations instituted by that body were published by Muñoz, *Recopilación.* The archives of the Royal Protomedicato were destroyed in a fire in 1939, during the Spanish Civil War. Fioravanti's original appeal was presumably also destroyed in the fire. By chance, he kept a copy—the one preserved in the British Library.
286 "When you consider": There is no record of Fioravanti's having obtained a degree from the University of Naples. Probably he was referring to a license to practice in Naples that he received from the Neapolitan Protomedico.
289 "This book": The identity of Fioravanti's "Abacue *hebreo"* is unclear; perhaps it was a corruption of the name of the prophet "Abacuc" (Habbakuk) or of some other alchemical figure.
290 Ausonio proved almost inexhaustibly inventive: Pereira, *Alchemical Corpus,* pp. 48-49.
290 The medicinal use: On blood, see Camporesi, *Juice of Life.*
290 He wrote about it at length: Fioravanti, *Della fisica,* pp. 165-67.
290 These bizarre ideas: Ferrari, "Public Anatomy," p. 101; Camporesi, *Bread of Dreams,* pp. 48-50.
292 "prepare quintessences": Quoted in Goodman, *Power and Penury,* p. 14. On Forte's activities in the court, see Rey Bueno, *Los señores del fuego,* pp. 51-57.

292 Olivares stood in his way: Rey Bueno, *Los señores del fuego,* p. 52.
292 Forte complained to Cardinal Granvelle: Rey Bueno, *Los señores del fuego,* p. 54.
293 Francisco Valles: Rey Bueno, *Los señores del fuego,* p. 92.
293 Valles vigorously promoted: On Valles, see Rey Bueno, *Los señores del fuego,* pp. 91-98.
293 Later, he was given the honorific title: Rey Bueno, "El informe Valles," p. 243.
293 The centerpiece of the laboratory: Fioravanti describes a *torre filosofal* in *Compendio,* p. 76v.

Chapter 33: *"Il mio sacco è vuoto"*

294 composed his final work: Fioravanti, *Della fisica*. Unless otherwise noted, all quotations in this section are to this work.
296 Then follows a lengthy discourse: On cosmography, see Portuondo, *Secret Science.*
297 a story by Iambulus: Ramusio, *Delle navigationi*, vol. 1, pp. 188-90.
298 it was generally understood: Findlen, "Jokes of Nature."
298 he had found the secret of making it: Fioravanti thought that he had discovered the secret to making the philosopher's stone in a manuscript that an Italian aristocrat named Lorenzo Granita showed him in Madrid. Fioravanti reports that Granita, a native of Salerno, was "the equal of Ramon Lull, Arnald of Villanova, and John of Rupescissa," and that he could make a philosopher's stone that would transform any metal into the finest 22-carat gold. Granita's manuscript contained a Spanish poem, "Coplas de la Piedra Filosofal" ("Verses on the Philosopher's Stone"), that so impressed Leonardo that he stole the manuscript and published the verses as an appendix to *Of Physic* so that "anyone might learn how to make gold." The poem may have held the secret of the philosopher's stone, but it doesn't give it up easily. The manuscript, in an ancient Castilian, is so opaque in its content, so profuse with multilayered images, and so deeply rooted in the Arabic alchemical tradition that Leonardo himself must have had difficulty understanding it. On the Coplas, see Castro Soler and Rodríguez Guerrero, "Luis de Centelles"; critical edition in Centelles. "Coplas."
298 "a secret with which you can very quickly extract": ASF, MdP 703, fols. 106r-1-7r.
299 John Dee's design: John Dee's "philosophical" device to find buried treasure is described in a letter to Lord Burghley, 3 October 1574, in Halliwell, *Collection of Letters,* pp. 13-18. On buried treasure, see Thomas, *Religion and the Decline of Magic,* pp. 234-37.
299 he completed a new book: Fioravanti mentions his *I dodici secreti remedii della gloriosa Nonciata di Napoli* in two of his works, *Della fisica,* p. 2, and *Specchio* (Venice, 1583), p. 359, where he claims that the work had been printed in Naples in 1578. A search of the national libraries in Naples and several other Italian cities failed to turn up the title.
299 "my sack is empty": Fioravanti, *Della fisica,* p. A1v.
299 "this will be the end of my labors": Fioravanti, *Specchio* (Venice, 1583), p. 59.
299 *"buena noche por siempre":* Fioravanti, *Specchio* (Venice, 1583), p. 281r.
299 the date of his death is unknown: The 18th-century literary historian Giovanni Fantuzzi dates Fioravanti's death as 8 September 1588 (*Notizie,* vol. 3, p. 328). I searched the *Necrologia* in the Venetian Archivio di Stato for the years 1582-1596 but failed to turn up any notice of his death. Nor did a similar search by the historian Davide Giordano in Bologna yield any results.
300 "He who lives well dies well": Fioravanti, *Della fisica* (Venice, 1594), p. 135.
300 he writes repeatedly, even expectantly: Fioravanti, *Della fisica* (Venice, 1582), p. 140v.
300 English alchemist George Ripley: Ripley, *Compound,* F2v (stanza 21).
300 Edmund Dickinson warned: Dickinson, *Epistola,* p. 208. Historians speculate that Isaac Newton's well-known periods of mental instability may have been caused by mercury poisoning resulting from his alchemical experiments: Johnson and Wolbarsht, "Mercury Poisoning"; Spargo and Pounds. "Newton's 'Derangement.'"

Chapter 34: The Judgment of History

302 "a preacher in the desert": Fioravanti, *Della fisica,* p. 136.
302 British historian Herbert Butterfield: Butterfield, *Whig Interpretation of History.*
304 "the most expert empiric": Donzelli, *Teatro,* p. 44.
304 Marcello Malpighi reported: Malpighi, *Correspondence,* vol. 3, p. 1117.
304 Fioravanti's medicines were still found: Brambilla, *Storia,* vol. 2, p. 37.
304 Hanover's *Official Pharmacopia*: López Pérez, *Asclepio renovado,* p. 319.
304 Hester translated Fioravanti's writings: Hester, *Three Exact Pieces.*
304 Fray Antonio Castell: Puerto Sarmiento, "La panacea aurea," p. 137.

305 Among the secrets that Hincapié recorded: AGI, sección Contratación, legajo 1135, f. 153-69v; Wellcome Library, WMS/Amer. 79, fols. 79-81 (my thanks to Mar Rey Bueno for calling this manuscript to my attention).
305 Roman physician Pietro Castelli named him: Castelli, *Emetica,* p. 207.
305 Dutch emigré physician Turquet de Mayerne: Mayerne's excerpts from Fioravanti's writings are found in the Sloane manuscripts at the British Library and include: Sloane MS 1991.6 ("Collectanea ex Thesauro vitae humanae Fioravanti," fols. 82-89); Sloane MS 1991.7 ("Antidotarium leonardi," fols. 90-99); and Sloane MS 2077.6 ("Collectanea ex libro Capricci medicinali," fols. 62-90).
305 Not until 1657: Webster, "The Helmontian George Thompson."
306 The Enlightenment dream: Porter, *Health for Sale.*
306 the long march of secularization: Gay, "Enlightenment as Medicine."
307 the "penicillin mode": The term "penicillin mode" is that of Golub, *Limits of Medicine,* p. 221.
308 *curing* has replaced *caring:* Golub, *Limits of Medicine,* p. 215.
308 The Bolognese humorist: Camporesi, *La carne impassibile,* p. 159.
308 the bizarre case of Costantino Saccardino: Ginzburg, "Dovecote." Although the records of Saccardino's trial are lost, the events are described in detail in Campeggi, *Racconti.*
308 "idle modern physicians": Saccardino, *Libro,* p. 10.
309 "In those days": Fioravanti, *Specchio,* pp. 41r-v.
310 "one of the most celebrated secretists": De Renzi, *Storia della medicina in Italia,* vol. 3, p. 75. De Renzi, who calls Fioravanti an "impudent charlatan," also quotes the 16th-century physician Johannes Crato von Krafftheim (1519-1585), who branded Fioravanti a *nebulo pessimus* (malicious rascal), p. 624. Crato, who served as a physician in the imperial court in Vienna, was one of the first to depict Fioravanti as a charlatan (De Renzi, *Storia della medicina in Italia,* vol. 3, pp. 624, 167).
310 "a man of ridiculous vanity": Jourdan, *Dictionaire,* vol.4, pp. 149-50.
310 "a clever man with the soul and temperament of a charlatan": Corsini, *Medici ciarlatani,* p. 79.
311 Fioravanti's doctrine was deployed: Fioravanti has not lacked sympathetic biographers. In 1920, the Italian historian Davide Giordano published the first biography of the Bologna empiric, and he was the first to challenge the assertion that Fioravanti was a charlatan (Giordano, *Leonardo Fioravanti*). More recently, the Italian historian Piero Camporesi wrote a highly sympathetic biography, *Camminare il mondo.*
311 it referred to the wandering empirics: Gentilcore, *Medical Charlatanism.*
312 to him the real quacks were the doctors: Fioravanti, *Capricci medicinali,* p. 225.
312 "rehabilitated wonders as useful objects": Daston and Park, *Wonders,* pp. 130-33, 137. In addition, see Eamon, *Science and the Secrets,* pp. 314-18.
313 the Elizabethan professor of secrets Hugh Plat: Harkness, *Jewel House,* pp. 216-41.
313 Ayesha Mukherjee has termed "dearth science": Mukherjee, "Dearth Science."
313 "The true end of all our private labors": Plat, *Jewell House,* p. 33.
314 stories about tricksters: Martines, *Strong Words,* pp. 203-205.
314 Galileo deployed it: Biagioli, *Galileo Courtier,* pp. 301ff.

Epilogue: Traces

317 one of the most important documentary sources: Louis-Courvoiser and Mauron, "'He found me very well.'"
318 "When I returned to Lausanne yesterday": I thank Micheline Louis-Courvoisier for permission to quote from her personal correspondence to me.

BIBLIOGRAPHY

Manuscript and Source Abbreviations

The following abbreviations of archival and manuscript sources and reference works are used in the notes:

AGI Archivo General de Indias, Seville

AGS Archivo General, Simancas

ASB Archivio di Stato, Bologna

ASF Archivio di Stato, Florence

ASMi Archivio di Stato, Milan

ASMo Archivio di Stato, Modena

ASP Archivio di Stato, Palermo

ASR Archivio di Stato, Rome

ASV Archivio di Stato, Venice

BAM Biblioteca Ambrosiana, Milan

BCAB Biblioteca Comunale dell'Archiginnasio, Bologna

BEM Biblioteca Estense, Modena

BL British Library

BMV Biblioteca Nazionale Marciana, Venice

BNM Biblioteca Nacional, Madrid

BUB Biblioteca Universitaria, Bologna

DBI *Dizionario Biografico degli Italiani,* Rome, 1960-

HMES Lynn Thorndike, *History of Magic and Experimental Science,* 8 vols. New York: Columbia University Press, 1923-1958.

MCV Museo Correr, Venice

MdP Mediceo del Principato

W Wellcome Library, London

BIBLIOGRAPHY

Primary Sources

Adams, John. *The Works of John Adams,* ed. Charles Francis Adams. Vol. 3. Boston: Little, Brown, and Company, 1865.

Adriani, Giovanni Battista, and Marcello Adriani. *Istoria de' suoi tempi.* Florence, 1583.

Agricola, Georgius. *De re metallica* , trans. Herbert Clark Hooker and Henry Lou Hoover. New York: Dover Publications, 1950.

Amaseo, Romolo. *Diarii udinesi dall'anno 1508 al 1541*, ed. G. A. Azio. Venice, 1884.

Andrés, Gregorio de, ed. *Documentos para la historia del monasterio de San Lorenzo el Real de El Escorial.* Vol. 7. Madrid: Imprenta Helénica, 1964.

Atanagi, Dionigi. *Il libro de gli Huomini Illustri di Gaio Plinio Cecilio, le vite d'Alessandro, di M. Antonio, di Catone Uticese, di Cesare & Ottaviano, aggiuntevi per M. Dionigi Atanagi. I costumi di Cesare ne fatti di guerra.* Venice, 1562.

——. *Le rime di diversi nobili poeti toscani.* Venice, 1563.

Augustine of Hippo. *The Confessions of St. Augustine,* trans. Rex Warner. New York: Mentor Books, 1963.

Bacco, Enrico. *Descrittione del Regno di Napoli* (1671). Trans. Eileen Gardiner, *Naples: An Early Guide.* New York: Italica Press, 1991.

Biringuccio, Vannoccio. *Pirotechnia,* trans. and ed. Cyril Stanley Smith and Martha Teach Gnudi. Cambridge, Mass.: MIT Press, 1959.

Boccaccio, Giovanni. *The Decameron,* trans. G. H. McWilliam. Harmondsworth, U.K.: Penguin Books, 1972.

_____. *Famous Women*, trans. Virginia Brown. Cambridge, Mass.: Harvard University Press, 2001.

_____. "Life of Dante," in *The Earliest Lives of Dante,* trans. James Robinson Smith. New York: Henry Holt and Company, 1901.

Bonner, Anthony. *Doctor Illuminatus: A Ramon Llull Reader.* Princeton, N.J.: Princeton University Press, 1993.

Borgarucci, Prospero. *La fabrica de gli spetiali.* Venice, 1567.

——. *Trattato di peste.* Venice, 1565.

Brambilla, Giovanni. *Storia delle scoperte fisico-medico-anatomiche-chirurgiche,* 2 vols. Bologna: A. Forni, 1977.

Bronzino, Giovanni, ed. *Notitia Doctorum sive Catalogus doctorum qui in Collegiis Philosophiae et Medicinae Bononiae laureati fuerunt ab anno 1480 usque ad annum 1800.* Milan: Giuffre, 1962.

Calvete de Estrella, Juan Cristobal. *El felicissimo viaje del muy alto y muy poderoso principe Don Phelippe*, 2 vols. Madrid: Sociedad de Bibliófilos Españoles, 1930.

Campeggi, Ridolfo. *Racconti de gli heretici iconomiasti giustiziati in Bologna.* Bologna, 1623.

Camporesi, Piero, ed. *Il Libro dei vagabondi.* Turin: Einaudi, 1983.

Cardano, Girolamo. *The Book of My Life,* trans. J. Stoner. New York: Columbia University Press, 1930.

Castelli, Pietro. *Emetica. . . . in qua agitur de vomotu et vomitoriis.* Rome, 1634.

Centelles, Luis de. "Las Coplas de la Piedra Philosophal (tres versimes)," ed. Elena Castro Soler. *Azogne* 4 (2001). Available online at www.revistaazogne.com.

Cervantes, Miguel de. *Don Quixote,* trans. Edith Grossman. New York: Harper Collins, 2003.

Concorreggio, Mercurio. *Risposte di Mercurio Concorreggio in sua difesa contra le calunnie dategli da Dionigi Atonagi sopra il libro de gli huomini sopra illustri di Plinio.* Brescia, Italy, 1562.

Cornejo, Juan. *Discurso y despertador preservativo de corrimientos y enfermedades dellos.* Madrid, 1594.

Corradi, Alfonso. *Annali delle epidemie occorse in Italia dalle prime memorie fino al 1850, 4 vols.* Bologna: Forni, 1973.

Cortese, Isabella. *I Secreti.* Venice, 1561.

Croce, Giulio Cesare. *Secreti di medicina mirabilissimi. Del poco eccellente, e tutto ignorante, il Dottor Braghetton.* Bologna, 1611.

_____. *Le Sottilissime astuzie di Bertoldo,* ed. Piero Camporesi. Turin: Einaudi, 1978.

Daciano, Gioseffo. *Trattato di peste.* Venice, 1565.

Dall'Osso, Eugenio. "Due lettere inedite di Leonardo Fioravanti." *Rivista di stria delle scienze mediche e naturali* 47 (1956): 283-91.

D'Amato, Cintio. *Prattica nuova et utilissima di tutto quello, che al diligente barbiero s'appartiene.* Venice, 1669.

Dante Alighieri. *The Divine Comedy: Purgatorio*, trans. Charles S. Singleton. Princeton, N.J.: Princeton University Press, 1973.

de Andrés, Gregorio, ed. *Documentos para la historia del monasterio de San Lorenzo el Real de El Escorial.* Vol. 7. Madrid: Imprenta Sáez, 1964.

Della Porta, Giambattista. *Magiae naturalis libri viginti*. Naples, 1589.

_____. *Magiae naturalis sive de miracalis revum naturalium libri IV.* Naples, 1558.

_____. *Natural Magick*. New York: Basic Books, 1957.

Dickinson, Edmund. *Epistola Edmundi Dickinson ad Theodorum Mundanum, Philosophum Adeptum.* Oxford, 1686.

Donzelli, Giuseppe. *Teatro farmaceutico dogmatico, e spagirico*. Venice, 1763.

Erasmus. *The Colloquies of Erasmus,* trans. Craig R. Thompson. Vol. 1. Chicago: University of Chicago Press, 1965.

Eriksson, Ruben, ed. *Andreas Vesalius' First Public Anatomy at Bologna, 1540: An Eyewitness Report.* Uppsala, Sweden: Almqvist and Wiksells, 1959.

Le essentione e franchezze. Nuovamente concesse dalla Serenissima Sig. di Venetia, a tutti quelli che di nuovo andaranno ad habitare nella citta di Pola, nella Istria, ultima Regione d'Italia, con le franchezze delle fiere, & altri beneficii da godere, la quelli che di nuovo ad habitare in detta città, e suo territorio. Venice, 1562.

Evelyn, John. *Diary and Correspondence of John Evelyn, F.R.S.,* ed. William Bray, 4 vols. London: George Bell and Sons, 1889.

Fantuzzi, Giovanni. *Notizie degli scrittori bolognese*. Vol. 3. Bologna, 1783.

Fioravanti, Leonardo. *Capricci medicinali*. Venice, 1561.

_____. *La cirugia*. Venice, 1570.

_____. *Compendio de i secreti rationali*. Venice, 1564; Venice, 1571.

_____. *A Compendium of the rational secrets,* trans. John Hester. London, 1582.

_____. *Della fisica*. Venice, 1580.

_____. *A Joyfull Jewell. Contayning as well such excellent orders, preservatives and precious practises for the Plague, as also such marvelous Medicins for divers maladies, as hitherto have not been published in the English tung,* trans. Thomas Hill. London, 1579.

_____. *Del reggimento della peste*. Venice, 1565; Venice, 1594.

_____. *Secreti medicinali*. Venice, 1561.

_____. *Secreti rationali*. Venice, 1561.

_____. *A Short Discours of . . . Leonardo Phioravanti Bolognese uppon Chirurgerie,* trans. John Hester. London, 1562.

_____. *Dello specchio di scientia universale*. Venice, 1567, reprinted 1583.

_____. *Il tesoro della vita humana*. Venice, 1570.

_____. *Three Exact Pieces,* trans. John Hester. London, 1562.

Fracastoro, Girolamo. *De contagione et contagiosis morbis et eorum curatione, libri III,* trans. W. C. Wright. New York: G. P. Putnam's Sons, 1930.

Galilei, Galileo. *Discoveries and Opinions of Galileo,* trans. Stillman Drake. New York: Anchor Books, 1957.

Garzoni, Tomaso. *La piazza universale di tutte le professioni del mondo,* ed. Paolo Cherchi, 2 vols. Turin: Einaudi, 1996.

Gerard, John. *Herball or Generall Historie of Plantes*. London, 1633.

Giannone, Pietro. *Civil History of Naples,* trans. James Ogilvie, 2 vols. London, 1729-31.

Glanvill, Joseph. *The Vanity of Dogmatizing.* London, 1661.

Halliwell, J. O. *A Collection of Letters Illustrative of the Progress of Science in England.* London, 1841.

Hernández, Francisco. *The Mexican Treasury: The Writings of Dr. Francisco Hernández,* ed. Simon Varey. Stanford, Calif.: Stanford University Press, 2000.

Hesse, Everett W., and Harry F. Williams, eds. *Lazarillo de Tormes*. Madison: University of Wisconsin Press, 1961.

Hippocrates. *Physician,* trans. Paul Potter. Vol. 8, Loeb Classical Library. Cambridge, Mass.: Harvard University Press, 1995.

Khalifa, Haji. *The History of the Maritime Wars of the Turks,* trans. J. Mitchell. London, 1831.

Lancellotti, Tommasino. *Cronica modenese,* ed. Carlo Borghi, 12 vols. Parma, Italy: Fiaccadori, 1863.

Latuada, Serviliano. *Descrizione di Milano*. Vol. 2. Milan, 1737.

Le Roy, Louis. *Of the Interchangeable Course, or Variety of Things in the Whole World,* trans. Robert Ashley. London, 1594.

Levi, Primo. *The Periodic Table,* trans. R. Rosenthal. New York: Schocken Books, 1984.

Machiavelli, Niccolò. *The Prince,* trans. George Bull. Harmondsworth, U.K.: Penguin Books, 1961.

Magni, Pietro Paolo. *Discorsi sopra il modo di sanguinare i corpi humani*. Rome, 1613.

Malespini, Celio. *Ducento novelle*. Venice, 1609.

Malpighi, Marcello. *The Correspondence of Marcello Malpighi,* ed. H. B. Adelmann. Vol. 3. Ithaca, N.Y.: Cornell University Press, 1975.

Marcora, Carlo. "Il diario di Giambattista Casale (1554-1598)." *Memorie storiche della diocesi di Milano* 12 (1965): 209-437.

Mattioli, Pietro Andrea. *I discorsi di M. Pietro Andrea Matthioli . . . ne i sei libri di Pedacio Dioscoride Anazarbeo Della materia medicinale*. Venice, 1563.

Mercurio, Scipione. *De gli errori populari d'Italia*. Verona, 1645.

Mersenne, Marin. *Correspondence du P. Marin Mersenne, religieux minime,* ed. Bernard Rochot, Cornelis de Waard, and Paul Tannery, 17 vols. Paris: G. Beauchesne, 1932.

Monardes, Nicolas. *Primera y Segunda y Tercera Partes de la Historia Medicinal de las Cosas que se traen de nuestras Indias Occidentales que sirven en Medicina.* Seville, 1574.

Montanari, V., ed. "Cronaca e storia bolognese del primo Cinquecento nel memoriale di ser Eliseo Mamelini." *Quaderni Culturali Bolognesi* 3 (1979): 3-70.

Morgan, Joseph. *A Complete History of Algiers*. London, 1731; reprinted New York: Negro Universities Press, 1970.

Moryson, Fynes. *Fynes Moryson's Itinerary,* ed. Charles Hughes. London: Sheratt and Hughes, 1903.

Muñoz, Miguel Eugenio. *Recopilación de las leyes, pragmaticas, reales, decretos, y acuerdos del Real Proto-Medicato*. Valencia, Spain, 1851.

Negri, Giovanni Francesco. *Annali di Bologna dall'anno di Cristo 1001 sino al 1600.* Bologna: Biblioteca Universitaria, MS 1107.

Nucula, Horatio. *Commentariorum de bello Aphrodisiensi libri quinque*. Rome, 1552.

Paracelsus (Theophrastus Von Hohenheim). *Selected Writings,* ed. J. Jacobi, trans. N. Guterman. Princeton, N.J.: Princeton University Press, 1951.

Pereira, Michela, and Barbara Spaggiari, eds. *Il "Testamentum" alchemico attribuito a Raimondo Lullo.* Florence: SISMEL, 1999.

Piemontese, Alessio. *I Secreti del reverendo donno Alessio piemontese.* Venice, 1555.

_____. *The Secretes of the reverende maister Alexis of Piemount,* trans. William Warde. London, 1558.

Plat, Hugh. *The Jewell House of Art and Nature. Conteining divers rare and profitable Inventions, together with sundry new experimentes in the Art of Husbandry, Distillation, and Moulding*. London, 1594.

Plinius, Gaius Secondus. *Natural History,* trans. H. Rackham. Vol. 3, Loeb Classical Library. Cambridge, Mass.: Harvard University Press, 1940.

Porreño, Balthasar. *Dichos, y hechos de el señor rey Don Phelipe Segundo, el prudente, potentissimo, y glorioso monarca de las Españas, y las Indias*. Madrid, 1748.

Ramberti, Benedetto. *Delle cose degli Turchi*. Venice, 1539.

Ramusio, Giovanni Battista. *Delle navigationi et viaggi*. Venice, 1550.

Rinieri, Valerio. *Diario*. Bologna: Biblioteca Universitaria, MS 2137.

Ripley, George. *The compound of alchymy. Or The ancient hidden art of archemie conteining the right & perfectest meanes to make the philosophers stone, aurum potabile, with other excellent experiments.* London, 1591.

Rodríguez Villa, Antonio. *Memorias para la historia del asalto y saqueo de Roma en 1527 por el ejército imperial.* Madrid: Biblioteca de Instrucción y Recreo, 1875.

Rostinio, Pietro, and Lodovico Rostinio. *Compendio di tutta la cirugia.* Venice, 1561.

Ruscelli, Girolamo. *Lettura di Girolamo Ruscelli sopra un sonetto dell'illustriss. Signor Marchese della Terza.* Venice, 1552.

_____. *Precetti della militia moderna.* Venice, 1572.

Saccardino, Costantino. *Libro nominato la verità di diverse cose, quale minutamente tratta di molte salutifere operationi spagiriche, et chimiche; con alcuni veri discorse delle cagioni delle lunghe infirmatà, & come si devono sanar con brevità.* Bologna, 1621.

Salazar, Pedro de. *Historia de la guerra y presa de Africa: con la destruycion de la vila de Monazter, y ysta del Gozo, y perdida de Tripol de Berberia: con otras muy nuevas cosas.* Naples, 1552.

Sandoval, Prudencio de. *The History of Charles the Vth,* trans. John Stevens. London, 1704.

Sansovino, Francesco. *Venetia città nobilissima.* Venice, 1663; reprinted Farnborough, U.K.: Gregg, 1968.

Scepper, Cornelius. *Rerum à Carolo V in Africa bello gestarum Commentarii,* Antwerp, 1554.

Selden, John. *Titles of Honor.* London, 1672.

Strozzi, Alessandra. *Selected Letters of Alessandra Strozzi,* trans. H. Gregory. Berkeley: University of California Press, 1997.

Valverde, Giovanni. *Historia de la composicion del cuerpo humano.* Rome, 1556.

Vegetius Renatus, Flavius. *Epitome of Military Science,* trans. N. P. Milner. Liverpool, U.K.: Liverpool University Press, 1993.

Secondary Works

Ady, Cecilia M. *The Bentivoglio of Bologna: A Study in Despotism.* Oxford: Oxford University Press, 1937.

Allegra, Luciano. "Il viaggio, fra Cinque e Seicento." In *Viaggi teatrali dall'Italia a Parigi fra Cinque e Seicento,* pp. 31-44. Genoa: Costa e Nolan, 1989.

Alvar Ezquerra, Alfredo. *El nacimiento de una capital europea. Madrid entre 1561 y 1606.* Madrid: Turner Libros, 1989.

_____. *Felipe II, la corte y Madrid en 1561.* Madrid: CSIC, 1985.

Armstrong, Walter. "Alessandro Oliverio." *The Burlington Magazine* 10, no. 44 (1906): 126.

Arnold, Thomas F. "Violence and Warfare in the Renaissance World." In *A Companion to the Worlds of the Renaissance,* ed. Guido Ruggiero, pp. 460-74. Oxford: Blackwell, 2002.

Arrizabalaga, Jon, John Henderson, and Roger French. *The Great Pox: The French Disease in Renaissance Europe.* New Haven: Yale University Press, 1997.

Bakhtin, Mikhail. *Rabelais and His World,* trans. H. Iswolsky. Indianapolis: Indiana University Press, 1984.

Baron, Frank. *Doctor Faustus: From History to Legend.* Munich: Wilhelm Fink Verlag, 1978.

Barrera-Osorio, Antonio. *Experiencing Nature: The Spanish American Empire and the Early Scientific Revolution.* Austin: University of Texas Press, 2006.

Bell, Rudolph M. *How to Do It: Guides to Good Living for Renaissance Italians.* Chicago: University of Chicago Press, 1999.

Belletini, A. *La popolazione di Bologna dal secolo XV all'unificazione italiana.* Bologna: Zanichelli, 1961.

Beltrami, Luca. *Vita di Aristotile di Bologna.* Bologna: Libreria Luigi Beltrami, 1912.

Benezit, E. *Dictionnaire critique et documentaire des peintres, sculpteurs, dessinateurs et graveurs,* 14 vols. New York: Library Reprints, 2001.

Benussi, Bernardo. *Pola nelle sue istituzioni municipali sino al 1797.* Miscellanea di storia Veneto-Tridentina. Vol. 1. Venice: R. Deputazione Editrice, 1923.

BIBLIOGRAPHY

Berti, Luciano. *Il Principe dello studiolo: Francesco I dei Medici e la fine del Rinascimento fiorentino.* Florence: EDAM, 1967.

Biagioli, Mario. *Galileo Courtier: The Practice of Science in the Culture of Absolutism.* Chicago: University of Chicago Press, 1993.

Biow, Douglas. *The Culture of Cleanliness in Renaissance Italy.* Ithaca, N.Y.: Cornell University Press, 2006.

Blanchet, Léon. *Campanella.* Paris, 1920.

Blastenbrei, Peter. *Kriminalität in Rom.* Tübingen, Germany: Max Niemeyer Verlag, 1995.

Bonaffini, Giuseppe. *Un mare di paura: Il Mediterraneo in età moderna.* Caltanisetta, Italy: S. Sciascia, 1997.

Boorstin, Daniel. *The Image: A Guide to Pseudo-Events in America.* New York: Harper and Row, 1961.

Braudel, Fernand. *The Mediterranean and the Mediterranea World in the Age of Philip II,* trans. Sian Reynolds, 2 vols. New York: Harper and Row, 1972.

Brockliss, Laurence, and Colin Jones. *The Medical World of Early Modern France.* Oxford: Oxford University Press, 1997.

Brody, S. N. *The Disease of the Soul: Leprosy in Medieval Literature.* Ithaca, N.Y.: Cornell University Press, 1971.

Brucker, Gene. "The Italian Renaissance." In *A Companion to the Worlds of the Renaissance,* ed. Guido Ruggiero, pp. 23-38. Oxford: Blackwell, 2002.

Burckhardt, Jacob. *The Civilization of the Renaissance in Italy,* trans. S. G. C. Middlemore. New York: Random House, 1954.

Burke, Peter. "Early Modern Venice as a Center of Information and Communication." In *Venice Reconsidered: The History and Civilization of an Italian City-State, 1297-1797,* ed. John Martin and Dennis Romano, pp. 388-419. Baltimore: Johns Hopkins University Press, 2000.

Butterfield, Herbert H. *The Whig Interpretation of History.* New York: W. W. Norton, 1965.

Butters, Suzanne. *The Triumph of Vulcan: Sculptor's Tools, Porphyry, and the Prince in Ducal Florence,* 2 vols. Florence: Olschki, 1996.

Calabria, Antonio. *The Cost of Empire: Finances in the Kingdom of Naples in the Time of Spanish Rule.* Cambridge: Cambridge University Press, 1991.

Calvi, Giulia. *Histories of a Plague Year.* Berkeley and Los Angeles: University of California Press, 1984.

Camporesi, Piero. *Bread of Dreams: Food and Fantasy in Early Modern Europe,* trans. David Gentilcore. Chicago: University of Chicago Press, 1989.

_____. *Camminare il mondo: Vita e avventure di Leonardo Fioravanti medico del Cinquecento.* Milan: Garzanti, 1997.

_____. *La carne impassibile. Salvezza e salute fra Medioevo e Contrariforma.* Milan: Garzanti, 1994.

_____. *Juice of Life: The Symbolic and Natural Significance of Blood,* trans. Robert R. Barr. New York: Continuum, 1995.

_____. *La maschera di Bertholdo.* Milan: Garzanti, 1993.

Campos Díez, María Soledad. *El Real Tribunal del Protomedicato Castellano (Siglos XIV-XIX).* Cuenca, Spain: Ediciones de la Universidad de Castilla-La Mancha, 1999.

Cañizares-Esguerra, Jorge. "Iberian Science in the Renaissance: Ignored How Much Longer?" *Perspectives on Science* 12 (2004): 86-124.

Carlino, Andrea. *Books of the Body: Anatomical Ritual and Renaissance Learning,* trans. John Tedeschi and Anne C. Tedeschi. Chicago: University of Chicago Press, 1999.

Carmichael, Ann. "The Last Past Plague: The Uses of Memory in Renaissance Epidemics." *Journal of the History of Medicine* 53 (1998): 132-60.

Castro Soler, Elena, and José Rodríguez Guerrero. "Luis de Centelles y las Coplas de la Piedra *Philosophal,*" *Azogue* 4 (2001). Available online at www.revistaazogue.com.

Cavallo, Sandra. *Artisans of the Body in Early Modern Italy: Identities, Families and Masculinities.* Manchester, U.K.: Manchester University Press, 2007.

Chastel, André. *The Sack of Rome, 1527.* Princeton, N.J.: Princeton University Press, 1983.

Cherchi, Paolo. "Leonardo Fioravanti e Antonio Guevara." *Esperienze Letterarie* 20 (1995): 13-36.

Chinchilla, Don Anastasio. *Anales historicos de la medicina en general, y biografico-bibliograficos de la española in particular* (1841). Sources of Science, no. 8. New York: Johnson Reprints, 1967.

Clarke, Georgia. "Magnificence and the City: Giovanni II Bentivoglio and Architecture in Fifteenth-Century Bologna," *Renaissance Studies* 13 (1999): 397-411.

Clubb, Louise George. *Giambattista Della Porta, Dramatist.* Princeton, N.J.: Princeton University Press, 1965.

Cochrane, Eric. "The Renaissance Academies in the Italian and European Setting." In *The Fairest Flower: The Emergence of Linguistic National Consciousness in Renaissance Europe*, pp. 21-39. Florence: Crusca, 1985.

Cohen, Elizabeth S., and Thomas V. Cohen. *Daily Life in Renaissance Italy.* Westport, Conn.: Greenwood Press, 2001.

Comparetti, Domenico. *Vergil in the Middle Ages.* Princeton, N.J.: Princeton University Press, 1997.

Conelli, Maria Ann. "The Ecclesiastical Patronage of Isabella Feltria Della Rovere: Bricks, Bones, and Brocades." In *Patronage and Dynasty: The Rise of the della Rovere in Renaissance Italy,* ed. Ian Verstegen, pp. 123-38. Kirksville, Mo: Truman State University Press, 2007.

Cook, Harold J. *Matters of Exchange: Commerce, Medicine, and Science in the Dutch Golden Age.* New Haven: Yale University Press, 2009.

Copenhaver, Brian P., and Charles B. Schmitt. *Renaissance Philosophy.* A History of Renaissance Philosophy. Vol. 3. Oxford: Oxford University Press, 1992.

Corsini, Andrea. *Medici ciarlatani e ciarlatani medici.* Bologna: Zanichelli, 1922.

Cosmacini, Giorgio. *Storia della medicina e sanità in Italia. Dalla peste Europea alla guerra mondiale, 1348-1918.* Bari, Italy: Laterza, 1987.

Covoni, P. F. *Don Antonio de' Medici al Casino di San Marco.* Florence: Tipografia Cooperativa, 1892.

Croce, Benedetto. *History of the Kingdom of Naples,* trans. F. Frenaye. Chicago: University of Chicago Press, 1970.

Dandelet, Thomas J. *Spanish Rome, 1500-1700.* Chicago: University of Chicago Press, 2001.

Dannenfeldt, Karl H. "Egyptian Mumia: The Sixteenth Century Experience and Debate." *The Sixteenth Century Journal* 16 (1985): 163-80.

Daston, Lorraine. "History of Science in an Elegiac Mode: E. A. Burtt's *Metaphysical Foundations of Modern Physical Science* Revisited." *Isis* 82 (1991): 522-31.

_____. "The Moral Economy of Science," *Osiris* 10 (2000): 3-24.

Daston, Lorraine, and Katharine Park, *Wonders and the Order of Nature, 1150-1750.* New York: Zone Books, 1998.

Davidson, Nicolas S. "An Armed Band and the Local Community on the Venetian Terraferma in the Sixteenth Century." In *Bande armate, banditi, banditismo e repressione di giustizia negli stati europei di antico regime,* ed. Gherardo Ortalli, 401-22. Rome: Jouvence, 1986.

Davis, Robert C. "Counting European Slaves on the Barbary Coast." *Past and Present* 172 (2001): 87-124.

Dear, Peter. *Discipline and Experience: The Mathematical Way in the Scientific Revolution.* Chicago: University of Chicago Press, 1995.

Debus, Allen. *The French Paracelsians: The Chemical Challenge to Medical and Scientific Tradition in Early Modern France.* Cambridge: Cambridge University Press, 1991.

De Renzi, Salvatore. *Storia della medicina in Italia,* 5 vols. Naples: Tipografia del Filiatre-Sebezio 1845-1848.

De Seta, Pietro. *L'accademia Cosentina.* Cosenza, Italy: Editrice Casa del Libro Dott. Gustavo Brenner, 1965.

Detienne, Marcel, and Jean-Pierre Vernant. *Cunning Intelligence in Greek Culture and Society,* trans. J. Lloyd. Chicago: University of Chicago Press, 1991.

De Vivo, Filippo. *Information and Communication in Venice: Rethinking Early Modern Politics.* Cambridge: Cambridge University Press, 2007.

De Vries, Kelly R. "Military Surgical Practice and the Advent of Gunpowder Weaponry." *Canadian Bulletin of Medical History* 7 (1990): 131-46.

DeVun, Leah. " 'Human Heaven': John of Rupescissa's Alchemy at the End of the World." In *History in the Comic Mode. Medieval Communities and the Matter of Person*, ed. Rachel Fulton and Bruce W. Holsinger, pp. 251-61. New York: Columbia University Press, 2007.

Dickie, John. *Darkest Italy: The Nation and Stereotypes of the Mezzogiorno, 1860–1900*. New York: St. Martin's Press, 1999.

Di Filippo Bareggi, Claudia. *Il mestiere di scrivere. Lavoro intellettuale e mercato librario a Venezia nel Cinquecento*. Rome: Bulzoni, 1988.

Di Giovanni, Vincenzo. *Le fortificazioni di Palermo nel secolo XVI giusta l'Ordini dell'Ing. Antonio Ferramolino*. Palermo, Italy: Lo Statuto, 1896.

Dobbs, Betty Jo Teeter. *The Foundations of Newton's Alchemy, or The Hunting of the Greene Lyon*. Cambridge: Cambridge University Press, 1975.

Dooley, Brendan. "Printing and Entrepreneurialism in Seventeenth-Century Italy." *Journal of European Economic History* (1997): 569-97.

Dupré, Sven. "The Dioptrics of Refractive Dials in the Sixteenth Century." *Nuncius* 18 (2003): 39-67.

_____. "Mathematical Instruments and the 'Theory of the Concave Spherical Mirror': Galileo's Optics Beyond Art and Science." *Nuncius* 15 (2000): 551-88.

Eamon, William. "Appearance, Artifice, and Reality: Collecting Secrets in Courtly Culture." In *The Gentleman, the Virtuoso, the Inquirer: Vincencio Juan de Lastanosa and the Art of Collecting in Early Modern Spain*, ed. Mar Rey-Bueno and Miguel López-Pérez, pp. 127-43. Cambridge: Cambridge Scholars Publishing, 2008.

_____. "The Canker Friar: Piety and Treachery in an Era of New Diseases." In *Piety and Plague in Europe: From Antiquity to the Early Modern Period*, ed. Franco Mormando and Thomas W. Worcester, pp. 156-76. Kirksville, Mo.: Truman State University Press, 2007.

_____. "The Charlatan's Trial: An Italian Surgeon in the Court of King Philip II, 1576-1577." *Cronos* 8 (2005): 1-30.

_____. "Court, Academy, and Printing House: Patronage and Scientific Careers in Late Renaissance Italy." In *Patronage and Institutions: Science, Technology and Medicine at the European Court, 1500-1700*, ed. Bruce Moran, pp. 25-50. Bury St. Edmunds, U.K.: Boydell, 1991.

_____. "Natural Magic and Utopia in the Cinquecento: Campanella, the Della Porta Circle, and the Revolt of Calabria." *Memorie Domenicane* n.s., 26 (1995): 369-402.

_____. *Science and the Secrets of Nature: Books of Secrets in Medieval and Early Modern Culture*. Princeton, N.J.: Princeton University Press, 1994.

_____. "Science as a Hunt." *Physis* 31 (1994): 393-432.

Eamon, William, and Françoise Paheau. "The Accademia Segreta of Girolamo Ruscelli. A Sixteenth-Century Italian Scientific Society." *Isis* 75 (1984): 327-42.

Edelstein, Ludwig. "The Dietetics of Antiquity." In *Ancient Medicine*, ed. Owsei Temkin and C. Lilian Temkin, pp. 303-16. Baltimore: Johns Hopkins University Press, 1967.

_____. "Empiricism and Skepticism in the Teaching of the Greek Empiricist School." In *Ancient Medicine*, ed. Owsei Temkin and C. Lilian Temkin, pp. 195-204. Baltimore: Johns Hopkins University Press, 1967.

Eisenstein, Elizabeth. *The Printing Press as an Agent of Change*, 2 vols. Cambridge: Cambridge University Press, 1979.

Élias de Tejada, Francisco. *Napoli Spagnola*. Vol. 2, *Le decadi imperiali*, ed. S. Vitale. Naples: Concorrente, 2002.

Ember, L. R. "Incredible Colors." *Science & Technology* 84, no. 37 (2006): 31-34.

Fanti, M., and G. Roversi, *Il santuario della Madonna del Soccorso nel Borgo di San Pietro in Bologna*. Bologna: Parrochia della Beata Virgine del Soccorso, 1975.

Favaro, Antonio. "Amici e corrispondenti di Galileo Galilei. XL. Giuseppe Moletti." *Atti del R. Istituto Veneto di scienze, lettere ed arti* 77, no. 2 (1918): 47-118.

Ferrari, Giovanna. "Public Anatomy Lessons and the Carnival: The Anatomy Theatre of Bologna." *Past and Present* 117 (1987): 50-106.

Findlen, Paula. "The Economy of Scientific Exchange in Early Modern Italy." In *Patronage and Institutions: Science, Technology, and Medicine at the European Court 1500-1750*, ed. Bruce Moran, pp. 5-24. Bury St. Edmunds, U.K.: Boydell Press, 1991.

_____. "The Formation of a Scientific Community: Natural History in Sixteenth-Century Italy." In *Natural Particulars: Nature and the Disciplines in Renaissance Europe,* ed. A. Grafton and N. Siraisi, pp. 369-400. Cambridge, Mass.: MIT Press, 1999.

_____. "Inventing Nature: Commerce, Science, and Art in the Early Modern Cabinet of Curiosities." In *Merchants and Marvels: Commerce, Science, and Art in Early Modern Europe,* ed. Pamela H. Smith and Paula Findlen, pp. 297-323. New York: Routledge, 2001.

_____. "Jokes of Nature and Jokes of Knowledge: The Playfulness of Scientific Discourse in Early Modern Europe." *Renaissance Quarterly* 43 (1990): 292-331.

_____. *Possessing Nature: Museums, Collecting, and Scientific Culture in Early Modern Italy.* Berkeley and Los Angeles: University of California Press, 1994.

Fiorentino, Francesco. *Bernardino Telesio ossia studi storici su l'idea della natura nel Risorgimento italiano,* 2 vols. Firenze, Italy: Successori Le Monnier, 1874.

Foa, Anna. *Giordano Bruno.* Bologna: Mulino, 1998.

Fontaine, Laurence. *History of Pedlars in Europe.* Cambridge: Polity Press, 1996.

Fontana, Jeffrey. "Duke Guidobaldo II della Rovere, Federico Barocci, and the Taste for Titian at the Court of Urbino." In *Patronage and Dynasty: The Rise of the della Rovere in Renaissance Italy,* ed. Ian Verstegen, pp. 161-78. Kirksville, Mo.: Truman State University Press, 2007.

Freedberg, David. *Eye of the Lynx: Galileo, His Friends, and the Beginnings of Modern Natural History.* Chicago: University of Chicago Press, 2002.

French, Roger. *Canonical Medicine. Gentile da Foligno and Scholasticism.* Leiden, Germany: Brill, 2001.

_____. *Medicine before Science. The Business of Medicine from the Middle Ages to the Enlightenment.* Cambridge: Cambridge University Press, 2003.

Galluzzi, Paolo. "Motivi Paracelsiana nella Toscana di Cosimo II e di Don Antonio dei Medici: Alchimia, medicina 'chimica' e riforma del sapere." In *Scienze, credenze occulte, livelli di cultura,* ed. Giancarlo Garfagnini, pp. 31-62. Florence: Olschki, 1982.

Gay, Peter. "The Enlightenment as Medicine and as Cure." In *The Age of Enlightenment. Studies Presented to Theodore Besterman,* ed. William Henry Barber, pp. 375-86. Edinburgh and London: Oliver and Boyd, 1967.

Gentilcore, David. " 'All That Pertains to Medicine': Protomedici and Protomedicati in Early Modern Italy." *Medical History* 38, no. 2 (1994): 121-42.

_____. *Healers and Healing in Early Modern Italy* (Social and Cultural Values in Early Modern Europe). Manchester, U.K.: Manchester University Press, 1998.

_____. *Medical Charlatanism in Early Modern Italy.* Cambridge: Cambridge University Press, 2006.

Gentili, Giuseppe. "Leonardo Fioravanti bolognese alla luce di ignorati documenti." *Rivista di storia delle scienze mediche e naturali* 42 (1951): 16-41.

Gilman, Sander. *Making the Body Beautiful: A Cultural History of Aesthetic Surgery.* Princeton, N.J.: Princeton University Press, 1999.

Ginzburg, Carlo. "The Dovecote Has Opened Its Eyes: Popular Conspiracy in Seventeenth-Century Italy." In *The Inquisition in Early Modern Europe: Studies on Sources and Methods,* ed. G. Henningsen and J. Tedeschi, pp. 190-98. Dekalb: Northern Illinois University Press, 1986.

_____. "High and Low: The Theme of Forbidden Knowledge in the Sixteenth and Seventeenth Centuries." *Past and Present* 73 (1976): 28-41.

Giordano, Davide. *Leonardo Fioravanti Bolognese.* Bologna: Editore Licinio Capelli, 1920.

Gnudi, Martha Teach, and Jerome Pierce Webster. *The Life and Times of Gaspare Tagliacozzi, Surgeon of Bologna 1545-1599.* New York: Herbert Reichner, 1950.

Goldthwaite, *Building of Renaissance Florence. An Economic and Social History.* Baltimore: Johns Hopkins University Press, 1980.

_____. *Wealth and the Demand for Art in Italy, 1300-1600.* Baltimore: Johns Hopkins University Press, 1993.

Golub, Edward S. *The Limits of Medicine: How Science Shapes Our Hope for the Cure.* Chicago: University of Chicago Press, 1997.

Goodman, David C. *Power and Penury: Government, Technology and Science in Philip II's Spain.* Cambridge: Cambridge University Press, 1988.

Goy, Richard. *Venice: The City and Its Architecture.* London: Phaidon Press, 1997.

Gracely, R. H. "Charisma and the Art of Healing: Can Nonspecific Factors Be Enough?" In *Proceedings of the Ninth World Congress on Pain: Progress in Pain Research and Management*, vol. 16, ed. M. Devor and M.C. Rowbotham. Seattle: ASP Press, 2000.

Green, Monica. "Women's Medical Practice and Medical Care in Medieval Europe." *Signs* 14 (1989): 434-73.

Greenblatt, Stephen. *Renaissance Self-Fashioning: From More to Shakespeare.* Chicago: University of Chicago Press, 1980.

Gregorovius, Ferdinand. *Storia della città di Roma nel medio evo,* 16 vols. Città di Castello, Italy: Unione Arti Grafiche, 1938-1944.

Grendler, Paul. *Critics of the Italian World, 1530-1560: Anton Francesco Doni, Nicolò Franco, and Ortensio Lando.* Madison: University of Wisconsin Press, 1969.

_____. *The Roman Inquisition and the Venetian Press, 1540-1605.* Princeton, N.J.: Princeton University Press, 1977.

_____. "The University of Bologna, the City, and the Papacy." *Renaissance Studies* 13 (1999): 475–85.

Guerra, Francisco. "Drugs from the Indies and the Political Economy of the Sixteenth Century." *Analecta medico-historico* 1 (1966): 29-54.

_____. "Juan de Valverde de Amusco." *Clio Medica* 2 (1967): 339-62.

_____. *Nicolás Bautista Monardes. Su vida y su obra (ca. 1493-1588).* Mexico: Compañia Fundidora de Fierro y Acero de Monterrey, 1961.

Guerrini, Olinda. *La Vita e le opere di Giulio Cesare Croce.* Bologna: Zanichelli, 1879.

Guglielmotti, P. Alberto. *La guerra dei pirati e la marina pontificia dal 1500 al 1560,* 2 vols. Florence: Successori Le Monnier, 1876.

Haller, Albrecht. *Bibliotheca chirugica,* 2 vols. Bern, 1774-1775; reprint Hildesheim, Germany: G. Olms, 1971.

Halleux, Robert. "Les ouvrages alchimiques de Jean de Rupescissa." *Histoire litteraire de la France,* vol. 41, pp. 241-84. Paris: Imprimerie Nationale, 1981.

Harkness, Deborah E. *The Jewel House. Elizabethan London and the Scientific Revolution.* New Haven: Yale University Press, 2007.

Headley, John M. *Tommaso Campanella and the Transformation of the World.* Princeton, N.J.: Princeton University Press, 1997.

Henderson, John. *The Renaissance Hospital. Healing the Body and Healing the Soul.* New Haven: Yale University Press, 2006.

Henke, Robert. "The Italian Mountebank and the Commedia dell'Arte," *Theatre Survey* 38 (1997): 1-29.

_____. *Performance and Literature in the Commedia dell'Arte.* Cambridge: Cambridge University Press, 2002.

Hoppen, Alison. "Military Engineers in Malta, 1530-1798." *Annals of Science* 38 (1981): 413-33.

Horodowich, Elizabeth. "The Gossiping Tongue: Oral Networks, Public Life, and Political Culture in Early Modern Venice," *Renaissance Studies* 19 (2005): 22-45.

_____. *Language and Statecraft in Early Modern Venice.* Cambridge: Cambridge University Press, 2008.

Howard, Deborah. *Architectural History of Venice,* rev. ed. New Haven: Yale University Press, 2002.

———. *Jacopo Sansovino: Architecture and Patronage in Renaissance Venice.* New Haven: Yale University Press, 1975.

Jardine, Lisa. *Worldly Goods: A New History of the Renaissance.* New York: Doubleday, 1996.

Johnson, L. W., and M. L. Wolbarsht. "Mercury Poisoning: A Probable Cause of Isaac Newton's Physical and Mental Ills." *Notes and Records of the Royal Society of London* 34, no. 1 (1979): 1-9.

Jourdan, A. J. L. *Dictionnaire des sciences médicales. Biographie médicales.* Vol. 4. Paris, 1821.

Kagan, Richard L. *Clio & the Crown. The Politics of History in Medieval and Early Modern Spain.* Baltimore: Johns Hopkins University Press, 2009.

_____. "Prescott's Paradigm: American Historical Scholarship and the Decline of Spain." *American Historical Review* 101 (1996): 423-46.

Kamen, Henry. *Imagining Spain. Historical Myth & National Identity*. New Haven and London: Yale University Press, 2008.

_____. *Philip of Spain*. New Haven: Yale University Press, 1997.

Katritzky, M. A. "Marketing Medicine: The Image of the Early Modern Mountebank." *Renaissance Studies* 15 (2001): 121-53.

Kern, Paul Bentley. *Ancient Siege Warfare*. Bloomington: Indiana University Press. 1999.

Kiernan, V. G. *The Duel in European History. Honour and the Reign of Aristocracy*. Oxford: Oxford University Press, 1988.

Kirkham, Victoria, ed. *Laura Battiferra and her Literary Circle: An Anthology*. Chicago: University of Chicago Press, 2006.

Klestinec, Cynthia. "A History of Anatomy Theaters in Sixteenth-Century Padua." *Journal of the History of Medicine and Allied Sciences*, 59 (2004): 375-412.

Knecht, R. J. *Renaissance Warrior and Patron: The Reign of Francis I*. Cambridge: Cambridge University Press, 1994.

La Cava, Francesco. *La peste di S. Carlo: Note storico-mediche sulla peste del 1576*. Milan: Editore Ulrico Hoepli, 1945.

Laird, W. R. *The Unfinished Mechanics of Giuseppe Moletti*. Toronto: University of Toronto Press, 2000.

Laughran, Michelle Anne. "The Body, Public Health and Social Control in Sixteenth-Century Venice. Ph.D. diss., University of Connecticut, 1998.

Lea, K. M. *Italian Popular Comedy. A Study in the Commedia dell'Arte, 1560-1620,* 2 vols. New York: Russell and Russell, 1962.

Lensi Orlandi, Giulio. *Cosimo e Francesco d'Medici alchemisti*. Florence: Nardini, 1978.

Lerner, Robert E. *The Feast of Saint Abraham: Medieval Millenarians and the Jews*. Philadelphia: University of Pensylvania Press, 2001.

Levi, Carlo. *Christ Stopped at Eboli,* trans. F. Frenaye. New York: Farrar, Straus and Giroux, 1947.

Levin, Harry. *The Myth of the Golden Age in the Renaissance*. New York: Oxford University Press, 1972.

Levin, Michael J. *Agents of Empire: Spanish Ambassadors in Sixteenth-Century Italy*. Ithaca, New York: Cornell University Press, 2005.

Lopez, Robert S. "European Merchants in the Medieval Indies: Evidence of Commercial Documents." *Journal of Economic History* 3 (1943): 174-80.

López Pérez, Miguel. "Algunos rasgos sobre la relación entre lulismo y pseudolulismo en la Edad Moderna." *Dynamis: Acta Hispanica ad Medicinae Scientiarumque Historiam Illustrandam* 22 (2002): 327-50.

_____. *Asclepio renovado: Alchimia y medicina en la España Moderna (1500-1700)*. Madrid: Ediciones Corona Borealis, 2003.

López Piñero, José María. *Ciencia y tecnica en la sociedad espanola de los siglos XVI y XVII*. Barcelona: Labor Universitaria, 1979.

López Piñero, José María, and José Pardo Tomás. *La influencia de Francisco Hernández (1515-1587) en la constitución de la botánica y la materia médica modernas*. Valencia, Spain: Universitat de Valencia, 1996.

López Terrada, María Luz, and José Pardo Tomás. *La primeras noticias sobre plantas americanas en las relaciones de viajes y crónicas de indias (1493-1553)*. Valencia, Spain: Universitat de Valencia, 1993.

Louis-Courvoisier, M., and A. Mauron. " 'He found me very well; for me, I was still feeling sick': The Strange Worlds of Physicians and Patients in the 18th and 21st centuries." *Medical Humanities* 28, no. 1 (2002): 9-13.

Mack, Rosamond E. *Islamic Trade and Italian Art, 1300-1600*. Berkeley and Los Angeles: University of California Press, 2002.

MacKenney, Richard. *Renaissances: The Cultures of Italy, c. 1300-c. 1600*. London: Palgrave Macmillan, 2005.

_____. *Tradesmen and Traders: The World of the Guilds in Venice and Europe, c. 1250–c. 1650.* London: Routledge, 1987.

Maczak, Antoni. *Travel in Early Modern Europe*. Cambridge: Polity Press, 1995.

Malgaigne, J. F. *Surgery and Ambroise Paré,* trans. W. B. Hamby. Norman: University of Oklahoma Press, 1965.

Malkiel, Y. "Italian *ciarlatano* and Its Romance Offshoots." *Romance Philology* 2 (1948-49): 325.

Manfroni, Camillo. *Storia della marina italiana,* 2 vols. Livorno: Tipografia di Raffaelo Giunti, 1897-1902 (reprint ed. Milan: Periodici Scientifici, 1970).

Marino, John A. "Economic Idylls and Pastoral Realities: The 'Trickster Economy' in the Kingdom of Naples." *Comparative Studies in Society and History* 24 (1982): 211-34.

Martin, John J. "The Imaginary Piazza: Tommaso Garzoni and the Late Italian Renaissance." In *Portraits of Medieval and Renaissance Living: Essays in Memory of David Herlihy,* ed. Samuel K. Cohn, Jr., and Steven A. Epstein, pp. 439-54. Ann Arbor: University of Michigan Press, 1996.

_____. "Inventing Sincerity, Refashioning Prudence: The Discovery of the Individual in Renaissance Europe." *American Historical Review* 102 (1997): 1309-42.

_____. "The Myth of Renaissance Individualism." In *A Companion to the Worlds of the Renaissance,* ed. Guido Ruggiero, pp. 208-34. Oxford: Blackwell, 2002.

_____. *Myths of Renaissance Individualism*. London: Palgrave Macmillan, 2006.

Martines, Lauro. *Power and Imagination: City-States in Renaissance Italy*. New York: Vintage Books, 1980.

_____. *Strong Words. Writing and Social Strain in the Italian Renaissance*. Baltimore: Johns Hopkins University Press, 2001.

Martinotti, G. *L'insegnamento dell'anatomia in Bologna prima del secolo XIX*. Bologna: Cooperativa Tipografia Azzoguidi, 1911.

Maylender, Michele. *Storia delle accademie d'Italia,* 5 vols. Bologna: Capelli, 1926-1930.

McCallum, R. I. *Antimony in Medical History: An Account of the Medical Uses of Antimony and Its Compounds since Early Times to the Present*. Edinburgh: Pentland Press, 1999.

McVaugh, Michael R. "Chemical Medicine in the Medical Writings of Arnau de Vilanova." *Arxiu de Textos Catalans Antics* 23-24 (2005): 239-64.

Milani, Marisa. *Antiche pratiche di medicina popolare nei processi del S. Uffizio (Venezia, 1572-1591)*. Padua: Centrostampa Palazzo Madura, 1986.

Moerman, Daniel E., and Wayne B. Jonas. "Deconstructing the Placebo Effect and Finding the Meaning Response." *Annals of Internal Medicine* 136, no. 6 (2002): 471.

Monchicourt, Charles. "Dragut, amiral turc." *Revue Tunisienne* (1930): 106-18.

_____. "Episodes de la carrière tunisienne de Dragut. I: Dragut dans l'Oued-Gabès et contre Gafsa (hiver 1550-1551)." *Revue Tunisienne* (1918): 35-43.

_____. "Episodes de la carrière tunisienne de Dragut. II: Le stratagème de Dragut à El-Kanatara de Djerba (avril 1551)." *Revue Tunisienne* (1918), 263-73.

_____. "L'insécurité en Méditerranée durant l'été 1550." *Revue Tunisienne* (1917): 317-24.

Moran, Bruce T. *Distilling Knowledge: Alchemy, Chemistry, and the Scientific Revolution*. Cambridge: Harvard University Press, 2005.

Mozzato, Andrea. "The Production of Woollens in Fifteenth- and Sixteenth-Century Venice. In *At the Centre of the Old World: Trade and Manufacturing in Venice and the Venetian Mainland, 1400–1800,* ed. Paola Lanaro, pp. 73-109. Toronto: Centre for Reformation and Renaissance Studies, 2006.

Muir, Edward. *Civic Ritual in Renaissance Venice*. Princeton, N.J.: Princeton University Press, 1981.

_____. *Mad Blood Stirring: Vendetta in Renaissance Italy.* Baltimore: Johns Hopkins University Press, 1998.

Mukherjee, Ayesha. "Dearth Science, 1580-1608: The Writings of Hugh Platt." *The Durham Thomas Harriot Seminar,* Occasional Paper No. 35. Durham, 2007.

Munger, R. S. "Guaiacum, the Holy Wood from the New World," *Journal of the History of Medicine and Allied Sciences* 4 (1949): 196-229.

Murdoch, John. "The Analytical Character of Medieval Learning: Natural Philosophy Without Nature." In *Approaches to Nature in the Middle Ages*, ed. L. D. Roberts, pp. 171-213. Binghamton, N.Y.: Center for Medieval and Renaissance Studies, 1982.

Muzzi, Salvatore. *Annali della città di Bologna dalla sua origine al 1796*. Vol. 6. Bologna: Tipi di S. Tommaso D'Aquino, 1844.

Navarro Brotòns, Victor, and William Eamon, eds. *Mas allá de la Leyenda Negra: España y la Revolución Científica. Beyond the Black Legend: Spain and the Scientific Revolution*. Valencia, Spain: Instituto de Historia de la Ciencia y Documentación López Piñero, 2007.

Newman, William. *Promethean Ambitions: Alchemy and the Quest to Perfect Nature*. Chicago: University of Chicago Press, 2004.

_____. "Technology and Alchemical Debate in the Late Middle Ages." *Isis* 80 (1989): 423-45.

Niccoli, Ottavia. *Prophecy and People in Renaissance Italy*, trans. Lydia G. Cochrane. Princeton, N.J.: Princeton University Press, 1990.

Norton, Marcy. *Sacred Gifts, Profane Pleasures: A History of Tobacco and Chocolate in the Atlantic World*. Ithaca, N.Y.: Cornell University Press, 2008.

Nummedal, Tara. "The Problem of Fraud in Early Modern Alchemy." In *Shell Games: Scams, Frauds and Deceits in Europe, 1300-1650*, ed. Richard Raiswell and Mark Crane, pp. 37-55. Toronto: Centre for Reformation and Renaissance Studies, 2004.

Oechslin, W. "La fama di Aristotele Fioravanti ingegnere e architetto." *Arte Lombarda* 44-45 (1976): 102-20.

Olmi, Guiseppe. "Farmacopea antica e medicina moderna. La disputa sulla teriaca nel Cinquecento bolognese." *Physis* 19 (1977): 197-245.

O'Malley, C. D. *Andreas Vesalius of Brussels, 1514-1564*. Berkeley and Los Angeles: University of California Press, 1964.

Padgen, Anthony. *The Fall of Natural Man: The American Indian and the Origins of Comparative Ethnology*. Cambridge: Cambridge University Press, 1982.

Paitoni, Jacopo Maria. *Biblioteca degli autori antichi greci, e latini volgarizzati*. Vol 4. Venice, 1767.

Palmer, Richard. "Medicine at the Papal Court in the Sixteenth Century." In *Medicine at the Courts of Europe, 1500-1837*, ed. Vivian Nutton, pp. 49-78. London: Routledge, 1990.

_____. "Pharmacy in the Republic of Venice in the Sixteenth Century." In *The Medical Renaissance of the Sixteenth Century*, ed. Andrew Wear, R. K. French, and Ian M. Lonie, pp. 100–17. Cambridge: Cambridge University Press, 1985.

Pane, Giulio. "Pietro di Toledo, vicere urbanista." *Napoli nobilissima* 14 (1975): 81-95, 161-82.

Park, Katharine. "Country Medicine in the City Marketplace: Snakehandlers as Itinerant Healers." *Renaissance Studies* 15 (2001): 104-20.

_____. "The Criminal and Saintly Body: Autopsy and Dissection in Renaissance Italy." *Renaissance Quarterly* 47 (1994): 1-33.

_____. "Medicine and Magic: The Healing Arts." In *Gender and Society in Renaissance Italy*, ed. J. Brown and R. Davis, pp. 129-48. London: Longman, 1998.

_____. *Secrets of Women. Gender, Generation, and the Origins of Human Dissection*. New York: Zone Books, 2006.

_____. "Stones, Bones, and Hernias: Surgical Specialists in Fourteenth- and Fifteenth-Century Italy." In *Medicine from the Black Death to the French Disease*, ed. Roger French, Jon Arrizabalaga, Andrew Cunningham, and Luis García Ballester, pp. 110-30. Aldershot, U.K.: Ashgate, 1998.

Park, Katharine, and Lorraine Daston. "The Age of the New." In *The Cambridge History of Science*. Vol. 3: *Early Modern Science*, ed. Katharine Park and Lorraine Daston, pp. 1-17. Cambridge: Cambridge University Press, 2006.

Parker, Geoffrey. *The Grand Strategy of Philip II*. New Haven: Yale University Press, 1998.

_____. *The Military Revolution. Military Innovation and the Rise of the West 1500-1800*, 2nd ed. Cambridge: Cambridge University Press, 1996.

Partner, Peter. *Renaissance Rome, 1500-1559: A Portrait of a Society*. Berkeley and Los Angeles: University of California Press, 1976.

Pastor, Ludwig von. *History of the Popes*. Vol. 15, ed. Ralph Francis Kerr. St. Louis: Herder, 1928.

Pastorello, Ester. *Tipografi, editori, librai a Venezia nel secolo XVI.* Florence: Olschki, 1924.

Pereira, Michela. *The Alchemical Corpus Attributed to Raymond Lull,* ed. Jill Kraye and W. F. Ryan. Warburg Institute Surveys and Texts. Vol. 18. London, 1989.

_____. "La leggenda di Lullo alchimista." *Estudio Lulianos* 27 (1987): 145-63.

_____. "Lullian Alchemy: Aspects and Problems of the *Corpus* of Alchemical Works Attributed to Ramon Lull (XIV-XVII Centuries)." *Catalan Review* 4 (1990): 41-54.

_____. "*Medicina* in the Alchemical Writings Attributed to Raimond Lull (14th-17th Centuries)." In *Alchemy and Chemistry in the 16th and 17th Centuries,* ed. Piyo Rattansi and Antonio Clericuzio, pp. 1-16. Dordrecht, Netherlands: Kluwer, 1994.

_____. "Teorie dell'elixir nell'alchimia medievale." *Micrologus* 3 (1995): 103-48.

_____. "Un tesoro inestimabile. Elixir e 'prolongatio vitae' nell'alchimia del '300.'" *Micrologus* 1 (1992): 161-87.

Pomata, Gianna. "Barbieri e comari." In *Cultura popolare nell'Emilia Romagna: Medicina erbe e magia,* ed. Piero Camporesi et al., pp. 161-83. Milan: Silvana Editoriale, 1981.

_____. *Contracting a Cure: Patients, Healers, and the Law in Early Modern Bologna.* Baltimore: Johns Hopkins University Press, 1998.

Porter, Roy. *The Greatest Benefit to Mankind: A Medical History of Humanity.* New York: Norton Books, 1997.

_____. *Health for Sale: Quackery in England, 1660-1850.* Manchester: Manchester University Press, 1989.

Porter, Roy, and Dorothy Porter. *Patient's Progress: Doctors and Doctoring in Eighteenth-Century England.* Stanford, Calif.: Stanford University Press, 1989.

Porter, Roy, and G. S. Rousseau. *Gout: The Patrician Malady.* New Haven: Yale University Press, 2000.

Portuondo, María. *Secret Science: Spanish Cosmography and the New World.* Chicago: University of Chicago Press, 2009.

Principe, Lawrence M. *The Aspiring Adept: Robert Boyle and His Alchemical Quest.* Princeton, N.J.: Princeton University Press, 1998.

Prosperi, Adriano. " 'Otras Indias': Missionari della controriforma tra contadini e selvaggi." In *Scienze, credenze occulte, livelli di cultura,* ed. Giancarlo Garfagnini, pp. 205-34. Florence: Olschki, 1983.

Puerto Sarmiento, Francisco Javier. "La panacea aurea. Alquimia y destilacion en la corte de Felipe II (1527-1598)." *Dynamis* 17 (1997): 107-40.

Puerto Sarmiento, Francisco Javier, and Guillermo Folch Jou. "Los manuscritos alquímicos seudolulianos conservados en la Biblioteca Nacional de Madrid." *Boletín de la Sociedad Española de Historia de la Farmacia* 30 (1979): 227-42.

Pullan, Brian. *A History of Early Renaissance Italy: From the Mid-Thirteenth to the Mid-Fifteenth Century.* New York: St. Martin's Press, 1972.

Quétel, Claude. *History of Syphilis,* trans. Judith Braddock and Brian Pike. Baltimore: Johns Hopkins University Press, 1990.

Quondam, Amedeo. " 'Mercanzia d'onore,' 'Mercanzia d'utile.' Produzione libraria e lavoro intellettuale a Venezia nel Cinquecento." In *Libri, editori e pubblico nell'Europa moderna,* ed. A. Petrucci, pp. 31-104. Bari, Italy: Laterza, 1977.

Rashdall, Hastings. *The Universities of Europe in the Middle Ages,* 3d ed., ed. F. M. Powicke and A. B. Emden, 3 vols. Oxford: Oxford University Press, 1936.

Rey Bueno, Mar. "El informe Valles: los desdibujados límites del arte de boticarios a finales del siglo XVI (1589-1594)." *Asclepio* 56, no. 2 (2004): 243.

_____. *Los señores del fuego: Destiladores y espagíricos en la corte de los Austria.* Madrid: Corona Borealis, 2002.

Richards, Peter. *The Medieval Leper.* Cambridge: D. S. Brewer, 1977.

Richardson, Brian. *Print Culture in Renaissance Italy: The Editor and the Vernacular Text, 1470-1600.* Cambridge: Cambridge University Press, 1999.

_____. *Printing, Writers, and Readers in Renaissance Italy.* Cambridge: Cambridge University Press, 1999.

Ringmar, Erik. *The Mechanics of Modernity in Europe and East Asia. The institutional origins of social change and stagnation* (Routledge Explorations in Economic History). New York: Routledge.

Roach, Joseph. *It*. Ann Arbor: University of Michigan Press, 2007.

Rodríguez Marín, F. *Felipe II y la alquimia*. Madrid, 1927.

_____. *La verdadera biografía del doctor Nicolás de Monardes*. Madrid, 1925.

Rojeck, Chris. *Celebrity*. Chicago: Reaktion Books, 2004.

Rosa, Edoardo. *Medicina e salute pubblica a Bologna nel Sei e Settecento. Quaderni culturali bolognesi*, vol. 2, no. 8. Bologna, 1978.

Rose, Paul Lawrence. "The Accademia Venetiana: Science and Culture in Renaissance Venice." *Studi Veneziani* 11 (1969): 191-241.

Rosenthal, Margaret. *The Honest Courtesan: Veronica Franco, Citizen and Writer in Sixteenth-Century Venice*. Chicago: University of Chicago Press, 1992.

Rossi, Paolo. *Philosophy, Technology, and the Arts in the Early Modern Era*, trans. S. Attansio. New York: Harper and Row, 1970.

Rowland, Ingrid D. *Giordano Bruno. Philosopher/Heretic*. New York: Farrar, Straus and Giroux, 2008.

Ruggiero, Guido. *Binding Passions: Tales of Magic, Marriage, and Power at the End of the Renaissance*. Oxford: Oxford University Press, 1993.

_____. "Introduction. Renaissance Dreaming: In Search of a Paradigm." In *A Companion to the Worlds of the Renaissance*, ed. G. Ruggiero, pp. 1-20. Oxford: Blackwell, 2002.

Ruggiero, Guido, ed. *A Companion to the Worlds of the Renaissance*. Oxford: Blackwell, 2002.

Ruiz, Javier. "Los alquimistas de Felipe II." *Historia 16* 12 (1977): 49-55.

Saffioti, Tito, and Gerardo Mastrullo. *E il signor duca ne rise di buona maniera: vita privata di un buffone di corte nella Urbino del Cinquecento*. Milan: La vita felice, 1997.

Scarpa, Tiziano. *Venezia è un pesce*. Milan: Feltrinelli, 2001.

Schutte, Anne Jacobson. *Aspiring Saints: Pretense of Holiness, Inquisition, and Gender in the Republic of Venice, 1618-1750*. Baltimore: Johns Hopkins University Press, 2001.

Segre, Michael. *In the Wake of Galileo*. New Brunswick, N.J.: Rutgers University Press, 1991.

Selwyn, Jennifer D. *A Paradise Inhabited by Devils. The Jesuits' Civilizing Mission in Early Modern Naples*. Aldershot, U.K.: Ashgate Publishing, 2004.

Simeoni, Luigi. *Storia della Università di Bologna*. Bologna: Zanichelli, 1940.

Siraisi, Nancy. *Avicenna in Renaissance Italy: The* Canon *and Medical Teaching in Italian Universities after 1500*. Princeton, N.J.: Princeton University Press, 1987.

_____. *Medieval and Early Renaissance Medicine: An Introduction to Knowledge and Practice*. Chicago: University of Chicago Press, 1990.

_____. *Taddeo Alderotti and His Pupils: Two Generations of Italian Medical Learning*. Princeton, N.J.: Princeton University Press, 1981.

Smith, A. Mark. "Knowing Things Inside Out: The Scientific Revolution from a Medieval Perspective." *American Historical Review* 95 (1990): 726-44.

Smith, Pamela. *The Body of the Artisan. Art and Experience in the Scientific Revolution*. Chicago: University of Chicago Press, 2006.

Smith, Pamela, and Paula Findlen, eds., *Merchants & Marvels: Commerce, Science, and Art in Early Modern Europe*. New York: Routledge, 2002.

Sorbelli, Albano. *Storia della Università di Bologna*. Bologna: Zanichelli, 1940.

Spargo, John Webster. *Virgil the Necromancer: Studies in the Virgilian Legends*. Cambridge, Mass.: Harvard University Press, 1934.

Spargo, P. E., and C. A. Pounds. "Newton's 'Derangement of the Intellect.' New Light on an Old Problem." *Notes and Records of the Royal Society of London* 34, no. 1 (1979): 11-32.

Spruit, Leen. "Telesio's Reform of the Philosophy of Mind." *Bruniana & Campanelliana: ricerche filosofiche e materiali storico-testuali* 3 (1997): 123-43.

Stannard, Jerry. "P. A. Mattioli: Sixteenth Century Commentator on Dioscorides," *Bibliographical Contributions*, University of Kansas Libraries, 1 (1969): 59-81.

Stössl, Marianne. *Lo spettacolo della triaca. Produzione e promozione della 'droga divina' a Venezia dal Cinque al Settecento.* Venice: Centro Tedesco di Studi Veneziani, 1983.

Strazzulo, Franco. *Edilizia e urbanistica a Napoli dal '500 al '70.* Naples: Artura Berisio, 1968.

Tadini, G. "Notizie della giovinezza di Antonio Ferramolino." *Atti dell'Ateneo di Scienze Lettere e Arti di Bergamo* 40 (1976-77): 33-54.

Tate Lanning, John. *The Royal Protomedicato in the Spanish Empire.* Durham, N.C.: Duke University Press, 1985.

Taylor, René. "Architecture and Magic: Considerations on the *Idea* of the Escorial." In *Essays in the History of Architecture Presented to Rudolf Wittkower,* ed. Howard Hibbard and Milton J. Lewine, pp. 81-109. New York: Phaidon, 1969.

Temkin, Owsei. The Falling Sickess: A History of Epilepsy from the Greens to the Bginnings of Modrn Nurology, 2nd ed. Rev. Baltimore and London: Johns Hopkins University Press, 1971. Tenenti, Alberto. *Piracy and the Decline of Venice, 1580-1615,* trans. Janet and Brian Pullan. Berkeley and Los Angeles: University of California Press, 1967.

Tergolina-Sislanzoni-Brasco, Umberto. "Francesco Calzolari speziale veronese." *Bolettino storico italiano dell'arte sanitaria* 33 (1934): 3-20.

Terpstra, Nicolas. "Confraternities and Local Cults: Civic Religion Between Class and Politics in Renaissance Bologna." In *Civic Ritual and Drama,* ed. A. Johnson and W. Husken. Amsterdam and Atlanta: Rodopi, 1997. *Ludus* 2 (1997): 143-74.

Thomas Keith. *Religion and the Decline of Magic.* New York: Charles Scribner's Sons, 1971.

Thompson, Stith. *Motif-Index of Folk-Literature*, 6 vols. Bloomington: Indiana University Press, 1955-58.

Thorndike, Lynn. *History of Magic and Experimental Science*, 8 vols. New York: Columbia University Press, 1923-1958.

Trovato, Paolo. *Con ogni diligenza corretto: La stampa e le revisioni editoriali dei testi letterari italiani (1470-1570).* Bologna: Il Mulino, 1991.

Truitt, E. R. "The Virtues of Balm in Late Medieval Literature." *Early Science and Medicine* 14 (2009): 711-36.

Van Deusen, Neil C. "The Place of Telesio in the History of Philosophy," *The Philosophical Review* 44 (1935): 417-34.

Villari, Rosario. *La rivolta antispagnola a Napoli.* Bari, Italy: Laterza, 1967.

Watson, Gilbert. *Theriac and Mithridatium: A Study in Therapeutics.* London: Wellcome Historical Medical Library, 1966.

Webster, Charles. "The Helmontian George Thompson and William Harvey: The Revival and Application of Splenectomy to Physiological Research." *Medical History* 15 (1971): 154-67.

Weinstein, Donald. *The Captain's Concubine. Love, Honor, and Violence in Renaissance Tuscany.* Baltimore: Johns Hopkins University Press, 2000.

Witcombe, Christopher L. C. E. *Copyright in the Renaissance: Prints and the "Privilegio" in Sixteenth-Century Venice and Rome* (Studies in Medieval and Reformation Thought). Vol. 100. Leiden and Boston: Brill, 2004.

Wood, George B., and Franklin Bache. *The Dispensatory of the United States*, 13th ed. Philadelphia: J. B. Lippincott, 1871.

Yates, Frances A. "The Art of Ramon Lull." *Journal of the Warburg and Courtauld Institutes* 17 (1954): 115-73.

_____. *Giordano Bruno and the Hermetic Tradition.* Chicago: University of Chicago Press, 1964.

Young, James Harvey. *The Medical Messiahs: A Social History of Health Quackery in Twentieth-Century America.* Princeton, N.J.: Princeton University Press, 1967.

Zilsel, Edgar. "The Sociological Roots of Science." *American Journal of Sociology* 47 (1941/42): 544-62.

Zinsser, Hans. *Rats, Lice, and History.* New York: Bantam Books, 1960.

INDEX

Illustrations are indicated by **boldface.**

A

IMAGE CREDITS

17, National Gallery of Art, Washington, D.C.; 44, Courtesy of the National Library of Medicine, Washington, D.C.; 50, From William Clowes, *A profitable and necessarie booke of observations* (London, 1637). Courtesy of the Wellcome Library, London; 55, Cintio d'Amato, *Prattica nuova, et utilissima di tutto quello, che al diligente barbiero s'appartiene* (1669). Courtesy of the Wellcome Historical Medical Library, London; 59, Museo del Prado, Madrid, Scala/Art Resource, NewYork; 97, Courtesy of the National Library of Medicine, Washington, D.C.; 104-5, Museo Nazionale di San Martino, Naples, Photoserve Electa; 119, From Hieronymus Brunschwig, *Liber de arte distillandi* (Strassburg, 1532). Courtesy of the Department of Special Collections, University of Wisconsin, Madison; 126, Folger Shakespeare Library; 158-59, Museo Correr, Venice, Erich Lessing/Art Resource, New York; 168, Photoservice Electa; 170, Courtesy of the Department of Special Collections, University of Wisconsin, Madison; 216, Leonardo Fioravanti, *Tesoro della vita humana,* Venice, 1582. Courtesy of the Department of Special Collections, University of Wisconsin, Madison; 221, Giuseppe Maria Mitelli, *Le arte per via* (Bologna, 1660). Courtesy of Arnaldo Forni Editore; 230, Courtesy of the New York Public Library; 232, Museo Correr, Venice, Ms. P.D.849C. Courtesy of the Fondazione Musei Civici Venezia; 253, Courtesy of the National Library of Medicine, Washington, D.C.